CW01395003

LIVES OF A LANCASHIRE MANSION
Alston (new) Hall

LIVES OF A LANCASHIRE MANSION – Alston (new) Hall

COLIN DICKINSON

The Hall in college days seen from the east with the Fylde plain beyond. The Hall nestles amid its woodland environs that would have been planned in the 1870s to eventually protect it from winter winds and to offer privacy in an agricultural and open landscape.

First published in 2023

by Palatine Books
Carnegie House
Chatsworth Road
Lancaster LA1 4SL
www.palatinebooks.com

Copyright © Colin Dickinson

All rights reserved
Unauthorised duplication contravenes existing laws

The right of Colin Dickinson to be identified as the author of this work has been asserted in accordance with the Copyright, Designs and Patents act 1988

British Library Cataloguing-in-Publication data
A catalogue record for this book is available from the British Library

Every effort has been made to trace copyright holders.

Paperback ISBN 13: 978-1-910837-48-1

Designed and typeset by Carnegie Book Production
www.carnegiebookproduction.com

Printed and bound by Halstan

Contents

List of Illustrations

Front cover

The Hall from the south soon after it had been sold in 2016.

Frontispiece

The Hall in college days seen from the east with the Fylde plain beyond.

Chapter 1

Fig. 1.1 Location of Alston Hall and Ribble View House near Preston.

Fig. 1.2 John Mercer.

Fig. 1.3 Helen Mercer, John's second wife.

Fig. 1.4 Stonyhurst College.

Fig. 1.5 The Mercer grave at St Oswald's and St Edmund's in Ashton-in-Makerfield of William Mercer (John's brother), Elizabeth Mercer (John's first wife), and William and John Mercer (infant sons of John Mercer and his second wife Helen).

Chapter 2

Fig. 2.1 Alfred Darbyshire (1839–1908) architect of Alston Hall.

Fig. 2.2 Early photograph of the Hall.

Fig. 2.3 Shield of Arms incorrectly indicating Mercer of Alston Hall, entrance hall (June 2015).

Fig. 2.4 John Mercer's 'Achievement of Arms' on the entrance tower.

Fig. 2.5 Skylight in the entrance hall (June 2015).

Fig. 2.6 'Discs' motifs around the base of the skylight.

Fig. 2.7 Column of polished Shap granite in the chapel (June 2015).

Introduction

I cannot think of a better way to begin this introduction than to quote from Vita Sackville-West's delightful book, *English Country Houses*, published in 1941.

> *There is nothing quite like the English country house anywhere else in the world. France has her chateaux, Italy her historic villas, Spain her gardens like the Generalife hooked on to the hillside, Germany her robber castles, but the exact equivalent of what we mean by the English country house is not to be found elsewhere. It may be large, it may be small; it may be palatial, it may be manorial; it may be of stone, brick, stucco, or even of beams and plaster; it may be the seat of the aristocracy or the home of the gentry – whatever it is, it possesses one outstanding characteristic: it is the English country house.*

Near the end of the book she would write:

> *––– a house which is still the home of men and women is a living thing which has not lost its soul. The soul of a house, the atmosphere of a house, are as much part of the house as the architecture of that house or as the furnishings within it. Divorced from its life, it dies. But if it keeps its life it means that the kitchen still provides food for the inhabitants: makes jam, puts fruit into bottles, stores the honey, dries the herbs, and carries on in the same tradition as has always obtained in the country.*

Alston Hall at times certainly became divorced from life but somehow managed to survive. Architecturally it was to be an eclectic mix of the Gothic Revival and Tudor style by Alfred Darbyshire of Manchester, and erected in the 1870s for John Mercer who had acquired his wealth from the mines of the south Lancashire coalfield. Yet for John Mercer and his second wife Helen, the Hall would never be a happy family home as before the building had been completed their two infant sons had died to leave Ellen, John's daughter of his first marriage as the future heiress of the Hall and its estate.

In 1881, Ellen married Edmund Waterton of a well-known Catholic family who had a long and impressive pedigree, his father having been a pioneer of natural history and who had died at Walton Hall near Wakefield, Yorkshire in 1865. In 1887 Ellen became a widow with two young daughters, Monica the elder becoming a novice nun in an East Sussex convent by 1905. After the death of John Mercer in 1893 and his wife in 1896, Ellen had chosen not to live at the Hall and in 1901 the mansion was in the care and residency of a caretaker then a widow with three children. The Hall would occasionally be the residency of John Mercer's brother-in-law Canon James Taylor who eventually lived there permanently until his death in 1908.

Following the death of her mother in London in 1909, Monica became the owner of the Hall and its estate, but having taken a vow of poverty she was unable to accept her inheritance and ceded the administration of the Hall to the nuns of her Order who realised they were not in a position as far as personnel, finance or apostolic work was concerned to accept the Hall on a permanent basis.

By 1912 the decision had been made to let the Hall to a local cotton manufacturer, William Eccles, who during his short residency at the Hall would organise a programme of modernisation that in some ways was to the detriment of the Hall's architecture. Yet on the positive side he would instigate the installation of electric lighting, a technical innovation welcomed in many a country house of the period.

In 1916 after Eccles had terminated his lease because of his bankruptcy, most of the Hall's furniture was sold by auction and during the following year the Hall and its estate came up for sale. At this particular period the Hall could well have become a military establishment or hospital for the remaining years of the First World War had it not been purchased by William Birtwistle, a local and prominent mill owner in the Lancashire cotton trade. A few years later in 1924 he would arrange for his managing director John Marsden to reside at the Hall for a term of five years, a term that would last until 1948 when Marsden retired.

Again the Hall had escaped from being commissioned by the government for wartime purposes unlike many a country house that having served such a honourable1 role would be returned in a condition requiring major and costly repair work. By 1949 after a sale of its contents the Hall stood empty waiting for yet another lifestyle. This arrived in the following year when it was to become a day continuation college of education and a few years afterwards an adult residential college of education.

Sixty-five years on after playing host to those who had found pleasure in the pursuit of social intercourse and knowledge within its walls, it would fall victim to the politics of the day in an atmosphere of financial restraints. Closure came just before Christmas 2015, and by May 2016 a buyer had been found whose intention was to convert the Hall back into a domestic dwelling. In March 2017 when such work was well advanced, fire broke out in the mansion to threaten its very existence but it would survive.

The first account of the Hall's history had been written by the late Marion Roberts and published by the Alston Hall Residential College for Adult Education in 1994, and although small in volume it was an inspiration to all who read it. During the summer of 2015 the 'Friends of Alston Hall' amid rumours of the Hall's pending closure as a college decided to produce an expanded version of Marion's account to include the Hall's 60-year history as a college of education. The well-known writer and a tutor at the college Alan G. Crosby was to write the new book that appeared in 2017, part of it presenting a detailed and memorable account of life at the Hall for staff, tutors and learners during college days.

Meanwhile as a tutor at the college in the history of Victorian/Edwardian architecture and technology, my thoughts had already focused on producing a new historical account of the Hall, part of which would include a detailed appraisal of its architecture and the life and career of its architect. As my intentions to write a new history of the Hall became known to college staff in the summer of 2015, I was given permission to carry out a photographic survey of the mansion with the help of college tutor Malcolm Tranter who performed the photography. I was also to receive the Hall's archives of sale catalogues, documents, plans, photographs, etc., on the understanding that when the proposed book was published such a collection would be offered to the Lancashire Archives in Preston.

Throughout 2016 researches began to shed new light on the Mercer and the Waterton families, in particular the life of John Mercer's granddaughter Etheburga who as the second daughter of Ellen Waterton was to be denied a considerable fortune. By March 2017 the book's manuscript was well on the way in readiness for publication when one received news of the major fire at the Hall. It soon became obvious that such a tragic event now had to be an important addition to the new book and in the following December I was invited to the Hall to inspect the fire and water damage. Once again Malcolm Tranter was available to undertake a photographic survey as well as for further visits during which 'hidden secrets' of the Hall were revealed during restoration work.

In extinguishing the fire, water had stripped paint from the stone arches in the entrance hall and those on the first floor landing to reveal Venetian style ones in keeping with an original Gothic style décor. Ceilings and floors had been destroyed to expose rolled steel girders that had been introduced during the early 1950s. Everywhere in the building was a scene of devastation but thoughtful and well-planned restoration work was slowly bringing the Hall back to life.

Of the country house in general Vita Sackville-West would write:

> Irrespective of grandeur or modesty, it should agree with its landscape and suggest the life of its inhabitants past or present; should never overwhelm its surroundings. The peculiar genius of the English country house lies in its knack of fitting in.

Alston Hall throughout its various lives in which it has experienced the many trials and tribulations of life has embodied such sentiments. The following is an account of those lives and also the lives of those who were fortunate to live and work within its walls. Hopefully this book will be enjoyed as much by the general reader as by those who knew the Hall well, particularly in college days.

Now approaching the third decade of the twenty-first century, the Hall faces yet another life with a new family who hopefully will be its guardians for many years to come. I wish them well in such an important role. On a personal front, having enjoyed the delightful and memorable position of being a tutor at the Hall over a number of years then to be given the opportunity to write and present a new and extended history of it, has indeed been a privilege and an exhilarating adventure.

Chapter one

John Mercer

On 20 September 1875, three-and-a-half-year-old John Mercer junior with a wooden mallet tapped the foundation stone of Alston (new) Hall. The ceremony had begun with the infant placing a sealed bottle containing current coins of the realm, copies of Manchester, Liverpool, Wigan, and Preston newspapers, a copy of the *Catholic Times*, and photographs of the Mercer family, into a cavity beneath the stone following which the space was filled with dry cement.

The contract for the stonework and the building of the mansion had been given to Messrs Isaac Wilkinson and James Kirby of Longridge, and it was Mr J. Kirby who would hand a silver-plated Gothic style trowel with ivory handle to the young John remarking that he had great pleasure in making the presentation. He hoped the young gentleman would use it well, that he (Master John) might grow to see the completion of the building he was commencing, so that in after years when he looked upon that trowel it would remind him of that memorable day. Mr Kirby also hoped the building might be brought to a successful completion without accident and that when so completed Master John might enjoy many happy days along with his honoured parents within its walls.

Following Mr Kirby's remarks, Master John then proceeded to spread the mortar upon which the stone would be laid, after which Mr Harrison of Messrs Harrison of St Helens who were the contractors for the joiners' work, plastering, slating, plumbing, painting, etc., presented him with a builder's level made of walnut, remarking that he hoped Master John's future would be so level as to be like the plum bob on that level, and then he would be a pleasure and a blessing to his parents and all about him.

Fig. 1.1 Location of Alston Hall and Ribble View House near Preston.

The architect of the new Hall, Alfred Darbyshire of Manchester, then presented a souvenir mallet to young John, and reiterated the sentiments expressed by the gentlemen who had preceded him, the silver-plated base of the mallet bearing the following inscription:

Presented to Master John Mercer by Alfred Darbyshire F.S.A. Architect, on the occasion of his laying the Foundation Stone of Alston Hall, September 20th 1875.

There would be a large Catholic presence at the ceremony including Father Lennon from Newton-le-Willows; Canon Taylor (John Mercer's brother-in-law) who was the Rector of St Augustine's Church, Preston; Father Walton from Alston Church and the school children from the Catholic school in Alston. Also present were a number of neighbouring farmers.

Father Walton was then called upon to say a few words, a part of which he expressed his hope that the Mercers would be happy in the new Hall and have many blessings and that John Mercer might live to see his son grow up before he left this world. John Mercer senior then thanked Father Walton for his remarks and the gathering for their attendance, and after several rounds of cheering young John handed out buns, cakes, and apples to the children present who then dispersed to enjoy themselves in numerous games and sports. A select party of friends and invited guests then retired to nearby 'Ribble View', the Mercers' holiday retreat and now a temporary home whilst the new mansion was being built, where they were dined and entertained whilst the contractors and their workforce along with the tenants of the Alston estate would enjoy an evening at the *White Bull* in Alston.

The Catholic faith in this particular region of Lancashire had been retained to some degree by an on-going resistance throughout the years since the beginning of the Protestant reforms of the late 1530s brought about by Henry VIII's severance from the Catholic Church in Rome thus allowing him to divorce, re-marry, and hopefully achieve a male heir. As the Protestant Reformation period got underway, Catholic places of worship were banned, and it was not until the second half of the eighteenth century when those of the Catholic faith were allowed to build new chapels.

A Catholic mission had been founded in Alston, south of Longridge in 1765 followed by a chapel in 1774 on the upper floor of a barn situated in a lane off the Longridge to Preston road, to be known as the Alston Lane Chapel. Such a humble meeting place served the Catholic community until 1854 when the present Church of Our Lady and St Michael was built, the architects being I. & C. Hansom, presumably the latter being Charles Francis (1816–88), the brother of Joseph Aloysius Hansom (1803–82) the inventor of the 'Hansom Cab' and architect of St Walburge's R.C. Church,

Fig. 1.2 John Mercer.
(By kind permission of
Wigan Archives)

Preston. The old chapel at Alston was to be used as a school until new school premises were built in 1927.

The land at Alston upon which the Mercer mansion and its estate were to appear had a long and complicated history of previous ownership. In 1230 William de Samlesbury had granted land in Alston to Adam de Hoghton, land that would remain under the de Hoghtons until the end of the eighteenth century when the family lost it due to non-payment of mortgages. From the fifteenth century the township of Alston was to consist of two manors; one held by the de Hoghtons of nearby Hoghton Tower, and the other by the Stanleys, Earls of Derby. In 1772 the Hoghton manor part was sold to a William Shaw and eventually descended to the Crosse family of Red Scar, near Preston.

Much of the freehold land in Alston was owned by families who were not manorial lords, one being the Nelsons who were of a minor Catholic gentry and resided at Fairhurst Hall, Wrightington, near Parbold. Even though the de Hoghtons had no manorial rights in Alston by the mid 1770s, they were to retain land, and in 1806 Sir Philip de Hoghton and John Assheton (or Ashton) Nelson (born 1769) transacted an exchange of land, Alston (old) Hall, a seventeenth-century stone building and its estate passing into the ownership of John Ashton Nelson who would die in 1822 having no direct heirs. His wife had died in 1804, less than five years after their marriage and as John did not remarry there were no surviving children. When the time came for John to make his Will, his older brother had died, his middle-aged sister was unmarried, and his other brother was in need of care, suffering from some kind of mental impairment.

Knowing that his sister and brother would die eventually without issue, John, as well as making provisions for his mother who would die two months after him, allotted his huge estate to trustees on behalf of his cousins which included his Riddell relatives, a leading Catholic family in

Fig. 1.3 Helen Mercer, John's second wife. (By kind permission of Wigan Archives)

Northumberland, his mother being the daughter of Thomas Riddell who died in1754 of Swinburne Castle not far from Hexham in Northumberland. She had two brothers, Thomas, the elder, who inherited the Swinburne estates, and Ralph who became the sole heir of his childless uncle, Ralph Widdrington of Cheeseburn Grange, ten miles northwest of Newcastle upon Tyne.

Ralph Riddell was to have two sons, Ralph and Francis, the first cousins of John Ashton Nelson, and it would be the latter Ralph who eventually following the death of John Ashton Nelson in 1822 inherited the Alston estate, and after his death in 1831, the estate passed to his son and heir Edward Riddell.

In 1837 the estate was still under the ownership of Edward Riddell, its Alston (old) Hall tenanted by Edmund Sagar who had been born at Mitton nearby in 1786, and who was still at the Hall in 1851 with his wife and three daughters, farming 154 acres. Ten years later Edmund is a widower at the Hall with his three daughters but in January 1867 he died leaving his two unmarried daughters as tenants of a farm of over 150 acres. It seems likely the two sisters may then have notified the Riddell estate of their intention to leave the farm in the near future because soon afterwards the estate decided to sell its entire landholding in Alston along with land in Hothersall and Parbold.

Fig. 1.4 Stonyhurst College.

In September 1868, these 470 acres mostly in Alston included almost 59 acres in Hothersall and 13 acres in Parbold were auctioned at the *Bull and Royal Hotel* in Preston, the total sale reaching a figure of just under £30,000 from which was deducted £4,400 for the value of the timber growing on the estate. Lot 10 of the sale consisted of the Alston (old) Hall and outbuildings etc., (to be known as Alston Hall Farm) and land amounting to a little over 173 acres upon which eventually the new Alston Hall would be built. Lot 10 fetched £7,400, the purchaser of this and the rest of the Riddell estate being Frank Chadwick who lived at Burholme, near Whitewell in the Forest of Bowland.

In November of the same year the remaining farm stock of the Sagar sisters at Alston (old) Hall farm was for sale comprising cattle, a horse, pigs and sheep with quantities of hay, oats, potatoes and swedes. The sisters then left and in 1871 were living at their old family home, Sagar Fold in Mitton, farming 24 acres. In that year James Blundell was living at Alston (old) Hall with his wife and four children, and also five living-in farm servants and a live-in girl in a farm then of 160 acres. Part of this land included all the area soon to be allotted for John Mercer's new mansion and its estate.

On 28 July 1870, most of the land including five working farms that Frank Chadwick had bought in Alston with the exception of Alston (old) Hall, its farm and estate, were auctioned at the *Shelley Arms* in Preston. At this sale John Mercer was to purchase land and properties in Alston, so it seems then that he had already set his sights on the area where he intended to build a house for his family. The opportunity for him to buy more land and property at Alston came on 25 August 1873 at the *Victoria Hotel* in Friargate, Preston, when the Alston (old) Hall freehold estate, including its manor house was to be sold by auction. After a successful bid that cost him a buying price of £8,000, John Mercer became the owner of about 420 acres plus property at Alston, acquired by the sales of 1870 and 1873. The stage was now set for Mercer to set into motion the building of his mansion to be called Alston Hall, the existing Alston (old) Hall, which he now owned to became known as Alston Old Hall Farm.

By the second half of the nineteenth century, agriculture had become economically less attractive with new wealth coming from industrialisation especially in Lancashire where coal mining and factory-based textiles were flourishing. The owners of the once great manorial estates now dependent to a large extent upon income from tenant farmers, were in many cases only too willing to sell land to the industrial entrepreneur who had 'new money' to buy or build an impressive house for his family away from the grime and chaos of the industrial town or city.

Such an entrepreneur was John Mercer who had been born on 23 December 1820 in Elm Grove, St Helens, in Lancashire, where his father had set up business as a mining surveyor. In the records of St Mary's Roman Catholic Church, Lowhouse, now preserved in St Helens, we find that John's baptism took place on Christmas Day 1820. John's father, Silvester Mercer had been born in 1780 in Kirkham and was eventually to move south, the 1851 Census recording him living in Paper Mill Lane, Eccleston, not far from St Helens.

At the time of John's birth, his parents, Silvester and Mary had a son William aged ten years and a daughter Elizabeth aged five years. Another daughter Mary was born in the mid-1830s, and by the time the 1841 Census was undertaken, Silvester is a land surveyor and a widower living in Eccleston with his sons William and John who are also land surveyors, daughter Elizabeth, and a servant girl.

After an education in one of the local schools John had entered his father's office at the start of the great railway-building period, a time when the services of the highly skilled land surveyor were in much demand. Land surveying for railways was no easy task with many problems arising among which could be opposition from landowners and work having to be kept to a tight schedule in order to meet the time limits presented for Parliamentary proceedings. It seems that John would undertake survey work on what is today the main west coast main line between Preston and Carlisle, working for the eminent engineer Joseph Locke, particularly on the length over Shap Fell, and also on the Caledonian line further north that was opened on 15 February 1848.

A fortnight after the opening of the Caledonian line John married his cousin Elizabeth Glover. A daughter Mary was born in the following December when the couple resided in St Helens. For the Census of 1851, John now 30 is listed as the surveyor of Sands Colliery. His wife Elizabeth is also 30 and daughter Mary is two years old. Ten years on in the Census of 1861 John is described as a 'Colliery Proprietor' residing at 'Cranberry Lodge', (which eventually became a hotel) Park Lane, Ashton-in-Makerfield, with his wife Elizabeth, a year when John Mercer is in a most respected position professionally as well as in a sound one financially. When opening a school for four hundred scholars, the entire costs of which he had borne himself, he would be described as an *example worthy of imitation*.

Fig. 1.5 The Mercer grave at St Oswald's and St Edmund's in Ashton-in-Makerfield of William Mercer (John's brother), Elizabeth Mercer (John's first wife), and William and John Mercer (infant sons of John Mercer and his second wife Helen).

The 1861 Census for the Mercer household does not list John and Elizabeth's daughter Mary and no mention of her has been found from when she was listed in the 1851 Census. However, in the 1861 Census is a daughter Ellen aged five years who eventually would become the heiress of Alston new Hall. Also in the household run by five servants was Mary E. Smith, a governess.

John Mercer's earliest partnership in the coal industry had been with a Mr Wright of Wigan. Eventually he would go into partnership with a Richard Evans who in 1847 had bought a share of Edge Green collieries near St Helens. Mercer and Evans would bring together under the same ownership the pits at Edge Green and those at Golborne and Haydock in the St Helens coalfield.

By the 1860s John Mercer's business career had been successful but not so his personal life. The year 1864 had brought about a double tragedy that began with the death of his brother William who on his way home in September from shooting on farmland, was thrown from a pony-drawn carriage as it abruptly turned a corner in Golborne, near Ashton-in-Makerfield, dying later as a result of his injuries. Then on 7 September the day after his brother's funeral, John's wife Elizabeth died suddenly at home. Both are buried in the same grave in the cemetery adjoining St Oswald's and St Edmund's Catholic Church in Ashton-in-Makerfield, the inscriptions on the grave reading:

William Mercer of Newton-le-Willows
Died 3rd September 1864
Aged 56 years
Elizabeth Mercer
Wife of John Mercer of Park Lane, Wigan
Died 7th September 1864
Aged 45 years

More tragedy followed in 1866 when on 23 January an explosion of firedamp occurred at Mercer and Evans's High Brook Colliery (mentioned as Highbrooks below) in Park Lane on the high road from Ashton-in-Makerfield to Wigan, claiming the lives of men and boys. At the time John Mercer was waiting to descend the pit shaft with the 'on-looker' a Mr Ashcroft who was preoccupied with superintending the lowering of a pony down another shaft, an operation that fortunately for Mercer and Ashcroft was taking longer than usual when the explosion happened. The pit was known locally as 'The Unfortunate Pit' because of its frequent minor accidents.

An inquiry was conducted in the following February into the cause of the disaster, the jury after a sitting of seven hours finding that

> James Marsh and 29 others came to their deaths by an explosion of firedamp at the Highbrooks Colliery … but by what means or by whom the gas was ignited there is no evidence to show. The jury are unanimous in stating that they are of opinion that the mine in which this calamity has happened has been properly conducted, and that there is no blame to be attached to the proprietors of the said colliery. A public meeting will be held in Wigan, on Monday evening, to take steps to provide for the families left destitute.

By April the verdict of the February jury was brought to question at a public meeting held in Wigan when it was believed there had been an infringement of the regulations allied to the storage of gunpowder in the mine and this had contributed to the disaster. From a Government Fund the widows of the disaster were to receive five shillings per week while they remained unmarried and one shilling a week extra for each of their children.

However some happiness would follow in John Mercer's life when in October of the same year the *Preston Guardian* announced John Mercer's marriage to Helen Taylor who was twenty years younger than him and the youngest daughter of the late George Taylor, a farmer of Lodge Hall, Lytham, in Lancashire, who had died in 1840, the year when his daughter Helen was born. John Mercer was about to become part of a family with a strong commitment to the Catholic Faith, this and the family's farming background would have a direct influence on his changing lifestyle at Alston Hall some years later. Helen's father had been born in 1797 in Warton, near Lytham, and in 1826 had married Ann Fayer (1806–83) whose father, William born in Wesham, near Kirkham was farming at Brown Moss, Kirkham in 1841.

With the onset of the Protestant Reformation, Lancashire became the heartland of Catholic resistance to the rules and proclamations of the newly established Protestant reforms. This resulted in fines, imprisonment, torture and even death to the recusants who defied such rules and proclamations, and in 1570 this resistance in Lancashire was described as *the very sink of popery where more unlawful acts have been committed and more persons holding secret than in any other part of the realm.*

In the Fylde area of Lancashire, prominent Catholic families such as the Westbys and the Cliftons as well as yeoman farmers, would to some degree preserve the Catholic Faith by providing centres for conducting Mass, the sons of which in some cases attended seminars abroad to become priests. By the start of the nineteenth century large numbers of Irish immigrants were arriving in the districts of Kirkham to take work in the local flax industries, such numbers strengthening the Catholic communities.

George Taylor and his wife Ann would have a family of nine, all born in Warton; Roger (b 1828), William (b 1830), James (b 1831), Mary (b 1832), Thomas (b 1833), Isabella (b 1834), John (b 1836), Henry (b 1839) and Helen (b 1840). Roger and James were to become priests, James (see chapter 9) going at 14 years of age to the Catholic college at Ushaw, Durham to train for the priesthood, whilst in 1851 Roger is studying theology there. In 1870–74 Roger is the priest at the R.C. Church of The Willows, Kirkham, and in 1881 before his death in 1885 is the priest at St Peter's R.C. Church in Lytham.

The Census of 1851 had found Ann Taylor (45) as a farmer in the village of Moss Side near Kirkham with six of her children including Helen, and two farm labourers. Ten years on, Ann, now with daughter Helen (20) was at the home of her father William (82) in Warton Street, Lytham.

The wedding of John Mercer and Helen Taylor was on 24 October 1866 at St Peter's Church, Lytham, where the ceremony was to be conducted by the bride's brother, the Rev. James Taylor. At this time John Mercer was living in Newton-le-Willows, and in 1871 the Census finds him as a county magistrate and colliery proprietor now aged 50 and still living in Newton-le-Willows at 'The Woodlands' in Ashton Road. Also listed for the Census were his wife Helen (30), his mother-in-law Ann Taylor (64), his sister Mary Lupton (36) and her husband William (35), a niece Mary E. Taylor (7), and two servants. At that particular time John Mercer's daughter Ellen from his first marriage, then aged 15 years was one of 79 girls boarding at the Convent of Notre Dame on the southern side of Clapham Common, London.

In March 1872 Helen Mercer gave birth to a son to be christened John. His birth may have influenced John Mercer to some extent in his decision to purchase land at Alston in September 1873, as his proposed mansion would be near the Roman Catholic public school at Stonyhurst where the young John might be educated.

The school had once been the great mansion of the Catholic Sherburnes. In 1717 the last of the Sherburnes, Sir Nicholas died, and having survived his son was to leave the Stonyhurst Estate to his daughter the Duchess of Norfolk who would die childless in 1754. The estate then passed into the family of Sir Nicholas's sister, Elizabeth, (who had married Humphrey Weld of Lulworth Castle in Dorset), in the person of Edward Weld. On the death of Edward in 1775, Thomas Weld inherited the Stonyhurst Estate, and having been educated by the English Jesuits at their college in St Omer, France, he offered the mansion and its grounds to the Jesuits of Liege for the continuation of their educational work.

Fleeing from religious persecution in Liege, Belgium, the Jesuits had arrived at Stonyhurst in 1794, the year when French Revolutionary armies were to march on Liege. The long and exhausting journey to Stonyhurst for priests and pupils had begun by riverboat to Rotterdam, then by sea to Hull followed by river-barge to Selby, where some local residents on seeing the pupils in their school uniforms mistook them for Frenchmen. From Selby the party walked to Leeds then on to Skipton by canal barge, from where they travelled on foot via Clitheroe to Stonyhurst, where they were to be confronted with a derelict and decaying mansion.

The Jesuits have always been innovators and up to date in improvements, installing during the 1830s the first gaslight in the district at Stonyhurst. In September 1841 the future husband of Ellen Mercer, Edmund Waterton would arrive as a pupil. Today Stonyhurst College is among the most modern of schools and known for its outstanding achievements in education.

Early in 1874, John Mercer's wife Helen had given birth to another son, to be named William, but nine months later on 26 November William died at 'The Woodlands' in Newton-le-Willows. The infant must have undergone much suffering in his final days, the death certificate listing croup 10 days, bronchitis 8 days, meningitis 3 days. The certificate was to be signed by a cross, the mark of John Pendlebury as the informant who was John Mercer's coachman at the 'The Woodlands'.

Shortly before William's death the *Preston Guardian Supplement* of 14 November had reported the death by drowning in the river Ribble of 31-year-old John Eddleston, a tenant farmer living at Alston old Hall. An inquest was held at the *White Bull*, Alston, following which a jury would return a verdict to the effect that the deceased had accidentally fallen into the river whilst in a state of intoxication.

These two tragic events came at a time when John Mercer would have been eagerly looking forward to the building of his new mansion at Alston. Less than two years later on the 17 July 1876, John Mercer junior who under a year earlier had taken part in the laying of the Alston mansion's foundation stone, died of scarlet fever. The death certificate states Alston as the place of his death and as the new Hall would not have been completed by then, John junior presumably died at 'Ribble View' the house on the Alston estate where the Mercers would then have been in residence whilst the new mansion was under construction.

In deep bereavement John Mercer who was present at the death is said to have cursed every stone in the new mansion and wished it would fall into the river. Now there would be no male heir to carry on the name of Mercer at Alston Hall. Ellen Mercer, John's daughter from his first marriage had now entered the role as the future heiress of the Hall and its estate and what would be a considerable fortune.

In the churchyard of Alston Catholic Church a memorial to John Mercer's two sons, William and John who had been buried in Ashton-le-Willows would appear on what would be the eventual grave of John

Mercer, his second wife Helen, and finally his daughter Ellen Waterton. The memorial reads:

IN LOVING REMEMBRANCE OF
WILLIAM MERCER
WHO DIED 26th of NOVEMBER 1874
AGED 9 MONTHS
ALSO OF JOHN MERCER
WHO DIED 17th of JULY 1876
AGED 4 YEARS and 4 MONTHS
SONS OF
JOHN AND HELEN MERCER
OF ALSTON HALL
AND WHO ARE INTERRED AT
ST. OSWALD'S ASHTON-LE-WILLOWS
GOD'S WILL BE DONE

Chapter two

The Hall's architect and its heraldry

Seemingly, John Mercer's choice of Alfred Darbyshire of Manchester as the architect for the new mansion at Alston had been influenced by his late brother William's acquaintance with the architect some years earlier. William had been a surveyor to Colonel Legh (later Lord Newton), a mine owner and a prime instigator, especially in the Newton-le-Willows area in the building of the Manchester to Liverpool Railway that opened in 1830. Legh of Lyme Hall near Stockport was to employ Alfred Darbyshire to undertake architectural work at the Hall, a time when Alfred would meet William, the two becoming friends. Most probably, William admired Alfred's work at the Hall, occasionally mentioning it to his brother John, who eventually chose Alfred to be the architect for the new Hall at Alston.

Alfred Darbyshire (1839–1908) F.I.B.A. (Fellow of the Institute of British Architects) in 1870 and Vice-President in 1902–5, and F.S.A. (Fellow of the Society of Antiquaries) in 1894, was to publish in 1897 his 'An Architect's Experiences: Professional, Artistic, and Theatrical' in which he would write:

> My recollections of Lyme Hall are very pleasant. I was entrusted with some important internal decorations. I designed and built on an Italian model left by Leoni, the large block of stables; improved the gardens on the south front by a series of terraces; planned farm buildings and model cottages. During the execution of these works I came in contact with Bailey Denton, Edward Kemp, cultured

Fig. 2.1 Alfred Darbyshire
(1839–1908) architect of
Alston Hall.

*gentleman, landscape gardener, author of the text-book "How to Lay
Out a Garden", and William Mercer, who was the steward of Lord
Newton's Cheshire and Lancashire estates, with whom I enjoyed
many years of pleasant friendship.*

Alfred Darbyshire was born at 8 Peru Street, Salford, on 20 June 1839
to Quaker parents, and in the 1840s, the Darbyshire family were to move
to Egerton, near Bolton, where Alfred's father, William, a cloth dyer was
to manage the dye works there. In 1849, the family moved to a village near
Pendleton, and after attending a Dame's school in Pendleton, Alfred was
sent to a Quaker school in Manchester.

In 1851 he visited the Great Exhibition in Hyde Park, London, with
his uncle, George Bradshaw of railway timetable fame, and later in the
same year was sent to the Quaker school at Ackworth, near Pontefract, in

Yorkshire. At Ackworth, under the direction of a master, Henry Sparkes, Alfred would begin to set his sights on becoming an architect and an artist. Years later in his *Experiences*, he wrote:

> Ruskin has said, "It is not necessary for an artist to be an architect, but it is necessary for an architect to be an artist." This is a true doctrine from the pen of the great art teacher, and it was a fortunate thing for me that my teacher at Ackworth School was not only an architect, but an artist, and a painter of considerable ability. He belonged to an artistic family, one of whom is now the Master of the celebrated School of Art at Lambeth.

To finish his education Alfred was sent to Lindow Grove Academy at Alderley, in Cheshire where he studied classics, modern languages and mathematics, following which on 31 October 1855 he began his articles

Fig. 2.2 Early photograph of the Hall. In the centre of the photograph are believed to be John Mercer and his second wife Helen, whilst on the left are Ellen Mercer (John's daughter by his first marriage) and Ann Taylor (Helen's widowed mother).

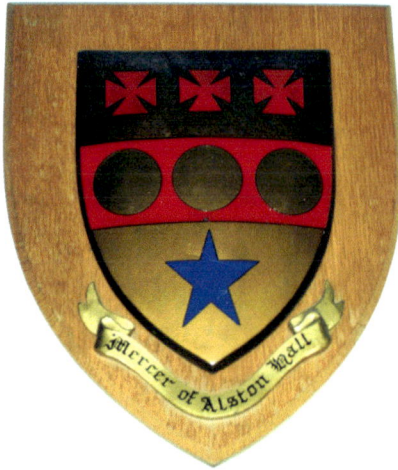

Fig. 2.3 Shield of Arms incorrectly indicating Mercer of Alston Hall, entrance hall (June 2015).

in architecture in the Manchester office of P. B. Alley who had been in partnership with Richard Lane, Manchester's leading architect. The office of Alley and Lane was at the corner of Chapel Walks and Cross Street where Lane was devoted to the Classical style. Alfred in his *Experiences* writes:

––– *the office at the corner of Chapel Walks and Cross Street was regarded in my young days with veneration and a certain amount of awe by the aspirants to architectural fame. Mr. Lane was a gentleman and a scholar. His practice was almost exclusively devoted to an attempt to force upon a commercial nineteenth-century town, with a sunless and humid climate, the refinement and perfect beauty of the art of the Greeks in the golden age of Pericles. Such was the school in which I was to receive my first impressions of architectural practice. It was a good school of study for a beginner; but its principles were impracticable for the time and climate. Mr. Waterhouse, R. A., was the first pupil to fall away from Mr. Lane and his severe classic work, and Gothic art in Manchester had its first great chance of exposition and application in the Assize Courts. This event was the death-blow to the repetition of Greek temples in banks, town halls, churches, Quakers' meetinghouses, and concert-halls. The principles of mediaeval architecture were seized upon with enthusiasm, and adapted to modern requirements.*

Mr Waterhouse mentioned above was Alfred Waterhouse (1830–1905) who had won the competition for the Assize Courts in Manchester in 1858 that brought him to national fame. This masterpiece of Gothic architecture was gutted by bombs in 1940 and stood as a ruin until cleared away in the late 1950s.

During his five-year pupillage with Alley, Alfred Darbyshire was to be engaged principally on the design of cotton mills that were to be filled with machinery from Messrs Platt Brothers of Oldham, one mill being the largest spinning establishment in the world on the Island of Narwa, near St Petersburg. Later, Alfred commented upon this kind of work:

> We tried hard to give some architectural character to the immense chimney-shafts and engine-house windows. We occasionally succeeded, when the cotton spinner had a soul that could soar beyond

Fig. 2.4 John Mercer's 'Achievement of Arms' on the entrance tower.

cotton; but it was uphill work, and one got heartily tired of it. Reward for this patient plodding came at last in some good domestic work; and when I left the office, in 1862, an interesting miscellaneous practice was established.

The fifties had been a time when Alfred was busily involved in the world of art as an accomplished artist. In 1857, he visited the great Art Treasures Exhibition in Manchester, and was in awe at what he saw.

That wonderful collection of representative examples of bygone art, and of typical specimens of the art of our time, was to me a revelation. Here I first came face to face with the Old Masters. My mind, in its process of throwing off the shackles of Classicism, was ready to

Fig. 2.5 Skylight in the entrance hall (June 2015).

Fig. 2.6 'Discs' motifs around the base of the skylight.

> *embrace the wonders of mediaeval and pre-Raphaelite art gathered*
> *in the first gallery of that ever memorable Exhibition.*

At the end of his pupillage with Alley, Alfred remained with him as his assistant for some months, his first holiday in this capacity being spent in the autumn of 1860 sketching amongst the abbeys and castles of Yorkshire during which he met the architect George Gilbert Scott at Ripon Cathedral. In 1862 Alfred began his own architectural practice in St James's Square, Manchester, and in 1864 made his first Continental tour through Belgium, Germany and Holland.

> *At this remote period my sketches and studies in these countries bring*
> *the details and adventures of that journey vividly before me; the sweet*
> *chimes of Antwerp are still ringing in my ear, –––. The architecture*
> *of the churches, town halls, and palaces of Belgium and the Rhine*
> *fascinated me. I returned convinced that there was no art equal in*
> *beauty and poetry to that of the Middle Ages. Shortly after arriving*
> *in England, I was elected an Associate of the Royal Institute of British*
> *Architects, and thus was fairly launched on a professional career.*

Alfred was then to enter a competition for the design of a town hall at Pendleton, for which he expressed his admiration for Gothic architecture but was advised by friends to produce an alternative design in the Classical style. To his surprise the latter won the competition, the Gothic one having no chance and by this experience he was to realise that mediaeval architecture required special treatment if it was to be adapted to nineteenth-century requirements.

Alfred Darbyshire was a fair-minded person and despised any form of unfair practice especially in the field of architecture. It was most probably due to his upbringing as a Quaker that made him this way, and with regard to architectural competitions he would write:

> The struggling architect is tempted to do all sorts of queer things in order to gather a practice together: he enters into competitions, and ultimately retires from this line of work disappointed and disgusted with unfair adjudication. There seems to be no cure for this competition curse. We may protest and attempt professional legislation, but human nature is too powerful: men will compete, and adjudication will often be partial, unfair, and illogical. If architects of repute would make a stand against the practice, there might be a chance of reform; and those who organise these competitions would be driven to liberality and fairness in order to secure the best talent in the profession.

Early on in his childhood on hearing his mother quoting from Shakespeare, Scott, Cowper, Byron and other well-known writers, Alfred developed a taste for poetry and poetic drama, and during the late 1850s he would visit the Theatre Royal Hotel in Manchester, the haunt of the star actors of the day. Here he would meet and secure a lasting friendship with Charles Alexander Calvert, the manager of the Theatre Royal, and soon Alfred would become involved with the theatre initially as an actor.

His first attempt at acting came in 1864 in the hall of the Athenseum, Bury, where he would recite the poem, 'Invocation to the Spirit of Shakespeare' following which began plays by Shakespeare to mark the three hundredth anniversary of his birth. Alfred was an instant success with the audience and later in his *Experiences* wrote:

> This was my first attempt at acting; but, strange to say, the newspapers said nice things of my effort, and I was seriously advised to throw up the "T square" and take to the sock and buskin. But no, I held true to

Fig. 2.7 Column of polished Shap granite in the chapel (June 2015). A row of 'discs' can be seen at the top of its carved stone capital.

my first love. I clung tenaciously to bricks and mortar, in spite of the tempting prospect held out.

In the same year Alfred appeared on stage at the Theatre Royal in Manchester as Jacques in *As You Like It* and was offered but refused a professional acting contract. At Bury in 1865 he played Polonius to Henry Irving's *Hamlet*, and in 1869 his friend Charles Calvert the actor-manager of the Prince's Theatre in Manchester employed him to redecorate the theatre. From then on Alfred spent much of his architectural practice in redecorating and designing theatres.

As the nineteenth century progressed, the fire hazard in the theatre domain was constantly in the minds of those responsible for the safety of audiences and actors. In 1884 Alfred Darbyshire and Henry Irving presented the Irving–Darbyshire Safety Theatre that called for the fitment of an asbestos safety curtain that in the event of fire would isolate the audience from the stage. There was also to be a louvered and glazed lantern to attract smoke and fire to its shaft. Emergency exits were to have easy access to the streets and escape staircases had to be absolutely fireproof; a safety plan that was to be readily recognised and accepted.

In the new Comedy Theatre in Manchester, opened in December 1884, Alfred was to carry out his 'safety in the theatre' ideas but later wrote:

> ––– but the nature of the site prevented their complete realisation. It was not till the awful disaster at Exeter in 1887 that people realised the fact that theatres were not properly planned and constructed. There was nothing unusual in the Exeter Theatre designed by my friend Mr. Phipps; it was as good a type as could be planned on existing lines; but the fearful loss of life when it was burned startled everybody into the conclusion that something must be done by which such fearful tragedies as those of the Ring Theatre at Vienna, and at Exeter, should be rendered impossible.

It would be at Exeter where people in the gallery had died in their seats by inhaling the poisonous gases given off by the fire, that Alfred was called upon to rebuild the theatre to his 'safety' plans. In 1889–91, he designed the Palace Theatre of Varieties on Oxford Road in Manchester where he would incorporate many of his safety features. Externally the stone-clad building was executed in a free Renaissance style with paired columns and pilasters on each of three floors, topped on the Oxford Street façade by a decorated gable, whilst in the centre of the first floor on Oxford Street was an open loggia. Sadly all was to go, this exterior being altered in 1913 and then clad in beige tiles in 1956, but thankfully the interior was beautifully restored in the 1980s.

Throughout his professional career Alfred attended social gatherings that brought him into contact with the cultural and artistic side of society. He was a member of the Brasenose Club, created in Manchester in December 1869, to *promote the association of gentlemen of literary, scientific, or artistic professions, pursuits, or tastes*, and would be where the painter, the poet, the actor and the musician would meet on a social standing. The first circular announcing the formation of the Club contained amongst others the signatures of Sir Charles Halle, Alfred Waterhouse R.A., and Edwin Waugh, the Lancashire poet. Alfred became a friend of Ford Madox Brown who created the great murals in Manchester town Hall, and visited the pre-Raphaelite artist and poet, Dante Gabriel Rossetti at his Cheyne Walk

Fig. 2.8 Cartouche of John Mercer's initials on a chimney stack, southwest-facing façade (June 2015). Re-pointing at some period has had a detrimental effect about the surrounding stonework.

home in Chelsea. Another pre-Raphaelite artist and friend of Alfred was Sir John Everett Millais.

The late 1860s saw Alfred doing two tours of the Continent that he would write about:

> Before closing the first decade of professional life, I may briefly allude to two visits to the Continent. In 1867 I went to the Paris Exhibition, held in the Champ de Mars; here I first saw the works of Millet, Jules Breton, Corot, and other artists, who influenced the methods of that wonderful trio of English painters, Fred Walker, George Mason, and George Pinwell: these men almost trod on the heels of another historic trio, the pre-Raphaelites, Millais, Holman Hunt, and Dante Gabriel Rossetti.

In 1868 I went through Normandy and Brittany, sketching the quaint domestic work, and studying the round-arched Gothic so beautifully illustrated in these northern French provinces.

The year 1870 was a good one for Alfred for as well as having two drawings exhibited at the Royal Academy illustrating the interior decorations carried out under his supervision at the Prince's Theatre in Manchester, he married Sarah Marshall with whom he was to have a son and three daughters. One of his last commissions in his declining years before he died on 5 July 1908 had been to design the triumphal arches for Queen Victoria's opening of the Manchester Ship Canal in 1894.

Amongst his many architectural works would be Heaton Moor Reform Club, Salford Police Station, the library at Knutsford, schools, and mock castles and hunting lodges in Ireland. Today, an example of his restoration work can be seen at Ordsall Hall, Salford. Erected centuries ago in brick and timber in spacious grounds, by the 1870s it was unoccupied and surrounded by industrial premises. In 1875 it was rented out as a working men's club, and when the lease ran out in 1896 the Hall was in urgent need of restoration. To the rescue came Earl Egerton of Tatton who asked Alfred to undertake the restoration work and also to design a church on the site as the Hall was to be used by the Church of England as a clergy training school. When finished the architecture of the church was in perfect harmony with that of the restored Hall, a tribute to the architect, but unfortunately the church (St Cyprian's) had to be demolished in 1967 because of subsidence.

Prior to the building of Alston Hall, Alfred had designed his own house that was to be built in Broughton Park on the outskirts of Manchester in 1871. Commenting on this he wrote:

I entered on this piece of extravagance for two reasons. In the first place I wanted to give expression to a few fanciful notions I had in regard to modern domestic architecture, and which I felt no client would ever be induced to allow me to realise; in the second place I thought that what might be looked upon as architectural eccentricities would arouse some criticism and draw the attention of the public to the fact that a young and struggling architect must advertise in some form in order to live. I was not disappointed in the result of this experiment; before the house was finished the historic Town Clerk of Manchester, Sir Joseph Heron, insisted upon renting it, and never rested content until he became the absolute owner of the property.

Such must have given Alfred confidence and pleasure as a domestic house architect, yet in his *Experiences* he does not mention in detail the building of Alston Hall and only presents a brief reference to it:

> *Passing over the alterations still going on at various intervals since 1869 at the Prince's Theatre, Manchester, the building of Alston Hall, near Preston, for my friend, the late John Mercer, I arrive at the springtime of 1878, when I made a tour, with two dear friends, through North and Central Italy.*

For the Alston mansion Alfred was to present an eclectic rendering of the Medieval–Baronial/Tudor–Elizabethan period, that appeared as Tudor Revival style in general for the outer façades and medieval Gothic for the entrance hall and first floor landing area. Inside the entrance hall with its medieval styled ceiling, Gothic arched doorways were to have at the headstops of their hoodmoulds carved plaster bosses representing the natural world of animals, fruits, flowers and leaves, two being symbolic of a colliery owner with one showing a miner at work, the other a pit-head

Fig. 2.9 Cartouche bearing the date 1876 on the entrance tower. Note the superb original pointing of the stonework in comparison to that seen in fig. 2.8.

winding wheel. The architect's passion for Gothic was to be clearly evident on looking up to the galleried landing with its two sets of Venetian style arches supported on polished pillars of granite hewn from the quarries of Shap away to the north in Westmorland, now Cumbria.

As one ascended the cantilevered staircase the first set of arches would be on the left (fig. 4.23) from where standing on the corridor behind, one could visualise a small Elizabethan audience looking down upon a performance of a Shakespearean play on the black and white marble floor below, a floor that could be seen as reminiscent of one belonging to a banqueting hall of the Middle Ages. In the base of the second set of arches on the landing (fig. 4.26) and also within the surround of the skylight above (fig. 2.6) decorative feature work was present by a row of discs within the stonework, each disc having a smaller disc recessed within it. On close inspection such decorative work was to be a common feature about the interior and exterior of the mansion.

The opportunity to establish the significance of these discs and why they had been incorporated within some of the design features about the mansion came when the Principal of the college, Graham Wilkinson was preparing a booklet *The Alston Hall Trail* published in 2000. He would ask me because of my long-standing study of heraldry if I could suggest why Alfred Darbyshire had presented these discs and why the shield of Arms on the entrance tower was different to the one on the wall in the Hall's entrance hall.

Fig. 2.3 shows the latter Arms with a scroll bearing the words Mercer of Alston Hall. Even though in heraldry a scroll in this position normally bears a motto, the one shown was incorrect in that investigations would reveal that the Arms belonged to a Scottish Mercer unrelated to John Mercer of Alston Hall. The Arms in the entrance hall compared to those on the entrance tower (fig. 2.4) had the addition of three gold discs referred to in heraldry as roundels representing bezants that were gold coins minted in Byzantium at the time of the Crusades.

In the language of heraldry a description (blazon) of the Arms in the entrance hall at Alston was:

> *Or, on a fess gules three bezants, between in chief three crosses paty of the second, and a mullet azure in base,* in which *Or* (gold or yellow) refers to the colour of the shield; *gules* (red); *azure* (blue); whilst *'of the second'* refers to the second colour mentioned in order, in this case, *gules*. These colours about the shield on the tower

were the same, represented by dots and lines in the stone, dots indicating *Or*, vertical lines representing *gules* and horizontal lines indicating *azure*.

To unravel the mystery of why the two shields differed in such a manner a letter was sent with a photograph of the Arms in the entrance hall to the College of Arms in London enquiring if John Mercer had been granted these Arms. A reply of 27 April 2000 revealed that it was most unlikely that such a grant had been made as in his reply Timothy H. S. Duke the Chester Herald was to state:

Dear Mr Wilkinson,

Searches have been carried out in the official registers of Arms to determine whether the Arms in your photograph, attributed to Mercer of Alston Hall, are on record and I now write to report the results.

There is no record of this precise design in the English and Welsh registers, although the same Arms within a border Azure were assigned to Douglas Mercer of Fordell House, Dalgetty co: Fife GB, Lt Gen in the army and Colonel of the 68th (The Durham Regiment) by Patent of Lord Lyon King of Arms dated 10 January 1853, and matriculated in the Public Register of All Arms and Bearings in Scotland. A transcript of the Patent has been entered in the College registers (Coll Arm Scotland 1 313). General Mercer was the son of George Mercer, Lt Col of First Life Guards, and grandson of George Mercer, who descended from a younger branch of the Mercers of Aldie co: Perth.

The simple Arms on the shield are therefore Scottish. They were matriculated for Mistress Gryssall Mercer, heretrix of Adie (rightly Aldie) in the Public Register of All Arms and Bearings in Scotland (1672–1677). The College has a manuscript copy of this part of the Register, in which the Arms are blazoned OR ON A FESS BETWEEN THREE CROSSES PATY IN CHIEF GULES AND ONE STAR IN BASE AZURE AS MANY BEZANTS. A modern blazon would describe the star as a mullet. The family's Crest was A CROSS OR and their motto Crux Christi nostra corona (Coll Arm Lyon Register First Vol p 272).

According to <u>Burke's Peerage</u> (1894), Aldie passed to a Mercer heiress named Jean, the wife of Robert Nairne, who was killed at the Battle of Culloden in 1746. Their descendant Emily Jane Mercer-Elphinstone-De Flahaut was Baroness Nairne in her own right, and brought the estate to her husband Henry (Petty-Fitzmaurice) Marquess of Lansdowne (died 1866).

The family is described in G R Mercer's <u>Our Seven Centuries, an account of the Mercers of Aldie and Meikleour, and their branches</u>. (Perth, 1868)

John Mercer of Alston Hall (1820–1893) is not on official record here. It is most unlikely that he was entitled to the Arms on the shield, which belonged to the senior line of the Mercers of Aldie. The family had no male heirs, which explains why the estate passed to an heiress in the 18th century. The assumption of Arms belonging to another family of the same surname was a common practice in the 19th century, although contrary to the Laws of Arms.

You asked about the significance of the charges, but I am afraid that I cannot offer an explanation. Crosses paty, mullets and bezants are all well known heraldic devices, which may not have a specific meaning in this context.

I am sorry to send such a disappointing report.

Yours sincerely,

Timothy Duke

Chester Herald

So the mystery surrounding the Arms in the entrance hall had now been solved along with the fact that John Mercer had never been officially granted Arms. The 1870s was a period when many 'new money' men applied for a coat of arms in a bid to illustrate their new status in life, some paying for the privilege of having them. The presentation of the Arms seen today on the entrance tower at Alston Hall was most probably the idea of Alfred Darbyshire who was well read in the science and art of heraldry and who decided that such a display of heraldry would be in keeping with the Hall's architecture. If so, during his searches to find Arms associated with the name of Mercer, Darbyshire discovered or had prior knowledge of the Scottish Arms as outlined in the letter above, and realised that he had to produce a slightly different blazon for John Mercer's shield of Arms in comparison to that of the Scottish Arms. Not to do so would be in gross contradiction to one particular rule of heraldry that in short declares that no two persons can have the same Arms. On page 9 in *Boutell's Heraldry* revised by C. W. Scott-Giles, one reads:

> *Since arms were primarily a means of identification, they necessarily aimed at being absolutely distinctive. At the same time there was a natural tendency for men allied by blood or feudal ties to bear similar arms, though with sufficient difference to prevent confusion between them. Furthermore, in the early days of heraldry, there was a likelihood of too close a similarity occurring between the arms of men in no way connected, due merely to the fact that a comparatively few devices and figures were in frequent use. "Differencing" of arms therefore became necessary not only to distinguish the shield of a cadet from that of the head of the family, and of a vassal from that of his feudal chief, but also to prevent identity between the arms of strangers who happened to have selected the same simple combination of form and colour.*

So it seems that Alfred Darbyshire made use of the Scottish Arms of Mercer by removing the three bezants on them resulting in the shield of Arms for John Mercer as seen today within the heraldic composition on the Hall's entrance tower. If John Mercer's ancestors had borne Arms, this heraldic composition would most likely have been in the form of a full 'Achievement of Arms' displaying a shield surmounted by an helmet bearing a Crest from under which 'mantling' in a plant-like form would have cascaded down each side of the shield. 'Supporters' in the form of human figures or members of the heraldic zoo, etc. might have been standing, one on either side of the shield, complete with a motto at the base of the Achievement.

As can be seen from the heraldic composition on the tower at Alston there is no Crest. Early shields and illustrated manuscripts show knights with their helmets bearing fan-shaped extensions upon which is painted the blazon to be seen on the knight's shield. Such fan-shaped devices were the early form of the Crest that to some extent gave protection against battleaxe and sword from cleaving through both helmet and the head within. By the time of the late medieval tournament ornate crests had appeared, some modelled in boiled leather supported by a wire cage to represent birds, heraldic beast etc., in keeping with the knight's rank and pedigree.

If there had been a Crest on display at Alston it would have been sitting on a 'torse' or 'wreath', the purpose of a wreath being to hide the join between helmet and Crest. Represented by a twisted ribbon of silk it would normally show two alternating colours beginning with that of the principal metal in the Arms, the other being the principal tincture. However, there appears to be no definite ruling for the colours in a wreath to correspond with that of the principal metal and tincture in Arms. For example the wreath for the Crest of Arthur Hillmen Birtwistle (fig. 14.5) has the colours or and gules whilst his Arms are *Sable, a chevron erminois, in chief two weasels statant, argent and in base a birt naiant, argent.*

The motto *Esse Quam Videri* on the entrance tower at Alston, translated reads: *To be rather than to see,* whilst the heraldic composition correctly signifies the rank of John Mercer as being that of an esquire or gentleman by portraying a steel helmet with its visor closed and turned sideways as shown.

'Mantling' depicted at Alston represents the cloth once worn by a knight to protect his armour and therefore himself from the sun's heat in foreign climates, for example during the time of the Crusades. This textile apparel soon became a decorative accessory for a shield and Crest in heraldic art appearing as a tattered garment to signify the sword cuts it would have received in battle. Its final form would be as a picturesque cascade of curling strands, plant-like in appearance as mentioned above, the outer surface being the principal tincture of the Arms whilst the lining being the colour of the principal metal. At Alston the mantling issues from behind the shield, the latter hanging by a strap, or in heraldic language, a guige, complete with buckle from a 'boss-like' object some distance above the helmet. Supporting a shield in this way is acceptable when there are no 'supporters'.

Arms often allude to the name of the person bearing the Arms, and sometimes the entire design on a shield can represent a pictorial pun on the name, a well known one being the Arms of De Ferres (*Argent, six horseshoes sable*). Making a 'play' on a particular name in this way was a favourite practice in heraldry during the Middle Ages. On the Scottish Arms of Mercer the three bezants could be seen as an allusion to or a 'play' on the name of Mercer as mercers in general were merchants who bought and sold goods and wares during which the bezant (gold coin) played an important part in the financial transactions. A good example to illustrate the bezant's association with financial transaction, in this case money lending, was the pawnbroker's sign consisting of three golden balls which from whatever angle one looked at them, they always appeared as flat discs representing bezants.

As to the many disc-like motifs presented externally and internally about Alston Hall, one came to the conclusion rightly or wrongly that Alfred Darbyshire having decided to remove the bezants from the Scottish Arms of Mercer, presented them in the form of discs-like motives thus making a 'play' on the Mercer name at Alston and its connection with this particular gold coin. No evidence has been found to support such a conclusion but Alfred Darbyshire with his comprehensive knowledge of heraldry had books on the subject that today are in the John Rylands Library in Manchester, and writing in his *Experiences* mentions his involvement with heraldry.

> *In December, 1861, the Prince Consort died. Manchester went into mourning; hatchments and other tokens of distress were hung out. I had turned my attention to Heraldry with a view to its use as an architectural adornment: the study of it had such a fascination for me that I went deeper and deeper in my investigations. At that time I knew enough to take exception to the absurd manner in which the hatchments of the Prince were painted and displayed on the public buildings of the city. I pointed out these absurdities in the columns of the Manchester Guardian, and a newspaper warfare ensued. I maintained my position by an appeal to "Lancaster Herald" (the post being then occupied by Mr. Albert W. Woods, now Sir Albert and "Garter King"), who most emphatically confirmed my statements. The discomfiture of my enemies was complete, and the absurd "heraldic anomalies" disappeared from the streets. My intercourse with the College of Arms has been maintained. The venerable Garter King is still on his throne, and in 1894 he conferred an honour upon me in connection with the Society of Antiquaries.*

> *Sometime after this heraldic dispute my relative C. Bradshaw, eldest son of George Bradshaw, of Railway Guide celebrity (before mentioned), introduced me to a gentleman who brought with him the great folio edition, 1724, of Guillims's "Display of Heraldry"; he wished to colour the blank shields: I instructed him in some of the mysteries of the science, and gave him the key to correct blazon.*

At Alston Hall one is constantly aware of the presence of these 'discs' motives, prominent ones to be seen on the base of the oriel window (fig. 3.6) on the entrance tower and those on the water tower (fig. 3.14). Inside the Hall such motives can be observed at the bottom of window and doorway casements, and perhaps the casual observer might be forgiven for overlooking those on the corner corbels within the porte-cochere (fig. 4.3).

During his involvement with the theatre, Alfred Darbyshire spent much of the time designing stage sets and costumes. When in 1872 his close friend Charles Alexander Calvert produced *Henry V* as part of a revival of Shakespeare's plays at the Prince's Theatre in Manchester, Alfred had designed the scenery, part of which would illustrate his comprehensive knowledge of the 'gentle science' of heraldry. Recalling this time he would say:

> *I had the good fortune to be intimately associated with my friend in this celebrated revival. When this work was in contemplation, I happened to be resident at Marple Hall, in Cheshire, formerly the home of Bradshaw, the regicide, and it was in this house, surrounded by armour, tapestry, old pictures, and quaint furniture, that I planned out and designed the architectural scenes; and it was here also that I conceived the idea of realising the correct blazon of the arms and banners, as they were actually used on the heroic field of Agincourt.*

On looking at the design of the heraldic display on the entrance tower at Alston, one instantly recognises it is the work of someone who 'knew his heraldry', and praise must also go to the sculptor who executed the work. The three exquisitely carved cartouches, one showing the date 1876 on the northeast face of the tower; one displaying John Mercer's initials on the Hall's southwest-facing façade; and another bearing his initials on an end gable of the stable block, bear testimony to an artist of some merit and a sculptor of superb dexterity and skill. Inside the entrance hall and down the main corridor the carved plaster bosses about the doorway arches again bear testimony to fine design and craftsmanship as do the decorated panels on the entrance hall's ceiling discovered in 2018 during restoration work following the fire of 2017.

Having designed his building the Victorian architect would consult his quantity surveyor who would supply figures on which the builder could base his tender for the work. After the plans and a price for the building had been accepted and construction was underway, the architect would rally his selection of artists and craftsmen. For example, Samuel Sanders

Teulon (1812–73), the architect of Bestwood Lodge, about five miles north of Nottingham for the 10th Duke of St Albans, had John Gregory Crace to undertake the interior decorations; Francis Skidmore of Coventry for the metalwork; and Thomas Earp to execute the fine carvings.

Skidmore was George Gilbert Scott's favourite metalworker, and for his Albert Memorial in Kensington Scott would rely on him for the railings; John Birnie Philip and Henry Hugh Armstead for carving the figures in the podium frieze; and John Clayton of Clayton & Bell, stained glass manufacturers, for 'Poetry', the mosaic in the pediment of the canopy above the figure of Albert. 'America', one of the four Continents placed at the outer corners of the monument is by John Bell whilst the gilded bronze of Albert is the work of John Henry Foley.

For his decorative feature work at Alston Alfred Darbyshire must have had easy access to artists and craftsmen for such work, most likely through his membership of the Brasenose Club and also as an architect recently involved in the design and decoration of a theatre in Manchester. In his *Experiences* he gives no indication as to the identity of such gifted persons that would work for him at Alston Hall, but does mention the names of two artists who would be engaged by him whilst enlarging the Prince's Theatre in Manchester during the 1870s. The theatre had been opened in 1864, Alfred's friend Charles Alexander being the manger, and owing to a successful series of Shakespearian Revivals being staged it was decided to enlarge the theatre and to decorate and equip the building in an artistic and luxurious manner. Alfred was called upon to undertake the task and recalling the time would write:

> *Thus commenced my association with theatre architecture, with the art of the stage, and with many distinguished men and women who have adorned their profession; and who have gained for the theatre an amount of respect hitherto unknown in its history.*

> *During the preparation and carrying out of these works at the Prince's Theatre in 1869 it was necessary that I should frequently visit London, as much of the artistic work was executed by Metropolitan artists and workmen. It was in this year that I made the acquaintance of H. Stacy Marks (now Royal Academician). He had painted a frieze of dancing figures for the theatre in Long Acre with such success that I determined to secure his valuable aid in the decoration of the Prince's Theatre; he accordingly undertook the commission to paint a Shakespearian frieze for the new proscenium. Marks entered into*

this grand decorative work heartily, and during its progress (it was painted on canvas in his studio in St. John's Wood), I had much pleasant intercourse with the art-world of the –––.

Later on in his *Experiences* he again recalls the alterations carried out at the Prince's Theatre and mentions the painter William Phillips.

The alterations were very extensive, and somewhat difficult of attainment. I was instructed to provide an additional circle without raising the roof, and to construct a new proscenium. I was allowed carte-blanche in the decoration; but the scheme was to be in accordance with the Shakespearian idea of the management. I accordingly induced H. Stacy Marks, R. A., to paint a proscenium frieze, the subject being Shakespeare enthroned between Tragedy and Comedy, and attended on either side by representative figures from the principal plays. This picture is one of the finest decorative paintings of our time, and retains its beauty and freshness to the present day. The box fronts were adorned by medallion portraits of the principal tragic characters, with incidents from the plays, all painted by William Phillips.

Once established in his own office, an architect would take on assistants and pupils, as did Alfred Darbyshire, but such persons belonging to his Manchester practice are not mentioned in connection with the building of Alston Hall. Commenting upon pupils and assistants he would say:

Another curious thing a young architect is tempted to do, is to take into his office pupils whose parents and guardians pay premiums which in many instances are thrown away, either because the pupil has no aptitude for his work, or because his master neglects him, and leaves him to shift for himself, or to the kind sympathy of some office assistant. By adopting the plan of never allowing a pupil to be articled without endeavouring to gauge his capacity, I have been singularly fortunate in turning out young men who have taken creditable and honourable positions in life. In cases where the artistic faculty has been strongly developed, it has received proper encouragement. Ruskin has said: "It is not necessary for an artist to be an architect, but it is necessary for an architect to be an artist." I take some pride, however, in the knowledge that some of my pupils, who have attained high positions in the world of art, have made good use of the architectural instruction they received. One of my earliest pupils and assistants was the late J. Moyr-Smith. Although he stuck manfully to the "T square", it was evident that he possessed artistic faculties of a high order. The development of these faculties was encouraged, and, acting on my advice, he went to London. If I remember rightly, he gained admission into the office of the late Sir Gilbert Scott. Although his experience in this office was principally confined to a study of Gothic art, he had by nature and inclination a Classic taste, which was expressed to the world through the columns of Punch.

There is no doubt that a good 'architect-cum-client relationship' existed at Alston, and in his *Experiences* Alfred Darbyshire was to comment on what he referred to as the curiosities of architectural practice.

The architect's professional life is little known, and often misunderstood by the general public; and this general public, as a rule, is no respecter of persons or professions when business has to be considered. ––– He has to fight with the client who knows what architecture is (or thinks he knows) better than himself; he has to humour the whims of the man who has to "pay the piper," and worse than all, he has to work for the client who has only a utilitarian soul;--- the man who says in effect, "Give me a good square thing with a middle entrance, and a room on each side, and I care nothing about skylines, grouping, or perspective effects; and none of your ornament for me." If the poor architect quarrels with these conditions he may starve, and somebody else does the work, as a mere matter of pounds, shillings, and pence. But oh! the luxury of having a client who puts his trust in you, and takes what you give him, as a man takes the physic prescribed by his doctor! He gets the best you have to give, and is satisfied; but if he should, in addition to his confidence and liberality, have an artistic mind, and strive after artistic things, then the architect's happiness is supreme. It is such conditions as these that make professional life pleasant, and which generate friendships never to be forgotten.

Chapter three

Architecture of the Hall – grounds and gardens

As mentioned above, Longridge stone would be the main building material for the new mansion at Alston. Readily available three miles north of Alston at Longridge, this carboniferous sandstone sometimes of a gritstone nature was looked upon as being most reliable for building purposes. It was a good colour and could easily be dressed for a variety of surfaces and shapes.

Sir Nikolaus Pevsner (1902–83), one of the most learned and stimulating twentieth-century writers on art and architecture, writing about North Lancashire in one of his county volumes on architectural guides, *The Buildings of England,* would say:

> *Sandstone plays a much more important part than limestone in the Lancashire picture. Some of the sandstone is Triassic, some Carboniferous. The Triassic (New Red) sandstone underlies the clays of a considerable part of southern and western Lancashire and reappears at the extremities of the Cartmel and Furness peninsulas (N); but usually it is at too great of depth to be quarried. The principal quarries, Woolton and Rainhill, were on the ridges in and near Liverpool (S). Stone from both these quarries is still being used for the Anglican Cathedral at Liverpool; the colour is a somewhat somber pink, by no means gay despite its comparatively warm hue. Triassic sandstone was also brought into south-west Lancashire from Runcorn and Storeton on the Cheshire side of the Mersey.*

The Carboniferous sandstones come partly from the Coal Measures and, outside the coalfields, from the immediately underlying Millstone Grit. These mostly dull buff or grey sandstones, although they lack charm, are much tougher and more reliable than those from the Triassic formation; moreover, they possess the inestimable property, in Lancashire, of being largely resistant to the disintegrating influence of a smoke-laden atmosphere. The sandstones of the Coal Measures are confined to a region well S of the Ribble, well N of the Mersey and well back from the coast, but they make an important contribution to the appearance of such cotton-spinning towns as Oldham (S), Rochdale (S) and Colne (N). The gritstone, often quarried in enormous blocks, is more characteristic of the rural areas; there is plenty of it in the Pennine villages, and everywhere between Morecambe Bay and the Trough of Bowland, not excluding Lancaster itself, which is largely built of pale yellow gritstone (all N).

Fig. 3.1 Alston Hall and its grounds as shown on the first edition (1893) map of the Ordnance Survey. Against the Hall's southwest-facing wall is a conservatory (hatched) whilst to the northwest are glasshouses (hatched), boiler house, coach house, stable block and walled garden, beyond which is the 'shamrock' pond.

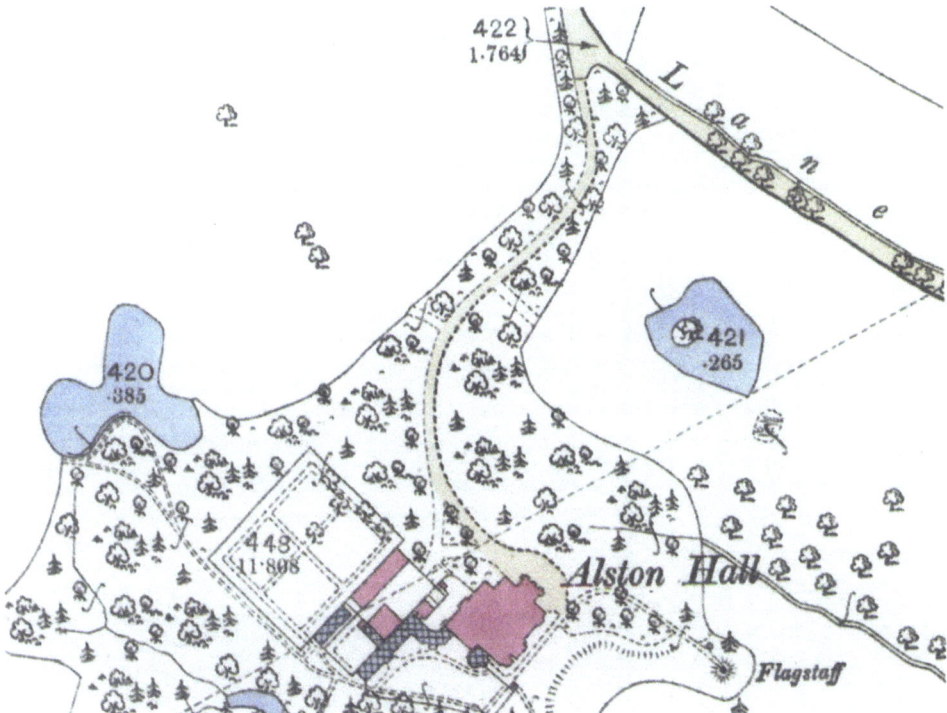

Prior to the nineteenth century in the Longridge area small delphs had been opened to extract the buff coloured carboniferous sandstone for local buildings, and by the early years of the nineteenth century rapid developments were to be seen in the Longridge quarrying industry as demand for the stone increased for the building of textile mills, housing, churches, and public buildings, etc. Eight quarries were to be worked, five of which were on the Tootle Height ridge northeast of the village, and when Alston Hall was under construction in the mid 1870s, somewhere in the region of 400 men were associated with the Longridge industry. Today in Preston, Fishergate Baptist Church, St Walburge's Church (its tower and spire to be erected later in limestone), St Mark's Church, Fulwood Barracks and the Harris Museum and Library building, are amongst the many impressive examples of Longridge stone construction.

The sandstone used for the exterior work at Alston would fall into two distinct categories, rock-faced for the walls and smooth ashlar as quoins for corners and mid-wall support around windows and doorways as well as a decorative element in certain areas. At Alston the dressed rugged appearance of the rock-faced stones convey a sensation of strength whilst the smooth surfaces of the ashlar can be seen (fig. 3.8) to act as an excellent foil to the vigour of the rock-faced walls.

Setting the stones at Alston would have been the responsibility of the fixer mason, more than likely adopting the established practice of setting each stone on a bed of mortar that would have been a mixture of fine gritty sand and 'putty lime'. For the joints a thin mortar grout would have been applied, its lime putty content being soft which allowed the stones to 'breathe' and dry out after being subjected to wet weather. If for some reason the mortar had to be harden slightly a small amount of white cement could be added to the mix, although no evidence has been found that the masons at Alston Hall used cement only with sand. At the time when the Hall was being built, Portland cement was available having been patented in 1824 but it did not come into widespread use until the turn of the century, but too much cement could produce a hard mortar that could impede the aeration of the joints with disastrous results. At Alston Hall putty lime was more than likely used in the plastering of its interior brick walls.

Basically the production of putty lime began with chunks of limestone being loaded between alternating courses of coal and wood inside a kiln, the resulting burn producing lump lime, known also as quick lime. By the nineteenth century quite a number of lime-burning kilns were operating

Fig. 3.2 The Hall illustrated in its contents sale catalogue of 1916. This photograph shows the result of some window re-modelling of *c*.1912–14 (compare with fig. 2.2) when transoms and mullions were removed. The Hall's water tower roof (centre left) still has its attractive ornamental cresting and lucarnes but sadly such features were removed in the 1950s to be replaced with a flat-roofed dormer window as shown in fig. 3.14.

about the countryside and the towns of north and east Lancashire to provide lump lime for farmers and their fields as well as for local builders. In Preston a double kiln arrangement once existed at the bottom of Aqueduct Street where it had been built against the embankment of the Lancaster canal that brought the limestone from the northern districts, the two kilns being loaded from the top (as was normal in any kiln) of the embankment.

The transport of the lump lime to wherever it was to be made into lime putty could be a hazardous journey if the utmost care was not taken as the smallest amount of water on the lump lime would start a reaction whereby the lime would give off much heat resulting in its boiling to threaten injury to those involved in its transportation.

To slake the lump lime into lime putty having made the safety precautions of wearing suitable clothing including goggles, mask and gloves, water was poured into a suitable container and the small lumps of lump lime added, never the other way round, following which there was

Fig. 3.3 Southeast-facing façade of the Hall (June 2015). On the ground floor from right to left is what originally had been the morning room; smoking room or study; drawing room; and the chapel, whilst on the first floor above had been (right to left) the pink bedroom; blue bedroom; and rose bedroom. Above the latter is what had originally been the bachelor's bedroom.

the immediate reaction of the mix soon boiling and bubbling. As the lime slaked it began to look like boiling white porridge and after a short while on settling down it had taken on a consistency similar to that of soft cream cheese. After standing for at least a fortnight, preferably even much longer, it was ready for use. At one time local building firms had huge beds of lime putty available for their own use and local sale, and I can remember one such firm where one could buy lime putty by the bucketful that when watered down could be used for whitewashing the backyards of terraced housing.

Skilful pointing of stonework plays a vital role in a building's aesthetic success and much care is needed in particularly to the colour of the mortar and how it is to be applied. The mortar should be as far as it is possible the same colour as the stone, especially in ashlar work where the joints are extremely thin (about one eighth of an inch), and should be flush with the wall-face. If mortared joints are much lighter or darker in colour, then the finished work will present a 'box of bricks' effect that unfortunately happened at Alston most likely during college days as seen in fig. 2.8. In this example even the pointing appears about the arrises (the sharp edges of the stones) so adding to the unsightly result.

At Alston in addition to the aesthetically pleasing exterior array of rock-faced and ashlar masonry would be the pillars of Shap granite about the porte-cochere and the surround of the main entrance and also within the interior of the Hall. The Westmorland quarry for this stone with its attractive large porphyritic crystals of pink feldspar had only begun to operate in about 1870. Apparently there was no local need for this granite as there was a plentiful supply of other stones that were possible to work a great deal more easily, nor was the granite ever to be used extensively in Westmorland, so the stone went elsewhere. Fortunately it had been possible to erect the quarry works beside the main London to Glasgow railway line.

What Alfred Darbyshire designed at Alston was not a mansion of palatial proportions but one representative of a medium sized country 'seat' for a new leader of industry wishing to have a house in the country well away from the heartland of industry. As mentioned above the overall style of the new mansion was to be that of the popular Tudor Revival period of the nineteenth century, with a careful selection of decoration in keeping with the Gothic Revival period that for domestic architecture had reached its zenith in popularity by the 1860s.

Fig. 3.4 One of two mythical creatures (similar to the gargoyles on the entrance tower) on the bay window of what had been the drawing room, southeast-facing façade (June 2015).

In Britain the Gothic Revival period is reckoned to have begun in the later years of the eighteenth century founded on the premise that medieval forms in architecture could be adapted within a modern setting for none secular buildings including country houses. In 1748 Horace Walpole, a Member of Parliament from 1741 to 1768 purchased a small house at Twickenham that he would remodel extensively from 1750 onwards in the Gothic style. The house to be known as Strawberry Hill was to be the first completely Gothic house of the revival period, having exterior and interior features as well as furnishings in the Gothic style. It was a time when the construction of follies and Gothic 'ruins' representative of medieval times would be popular. Even literary circles would be influenced by the air of romanticism of Gothic and also that of the melancholy element to be associated with it.

Part of Pope's poem, *Eloisa to Abelard* of 1717 expresses this melancholy:

> *In these lone walls (their days' eternal bound)*
> *These moss-grown domes with spiry turrets crowned,*
> *Where awful arches make a noonday night,*
> *And the dim windows shed a solemn light;*

A century later, novelists were adding horror to the Gothic scene such as Mary Shelley with her novel *Frankenstein*, published in 1818, and Polidori's *Vampyre* of 1819.

Before the period of its revival, Gothic architecture had always been considered and believed to be England's long established and adopted style, its cathedrals and churches supporting such a belief. But as the Gothic Revival got underway in the second half of the eighteenth century another style of architecture was running parallel to it in the popularity stakes, the Classical style. Such had long since made its debut on the English scene for secular and non-secular buildings including large mansions. The first predominantly Classical style building in Cambridge had been the Fellows Building (1640–43) at Christ's College. Before then Cambridge had seen both medieval Gothic and Classicism combined in some of its buildings. As to the Gothic Revival style, this had made its Cambridge debut between 1821–33 when Sir Jeffrey Wyatville re-designed Sidney Sussex College, transforming the original buildings from their authentic Elizabethan state into neo-Elizabethan Gothic.

Classical architecture was to be comprised of ancient Greek and Roman styles like the later sixteenth-century Palladian style associated with the Italian Renaissance period. It was architecture that stood for ideas of order

Fig. 3.5 Carriage court and entrance tower (June 2015). To the right of the tower's porte-cochere is the gable of what had been the hall lounge; the butler's pantry; and the later addition of a servant's hall.

and harmony derived from gods, nature and the universe. Decorative details such as columns with their bases, capitals and architraves belonged to a rigid system governed by the 'orders', the Doric, Ionic, Corinthian and the Composite.

Georgian architecture based on Classical style models would result in many Anglican churches being erected on such models in the closing decades of the Georgian age, the first Greek Revival style church in London being St Pancras' (new) Church (1822–24) by the architects H. W. and W. Inwood. In the Victorian era Classical architecture was a popular choice for Nonconformist places of worship but it was for monumental public buildings such as corn exchanges, art galleries and museums etc., that the Classical style throughout the nineteenth century and the years leading up to the 1930s would make its greatest impact on the architectural scene in Britain.

According to Sir Nikolaus Pevsner in his *The Buildings of England* for North Lancashire, for its early nineteenth-century houses he would write:

> *Although Gothic seems to have dominated more in North Lancashire than in other counties (because the men who commissioned the houses were short of known medieval ancestors?), the Grecian and otherwise classical contingent is substantial.*

Many of these Classical-style houses erected during the early to mid-Georgian era had ashlar-faced stone elevations, windows without mouldings, and porches with columns etc., plain and rather dull-looking buildings, and by the early nineteenth century quite a number were in need of structural attention and facelifts. Some of the owners of these houses would decide to Gothicise the exteriors, one striking example being Leighton Hall at Yealand Conyers about eight miles north of Lancaster. Its Georgian façade of 1759–61 executed in white local limestone was Gothicised in 1822–5 with pinnacles, decorated battlements and turrets etc. In 1870 Paley & Austin of Lancaster added an extension on the left flank of the main façade that with its tall tower was to give a pleasing picture of controlled asymmetry to the front elevation.

After 1870 Paley & Austin and their clients would turn away from any hint of Gothic for their houses as the popularity of Gothic had already begun to wane and by the dawn of the eighties a new style had appeared in domestic architecture, 'Old English'. This was to be a style associated with Richard Norman Shaw (1831–1912) as could be seen at 'Allerton Beeches' (1883–4), Allerton, Liverpool, prior to its demolition in c.1930, Shaw having designed the house for Henry Tate junior. Shaw was to be the most influential domestic architect of the late Victorian period, his early career coinciding with the heyday of the Gothic Revival. His 'Old English' domestic style of brick-built houses with massive chimney stacks, tile-hung storeys, half-timbered work, mullioned windows with leaded lights, and hipped and complex rooflines were to some extent fashioned on the old manor houses, farmhouses and cottages in Kent.

Another style of architecture that was becoming popular during the time when Alston Hall was under construction was the so-called 'Queen Anne' Revival style based on seventeenth-century vernacular Classicism as seen in Holland, France and Germany as well as England. With its red brick walls and sash windows with wooden panes painted white, it

Fig. 3.6 'Discs' on the base of the oriel window of the boudoir, entrance tower.

presented many of the elements to be seen in the Classical style but without the Classical laws of proportion. But 'Queen Anne' would be considered unsuitable for new country houses, its style not dignified enough and its image too much a middle-class one, only suitable in town and city. It was in this domain that 'Queen Anne' was to flourish in the eighties in London's Kensington area of Harrington and Collingham Gardens where Ernest George (knighted in 1911) and his practice partner Harold Ainsworth Peto were to design homes for the middle classes in the style's Flemish variant. Number 39 Harrington Gardens of 1882 built of red brick with stone dressings, its high and stepped front gable with leaded-lights windows, was to be the house of W. S. Gilbert of Savoy Opera fame.

Richard Norman Shaw would also adopt 'Queen Anne' in its many variants as seen at Albert Hall Mansions that were middle class flats of 1879–86, and for the new salubrious suburb of Bedford Park on the western edge of London in the late 1870s and early 1880s. Like many architects of the period, Shaw would copy past styles of architecture and in a letter to his friend and architect John Dando Sedding in November 1882 would write:

Fig. 3.7 A gargoyle on the entrance tower.

If I could get myself to believe that my half-timbered work and tall chimneys were in any way my own, I should sit up on my hind legs and purr away like our Tom cat John, but common honesty compels me to own that they are simply indifferent copies of old work.

By the 1880s the effects of a depression in agriculture was to see a slowing down of new country house building and where new houses were to appear they would in the main be within the rich and prosperous counties of Middle England and its southern ones. This was a period when Ernest George with Harold Peto would design some of the finest large country houses to be seen in England to be executed in the Tudor, Elizabethan and Jacobean Revival styles. By the eighties, Gothic for domestic architecture had 'run its course', having presented a legacy of country houses whose architecture today still attracts much admiration.

The year 1817 had seen the publication of what has been considered to be the first accurate account of the development of the Gothic style. It had been written by Thomas Rickman who later in the 1820s as a leading architect of the early Gothic Revival period would be the architect of St

Peter's Church in Preston, the foundation stone laying ceremony taking place during Preston Guild Week 1822, whilst its later tower and steeple would be an addition of 1851–2 by Joseph Mitchell of Sheffield.

The second decade of the nineteenth century was a time of social unrest within the labouring classes especially in the North of England. Only a few years had passed since the revolution in France, and in parts of Britain atheism and revolution was in the air so it was thought that an increase in religious worship might ease the problem. A sum of one million pounds was extracted from the French as reparations and channelled to a Church of England Commission for disbursement, 1818 seeing an Act for the building of additional churches in populous parishes. The sum of one million pounds was to be added to, and two hundred and fourteen churches of these so-called 'Waterloo Churches' were commissioned throughout

Fig. 3.8 The porte-cochere. At each headstop of the hoodmould of the outer arch is a 'grotesque', each one shown respectively in fig. 3.9 and fig. 3.10.

Fig. 3.9 A 'grotesque' on the porte-cochere.

Fig. 3.10 A 'grotesque' on the porte-cochere.

Architecture of the Hall – grounds and gardens

the United Kingdom, of which twelve were to be designed by Thomas Rickman, two in Preston, one being St Peter's and the other St Paul's of 1823–5 which is still extant (but not as a church) opposite the present bus station. St Paul's was the result of the Vicar of Preston pleading for two new churches but the £12,500 that had been allotted for the building of St Peter's was to be the sum granted for both churches.

Thomas Rickman had been born in Maidenhead in 1776, the eldest son of a Quaker and grandson of an apothecary/surgeon, and would first train as an apothecary before going on to study as a medical practitioner working in London hospitals that he found most unsuitable. Eventually he found work as an assistant to a Midlands grocery concern before returning home to complete his medical training to become his father's partner for two years. Dissatisfied with provincial life and medicine he returned to London to work as an office clerk, teaching himself book keeping, and in 1807 sought a living as an accountant/clerk in Liverpool.

During his time in Liverpool Rickman began to write articles on architecture and gave deeply researched lectures that would result in his election in 1812 as Professor of Architecture of the Liverpool Academy of Arts. Although he would continue to be nominally an accountant, he would engage himself in the designing of three Liverpool churches and several public buildings, and between 1813–16, he was to Gothicize a run-down sixteenth-century Lancashire manor house, Scarisbrick Hall near Southport for Thomas Scarisbrick. It has been thought that the Liverpool architect John Foster was involved in this work at Scarisbrick but Rickman's diaries (RIBA MSS Collection) make it clear that this was not so. The Hall was refaced in stone, new windows made, the porch re-designed, and Gothic detailing in the form of battlements, pinnacles and crockets added.

In 1817 Rickman was to commence practice as an architect, his first two buildings being 'cast iron' churches in Liverpool, a material he would use to some extent at St Peter's in Preston by way of window mullions and tracery, pew ends and columns supporting the gallery etc. Even the pulpit was of cast iron but sadly was removed and sold for scrap in 1975. The use of cast iron instead of carved stone would considerably lower the building cost, the various patterns for the casting moulds being used time and time again thereby resulting in large numbers of each type of cast iron elements and fittings being available. Today, St Peter's is part of the University of Central Lancashire and is used for a variety of secular activities.

In 1820 Rickman's practice in Liverpool had expanded sufficiently to warrant a second office to be opened in Birmingham under the control of Rickman's assistant, Henry Hutchinson. By the end of 1821 with his Liverpool practice having become of lesser importance, Rickman closed his Liverpool office and taking on Hutchinson as a partner moved to Birmingham. Over the next ten years the practice was successful, two major achievements being the New Court (1826–31) in Tudor–Gothic of St John's College, Cambridge, by Rickman and Hutchinson (to be known as the 'wedding cake building') and the 'Bridge of Sighs' designed in 1831 by Hutchinson, a bridge to connect New Court with the older courts of the college. Rickman would retire from practice after many illnesses three years before his death in 1841.

In 1833 Thomas Scarisbrick of Scarisbrick Hall died, to be replaced at the Hall by his brother Charles Scarisbrick who by 1837 had appointed Augustus Welby Northmore Pugin (1812–52) to further Gothicise the Hall. Pugin, the only son of a French émigré Auguste Charles Pugin and Catherine Welby Pugin, the daughter of a barrister and a relative of Sir William Welby, baronet, of Denton Hall in Lincolnshire, was born on 1 March 1812 at 39 Keppel Street, off Russell Square in Bloomsbury, London. As can be seen his Christian names were to be taken from his father's name, his mother's maiden name and the third one, Northmore, from that of Thomas Northmore, a distant cousin on his mother's side of the family.

Pugin's father was to work as an architectural draughtsman for the London-based architect John Nash, architect of the Brighton Pavilion, London's Regent Street, Regent's Park and Buckingham Palace, and it would be in his father's drawing office, a powerhouse of research into the architectural sources of the Gothic Revival that the young Pugin would be introduced to Gothic design and architecture. By 1827 as a teenager he was designing Gothic furniture for Windsor Castle and employed by Rundel & Bridge, the royal goldsmiths. Eventually he would advocate that everything should be built with Gothic in mind and his conversion to Catholicism in 1835 gave him a raison d'être to become a church architect for the Catholic cause. A prolific designer of furniture, metalwork, silver and jewellery, textiles, wallpapers and books, he was to be the architect of cathedrals, parish churches, schools, colleges and private houses, and with Charles Barry was the joint architect of the new Palace of Westminster, now known as the Houses of Parliament.

Pugin was to do more than anyone else to make the Gothic Revival the national style in Britain and elsewhere in the world, and could never bear

Fig. 3.11 On the roof of the entrance tower (May 2019). Of the two chimney pots seen on the tower's parapet, one presumably belongs to the flue of the morning room, the other to that of the pink bedroom.

to be idol. There was talk of his father, Auguste Charles, once being of the nobility having been 'le comte de Pugin', ruined by the French Revolution, although Auguste Charles would conceal many facts about his origins. However, he was to have a shield of Arms bearing a martlet, the blazon being *'Gules, a bend dexter Or charged with a marlet sable'*. Of the birds in heraldry the martlet is considered to be the swallow, a bird seen to be most active on the wing and almost never seen at rest. Following the death of his father, A. W. N. Pugin would present the Arms in many of his design projects, one example being the wallpaper for his new house in Ramsgate, and many writers have seen the martlet on the Arms as being so appropriate to A. W. N. Pugin's hyperactive lifestyle.

For the design of country houses A. W. N. Pugin would make a considerable contribution to be acknowledged and used in architectural practices throughout Britain for the rest of the nineteenth century. Scarisbrick Hall near Southport was his first independent commission on the domestic house front, and using his knowledge of medieval architecture and the decorative arts, he created at Scarisbrick both externally and internally a Gothic Revival masterpiece. On 24 April 1837, he noted in his diary: *Began Mr. Scarisbrick's house.*

At Scarisbrick work started on Rickman's existing west wing during which a library bay window, garden porch and a turret were added. The

Fig. 3.12 The boudoir during post-fire restoration work (January 2019).

following year Pugin proceeded to design the north elevation to which he added a clock tower built in 1839, the tower said to have been the prototype for the clock tower on his Houses of Parliament building in London. On the death of Charles Scarisbrick in 1860, his widowed sister Ann inherited Scarisbrick Hall, and the following year brought in Edward Welby Pugin, the son of A. W. N. Pugin to re-decorate the Hall and extend it by the addition of an east wing. The clock tower was taken down and replaced by a much taller tower with a spire, executed in the French Gothic style, whilst the new west wing was joined to the original Hall by an octagonal tower crowned with eight doves, the heraldic bird of the Scarisbricks.

A. W. N. Pugin felt that all parts of a house should express their function:

--- *not masked or concealed under one monotonous front, but by their variety in form and outline increasing the effect of the building.*

When one studies the massing and the positioning of detail on the façades at Alston Hall, particularly on the southeast-facing façade (fig. 3.3), one is reminded of this statement from Pugin. Up to the mid-nineteenth century the Gothic style was still to be seen as the architecture of heaven, and Tudor that of the home, and from the 1850s onwards the marriage of the two was to be a popular choice for new country houses, Alston Hall being an impressive example.

The year 1857 had seen the publication of George Gilbert Scott's influential book *'Remarks on Secular & Domestic Architecture, Present & Future'*, its title page illustrating Continental examples; the Cloth Hall at Ypres for the North of Europe, and the Doge's Palace in Venice and the Palazzo Pubblico in Siena for the South. Scott (1811–78), knighted in 1872, was to become the most famous and most prolific architect of the Victorian Age. Today in London, the Albert Memorial (1864–72) with its gilded bronze figure of Prince Albert installed under its canopy in 1876, and the

Fig. 3.13 The chapel in college days.

Midland Grand Hotel at St Pancras completed in 1876, serve to illustrate his genius as an architect.

Many of his commissions were for churches and restoration work on many of England's ancient cathedrals. He had a modern approach toward domestic house design, adopting Gothic to fit in with modern improvements. In his book mentioned above he argued that windows need not be pointed, and in many of his houses where he adopted the Tudor Revival style, square-headed window areas of the style encompassing the welcoming Victorian invention of plate glass were adopted. At Alston Hall Alfred Darbyshire would also adopt a modern approach by presenting mullioned windows representing large areas of plate glass instead of the Tudor style's traditional multi-paned leaded-lights windows, thus allowing a considerable amount of natural light to enter the main rooms.

As for the use of cast iron as a structural element in domestic architecture Scott was always keen to adopt it until wrought iron became available, and following the publication of his influential book on secular Gothic in 1857 commissions for large country houses would come his way, one being Kelham Hall near Newark-on-Trent, Nottinghamshire. In 1857 the house

Fig. 3.14 The Hall's original water tower (June 2015). The 1950s addition of a dormer window for a bathroom is seen to be at odds with the Hall's architecture.

Fig. 3.15 An early photograph of the impressive glasshouse. On the immediate right is the original conservatory to be replaced in college days, whilst in the background is the coach house, the ridge of its roof adorned by decorative feature work.

had been largely destroyed by fire and in 1858 Scott prepared his designs for its rebuilding, work beginning in the following year. In the rebuild Scott was able to carry out his modern ideas, plate glass and iron beams appearing at the new mansion. Years later in the 1870s at Alston when Alston Hall was under construction, iron beams as structural elements were not to appear. Instead Alfred Darbyshire used what had been traditional wooden beam construction, most likely because the Hall as a medium size mansion would not warrant metal structural work (see next chapter).

In 1912 a local textile manufacturer, William Eccles, was to take on the lease of Alston Hall and grounds for a period of fourteen years at an annual rent of £280 (see chapter 12), and between c.1912 and 1914 a major modernisation of the Hall was undertaken by him, part of the work involving the re-modelling of some of the windows about the Hall's southeast-facing façade.

Such work unfortunately saw the removal of a number of stone transoms and mullions, the result of which can be seen by comparing figs 2.2 and 8.3 with fig. 3.2. Fig. 2.2, a photograph of the Hall soon after it had been built, and fig. 8.3, the Hall in *c.*1896, shows the ground floor window of the drawing room seen on the left gable, like the window above, having transoms and three mullions. Fig. 3.2 shows the same windows after re-modelling, each one now having a single mullion only. It can also be seen that the windows on the next gable, that is the ground floor window and the one immediately above it, as well as the window above the ground floor bay window seen on the right, had also been re-modelled.

In 1911 before his arrival at Alston Hall with his wife and four young daughters, William Eccles with his family was living at 'West Bank', Lytham, the house having twenty rooms and where a cook, two housemaids, a general maid, a kitchen maid, a footman and a butler were employed. When Eccles arrived at Alston, the Hall must have been in need of modernisation and re-decoration. It had not been a family home since the deaths of John Mercer and his wife Helen in the 1890s, following which a caretaker would be in residence and occasionally Helen's brother, Canon Taylor, who in his final years lived there permanently before his death in 1908.

Among Eccles's first priorities to modernise the Hall was to install electric lighting following which the re-decoration of the principal rooms would bring about a Georgian style décor with wall panelling and impressive plasterwork. It seems that the re-modelling of the windows was simply to blend in with the new décor and allow more natural lighting to enter the principal rooms that were to have new Adam style fireplaces and new mahogany doors. Most likely the original doors would have been of oak with linen fold decoration in keeping with what would have been a Gothic style décor in the entrance hall and possibly the main ground floor rooms.

Why Eccles was allowed to bring about such an intensive programme of modernisation employing a local architect to undertake the work, especially the drastic alterations to some of the windows, one is unable to comprehend. But this was a period when the Hall, like a number throughout the country, had been abandoned for various reasons by surviving family members. In some instances an abandoned country house could languish into a state of deterioration resulting in demolition being the only option left. It is so easy to criticise William Eccles in exercising his intentions to modernise the Hall, but had it not been for his arrival in 1912 demolition of the Hall may well have taken place soon after the First World War.

Fig. 3.16 Looking in the same direction as in fig. 3.15 (June 2015). Some years have passed since the glasshouse was demolished, the outline of its end portion still to be seen on the scullery wall. On the left is the extended coach house and to its right the boiler house.

Following the First World War, trends in capital taxation and the loss in some country house families of an immediate heir killed in the war led to the situation of some country houses becoming unwanted, many being demolished in the 1920s and 1930s.

On her mother's death in 1909, Monica Waterton, John Mercer's granddaughter, had inherited the Hall and its estate, and as a nun having made a vow of poverty, was to cede the administration of the Alston Hall property to the nuns of her religious Order based in Mayfield, East Sussex, who did not wish to accept the property on a permanent basis. Monica and her sister Ethelburga had gone their separate ways, Ethelburga to lead a contrasting lifestyle in the south of England. So it would seem that the one option left was to offer the Hall on a leasehold arrangement in which

William Eccles was allowed to carry out the programme of modernisation work provided he honoured the cost. Clarification of this is seen in the amount of money he would spend on such work that partly would be responsible for his bankruptcy. Clearly the long-term lease of fourteen years would encourage Eccles to bring the Hall into the twentieth century but on arrival at Alston in 1912 he was already overdrawn at his bank.

The modernisation of the Hall must have been of some magnitude as Eccles and his family were to live there for only about twelve months before having to leave in *c*.1915 due to Eccles's bankruptcy. Sadly much of the modernisation work was to destroy and in some instances hide for decades many of the original design features about the mansion until ironically they were exposed by the fire of March 2017.

Due to the absence of photographs of the Hall's interior prior to the arrival of Eccles it is not possible to comment upon the original types and designs of wallpapers used in the private rooms. Wallpapers only became available soon after the introduction of the papermaking machine that had been invented in 1799 by Nicolas Louis Robert following which the machine was developed in England by the Fourdrinier brothers who were London stationers, and the engineer Bryan Donkin. Before then paper was

Fig. 3.17 Southwest-facing wall of the scullery (May 2019). In the centre of the photograph is the ventilation aperture of the pantry whilst on the right is the dining room window.

hand made, the process beginning with a vat containing a mash of pulp (linen, cotton or other materials) and water into which the vat man dipped a mould of wire mesh within a wooden frame to form a sheet of paper. The sodden sheet with others was then passed to a hand-operated press from which it was then hung up to dry. In the Fourdrinier machine each manufacturing process was done mechanically, the paper being formed on an endless wire cloth then passed between rollers to drain it of superfluous water. Steam heated cylinders then completed the drying process following which the finished paper was cut into lengths.

The introduction of machine-printed wallpapers from 1839 led to brightly coloured designs depicting artificial realism made up of floral and rococo scroll motifs seen by some as florid and gaudy compositions. By the end of the 1850s more subdued papers in colour and design were in fashion, wallpapers now being viewed as a background to the furnishing in a room rather than a decoration in their own right.

Charles Locke Eastlake the author of the popular manual *Hints on Household Taste*, London, 1867, was to give detailed advice on choosing wallpaper.

> *The choice of wallpaper should be guided in every respect by the destination of the room in which it will be used. The most important question will always be whether it is to form a decoration in itself, or whether it is to become a mere background for pictures. In the latter case the paper can hardly be too subdued in tone. Very light stone colour or green (not emerald), and silver grey will be found suitable for this purpose, and two shades of the same colour are generally sufficient for one paper. In drawing-rooms, embossed white or cream colour, with a very small diapered pattern, will not be amiss, where water-colour drawings are hung. As a rule, the simplest patterns are the best for every situation; but where the eye has to rest upon the surface of the wall alone a greater play of line in the ornament may become advisable. It is obvious that delicate tints admit of more linear complexity than those which are rich or dark. Intricate forms should be accompanied by quiet colour, and variety of hue should be chastened by the plainest possible outlines. In colour, wall-papers should relieve without violently opposing that of the furniture and hangings by which they are surrounded.*

By the time Alston Hall was under construction the use of dado and picture rails to divide the wall into dado, filling and frieze had become a hallmark of 'artistic' taste, and wall coverings were being produced in sets of three, one for each compartment of the wall. When Richard Norman Shaw was restoring Sutton Place in Surrey in 1875, for the four-foot dado he suggested a hard-wearing Japanese leather paper, and above the dado a light William Morris paper followed by a frieze showing fruit along the top; a typical scheme for many a country house drawing room during this period.

Japanese embossed papers were also in vogue and for those who could not afford them new relief papers imitating stucco, embossed leather etc., were becoming available, one being Lincrusta introduced in 1877 when the building of Alston Hall would have been nearing completion. The first of these relief papers had been produced by Frederick Walton under the name of 'Lincrusta-Walton' using the same ingredients that had gone in his previous invention linoleum, made up of linseed oil, gums, resins and wax, although mixing them with wood pulp instead of cork dust. The resulting mixture was then pressed between heavy metal rollers, one of which bore the engraved pattern to create the embossed effect of the finished wall covering.

Lincrusta could imitate any kind of relief decoration including linen fold panelling, a type of decoration that could well have appeared at Alston Hall in keeping with its Gothic theme. Relief wall coverings were most suitable for the dado as they could stand up to the wear and tear inflicted on this particular area that was usually painted a dark colour.

Frederick Walton failed to register linoleum as a trademark and lost the right to the exclusive use of the name but was to take care that his name was securely attached to Lincrusta and properly registered. One of his employees, Thomas J. Palmer, approached Walton with the idea of producing a lighter, more flexible wall covering made of wood pulp but Walton showed no interest, so Palmer was to take out a patent for his new wall covering to be called Anaglypta in 1886, and two years later it was on sale to the public.

The time approaching the end of the period 1900–14 has been described as the 'Indian Summer' of the country house when it found a new *raison d'etre* as a place of recreation and entertainment for those who had the capital to live such a lifestyle. In many instances those who fitted into this category decided to rent a country house where the owner could no longer afford the expense of maintaining the property. If William Eccles had been more careful with his money, he and his family could have enjoyed living out the fourteen-year lease at Alston Hall with a possible extension of the lease.

Of the principal rooms that would escape from the re-modelling of their windows and the installation of new Adam-style fireplaces were the morning room and the hall lounge. Today at the Hall with its Grade 2 preservation status, the very hint of removing transoms and mullions from its Tudor style window areas would certainly raise eyebrows in architectural circles and be seen as a complete disregard of fine architecture. One little wonders what Alfred Darbyshire would have said had he lived to see the disfigurement of his masterpiece.

The Tudor Revival style suggested the permanence of an established order representing the golden age of Elizabeth I, and the time when the style appeared at Alston it was considered to be appropriate for a leader of industry or financier whose Tudor Revival house might be seen to suggest his assimilation into a traditionally structured and peaceful rural community. Today the eclectic creation of Tudor and Gothic at Alston Hall can also be seen at Wyresdale Hall (1856–8) at Scorton, a few miles north of Alston. Enlarged in 1863, Wyresdale Hall (known today as Wyresdale Park) was built for Peter Ormrod (1795–1875), a cotton spinner and banker who resided at Halliwell Hall, near Bolton. The architect was Edward Graham Paley of Lancaster who in 1838 had begun his articles in

Fig. 3.18 Interior photograph of the pantry's ventilation grille (January 2019).

Fig. 3.19 Rear of the Hall in college days. In the centre is the servants' hall and its chimney from which is the extension of what had been ground floor service rooms that like the servants' hall was an addition of *c*.1913–14.

Lancaster as a pupil of Edmund Sharpe. On completion of his training, Paley became a partner in the Lancaster practice, and in 1851 Sharpe transferred the chief charge of his practice to Paley thereafter pursuing other interest and spending the years 1856–67 outside Lancaster, chiefly in Wales.

When Paley was working on the design of Wyresdale Hall, John Douglas (1830–1911) was his chief assistant and it is thought that he was very much involved with the design of the Scorton mansion. He was to leave Paley some time before his marriage in January 1860 to set up his own practice in Chester, and in 1886, along with D. P. Fordham, designed a mansion at Abbeystead near Scorton for the Earl of Sefton. By the 1880s architects of new country houses, Edward Graham Paley being amongst them, had moved away from the Gothic style.

During his time with Alley in Manchester from 1855 onwards, Alfred Darbyshire like all trainee architects of the period more than likely would have been introduced to the writings and architecture of A. W. N. Pugin and George Gilbert Scott. Whilst establishing his manifesto on Gothic architecture, he would know of and probably visited the Pugin mansion at Scarisbrick and sometime later admired its extension by Pugin's son Edward with its brilliant 'spiky Gothic' appearance. On receiving the commission to design Alston Hall, Alfred Darbyshire may well have visited Paley's mansion at Scorton, and would have known about 'The Grange' of 1843–4 in Ramsgate, the house designed by A. W. N. Pugin for himself and family, a house that became a model for detached middle class housing.

Like Alfred Darbyshire, A. W. N. Pugin was to be involved with the theatre in the design of stage sets and stage mechanisms with their array of pulleys, counterweights etc., used in scenery changes. Well before his teens Pugin had been pre-occupied with the theatre, and by his teenage years was working in London's theatre land having begun at Convent Garden as a stage-hand before becoming a designer of stage sets, scenery and costumes.

Fig. 3.20 Stable yard in college days with boiler house (centre left) and garage with washdown canopy. On the right a vehicle is parked in front of the stable block, see fig. 3.21.

His triumph in the stage set and scenery domain materialised in 1831 with the success of the opera *Kenilworth*, but during his time in the theatre Pugin still had a growing passion for Gothic architecture and design and by 1832 was concentrating on training himself as an architect, principally by making intensive tours of medieval buildings. On 26 February 1833 he wrote a letter to E. J. Willson to say:

> After mature consideration and consulting my best friends I have resolved to give up my theatrical connection altogether and to devote myself entirely to the pursuit of Gothic architecture.

Pugin would have been Darbyshire's mentor in the field of Gothic architecture, and the common bond they had relating to artistic design in the theatre may have influenced and encouraged Darbyshire to become one of the leading theatre architects of his day. By carefully studying Alston Hall's architecture one is reminded of the ideas put into practice by Pugin during his short time as one of the foremost architects of Gothic design in its revival period.

Today as one looks at the Tudor style entrance tower of the Alston mansion one is readily drawn into recognising the elements of Gothic in its machicolated parapets, gargoyles and grotesques, the latter being extravagantly formed non-existent creatures that on a Gothic building are supposed to ward off evil spirits; four grotesques to be seen on the entrance tower's porte-cochere. Two mythical creatures similar to the gargoyles at the top of the entrance tower appear one at each corner of the projecting ledge above the drawing room window of the Hall's southeast-facing façade (fig. 3.4).

At Alston Hall as well as the impressive entrance tower even the chimney stacks are adorned with machicolated parapets, and such Gothic elements are a delight to see and represent the masterly artistic touch of the architect. Centuries ago as a means of fortification to a building machicolated parapets had openings within their arched corbels for pouring molten substances upon an attacking force below. Eventually the parapets simply became a common architectural feature on buildings especially in Northern Italy, Florence having some striking examples. William Burges (1827–81) adopted them in many of his architectural commissions, for example at Cardiff Castle (1868–81).

At Alston Hall its tall chimney stacks breaking through the roof in various positions add to the well-balanced composition of the mansion's architecture, and to achieve this Alfred Darbyshire would have given much thought to the positioning and tracking of their flues.

Fig. 3.21 Stable block (June 2015). On the left is the blocked-up entrance (brick and window) to what had been four-stalled stables.

The placing of fireplaces on outer facing walls was considered a wasteful practice in that warmth was dissipated to the outside. This was the situation at Alston Hall where the morning room's fireplace and that of the fireplace of the pink suite's bedroom above were positioned on the wall of the northeast-facing façade. To avoid a chimney stack appearing on the façade, Darbyshire tracked the chimney flue of both morning room and bedroom within the roof space to emerge adorned by two chimney pots on top of one of the entrance tower's parapets (fig. 3.11). Further along the same parapet would be the chimney pot of another flue, presumably for the corner fireplace of the pink suite's dressing room.

Each one of the three rooms of the entrance tower was to have a fireplace, the tower's first floor room (the boudoir) and its third floor one each having a corner fireplace whilst the fireplace in the second floor room was to be against the tower's northwest-facing wall. Their chimney flues were to be tracked to terminate within the tower's turret, the chimney pots appearing discreetly almost out of view. By using the entrance tower to provide outlets for these flues, Alfred Darbyshire avoided the building of numerous chimney stacks in the immediate vicinity of the tower so presenting it as a prominent and impressive architectural feature of the mansion.

External chimney stacks were nearly always to become a major feature of A. W. N. Pugin's domestic architecture; he had two about the tower of his house 'The Grange' in Ramsgate. He recommended for practical reasons that external chimney stacks gained space in a building, added stability to it and avoided fires in roofs. To him they presented a great variety of light and shadow and by them a succession of bold features was to be gained on a building.

At Alston Hall Alfred Darbyshire presented one on the gable of the hall lounge as seen in fig. 3.5. Beginning a few feet from ground level similar to the base of an oriel window, the chimney stack continues up the gable to well above roof ridge level to be topped with a machicolated parapet, referred to as an oversailer in such a position.

The presence of an oversailer on a chimney stack is essential for the efficient working of the chimney and the protection of the stack during certain wind conditions, that is, when the wind velocity is exceeding that of the smoke plume leaving the chimney. In these conditions an area of reduced pressure on the stack's leeward side to the oncoming wind is created to produce a suction effect, that without the protective overhang of the oversailer, would draw the sulphur laden smoke plume downwards against the sides of the chimney stack, rain soon converting it into an acidic layer to bring about its destructive effect upon stonework, brickwork and mortar.

Some of the most impressive oversailers were those designed to adorn factory and textile mill chimneys of the nineteenth century, and during his time with Alley in Manchester in the 1850s and early 1860s whilst working on mill chimney architecture, Alfred Darbyshire would become well experienced in the use of the oversailer. This is evident on his chimney stacks at Alston where the oversailers offer a substantial overhang and have a bottom and top sloping surface upon which wind eddies presumably help to lift the smoke plumes well into the surrounding air.

Where possible the tops of chimney stacks should be above the line of roof ridges as the latter in windy conditions can create air eddies to bring about down draughts in chimney flues and thus problems in the area of the fireplace. At Alston Hall one chimney stack to be seen in a somewhat odd position before its demolition in 2019 was the one for the servants'

Fig. 3.22 View from the 'pleasure ground' terrace in college days. To the left the terrace sweeps away to the mound seen at upper centre.

hall, a building addition to the Hall sometime between *c*.1913–14 when the architect Edwin James Andrew was involved with alterations and additions for William Eccles. Its chimney stack was to be positioned not far from the gable of the butler's pantry with the school room above, and was well below the roof ridge line; not a good position for avoiding down draught problems that may have come about. Most likely this is the reason why the chimney stack was to be adorned by such an interesting design of chimney pot (see fig. 3.19). Had the servants' hall been built in the same position in the 1870s, more than likely Darbyshire would have tracked its chimney flue to emerge within a stack in a more favourable position.

The architect Edwin Andrew would have encountered many problems at Alston Hall during the programmes of modernisation brought about by William Eccles, and the positioning of the servants' hall's chimney may well have been one. If he had placed the fireplace of the servants' hall against the

Fig. 3.23 Ribble Valley scene from the 'pleasure ground' terrace. In the far distance can be seen the village of Mellor.

existing wall of the butler's pantry, a room that had a corner fireplace (see fig. 100), then Andrew would have had to track its chimney flue within this existing wall, thereby presenting construction work of some magnitude. So this is probably why Andrew, with little or no choice, decided to place the chimney of the servants' hall in such an odd position as seen in fig. 3.19 and fig. 3.24.

The large number of roof surfaces of varying shapes and sizes angled in different directions as seen at Alston Hall could well have presented chimney down draught problems in certain wind conditions. A close study of fig. 3.2 a photograph of 1916, shows to the left of the water tower with its truncated pyramidal roof, the chimney stack of the kitchen and scullery adorned by two very tall chimney pots. On the extreme left of the photograph and beyond the roof of the conservatory is the stack of the boiler house, again with two extremely tall pots, most likely having been fitted to avoid down draught problems. The Hall's accumulation of chimney pots varying in size and shape to solve flue draught problems would eventually to some extent compromise the Hall's pleasing arrangements of its rooflines and the attractive lines of its chimney stacks.

But Alston Hall was not alone in being subjected to such later additions to its impressive stacks. Today on many a country house, chimney pots that would have originally been the same size and shape, some to be arranged in groups, have been replaced by ones varying in design with some unfortunately looking like obelisks.

The purpose of a chimney pot was to produce an effective exit of the flue gases thus establishing a good draught at the fireplace end, the much reduced cross-sectional area of the chimney pot compared to that of the flue so producing a necessary velocity for the rising flue gases.

Even the boiler house chimney stack at Alston Hall seems to have been a victim of a change for the worse that probably came with the installation of new boiler plant with oil fuel feed in college days. Originally the chimney stack would most likely have been of brick construction like the rest of the stable yard buildings, only to be rebuilt in what seems to be reconstructed stone, each block being the same size and shape and therefore seen to be completely at odds not only with the brick of the stable yard area but also with the stonework of the Hall.

One aim of a country house architect was to avoid having chimney stacks appearing on roof ridges that would not only be seen to clutter a ridge line but also could present the impression of them having a crushing effect on the building. Instead, the recognised practice of having stacks appearing at seemingly unrelated positions about the slopes of roofs had the desired effect of these stacks 'tying down' the whole architectural composition of a building. Such a practice would entail the careful tracking of flues and at Alston Hall Alfred Darbyshire certainly achieved the 'tying down' effect in a remarkable way.

One particular pleasing architectural feature of the Hall that would deserve much merit would be the roof of its water tower before its reconstruction during the 1950s. Initially domestic water supply to the Hall most probably had been by gravity feed via pipes from the Shamrock pond named because of its shape (see fig. 3.1) and one to be a reserved water supply in case of fire.

On reaching the Hall's water tower the water would have presumably been pumped to its tank using a force pump unless the water pressure without a pump was adequate to feed the tank in order to establish the necessary water pressure for bedrooms, bathrooms and domestic services etc. Only after an agreement had been made on 14 June 1912 between Preston Corporation and John Mercer's granddaughter Monica Waterton, was Alston Hall and its outbuildings to receive a water supply from the reservoirs of the Corporation. Presumably such an agreement was made in readiness to lease the Hall.

In 1832 the Preston Waterworks Company had been established following which the Company began constructing a series of reservoirs, the first being the Fulwood one fed by springs and situated on the outskirts of Preston on the east side of the Preston–Longridge road. Grimsargh reservoir was completed in 1835 and about the same time the Upper Dilworth one at Tootal Heights in Longridge was completed to be followed by the first Alston reservoir constructed in 1842. In 1853 the Corporation of Preston purchased the Preston Company, acquiring the reservoirs at Fulwood, Grimsargh, Dilworth and Alston, and began work in Longridge to construct more reservoirs.

Before the conversion of Alston Hall into a college of adult education the top of its water tower's roof had been adorned with feature work (see fig. 3.2) in keeping with the Gothic style, whilst upon each of its four-slated roof surfaces was a lucarne, that is, a small dormer-shaped ventilator to be seen on church steeples. During the work of converting the tank room into a bathroom, when presumably a water tank was fitted in the top room of the main entrance tower, this feature work and lucarnes were removed and not replaced following which a flat-roofed dormer window (fig. 3.14) incongruous to the Hall's architecture appeared on the new roof.

One has to admit that on the several occasions when observing the window, one was reminded of the story in connection with Sir Edwin Landseer Lutyens (1869–1944), the great British architect of the Edwardian period and throughout the years up to his death. His masterpiece was the Viceroy's House in New Delhi, India, completed in 1929, and in 1938 he was to return to Viceroy's House to help the then Viceroy, Lord Linlithgow, undo the gratuitous damage wrought by the preceding Vicereine whom Lutyens had once told that if she possessed the Parthenon she would add bay windows to it.

Most likely the reason behind the decision to convert the tank room into a bathroom was in order to use the existing plumbing arrangement of the bathroom below; but for whatever reason the conversion would entail the installation of steel girder work as shown in fig. 16.9. The dormer window remained on the water tower until after the fire of 2017 when during the re-roofing of the Hall it was replaced by a Velux-type window.

Velux-type skylight windows had become popular when the Hall's second floor rooms were being converted to present more bedroom space and associated facilities for the residential college. One would unfortunately appear near an original roof dormer on the Hall's southeast-facing façade as seen in fig. 3.3, the new window providing natural lighting to a room created by the partitioning of an original bedroom situated directly above what had been the pink bedroom. When a new roof to the Hall was being constructed after the fire, this dormer and the Velux one was replaced by a much larger Velux window as seen in fig. 16.12. Today Alston Hall having survived the inferno of 2017 has a new roof about which are number of Velux-type windows.

Another roof at Alston Hall that originally had supported pleasing architectural work was that of the coach house (see fig. 3.15), its roof ridge having decorative cresting and finials. Sometime following the arrival of Brian Leighton as Principal in May 1988, essential refurbishment work would come about, a part of which the coach house was extended on its western side where a new entrance and stairwell was constructed (see fig. 15.30), the area to be lit by natural lighting by the addition of a window at first-floor level. This major construction work was responsible for the roof having to be rebuilt with the loss of its cresting and finials as seen in fig. 3.16 and the unfortunate external rendering to the brickwork of the coach house.

Yet after these many losses to its original architecture the Hall was given grade 2 building status on 20 September 2016 (entry number 1434771), and the following architectural assessment is from the English Heritage document which sets out the reasons for giving the Hall listed building status:

> Alston Hall makes good use of the progression of elevations, in particular on its garden front (south elevation). In addition, the varying height of the different projecting elements on that elevation helps to create a harmonious composition and to identify principal internal spaces. This careful use of recession extends to other elevations; for example through the tower projecting from the east front, which in turn sits forward of the east wall of the north range. This lends the square house an aspect similar to the phased, courtyard-plan houses built when the style was new. The overall Tudor Revival style is plain, but close inspection reveals substantial detailing beyond the obvious hoodmoulds to windows. This includes chevron courses and blind

oculi in the gables, scrolls to the kneeler corbels, and even gablets to the shoulders of the tall chimney stacks and machicolations to their corbelled tops. The detailing to the tower is particularly fine, with machicolations, gargoyles and elaborate stops to the hoodmoulds of the (projecting) porte-cochere arches.

The high standard of detailing is continued internally with Gothic details (mainly in the public spaces) mixing with what Darbyshire called the French-Italian style in the rooms. Together, the Entrance Hall, galleried staircase, Billiard Room, Dining Room, Drawing Room and Chapel make a very good suite of high-status spaces, with very finely-detailed plasterwork, good joinery and good use of high-quality stone such as marble and granite. Good detailing is also found in private and lower-status spaces such as bedrooms and the service stair, not just in the more prestigious areas, Overall, the design is carefully considered and well executed, and above the ordinary standard for its time. It compares well, for example, with the larger but similar-style Crookhey Hall … of 1874 by Alfred Waterhouse.

Crookhey Hall mentioned is situated about three-quarters of a mile southeast of Cockerham village in north Lancashire and was to be the residence of Colonel C. H. Bird, the son of a Cockerham mother and a Massachusetts father. Work began on the Hall in 1874 and was completed in 1878, and according to Nikolaus Pevsner it is in the domestic Gothic style. A drawing of the Hall is shown in Anthony Hewitson's *Northward*, published in 1900, in which its architecture is described as being Elizabethan. Its elevations were to be asymmetrical with the presence of a porte-cochere and a tower with a steep French style hipped roof, the latter to be a feature on many of Waterhouse's buildings, whilst the Hall was to have a central hall with a gallery and skylight.

At Alston Hall good proportion was to be a key factor in all of its elevations, an essential part of fine architecture allied to any kind or type of building. The architect Sir Ernest George (1839–1922) believed that *'Proportion is perhaps the most essential element of good architecture. It cost nothing and is applicable to the humblest as well as to the noblest of works'*. When Richard Norman Shaw had completed his last new country house in 1895, George became the leading English architect for new country houses until the arrival of Edwin Landseer Lutyens who was once a pupil in his practice.

The site chosen for the Alston mansion alone amounted to four acres on a building platform almost on the edge of a series of steep slopes leading to

Fig. 3.24 Hall and stable yard area photographed by drone following the sale of the Hall in 2016. At the bottom is the stable block to the right of which is a glasshouse adjacent to the wall of the kitchen garden. A fuel tanker is parked in front of the garage's washdown canopy.

the river Ribble in the valley below. Beyond in the distance is the village of Mellor with Rickman's 'Commissioners' church of St Mary (1825–7) sitting astride on a ridge that is a part of one of the most beautiful of views in Lancashire. About eight acres had been allotted for the mansion's grounds that in the main were to be laid out eventually as woodland so sheltering the house from the wet west winds and cold east ones in winter, and also to offer privacy.

It would seem that parterres, mass bedding of annuals and deep and lengthy herbaceous borders were not to appear within the layout of the

Hall's gardens. On the western side of the Hall the land was at a much lower level than the Hall's building platform and contained a natural clough with a small stream, the Ordnance Survey map (surveyed in 1892) showing this land as an area of rock gardens with inter-connecting ponds and waterfalls, and at the far side of the top pond was to be a small grotto. Presumably Alfred Darbyshire would have been the landscape architect at the Hall as he was well experienced in the art of landscaping having improved the gardens at Lyme Hall in Cheshire, and was the designer of Alexandra Park in Moss Side, Manchester.

From the Hall's entrance gates the eventual tree-lined drive would take a slightly serpentine line to the Hall so enabling the latter to be hidden from public gaze. On reaching the Hall two paths from the main drive (fig. 3.1) would lead to the gates of a high wall behind which was the stable yard and domestic facilities, the wall discreetly hiding such from guests arriving at the mansion. Straight ahead was the Hall's impressive entrance tower and carriage court (fig. 3.5).

In the stable yard was an attractive brick-built block housing a four-stall stable arrangement, harness room, hayloft etc., as well as an impressive brick-built coach house, its upper floor probably having been designated as a dance floor, a common addition for medium size country houses of the 1870s for coming of age parties and estate tenants' annual dances. At the side of the stable yard was the boiler house for the Hall's central heating system and one can imagine this area once presenting a busy scene of horses being fed and watered, groomed and harnessed, new hay arriving and carriages at the ready, a scene soon to change with the advent of the motorcar.

By the time the Hall was to be sold by auction in July 1917 the buildings of the stable block and that of the coach house had undergone a transformation to meet the motorcar age. When William Eccles arrived in 1912 he would employ three to five gardeners, five indoor servants and a chauffeur, and it seems that among his priorities to modernise the Hall would be the conversion of the coach house into a garage and part of the stable block into living accommodation (to be known as the bungalow cottage) for his chauffeur. The sale particulars for the sale of 1917 mention the garage as well as the stable block's harness room and living rooms with lofts over. The four-stall stable was still extant by this time and most likely would be available for stabling horses purely for recreational pursuits unlike stables in towns and cities that still had horses for transporting loads of all descriptions.

In the world of the country house leading up to the First World War motoring had become a new and important element, and to own a motorcar was a sign of wealth and status. At Alston Hall in keeping with this national trend the conversion of the coach house into a garage more than likely saw the fitting of two sets of double entrance doors and a glass-covered canopy at the front to be known as a 'washdown', all being mentioned in the sale of the Hall in 1949. Inside the new garage during the sale of 1917 would be all that was necessary for the repair work and general maintenance of a motorcar, as during the Edwardian period and that of the First World War the fragility of these early motorcars and a general absence of wayside garages, meant that country house garages had to be well equipped for such work that in many instances would be carried out by the chauffeur.

A number of coachman were to undertake training to become chauffeurs whilst in some instances chauffeurs were to be drawn from the artisan class of skilled mechanics having had experience in this role in the new car factories of the period. In consequence many chauffeurs of this particular class were not considered as domestic servants but as skilled professionals desiring respect and some degree of status. In his special uniform the chauffeur could even be seen as a dashing 'knight of the road'.

The particulars of the 1949 sale list the garage premises capable of accommodating six motorcars, and had an inspection pit, hot water pipes, and electric light. The mention of the hot water pipes is interesting in that at the beginning of the motorcar era vehicles on very cold nights had to be kept in heated garages to ensure that their radiator water did not freeze. If heating was not available the tiresome task of draining radiators had to be carried out. To provide heating, devices known as heating chambers were installed separated from the car area by a wall to minimize the risk of fire, the heat being carried through by hot water pipes. Such an arrangement may well have been adopted during the conversion of the coach house at Alston Hall. An inventory of 1940 lists a radiator cover in the garage and amongst the list of contents for the various greenhouses, the main one being in close proximity to the garage, were two separate heating facilities, one listed as 'heating apparatus chamber' with boiler, firing tools and pipe connections; the other listed as 'heating apparatus' which also had a boiler and pipe connections. However, one presumes that both heating sets had initially been installed solely for the greenhouses and were not heating devices of the early motorcar era as mentioned above.

How much conversion for the motorcar age had been undertaken at the Hall from William Eccles's time there to when John Marsden (see chapter

14) left towards the end of the 1940s is difficult to assess. By the time of the 1949 sale the stables had been converted into a garage for two cars, the entrance having a roll-up steel shutter door. Sometime later this entrance would be sealed up by the combination of brick wall and window, and during one period the glass-covered 'washdown' canopy was to be replaced by a slated one.

Adjacent to the stable block was a storeroom that originally had been the end of the block until a small lean-to building had been built onto it to house a diesel engine and a generator to produce electricity at the Hall (see chapter 13). In 1949 it was a sub station maintained by the Preston Corporation Electricity Department (see fig. 15.6); electricity from an outside source apparently having been installed in the 1930s.

As can be seen in fig. 15.6 the 'bungalow cottage' in the stable block was still available for accommodation, and when the Hall became a college the stable block would be converted into a variety of uses, a part of the 'bungalow cottage' it seems becoming the domestic science room. Prior to 1974, on entering the doorway at the centre of the block, on the left was the astronomy room that was the laboratory of Dr V. Barocas, an astronomer, whilst next door was his bedroom. Dr Barocas looked after both the Moor Park Observatory in Preston and the Alston Lane one near the Hall, and went on to become Professor of Astronomy at Preston Polytechnic, now the University of Central Lancashire. One remembers tutoring a class in what had been the astronomy room whilst opposite across the entrance passage was the domestic science room.

Most Victorian country mansions and Alston Hall was no exception had a pleasure ground area, an intimate environment for dalliance in the outdoor air enabling one to walk straight out of the house to enjoy gentle exercise and views from gravel and grass laden paths, suitable for damp days and those with long skirts, delicate shoes and constitutions. The Hall's pleasure ground began on a terraced pathway on what was left of the building platform immediately alongside the Hall's southeast-facing façade and continued in a southeast direction to terminate on a mound (fig. 3.22). From the pleasure ground terrace steps led to two large areas of lawn, whilst another pleasure ground area would be the dell area with its ponds and waterfalls. Perhaps the path from the terrace leading to the shamrock pond was also a favourite walk.

As was a common feature of country houses Alston Hall had its walled kitchen garden, a portion of one of its walls being that of the stable block, and at a little under an acre in size its plan layout was of the type popular in

Elizabethan times, made up of four quadrants divided by pathways. By this simple arrangement effective management of the quadrants could be made in deciding what should be planted and where. In some walled gardens storing sheds, potting sheds and glasshouses were to be part of the garden, but the Alston one was to remain free of such, the assortment of garden sheds being amongst the separate area of the plant houses.

Some walled gardens as well as providing food for the dining table grew flowers for garden display and cut flowers for the house. At Alston Hall its walled garden specifically catered for vegetables and fruit in season whilst cut flowers in the form of carnations, as well as plants and exotic fruits were to be grown within the Hall's glasshouses.

After its introduction in 1745, the tax on glass was abolished in 1845, and six years later saw the end of the window tax (1696–1851), both taxes having hampered the development and production of glass. Three years after the abolition of the glass tax, plate glass was invented and with the ending of the window tax the cost of glasshouses fell to bring about a revolution in their manufacture. Alston Hall was to have a peach house, a vine house, a greenhouse, two carnation houses and a tomato house, one of these being known as a hothouse that was a lean-to one on the outer and southeast-facing side of the kitchen garden wall.

A variety of decorative plants was to be grown in the hothouse and during the 1950s, when Preston Borough Council owned the Hall, these would be taken to important civic events in the town. Raised cold frames were to run alongside the front of the hothouse but just before the closure of the college in December 2015 all was in a state of disrepair. Heating for the hothouse had been from a boiler housed in a small building alongside the end of the stable block and by 2019 the hothouse under new ownership had been rebuilt. Opposite it had formerly stood the coldhouse where carnations were once cultivated, and which was demolished in the 1990s due to maintenance problems, the site becoming a staff car park.

Some walled kitchen gardens had 'slip gardens' made up of the land immediately outside and adjacent to their walls, a profitable area for growing hardy root vegetables and fruit that did not require the all-round protection found within the walled enclosure. Whether the strip of land alongside the kitchen garden wall facing the dell at Alston was ever used as such remains questionable, in college days it supported a row of rhododendrons. During the Second World War the quadrant in the wall garden's west corner supported a fowl house and its enclosure and eventually an air raid shelter. Another shelter was to be built at the far end of the stable block and in 1940 there was also a fowl house mentioned and situated *'at end of rose path'*. During the 1990s the walled garden was taken out of vegetable production and converted into an area of paths and lawns with a mound surmounted by a water feature.

The 1893 map shows the walled garden that presumably at the time would have had wall-trained pear and plum trees, cooking and dessert apple trees and soft fruit trees etc. Shown is the extensive range of glasshouses mentioned above for the cultivation of melons, cucumbers, peaches, nectarines, grapes, carnations and plants etc. The main plant house (fig. 3.15) was demolished when the Hall was a college, one end of it having been joined onto the wall of the scullery where its outline can still be seen (fig. 3.17). A water tank was located near the entrance to the potting shed from which the gardener would siphon water by means of a syringe, using it to spray onto the hot water pipes of this impressive plant house, the resulting heated vapour providing the necessary humidity.

In April 1950 prior to the Hall being converted into a day continuation college, the *Lancashire Evening Post* would write:

> *In the conservatories of the Hall are magnificent plants, carefully tended for 25 years, which will produce about 500 peaches and nectarines this summer. But the doors to the conservatories will be locked!*

Chapter four

Layout of the Hall

In planning the layout of a country mansion one aim of the Victorian architect was to segregate family and guests from servants to allow privacy for the former but at the same time present for the latter suitable routes of movement during the execution of their duties. Servants were required to blend discreetly into the background when not actually serving their so-called betters and in some of the grandest of country houses this invisibility of servants was taken to an extreme level. For example when Cliveden was rebuilt in 1851 after a fire the architect Charles Barry installed a tunnel under the middle courtyard for servants to walk from one wing to another unseen by the family of the house.

At Alston Hall ground floor family living rooms were to be separated from kitchen and scullery and other service facilities by a main entrance corridor aligned on a northeast to southwest axis. Such an alignment enabled some of the family rooms and those of the principal bedrooms directly above them to look upon a southeast aspect enabling them to receive the sun's light and warmth from sunrise to sunset and also to have the Ribble Valley view. On first floor level as well as the principal bedrooms with dressing rooms and bathrooms, were guest bedrooms, a sewing room, a school room, and a boudoir in the entrance tower. The second floor had servant bedrooms, a bachelor's bedroom, and the tower's middle room. Stairs from this level led onto the Hall's roof and also into the tower's top room where stairs and trap door presented access onto its roof.

It is difficult to offer an accurate description regarding the interior layout of the mansion as well as its service facilities during the time when John Mercer and his family were in residency. Even though photography

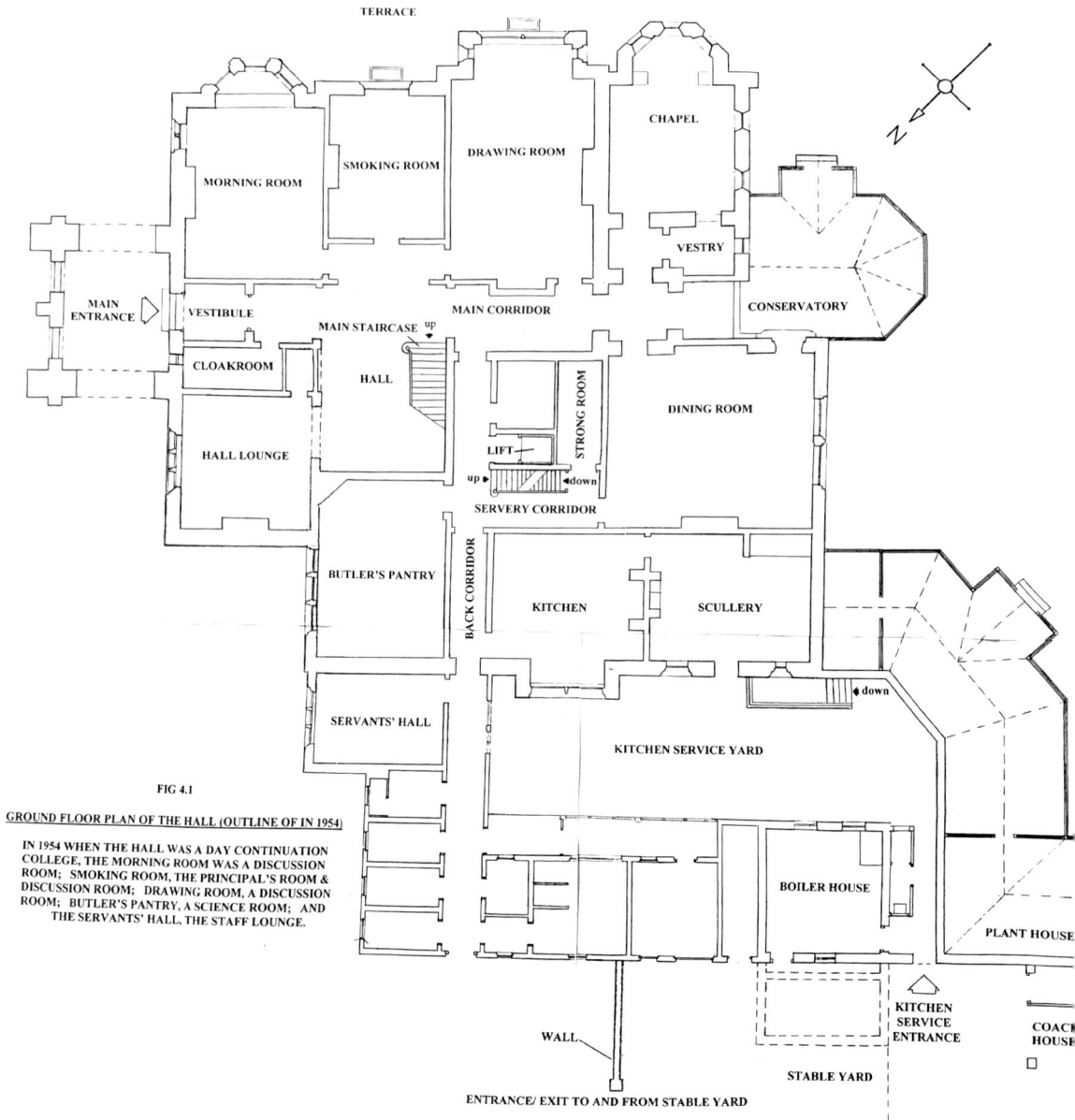

TERRACE

DRAWING ROOM

CHAPEL

SMOKING ROOM

MORNING ROOM

VESTRY

CONSERVATORY

MAIN ENTRANCE

VESTIBULE

MAIN CORRIDOR

MAIN STAIRCASE up

CLOAKROOM

HALL

DINING ROOM

STRONG ROOM

HALL LOUNGE

LIFT

up ► ◄down

SERVERY CORRIDOR

BACK CORRIDOR

BUTLER'S PANTRY

KITCHEN

SCULLERY

◄down

SERVANTS' HALL

KITCHEN SERVICE YARD

FIG 4.1

GROUND FLOOR PLAN OF THE HALL (OUTLINE OF IN 1954)

IN 1954 WHEN THE HALL WAS A DAY CONTINUATION
COLLEGE, THE MORNING ROOM WAS A DISCUSSION
ROOM; SMOKING ROOM, THE PRINCIPAL'S ROOM &
DISCUSSION ROOM; DRAWING ROOM, A DISCUSSION
ROOM; BUTLER'S PANTRY, A SCIENCE ROOM; AND
THE SERVANTS' HALL, THE STAFF LOUNGE.

BOILER HOUSE

PLANT HOUSE

KITCHEN SERVICE ENTRANCE

COACH HOUSE

WALL

STABLE YARD

ENTRANCE/ EXIT TO AND FROM STABLE YARD

Fig. 4.1 Ground floor plan of the Hall (outline of in 1954).

was well advanced by the late 1870s when the building of the Hall had been completed, no photographs have been found to illustrate its interior layout and decoration during this period. As mentioned above the extensive programme of modernisation undertaken from c.1912 onwards would bring about considerable changes to structure and décor, and if further changes did come about during the interwar years when the Hall was still a private residence, they must have been minor. However, what was to be the second extensive programme of modernisation came during the 1950s when the Hall was converted into a college of education. During the second half of this decade especially on the first and second floors, much structural alteration was to take place to bring about a maze of new residential accommodation. The layout for what had been ground floor living rooms and principal bedrooms on the first floor with the exception of the rose suite's bedroom, its dressing room and bathroom (see later), would remain unaltered.

By the aid of floor plans drawn during the 1950s; a sale catalogue of 1916 listing the Hall's rooms, furniture and appointments; and an inventory listing room contents in 1940 for fire insurance purposes, one was able to establish to some degree of accuracy the layout of the principal living rooms, bedrooms and service facilities when the building of the

Fig. 4.2 Entrance tower. On the right is the oriel window of the boudoir facing the carriage court, whilst above the window is the 'Achievement of Arms' of John Mercer.

mansion was completed in the 1870s. The floor plans drawn in the 1950s and in 2003, copied for this publication show errors with regard to some of the window openings where mullions have not been shown. In the ground floor plan of 1954, the butler's pantry is shown as having two separate windows that must be an error. Such an error has been corrected to show a triple window arrangement divided by two mullions as seen in fig. 3.5.

On entering the Hall via a Gothic arched doorway one passed into a small vestibule area, part way along of which were doors before finally entering the entrance hall, such an arrangement ensuring that the latter would be relative free of winter draughts. For this reason the idea of the vestibule for new, small and medium size country houses had grown in popularity from the mid-nineteenth century onwards. Presumably the original inner vestibule doors, the main entrance doors and those about the private rooms would be of oak to be replaced by mahogany ones soon after William Eccles's arrival in 1912. The new glazed inner vestibule doors would admit a considerable amount of natural lighting to the vestibule area, especially when the main entrance doors were open, but their modern style would be at variance with the Gothic arches about the Hall. Another replacement during this modernisation period must have been the skylight in the entrance hall as its design was to be in keeping with the Art Nouveau period of 1890–1914.

Just before entering the entrance hall, on the right was a cloakroom and toilet, part of which eventually became a telephone room accessed from the hall lounge. In large country houses entrance halls were sitting rooms complete with fireplace to be referred to as 'living halls', the one at Holker Hall of 1874 by Paley and Austin in south Cumbria being a prime example. At Alston Hall its entrance hall was not to have a fireplace and would simply be an area to receive and no doubt impress visitors on their arrival, its elegant staircase leading to a landing whose architectural décor like the hallway below being in the Venetian Gothic style, the overall effect rekindling the bygone days of 'Merry England'.

On the staircase wall was a set of arches (fig. 4.23) from where with some imagination one could visualise an Elizabethan audience peering through them to enjoy a Shakespearean play being enacted on the black and white marble floor below. Perhaps Alfred Darbyshire had one of his Shakespearean plays in mind when designing the arches, with a vision of Juliet on her balcony. The arches were also to have a functional purpose in that they allowed natural lighting from the skylight above to illuminate to some extent the corridor behind them.

Fig. 4.3 Ceiling of the porte-cochere, a corner of displaying a row of 'discs' motifs.

During the time when Alfred Darbyshire was drawing up his design plans for the interior of the Alston mansion, Italian Gothic was enjoying its final period of popularity for new English country houses. In the 1850s and 1860s English trainee architects during their grand architectural tours of Europe had admired the medieval Gothic architecture of Northern Italy and that of Venice on Italy's eastern coastline. Venetian Gothic was colourful and picturesque with its use of different coloured bricks and stones to form surface patterns to buildings both internally and externally. Such decorative work was to be known as 'constructional polychromy' or 'permanent polychromy', and in Britain it became a trademark of the 'High Gothic' period of the 1860s and 1870s.

John Ruskin (1819–1900), inveterate traveller to European places, sketcher and writer, was to draw attention to the Gothic buildings of Verona and Venice in his *The Seven Lamps of Architecture* (1849) and *The Stones of Venice* (1851–53). In his *The Stones of Venice* he would illustrate the dullness of the monochrome and uniform stone surface of a Regency Classical building in comparison to a medieval wall in Northern Italy with its constructional polychromy.

An outstanding example of constructional polychromy using the combination of marble, brick and stone, is to be seen inside the University Museum in Oxford (1855–60) by Deane and Woodward. For his Grand Midland Hotel at St Pancras, London, George Gilbert Scott would apply constructional polychromy for the voussoirs of its many Gothic arches to present a distinct decorative element to this iconic building.

In a similar way for Alston Hall Alfred Darbyshire had selected constructional polychromy using light and dark coloured stones for the

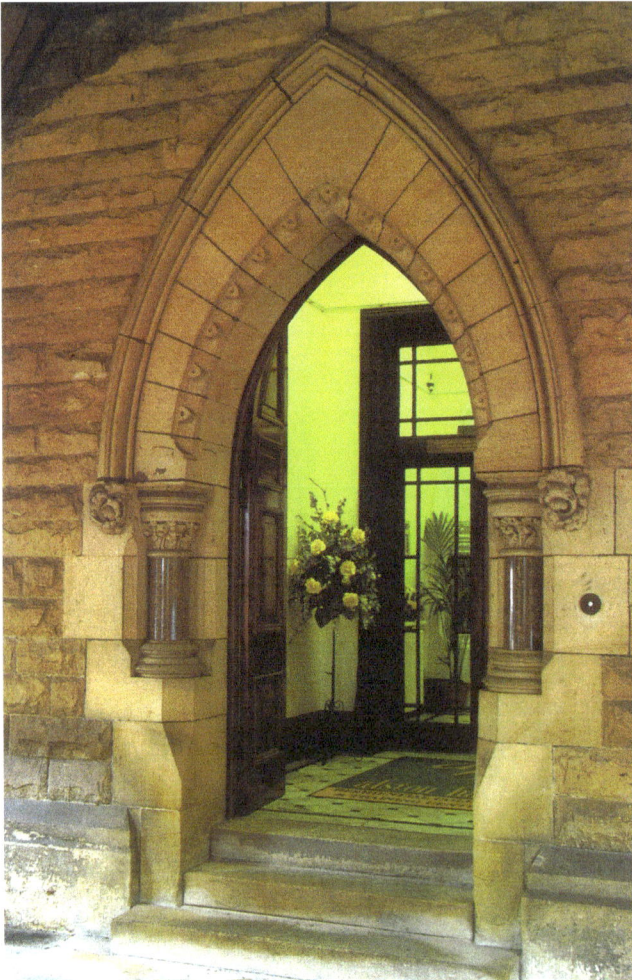

Fig. 4.4 Main entrance and vestibule.

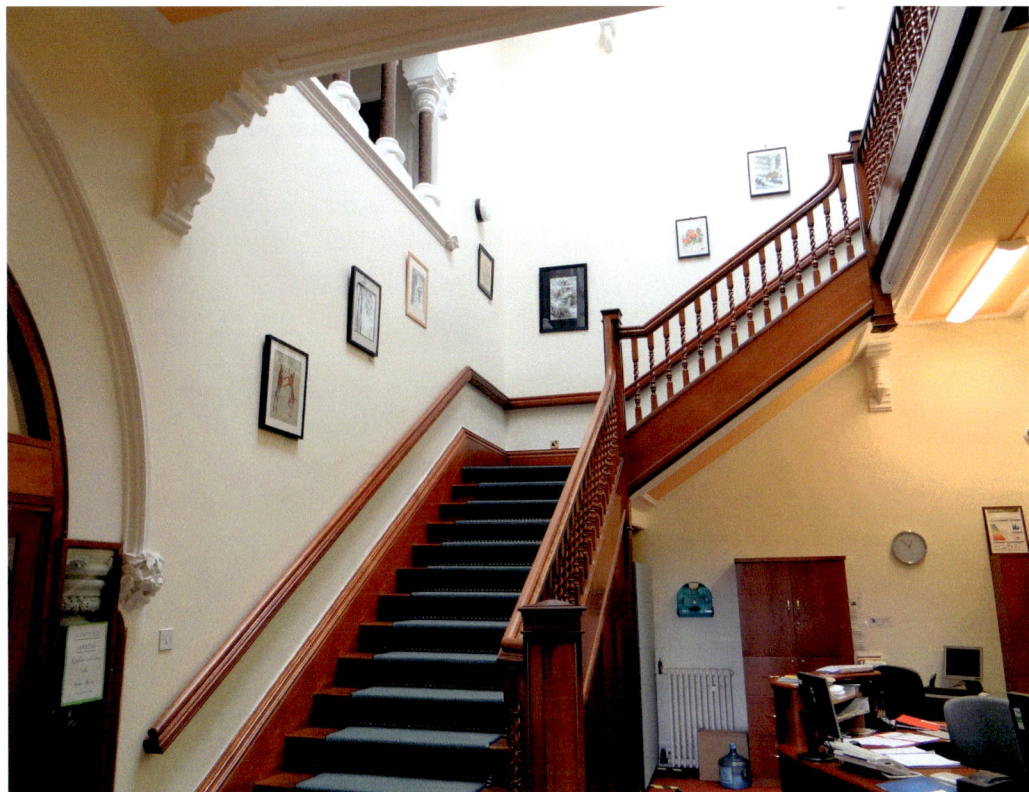

Fig. 4.5 Main stairs to the first floor landing (June 2015).

arches of doorways about the entrance hall, main corridor and first floor landing, and also for the set of arches on the main staircase wall as well as the set on the first floor landing. In selecting the darker stones Darbyshire would be presented with a wide field of possible quarries although nothing has been found in researches to indicate a specific one. Pevsner mentions some possible ones at the beginning of chapter three that may have been working in the 1870s. However, many of the dark coloured sandstones can be structural deficient in strength and can react badly to the rigours of our English climate with flaking and crumbling of the stone being all to common. Darbyshire would be well aware of this and was most probably the reason why he only used the dark coloured stones about the interior of the Hall.

But alas, such decorative stonework was to be painted over presumably between 1912–14 as part of the 'modernisation' of the Hall, to be hidden for years until exposed (fig. 4.7) by water damage following the fire of 15 March 2017. Even the plaster bosses on the headstops of the hoodmoulds of doorway arches in the entrance hall and along the main corridor as well as those on the galleried landing depicting the natural world of animals and fauna in which Ruskin in his writings was to illustrate and celebrate as being the very work of God, were to be subjected to the horror of the paint brush (figs 4.12 and 4.14). In the 1950s when the Hall became a college, further redecoration would take place to add more coats of paint to these plaster bosses, and in consequence their intricate and fine details would be almost obliterated.

Alfred Darbyshire had also applied decorative polychromy to the roof of the Hall and that of the chapel upon which horizontal bands of blue slates ran across an expanse of green ones. These presumably were to be Westmorland slates, available in blue or green and having a more grainy texture as well as being thicker and less uniformly flat than North Wales slate. Little wonder that architects admired Westmorland ones for their colour, texture and character. William Burges used them for his own house

Fig. 4.6 View from the hallway along the main corridor to the conservatory (June 2015). The painting of doorway arches and decorative plaster bosses have presented a somewhat stark-looking décor.

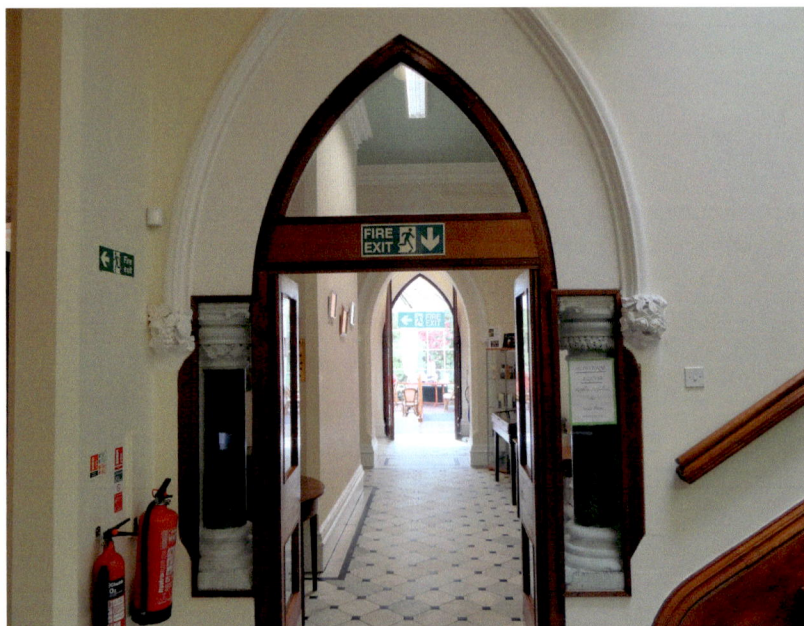

Fig. 4.7 Post-fire scene (January 2019) from the vestibule area showing the original Gothic splendour of the arches and hallway ceiling.

in Melbury Road, Kensington in 1882, their texture and beautiful grey-green aqueous colours were to be in striking contrast to the slates used on neighbouring houses. The fire at Alston Hall was to destroy much of the roof, and slates from America similar in texture and colour to the old ones were to be used for the new roof due to the high cost of Westmorland slate and problems in its availability.

In the entrance hall Alfred Darbyshire had set about to show an overall desire to recapture the Gothic idiom, its ceiling consisting of wooden beams between which ceiling panels had been covered by designs illustrating Gothic style decoration (figs 4.10 and 4.11). This beautiful ceiling had been boarded over presumably during the modernisation period of 1912–14 to be hidden for just over a century until exposed during restoration work following the fire of 2017. Another unfortunate event in the entrance hall during this period of modernisation was the painting of the main wooden ceiling beams and their carved wooden corbels (fig. 4.9).

Fig. 4.8 Post-fire scene (January 2019) in the entrance hall. Under the stairs is the bricked-up doorway into what had been the butler's pantry. On the right is the open arched entrance into what had been the hall lounge, eventually to be the college office.

Looking up at the original ceiling during a visit in September 2018, instantly brought to mind some elements of ornamentation that A. W. N. Pugin had presented for his encaustic tiles to be manufactured by Minton of Stoke-on-Trent during the 1840s. Unfortunately some of the ceiling panels at Alston Hall had suffered slight damage when electric lighting had been installed prior to or during the outbreak of the First World War.

In 1916, suspended from the ceiling of the porte-cochere, was an iron lantern designed to be a part of this new technology of electric lighting whilst in the vestibule area were two antique satin brass suspension lamps with bulbs and frosted shades. Three similar suspension lamps provided lighting for the entrance hall that at this time was well endowed with furniture and appointments of which in April of that year were to be sold by auction. Among the pieces of furniture was a rare antique walnut Queen

Anne table with two drawers; an exceptionally fine and valuable Charles I oak table with date 1635 that in the sale catalogue had been noted as: *This table was the property of the Chapman family and was purchased from the Rev. F. D. Chapman on his retirement from St. Peter's Vicarage*; an Early English oak court cupboard, noted in the sale as: *Purchased from the Sale of the Collection of the late Paul Catterall, Esq., Lytham*; an antique oak chest; an exceptionally fine antique oak armchair with high back surmounted with a frieze dated 1688; and a rare and valuable antique walnut gate legged table.

Among other appointments and pieces of furniture in the entrance hall was a Florentine bronze group, 'The Bacchanalian Revel' 24 inches in height by the French sculptor Clodion (1738–1814) depicting two Satyrs dancing with Bacchante on a Carrara marble base mounted on ormolu. Also a Louis Quatorze impressive bracket clock of total height 4ft 6in., whilst the Far East was represented by an Oriental carved-wood stand, and a Japanese four-fold screen, its panels exquisitely decorated in Shibiyama work – birds and flowering shrubs in tinted ivory and mother of pearl surrounded with black and gold lacquer in a richly carved frame. There was also a Burmese bronze dinner gong in an Indian pierced carved frame, and among a collection of curios was a Persian sword in a chased

Fig. 4.9 The original decorated ceiling in the entrance hall exposed during post-fire restoration work. Damaged paint on the arch is beginning to reveal the 'constructional polychromy' of the arch.

Fig. 4.10 Original ceiling panels in the entrance hall (October 2018).

Fig. 4.11 Original ceiling panels in the entrance hall (October 2018).

brass scabbard. Among other items on display were a pair of buffalo horns mounted on an oak shield; an antique mahogany case barometer by G. Tagliabue; two umbrella stands, one of which was fitted with a brush box; a newspaper box; and a letterbox and stand. On the floor was a costly 12ft by 9ft. Persian bordered carpet, Oriental in design in rich colours; a black skin rug 6ft by 4ft; and two pairs of black skin doormats mounted on green cloth.

However, Alfred Darbyshire had provided a hall lounge of a sort, a sitting room with fireplace to be known simply as the lounge, situated off the northern corner of the entrance hall as part of an open-plan arrangement whereby one entered the room under a large open arch fitted with curtains. Like its entrance hall in 1916 this room was richly furnished. At its window looking upon the main driveway were three Holland blinds with spring rollers and Swiss lace curtains. The main curtains with fadeless linings were made of old gold striped linen plush with pelmet to match. Holland blinds were a common fitment in the principal rooms at this time and most

Fig. 4.12 Carved plaster boss at the bottom of a doorway arch in the entrance hall (June 2015) showing a coal miner at work. Periods of painting have almost obliterated the carving's fine details.

probably were those that had been fitted when the mansion had initially been furnished for John Mercer and his wife.

Electric lighting was provided by a copper bronze electrolier, its suspension chain supporting four lamps with English cut glass shades, and there was also an electric table lamp with a flexible connection. The furniture included a fine Early English walnut bureau; a Chesterfield settee; two divan lounge chairs; a rare Queen Anne cabinet of richly figured walnut; a grandfather clock by J. Fisher of Preston; an antique rosewood card table; an old oak gate legged table; a set of four mahogany Chippendale chairs; an antique walnut stool; a mahogany rocking chair; three cane coffee tables; and a wicker work paper basket. The fireplace had a special antique designed brass kerb with three fire implements and extra cinder tongs, with a brass coal vase to match, and there was also a copper coal bucket. Extra thick linoleum of oak parquet pattern covered the floor upon which were a Persian carpet, a Wilton carpet surround, and a tiger skin rug mounted on bear fur. During college days this room would become the college office.

Having entered the entrance hall, to the immediate left were three principal living rooms beginning with the morning room. One of its windows faced the entrance drive and in this position the room would receive the soft morning light making it ideal as a sitting room prior to lunch, and where breakfast might be served.

In 1954 the room was a discussion room for the day continuation college and when the Hall closed as a residential college in December 2015 the room had long been a bar lounge. One remembers with affection those Sunday evenings when one was to present an illustrated talk, first welcoming those arriving who would partake of a drink in the bar lounge before making their way to the dining room on hearing the sound of the dinner gong. After a superb meal we would assemble in what had originally been the rose bedroom for the evening's performance.

The arrangement for daytime classes was first to meet for tea, coffee and biscuits in the conservatory followed by the start of the day's morning session in what had been the drawing room or perhaps in the original bedroom of either the pink or rose suite. During the morning session would be a short break and at lunchtime a buffet meal was to be had in the dining room followed by tea or coffee in the conservatory after which, weather permitting, a gentle stroll in the grounds could be taken. The afternoon session ended about 4pm when tea, coffee, and college-made cakes and scones were available in the dining room.

Fig. 4.13 The same carved plaster boss shown in Fig. 4.12 after the fire. Having been stripped of paint by water damage during the fire, the exquisite detail work is revealed.

Adjacent to the morning room would be a smaller room (the Principal's room as well as a discussion room in 1954). Initially it seems to have been planned as a billiard room as in the newspaper report of the September 1875 stone laying ceremony, one of the ground floor rooms mentioned for the new Hall was to be a billiard room. By the time Alston Hall was under construction a billiard room was being seen as an essential addition to a country mansion as it was where gentlemen following dinner and after lingering to finish their port in the dining room might assemble to play a game or two and smoke, their ladies having withdrawn to the drawing room where the gentlemen would eventually join them.

Within the principal rooms of the Victorian country house smoking was frowned upon and normally prohibited altogether except of course outside or in a designated smoke room. The conservatory in some houses was also where smoking might be permitted which seems to have been the case at

Alston Hall where there was once a door between the conservatory and the adjacent dining room. When a ramp was built in 1997 from corridor to conservatory enabling wheelchair easy access between the two, the door had to be sealed off.

No evidence has been found to say that the planned billiard room at Alston Hall had from the outset accommodated a billiard table. Instead the room may have become a room for smoking or even a study during John Mercer's time there. In a sale of the Hall in 1917 it is listed as a study and years later in a sale of 1949 is considered to be a smoking room.

However, the Hall did have a billiard table in 1940 when it is a part of the inventory of that year for what had been the drawing room (see chapter 14). By the time of the 1949 sale the drawing room presumably would still have the full-sized billiard table by Orme & Sons Ltd., and to establish when the table might have arrived at Alston reference to the history of this Manchester firm was made.

Founded in 1845, by 1856 the firm was trading in Manchester as Thomas and James Orme, billiards and bagatelle table manufacturers

Fig. 4.14 Carved plaster boss on an arch in the main corridor (June 2015); another victim of the paint brush.

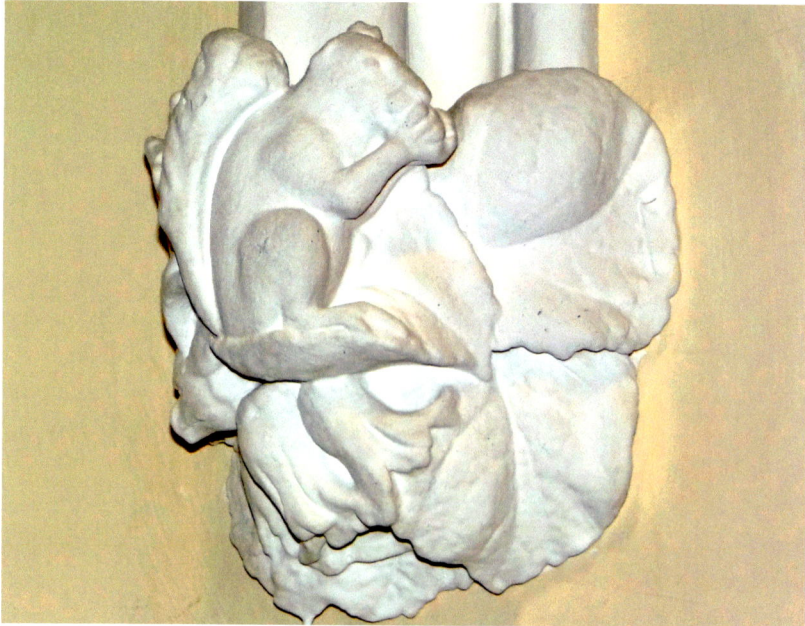

Fig. 4.15 Smoking room / study fireplace (June 2015).

from premises at 1 St Ann Street and 27 Littlejohn Street, and in 1874 the company was trading as Orme & Sons. In 1880 the firm expanded its operations to Glasgow, its branch office there being at 53 Vincent Street, a time when the firm had acquired royal patronage to show the three feathers emblem of the Prince of Wales in its advertisements and products. The firm was always keen to adopt new innovations and its promotion of Ivorine billiard balls was to appear in the *Scotsman* newspaper a year later, such composition balls being half the price of ivory ones.

In 1887 the firm was commissioned to make a billiard table for Queen Victoria's Jubilee Exhibition in Manchester, the price of the table and fittings being 1,000 guineas, a label on the table showing by this date that the firm was trading as Orme & Sons, Ltd. of Manchester, London and Glasgow. In 1890 Orme & Sons Ltd. had showrooms and a matchroom in Blackfriars Street, Manchester, and had a similar facility at 16 Soho Square in London. By 1909 the firm had new showrooms in Liverpool and after the death of Edward VII in 1910 Orme and Sons Ltd. continued to receive royal patronage obtaining a warrant from George V when some of their finest work was done.

Fig. 4.16 The impressive mirror in the drawing room (June 2015).

In 1928 with many businesses struggling, Orme & Sons Ltd. who had already acquired a controlling interest in Messrs. Camkin Ltd. of Birmingham, joined with George Wright and Co. of London and Fred Heyes of Preston. The new company continued to trade as Orme & Sons Ltd. with headquarters in Manchester and branches in London, Glasgow, Hull, Liverpool, Birmingham, Cardiff, Belfast, and Dublin. Even by this amalgamation the new company continued to struggle, and in 1931 made an arrangement with Burroughes & Watts to share their distribution facilities whilst continuing to trade independently. As a consequence the London Showrooms at 16 Soho Square was relinquished and business conducted from the Burroughes & Watts amenities across the road at 19 Soho Square, an arrangement that was sustained until the outbreak of war when all manufacturing came to a standstill.

Most probably the billiard table arrived at Alston soon after William Birtwistle had bought the Hall in 1917 or sometime after 1924 when John

Marsden was in residency, the table on its arrival to be installed in the drawing room, a room whose initial function had changed considerably over the years.

In the Victorian country house the drawing room and the dining room were usually the most lavishly decorated of all the rooms, so reflecting the wealth and status of the owner, the drawing room being where the mistress of the house received callers in the afternoon, and where it was possible its window faced south or southwest to receive the afternoon sun as at Alston. But not so if possible the dining room, as the Victorians disliked their main meal of the day in a sunny environment. At Alston Hall its window was to face southwest with a view of the dell thus enabling the evening meal to be enjoyed in natural lighting especially on a fine summer evening from a weakening and setting sun.

On entering the private rooms of a country house the focus of attention in most instances would be the fireplace, the ones fitted at Alston Hall during William Eccles's time there being most attractive and in keeping with the new décor. Yet the fireplace in the morning room (fig. 16.6) and that of the hall lounge, similar in design with a high wooden mantel and

Fig. 4.17 Drawing room fireplace (June 2015).

Fig. 4.18 Dining room in college days.

surround, inner tiling and metal canopy were to be in marked contrast to the Adam style fireplace of smoking room, drawing room, and dining room as well as those in the private bedrooms. Such a contrast could possibly be an indication that the fireplace in the morning room and the one in the hall lounge were original.

Adjacent to the drawing room at Alston Hall was the chapel where following the death of John Mercer and until his funeral, Mass was said each morning by Mercer's brother-in-law, Canon Taylor. The raised alter area in a bay with three leaded-lights windows and the chancel arch supported by columns of polished pink Shap granite, were to be appropriate features of the chapel. Entrance to the chapel from the main corridor was via a short passageway, a door on the right giving access to the vestry where the priest would have dressed appropriately prior to conducting the religious service.

This small room that at one time had a door leading directly into the chapel had a sink and was also known as the flower room as it was here that flowers were prepared for the chapel.

Opposite the chapel and across the main corridor was the entrance to the dining room. From this room as well as the door into the conservatory, another gave direct access to the servery corridor associated with the kitchen. As well as the unpleasant odours from smoking, the Victorian gentry treated food smells from the dining room with the same intensity of dislike, and in general for this reason the dining room was positioned a reasonable distance but not too far away from the principal living rooms. At Alston Hall this was achieved to some extent by the use of its main corridor.

A visit in December 2017, six months after the fire, found the ceiling of the dining room had been totally destroyed to reveal a rolled steel girder as well as a large wooden beam that together had been the main supports of the floor above (fig. 4.20). As to when the steel girder had arrived at Alston Hall would initially present some thought as the 1870s when the Hall was built seemed a little too early for the use of steel girders in country

Fig. 4.19 Dining room fireplace (June 2015).

house construction. Further exposure of steel girders about the fire-damaged mansion and then evidence of their place of manufacture were soon to remind one of the 1950s period when the Hall underwent major construction work for its conversion into a residential college.

Steel girders, apparently the first in the world were being manufactured in 1860 in Sheffield. Prior to this date cast iron and wrought iron beams or girders perceived for their 'fireproof' qualities were the only metallic structural elements available to architects. Cast iron beams of the inverted T-section form had been used in London's National Gallery (1833) and the Houses of Parliament (1838–41), but in certain situations where large tensile loads were present the use of cast iron with its brittle and crystalline nature could end in disaster. Its inability to cope with large tensile stresses and then fail without warning would come to the fore as in the collapse of a number of multi-storeyed textile mills internally framed in cast iron such as Radcliffe's mill in Oldham in 1844. In compression, cast iron presented no problems and was used extensively in supporting columns in all kinds of buildings during the nineteenth century and the early years of the next.

In contrast to cast iron, wrought iron was a ductile material and much stronger when subjected to tensile loading, but the restricted volume of the semi-molten bloom of iron (due to its weight) coming out of the furnace to be rolled to form the girder, was insufficient to produce a girder of considerable length. This led to the manufacture of fabricated I-section wrought iron girders of substantial length whereby riveted iron angle brackets secured top and bottom flanges with the central vertical plates of the finished girders. George Gilbert Scott was always keen to adopt the fabricated wrought iron girder with its array of rivets as can be seen at his St Pancras Station Hotel in London and also Glasgow University. Alfred Waterhouse for the construction of his Manchester Town Hall opened in 1877 used wrought iron beams.

Although Henry Bessemer's 'converter process' of the 1850s converting molten pig iron directly into steel was ailed as a breakthrough in the production of steel, it was the open-hearth system of Siemens and Martin in the mid-1860s that made steel an economic choice for structural work in buildings from 1870 onwards, and about this time large steam-powered steel rolling mills were producing standard sections.

Early on in his career as an architect Alfred Darbyshire was involved to a considerable extent with structural work in buildings and was to receive a commission to provide plans for the erection of a multi-storey sugar refinery in the city of Dublin.

Fig. 4.20 The dining room (December 2017). At ceiling level is a rolled steel girder that had been installed in the 1950s. Further along towards the window had been an original wooden beam, sawn-off lengths of which are seen in fig. 16.5.

As he would mention in his *Experiences*, Alfred had considerable experience in mill architecture under his old master, Alley, and had worked on the plans of some large cotton mills in Lancashire. He had also been engaged on the drawings of the largest spinning and weaving mill in the world, built on a river island near St Petersburg. Such buildings had been erected on the fireproof principal and his clients for the sugar refinery were determined it should be constructed in a similar manner.

Alfred would mention that cast iron was then exclusively used in girders and beams as well as in the supporting columns, but there appears to be an indication in his account that he was planning to use wrought iron girders and beams for his sugar refinery building, and this was most likely the reason why his clients for the sugar refinery were anxious to have the constructive portion of the scheme submitted to an engineer of some eminence. Alfred suggested a consultation with one of the greatest structural engineers of the day, Sir William Fairbairn who with mathematician Eaton Hodgkinson was to carry out tests on iron beams that would result in mathematical equations and tables becoming available to architects in the preparation of their building plans.

On 17 August 1862 Alfred met Sir William and was impressed by his immense knowledge of mechanics and mathematics. After listening to Alfred's story about his sugar refinery and examining its plans, Sir William was to say something like the following lines as Alfred could not recollect the exact words: *"I am convinced the time has arrived for the introduction of wrought iron for bearing purposes, and would like to try the result of my thoughts and scientific investigations on your Sugar Refinery."*

The result of the meeting with Sir William, according to Alfred, was that his sugar refinery building was the first example of the new departure in wrought iron construction. In the third edition (1864) of Sir William's book, *On the Application of Cast and Wrought Iron to Building Purposes*, Sir William would mention the Dublin sugar refinery.

> *Since the last edition of this work was published I have had several opportunities of testing the value of wrought iron beams; and in proof of their greater security and adaptation for buildings, such as mills, warehouses, c., where great weights have to be supported, I have selected a fire-proof building eight storeys high, erected for Messrs. Bewley, Moss, Co., for illustration. It is built for a Sugar Refinery, and the weight which these floors and beams have to sustain, when loaded with moist sugar, has been calculated at 400lbs. on the square foot,*

Fig. 4.21 Scene from the servery corridor into the kitchen area (January 2019). Positioned back-to-back rolled steel girders installed in the 1950s support the kitchen wall. In the background is the bricked-up original kitchen doorway into the back corridor.

and the breaking weight of the beams is computed at 106 tons equally distributed.

This building is probably one of the most important yet constructed with arches in wrought iron beams, and we may here refer to it as an example of what may be done by the introduction of a material free from flaws, and much lighter than cast iron.

In his *Experiences*, Alfred Darbyshire does not mention steel as a structural element in his architectural commissions, even though by the beginning of the 1890s when he was designing the Palace Theatre of Varieties in Manchester, the use of steel as a major structural component would have become the norm in the construction of theatres. In 1869 he was well involved with what was to be his first association with the architecture of the theatre. As already mentioned, in 1864 the Prince's Theatre in Manchester had opened and following a successful series of 'Shakespearian Revivals' beginning with *The Tempest*, it was decided that the theatre needed to be enlarged, decorated and equipped in an artistic and luxurious manner. Alfred was called upon to undertake the work and in 1869 felt it necessary to visit London where artists and workman who

Fig. 4.22 Scene from the kitchen into the servery corridor (January 2019). On the right is the strong room and its safe, the scaffolding being a safety barrier to the stairwell leading to the basement, whilst over and above the stairwell had been staff stairs to and from the first floor level. On the left is the back corridor and the doorway into what had been the butler's pantry.

had the expertise of decorating theatres could be found. There he met H. Stacy Marks, a painter who would undertake the commission to paint a Shakespearian frieze for the new proscenium (the front of the stage) at the theatre in Manchester.

By 1878 Alfred was in London again on theatre work inspecting the Lyceum for Henry Irving, then Sir Henry, who had taken out a lease on the theatre. In October of that year Sir Henry expressed his wish that Alfred should undertake extensive alterations, repairs and decorations at the London theatre. The scheme was embodied in a set of drawings and by 4 November the work was well in hand, the theatre opening the following month on 28 December.

By this time the building of Alston Hall had been completed or was nearing completion and it would seem that Alfred Darbyshire had decided to install wooden beams to support the various floors rather than iron or steel girders. It is most doubtful that steel girders were to appear at the London Lyceum in 1878 when Alfred was there undertaking extensive alterations as some years were to elapse after this date before steel in the form of box girder construction was to make its debut in theatre architecture.

The first theatre in London to adopt the new technology of steel construction was the Royal English Opera House (now the Palace Theatre) in Cambridge Circus (1888–91). Built for Richard D'Oyly Carte and to the designs of architects T. E. Collcutt and Collings B. Young, the theatre was to have prefabricated box steel girders acting as cantilevers fixed to and radiating from the walls of the building to support three tiers of seating. With this new technology there was no need for cast iron columns supporting the far extension of the tiers, columns that had been to some varying degree in the sight line of some of the audience. Now there was an auditorium offering unrivalled sightlines of the stage. The stepped floors of the tiers were of concrete, whilst incombustible concrete and Portland cement encased the steelwork to form floors, ceilings, stairs and partitions. Glazed brick was used to clad interior walls, whilst window frames were of steel; such was the extensive employment of 'fireproof construction'.

Fig. 4.23 Arches within the wall of the main staircase (June 2015). Coats of paint have obliterated to some extent the true magnificence of this superb architectural composition.

By the early 1900s throughout Britain many theatres that had been erected on iron structure lines were being modernised using the new steel technology with audience safety and comfort in mind. In 1904 the Lyceum in London that Alfred Darbyshire had worked upon for a short while in 1878 was undergoing column-free tier construction, Bertie Crewe being the architect. There, rolled-steel joists were to act as cantilevers supported by prefabricated steel-plate girders. When designing the Palace Theatre of Varieties (1889–91) in Manchester, Alfred Darbyshire may well have adopted the new steel technology thereby eradicating the use of supporting columns at the extremities of the tiered floors.

A visit to Alston Hall on 23 July 2018 found two rolled steel girders exposed in the ceiling area of what had been the pink bedroom. Unable to inspect them closely at the time, it seems according to a workman's description that they were two channel type girders fastened web to web to present an I-section arrangement. Also exposed was girder work in what had originally been the ceiling of the rose suite's bathroom, the girders (fig. 16.9) having been installed to support the floor of a bathroom that had been fitted in the tank room of the water tower as mentioned above in chapter 3. During the same visit the steel girder that had been in the ceiling area of the dining room was in the stable yard having been cut into pieces, and on one piece could be seen in capital letters the words GLENGARNOCK STEEL.

Soon after the July visit to the Hall in 2018 a chance conversation with retired civil engineer Eric Waterhouse would confirm the period when Glengarnock girders had arrived at Alston. On his retirement in 1998 Eric had been Chief Engineer responsible for policy and schemes with Lancashire County Council. In early June 1956 he had been a member of a group of civil engineering students from the Faculty of Science at Manchester University to arrive at Alston Hall to undertake a topographical survey of the area. The group was one of the first residential parties at the Hall, accommodation being on the first and second floors, so recent engineering work about these floors had been completed by this time. In our conversation Eric would recall the mention of Scottish steel being used in such engineering work.

Glengarnock in North Ayrshire and about eight miles northeast of Ardrossan was but a village in 1840 that soon would support one of the largest steel-making works in Scotland. In 1841 James Merry and Alexander Cunningham, coalmasters and ironmasters, had second thoughts about black band, mussel band and clay band ironstones in the district. The ores

Fig. 4.24 Wall of the main staircase (April 2018). Water-sodden plaster had been removed to aid the process of drying out the wall.

had been discovered some years earlier but there were doubts about the suitability of local coal for smelting them. They had not been prepared to take the gamble, for if the coal proved unsuitable they would have been marooned many miles from the nearest alternative supply. However, the situation changed when the Glasgow to Ayr Railway was built along the shore of Kilbirnie Loch nearby that could also provide reserves of water, and in 1843 the Glengarnock Iron Works was founded.

Initially the works had eight blast furnaces, which by 1872 had increased to fourteen, and considerable tonnages of Glengarnock pig iron were exported to America. But with the increasing production in pig iron in the importing countries it became necessary to introduce steel making as an outlet for the surplus pig iron produced at Glengarnock.

The aim was to manufacture steel plates and angles, and in 1884 the blast furnaces were reconstructed for a higher output of 250–300 tons per week. Four eight-ton Bessemer converters and a steam hammer were installed, the hammer being installed because there was some doubt whether the Admiralty would accept rolled rather than hammered slabs.

In early 1885 the first casts of steel were made and later a cogging mill and a plate mill were installed. An extensive trade was then developed for the delivery of tinplate bar to the tinplate mills of South Wales. This mill at

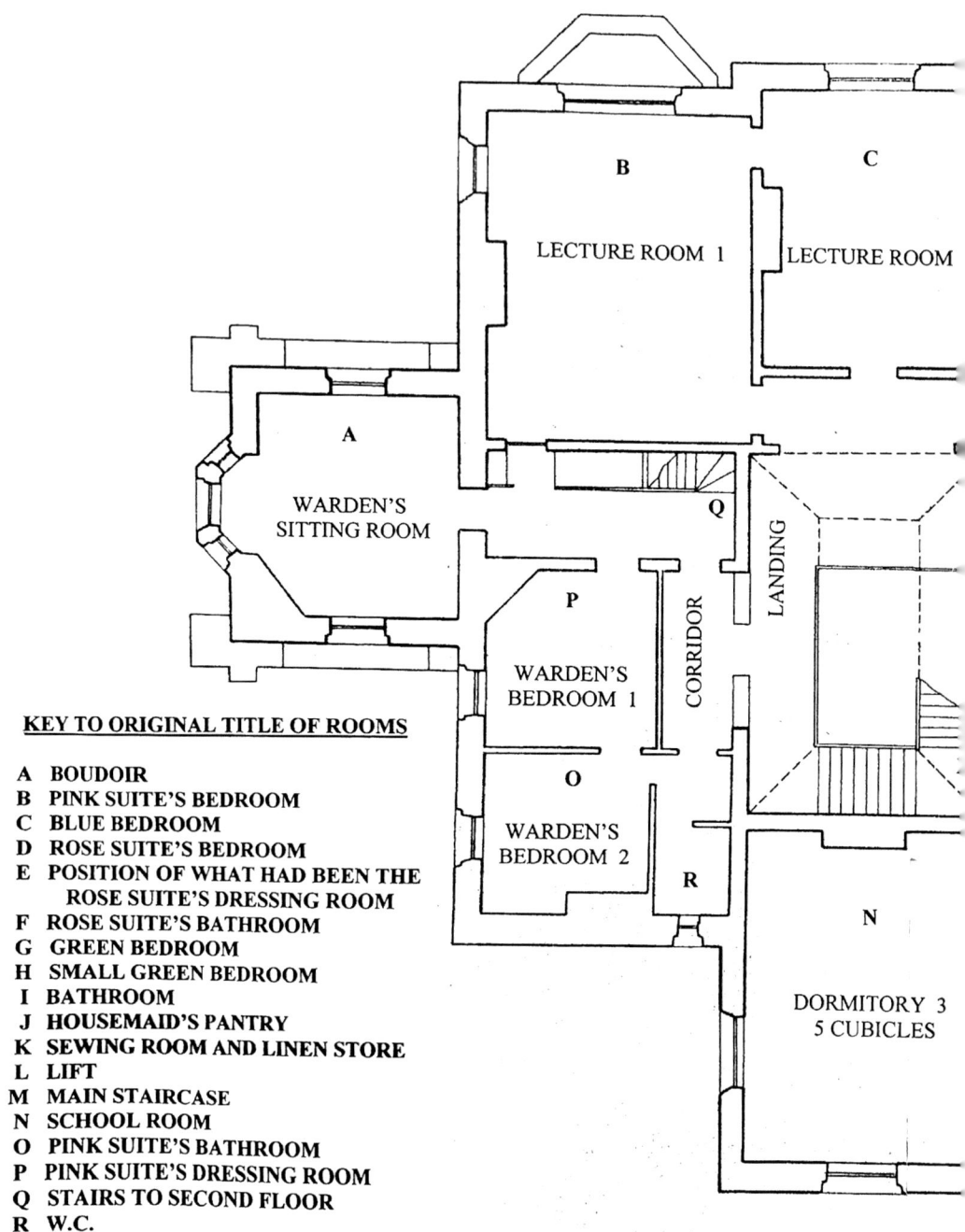

Fig. 4.25 First floor plan of the Hall (second half of the 1950s).

KEY TO ORIGINAL TITLE OF ROOMS

A   BOUDOIR
B   PINK SUITE'S BEDROOM
C   BLUE BEDROOM
D   ROSE SUITE'S BEDROOM
E   POSITION OF WHAT HAD BEEN THE
      ROSE SUITE'S DRESSING ROOM
F   ROSE SUITE'S BATHROOM
G   GREEN BEDROOM
H   SMALL GREEN BEDROOM
I   BATHROOM
J   HOUSEMAID'S PANTRY
K   SEWING ROOM AND LINEN STORE
L   LIFT
M   MAIN STAIRCASE
N   SCHOOL ROOM
O   PINK SUITE'S BATHROOM
P   PINK SUITE'S DRESSING ROOM
Q   STAIRS TO SECOND FLOOR
R   W.C.

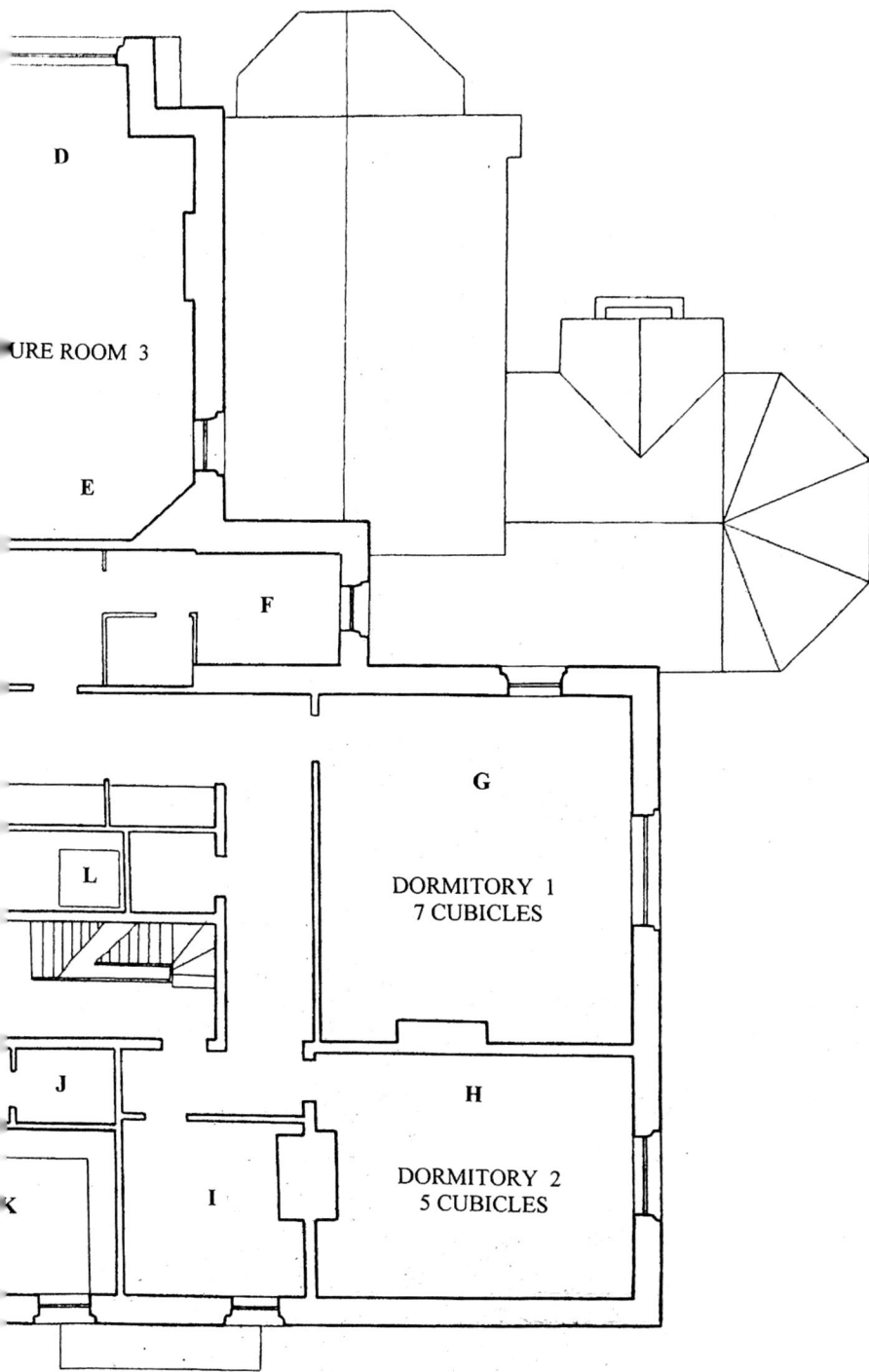

D

URE ROOM 3

E

F

G

L

DORMITORY 1
7 CUBICLES

J

H

I

DORMITORY 2
5 CUBICLES

K

Glengarnock also pioneered the rolling of steel joists that were to acquire a high reputation among structural engineers. However, tariffs in the United States soon ended the trade in tin plate and the Glengarnock works was the first in Scotland to move into making H beams for structures and bridges. Most structural work at that time was done with Belgian iron, but the cheap and strong Glengarnock girders soon replaced the imported girders. The works went on to modernise and expand and by the 1950s their steel girders would be a popular choice in many a building project, one being for the conversion of Alston Hall into a residential college.

Soon after the sale of the Hall to Preston Borough Council in August 1950 and the opening of a day continuation college on its ground floor in the following month, work had begun to convert the Hall into a residential college that had been completed by the beginning of 1956. During this lengthy period of work steel girders had to be fitted under floors before additional bedroom accommodation, toilet and washing facilities could be installed. Figs 4.25 and 4.30 show the general layout on the first and second floors respectively following this conversion work.

On the first floor the green bedroom was now dormitory 1 with seven cubicles, the small green bedroom, dormitory 2 with five cubicles and the school room, dormitory 3, with five cubicles. On the second floor six dormitories had been established, the bachelor's bedroom having been converted into a lecturer's room. Within the dormitories were curtained

Fig. 4.26 Arches with Shap granite columns on the first floor landing (June 2015). Behind them is the corridor giving access to what had originally been the dressing room and the bathroom of the pink suite; the boudoir in the entrance tower; and staff stairs to and from the second floor.

Fig. 4.27 Pink bedroom fireplace (June 2015).

cubicles each with a dressing table-cum-wardrobe whilst at each end were washbasins with screens; toilets and bathrooms would be in a separate section. On the reorganisation of local government in 1974 Lancashire County Council would take on the responsibility for supporting and developing Alston Hall as a college and the dormitories were rearranged into single and twin-bedded rooms, whilst the science laboratories on the ground floor became bedroom accommodation. During the 1980s and 1990s further major improvement programmes saw the formation of a number of en suite bedrooms.

On 2 January 2019 during yet another much appreciated visit to the Hall, more rolled steel girders could be accounted for including those supporting the kitchen wall in the servery corridor (see figs 4.21 and 4.22) where in the 1950s a new entrance to the kitchen had been made and probably the construction of a larger serving hatch from the kitchen, as a serving hatch was in situ in 1949 and may well have been an original feature. The 1954 ground floor plan (fig. 4.1) drawn on 30 March to show the electrical layout in rooms before structural alterations were to take place, shows the kitchen entrance-cum-exit being off the back corridor opposite the wall of the butler's pantry, such a position ensuring the smell of cooking did not enter the dining room.

By the 1950s college kitchen staff had to deal with mass catering in the dining room, and the construction of a more conveniently placed kitchen entrance-cum-exit door in the servery corridor would have been a priority. A drawing (now in the Lancashire Archives) of December 1980 when new fire regulations were in place, shows the serving hatch and presents instructions to take out its existing Colorastic roller shutter and fit a steel roller shutter to give half an hour fire protection. In the background of fig. 4.21 can be seen the blocked up original doorway into and from the kitchen.

On approaching the dining room along the servery corridor, a door on the left gave access to the strong room, immediately before which stairs led down into the wine and other cellars (fig. 4.22), the emergency exit from these cellars leading onto the terraced pathway alongside the Hall's southeast-facing façade. Above the stairwell staff stairs gave access from back corridor to the first floor. A sale of 1917 mentions the strong room having an iron safe and shelving for silver etc., and in 1949 the room contains a steel safe and has a steel entrance door followed by a grill arrangement. There had been another entrance to the strong room, one from the dining room that for some reason had been blocked-up at one period, probably between 1912–14, to be exposed during restoration work in 2019. Such a connection between the two rooms would have allowed the direct and easy transfer of silver and other expensive tableware from strong room to dining table.

Next to the staff stairs in the back corridor was a hand-operated service hoist (lift) to the first floor level, presumably an original feature (see fig. 4.1) for transporting small items such as linen and maybe luggage, and when required, breakfast to the private bedrooms.

Adjacent to the lift entrance on the ground floor was a room at the corner of the main corridor and that of the back corridor whose original purpose has never been established during researches. First thoughts focused on it being a storeroom for luggage awaiting its transportation by coach or having returned to the Hall awaiting the service of the lift.

But a number of country mansions were to have a storeroom known as the plate-room for the storage of valuable tableware made up of silver and plate, glass and china, specifically used for entertaining purposes such as dinner parties. For the safety of this tableware it was usual to have the plate-room as near as possible to the butler's pantry, the butler being

Fig. 4.28 Blue bedroom fireplace (June 2015).

responsible for the upkeep of such items. At Alston the position of the room being so close to the butler's pantry could be an indication that it was a plate-room, its contents presumably being those listed as silver and plate, glass and china, in the inventory of November 1940. The list was huge but no indication was given as to where this collection of valuable items was being stored.

It was also a common arrangement to have the butler's pantry as close as possible to the family part of the house since the butler would have to frequently use the area between both domains in the execution of his daily duties. Some houses did not have a butler but had a housekeeper instead which was the case in 1881 when John Mercer was in residency.

The butler's pantry at Alston once had a door into the entrance hall near to the open arched entrance to the hall lounge, a room where most probably had there been a butler he would have received his instructions. The door would also have given the butler easy access to the front door especially when guests arrived to welcome them.

The removal of plaster during the aftermath of the 2017 fire revealed the bricked-up doorway (see fig. 4.8) across which a new skirting board had been placed. It seems that the bricking-up of the doorway from the butler's

Fig. 4.29 Rose bedroom fireplace (June 2015).

pantry occurred during William Eccles's time at the Hall as behind the skirting board was a delivery label addressed to Eccles for some decorating product or products to be used for the school room. It was from Goodalls (see chapter 12 and 13), decorators of 8 Albert Street, Manchester, who had showrooms in King Street and Police Street.

In 1954 the butler's pantry was a science room for the day continuation college, and adjacent to it was the servants' hall as shown in fig. 4.1. Evidence that the latter was a later edition is seen when inspecting the Ordnance Survey Maps of 1893 and 1912 on which the building is absent. This was to be an unusual omission for a medium sized country house thus leading one to suggest that if it had been present on the original plan of the Hall, it was most likely cancelled following the deaths of John Mercer's two sons when the Mercer family probably had decided not to have a large number of servants. In 1954 the room was the staff lounge of the day continuation college.

For the Census of 1881 John Mercer was still a J.P. and a colliery owner and was now farming 420 acres employing ten men. With him at the Hall are his wife Helen, his daughter Ellen and his mother-in-law Ann Taylor. Indoor staff consisted of four females made up of a Northumberland-born cook, a waitress (born in Lancaster), a kitchen maid (born in Lytham), and a housemaid (born in Garstang). The gardener was from Bold near St Helens and lived at 'Ribble View' with his wife and six children together with their lodger the coachman Piers Pendlebury (20) from Ashton-in-Makerfield.

In the Victorian era country houses employing a substantial number of servants would have a system of bells operating on a mechanical arrangement whereby bell pulls in the main living rooms and bedrooms connected to wires and pulleys running along corridors to bellboards in a servants' hall could summon staff where their services were required. In 1881 when John Mercer was only employing a small number of servants it is most unlikely that such a system of bells existed, if so the bellboard would have possibly been in the back corridor. When the servants' hall was built sometime between 1912 and 1914 it may well had a system of bells operating on electricity to be removed when the Hall was converted into a day continuation college in the early 1950s.

Following on from the addition of the servants' hall were to be four small pantries for which the inventory of 1940 respectively lists as containing bottled fruits and cooking utensils etc.; bread bins, bottles and jars etc.; tinned goods etc.; wood stillage and a barrel of cider. By 1954 these four pantries had been converted into respectively, a cleaners' toilet; caretaker's store; and two cloakrooms, and when the Hall closed as a residential college just before Christmas 2015 these rooms had long been converted into bedrooms.

This was the end of the back corridor (see fig. 4.1) giving access outside to the area in front of the brick wall behind which was the stable yard; the ground floor extension of the four pantries then continuing alongside the stable yard to have an assortment of rooms including housemaid's pantry; a lavatory; firewood and sundries store etc.; rooms to be converted in the 1950s to include toilets and a cloakroom.

Back in the entrance hall the cantilevered staircase led onto to the first floor landing with its three decorative and impressive arches, the centre one giving access to a corridor behind the arches (see fig. 4.26). On turning left into the corridor straight ahead was a W.C. adjacent to the bathroom of the pink suite. With its fireplace on the gabled wall facing the entrance drive and its window overlooking the drive, the bathroom had a communicating door into the suite's dressing room that had a corner fireplace, its window also overlooking the main drive. From the dressing room a passage gave access to the suite's bedroom and also the boudoir situated in the Hall's entrance tower as well as staff stairs to the second floor level (see fig. 4.25).

The boudoir was a private sitting room for the lady of the house where she might entertain female friends, read or perhaps be engaged in some form of artwork. At Alston the boudoir with corner fireplace was to have a window bay projecting as an oriel window on the entrance tower, and for the Hall's contents sale of 1916 the furniture and appointments in the

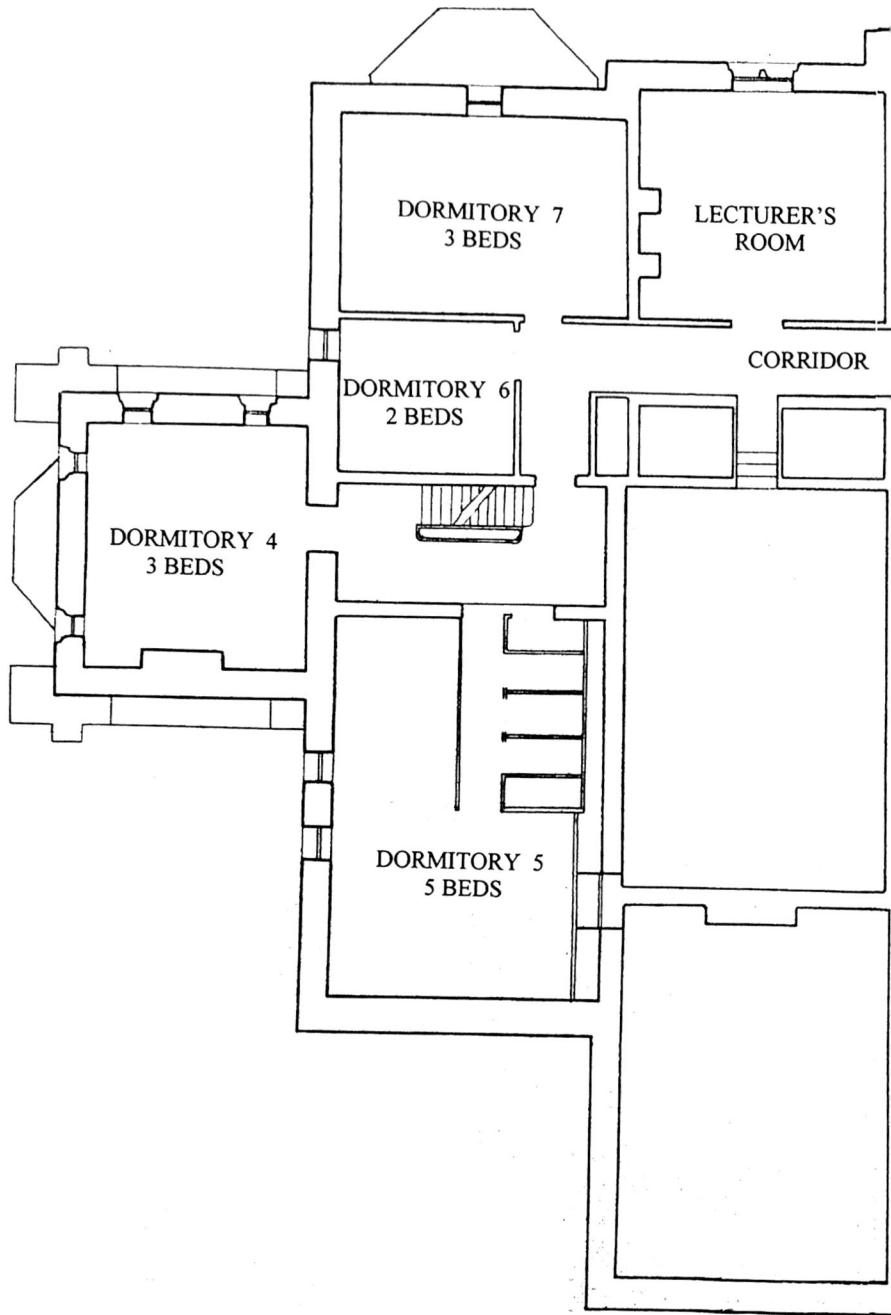

DORMITORY 7
3 BEDS

LECTURER'S
ROOM

DORMITORY 6
2 BEDS

CORRIDOR

DORMITORY 4
3 BEDS

DORMITORY 5
5 BEDS

Fig. 4.30 Second floor plan of the Hall (second half of the 1950s).

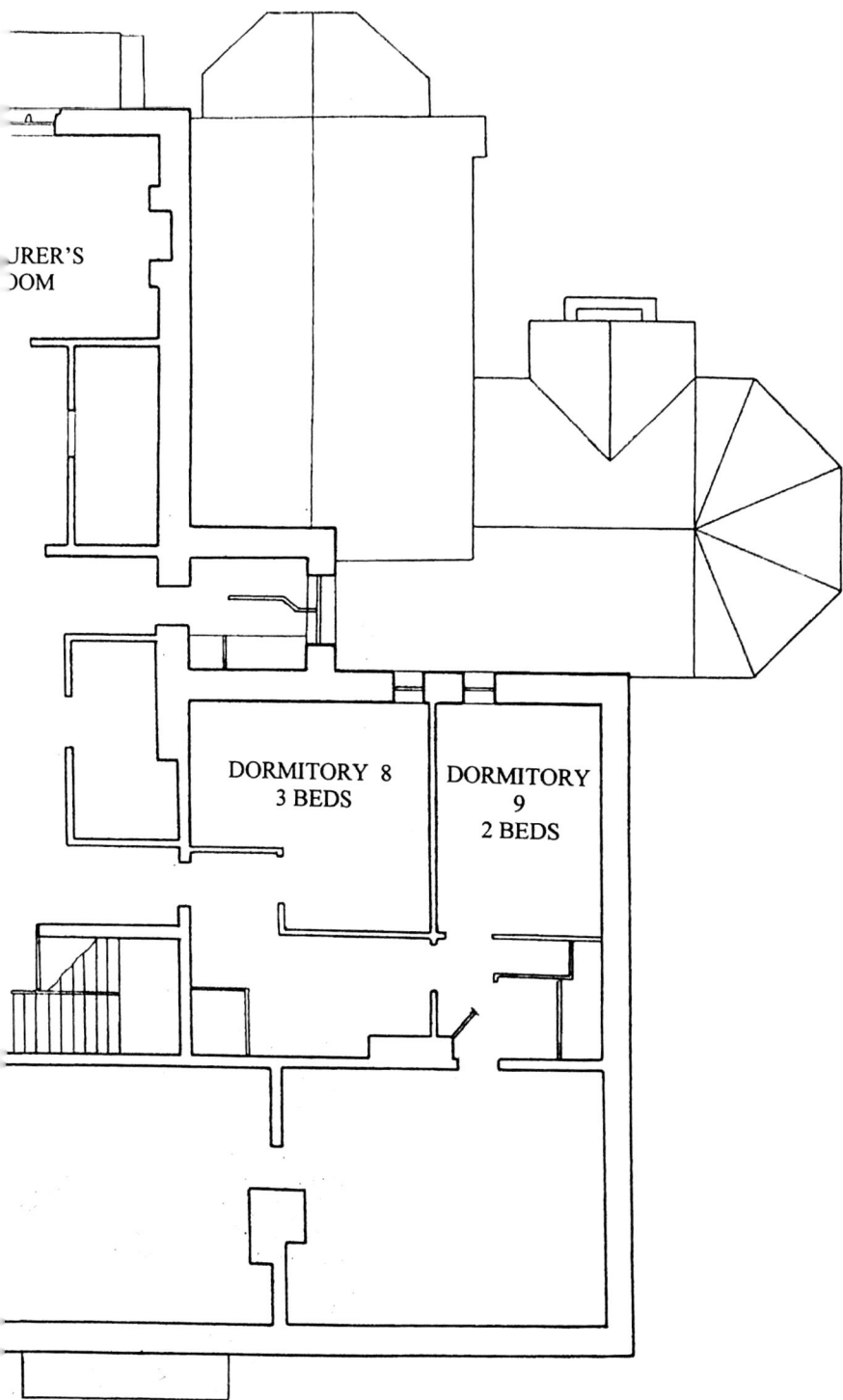

JRER'S
)OM

DORMITORY 8
3 BEDS

DORMITORY
9
2 BEDS

boudoir presented the height of sheer luxury. Its windows with Holland blinds had Swiss lace curtains in two tone shading on Brussels net, whilst the main curtains with fadeless linings were of poplin, soft pink with cream appliqué embroidery, and had draped valances trimmed with cords and tassels.

Amongst the lots on sale in the room was an antique mahogany Chippendale bookcase and secretaire; a rare antique mahogany Adam bookcase; an antique mahogany pole screen with oval silk panel; a four-fold screen 7ft wide by 5ft 10in. high; a Spanish mahogany centre table with circular top and an oval table to match; a Chesterfield settee covered in fawn silk tapestry with a pair of cushions to match; a divan lounge chair with two single chairs and an armchair, all *en suite*; an antique mahogany writing table, whilst an elegant mirror added to the luxury of the room. Other lots included watercolour paintings and an impressive array of china – Dresden, Spode, Vienna, Sevres, Worcester, and Royal Worcester. On the ceiling was a steel bronze electric two-light fitting with cut glass bowl, and as part of the electric light fittings were a pair of steel bronze electric light brackets in Adam design, each arranged as a two-branch candelabra fitted with lamps and pink silk shades.

For the corner fireplace was an oxidized silver hearth suite comprised of a 4ft kerb with shaped and pierced front, ornamented with bosses and beaded moulds; a set of three fire implements and extra under tongs, and a cabinet coal box to match. There were also two ornamental paper baskets, covered with green watered silk, worked with panels of flowers in rich colours. On the floor as well as linoleum was an extra-super quality Axminster carpet complete with underfelt.

When in 1966 Ann Lightfoot became Warden of Alston Hall Residential College she would incorporate the boudoir as her sitting room and the dressing room and bathroom of the pink suit to form a self-contained flat. On her arrival in 1962 as Deputy Warden her room was what had originally been the bachelor's bedroom on the floor above with its a battlemented balcony and the view of the Ribble Valley. Soon after arriving at the college in 1988 as her replacement Brian Leighton was to convert the boudoir into the Principal's room before which the original smoking or study room downstairs had been used as such.

Like the boudoir, the contents of the pink bedroom in 1916 represented almost unbelievable luxury. Adjacent to the room was the smaller blue bedroom that was to have two communicating doors, one with the pink bedroom and one with the rose bedroom. If this two-door arrangement had been a part of the 1870s construction schedule, perhaps the blue bedroom had been intended to be a bedroom for John Mercer's two infant sons, or perhaps it had been William Eccles's idea for his children. Eventually the blue bedroom accommodated the college library.

The rose bedroom with its large bay window was like the pink bedroom in that it had a dressing room and a bathroom, but the original layout of this suite of rooms is not shown on the Hall's first floor plan (fig. 4.25) of the early 1950s. This is because when the plan was drawn the rose bedroom had been or was being enlarged to convert it into a large lecture room for residential college purposes by extending it into the suite's dressing room area, when the latter's corner fireplace was removed to leave behind its chimney breast and what had been the room's small window.

In 1940 when the inventory for insurance purposes was undertaken the rose bedroom still had its original adjacent dressing room with its corner fireplace. In October 2000 Gwen Marsden in presenting her personal reminiscences of wartime Alston Hall in the 1940s (see chapter 14), in referring to the rose bedroom mentions the rose suite's dressing room being in *the rear part of the room, the wall etc. removed sometime in the last 50 years*. Entry into the rose suite's bathroom from its dressing room seems to have been via a doorway or opening, to be exposed by the 2017 fire as seen in fig. 16.4.

Off the corridor behind the four decorative arches on the wall of the main staircase were the Hall's original two main guest bedrooms to be known respectively as the green bedroom and the small green bedroom (see fig. 4.25). Adjacent to the small green bedroom and overlooking the stable yard was a bathroom followed by a room made up of the housemaid's pantry and the sewing room and linen store, the pantry being a storeroom on the left on entering the room

The housemaid in a country house was the workhorse of the household staff, usually the first to rise in the morning to open window shutters and raise blinds, clean out fire grates to relay and light fires, followed by what seemed countless tasks to keep the house clean and tidy. Little wonder the term 'housemaid's knee' came about when one considers the repetitive movements causing inflammation of the joints the housemaid had to endure during the execution of her work.

The housemaid's pantry was where she could keep her cleaning materials conveniently close to the floor upon she was working, and the 1916 sale catalogue in presenting the contents of the housemaid's room give some idea of her enormous work load. Amongst the assortment of cleaning aids were a number of housemaid's boxes containing brushes; five cane carpet beaters; carpet brushes; two closet pan brushes; a mattress brush; three ceiling brushes; two enamelled slop pails with covers; and three brass hot water supply cans, etc. Lot 274 was made up of a number of items, one being a tin of 'Ronuk' floor polish.

With the pantry to the left, straight ahead was the entrance to the sewing room and linen store, a most important room in the country house scene where articles of linen were kept in large cupboards having labelled shelving. The purchasing of household linen was the responsibility of the housekeeper who took stock of it and would examine it to see if repairs were necessary on its return from the laundry, the repairs in general undertaken by the housemaid or some other members of the household staff in the sewing room. Fig. 4.25 shows the room at Alston, its corner fireplace facing two opposite walls about which can be seen the outline of the cupboard area for the storing of linen fabrics. The sixth and final day of the 1916 sale saw the sale by auction of numerous lots of linen including bath towels and mats; bedspreads; sheets and pillowcases; tablecloths and covers; tray cloths etc.

The sale catalogue refers to the room as sewing room and linen room for which lot 298 was a wardrobe or linen store cupboard constructed in solid walnut, its interior fitted with six sliding trays enclosed by three folding doors, the under part containing three long drawers and three short drawers. Lot 299 for the same room was a range of walnut cupboards containing nine sliding trays and convenient shelves enclosed by six carved panel doors, the under part fitted with six long drawers and two deep centre drawers. Lot 300, again for the same room, was a range of walnut stained store cupboards fitted with nine shelves enclosed by three sliding panel doors.

The sewing room portion was set out to what seemed to be a comfortable workplace among the contents being a suite of six solid walnut chairs; a stained mahogany table 3ft by 3ft 9in with a hardwood top and supported on four turned legs with brass castors, and a stained walnut table 5ft 3in. by 3ft 3in. having a sycamore top and supported on four massive turned legs with castors. There was also a box Ottoman, 4ft long by 2ft 6in. deep, lined and covered with floral tapestry, an Ottoman being a seat for several persons sitting with their backs to one another. The room had an ironing board, an electric iron (the room having electric lighting) and a box iron with two heaters. Lot 306 was linoleum that had been planned to the floor whilst lot 307 was again linoleum planned to the housemaid's room; airing chamber; landing and hoist room.

By the time of the 1940 inventory these service rooms seemed to have taken on a new name for the listing of their contents. The airing room with its three square yards of linoleum is mentioned, as is a boot and sundries storeroom with its array of travelling cases; a cabin trunk; a Gladstone bag; tennis rackets; etc., but there is no mention by name of the sewing room and linen store. Listed is the housemaid's pantry having cleaning utensils; aluminium and rubber hot water bottles; carpet sweepers, etc.

Next to the housemaid's pantry, sewing room and linen store would be the school room situated at the north corner of the Hall, one of its windows overlooking the stable yard, the other looking upon the main drive; a room in 1940 to be well-furnished as a bedroom (see chapter 14).

On the second floor level were servant bedrooms along with bathroom and toilet facilities whilst on the side facing the Ribble view were three large bedrooms, one above the rose bedroom, one above the blue bedroom and opposite the stairs to the roof, and the bachelor's bedroom above the rose bedroom. In the sale of 1916 among the contents of the bachelor's bedroom were; a satin brass three light electrolier with cut-glass shades; a satin brass 3ft 6in. kerb fender; an all-brass Sheraton bedstead; wardrobe; dressing chest; washstand; two cane-seated chairs; a cane armchair, and a Chippendale occasional table. On the floor were linoleum and an Axminster carpet.

It was not unusual to have a bachelor's bedroom somewhat isolated from guest bedrooms as at Alston Hall, guest bedrooms perhaps where unmarried female visitors might have to be accommodated. In the Victorian country house in general, bedroom accommodation for single males and females were to be kept as far apart as was possible. Male and female servants were also separated in a similar way and the only common territory for both sexes in the servant domain would be the servants' hall.

After the bachelor's bedroom and overlooking the dell area was the tank room in the Hall's water tower. Fig 15.29 shows the room in 2003 having long been converted into a bathroom. In 1940, next to the tank room was an empty room, then came a room listed as a sundries store room adjoining which what had become a dark room for photography (see chapter 14), Next came a bathroom with lavatory, then a W.C.

Chapter five

A marriage into a Yorkshire family

The Census of 1881 had found "John Mercer J.P. of Alston new Hall, Colliery Proprietor and Farmer of 420 acres, employing 10 men" living in his new mansion with wife Helen (40), daughter Ellen (25), Ann Taylor (74, widowed mother-in-law), and four unmarried female servants; cook, waitress, kitchen maid, and housemaid. This was the year that would define the future of John Mercer's daughter Ellen and eventually that of Alston Hall, as on 15 November Ellen became a member of a Roman Catholic family whose ancestors had been living as aristocrats for centuries when she married Edmund Waterton of Deeping Waterton Hall, near Market Deeping in Lincolnshire.

Arranged to take place in London instead of Alston Hall it is said because of a recent bereavement, the marriage ceremony would take place in St Mary's Chapel in Horseferry Road, Westminster. Attended by six bridesmaids Ellen wore a dress of rich, white satin whilst her ornaments were gold and diamonds, the gift of her father. The Pope had blessed the bride's ring and Cardinal Manning, Archbishop of Westminster, of the Brompton Oratory performed the ceremony, the wedding reception afterwards being in the Buckingham Palace Hotel, London, where the dining table had been arranged for 32 settings, and where the Rev. Father Purbrick, former Rector of Stonyhurst College would propose a toast.

At the time of his wedding Edmund had been staying in London's Westminster Palace Hotel, and because he was well known in the Catholic Church hierarchy and enjoyed being part of grand religious and ceremonial

Fig. 5.1 Edmund Waterton.

occasions, the Brompton Oratory could well have become the venue for the wedding had it not been undergoing a major re-build at the time.

To be known as the Church of the Immaculate Heart of Mary, the Brompton Oratory in Brompton Road was built between 1880 and 1884 replacing an earlier church of the Oratorians on the same site. Following the rule of Saint Philip Neri, the Oratorians were a community of Catholic worshippers that Cardinal John Henry Newman had introduced in Birmingham after his resignation from St Mary's Church, Oxford in 1843 to join the Roman Catholic Church. A London congregation was founded in 1849 that worshipped in a temporary church on the Brompton Road site in 1854, and in 1874 to mark the congregation's Silver Jubilee an appeal was launched to replace the church with the present one. After an architectural competition, Herbert Gribble, a convert to the Catholic faith was appointed as architect, the new church eventually being erected in an Italianate style seen to have been a deliberate attempt to bring the Vatican in Rome to a nineteenth-century London congregation, many of which who would have been unable to visit the real thing. A few days after the consecration of the church in April 1884 Cardinal Henry E. Manning officially opened it. Before the building of London's Westminster Roman Catholic Cathedral (1895–1903) the Brompton Oratory was the largest Catholic Church in the Capital with later additions such as the southern façade in 1893 and its impressive dome in 1896.

The place for the wedding, St Mary's Chapel, was a chapel of ease served by the Jesuits before it became redundant following the building of the Roman Catholic Cathedral in Westminster, the parishioners of St Mary's attending the Cathedral on St Joseph's Day 1903. Salvaged from St Mary's were the Stations of the Cross, seating, pulpit and statues, one statue being that of St Joseph made in Germany and re-erected in the Church of St John the Evangelist in Duncan Terrace, Islington. Today the Roman Catholic Church in Horseferry Road is that of the Sacred Heart near the bend in the road some distance from the river. Presumably this was the site of St Mary's Chapel that was to be replaced by the Church of the Sacred Heart that today serves as a chapel of ease for Westminster Cathedral.

Cruchley's Map of London of 1829 (fig 5.2) in the British Library's collection in London shows the site and another one in the road but further along towards Marsham Street. Each have a building at its centre, the one on the site backing onto Medway Street is presumably St Mary's Chapel, the other one maybe its school as a map of c.1870

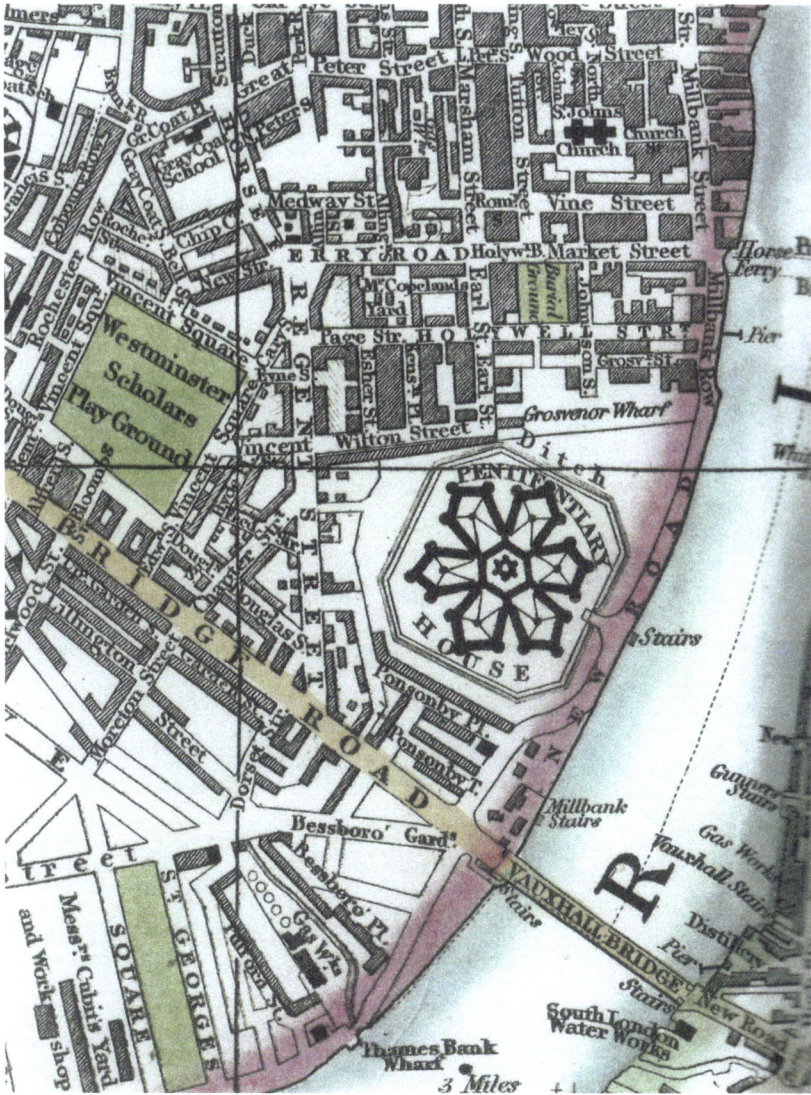

Fig. 5.2 Part of Cruchley's London Map of 1829. Horse Ferry (then, two words) Road is shown in the upper half of the map, where near the bend in the road is presumably St Mary's Chapel at the centre of a site backing onto Medway Street where Ellen Mercer married Edmund Waterton in 1881.

shows both sites having been redeveloped and indicated by a religious cross symbol.

At the time of his wedding Edmund was 50 years of age whilst Ellen was 26, and among those who were to sign the marriage certificate as witnesses were the bride's father; Mary and Agnes Waterton (Edmund's daughters by his first marriage); Catherine Thompson; Mary Pyke; and Eleanor Parsons. Following the wedding celebrations the newly weds left the Buckingham Palace Hotel amid a deluge of rice and old shoes for Victoria Station and then to the south coast.

A few weeks later on 17 December, the *Grantham Journal* presented a lengthy and delightful account of the couple's return from their honeymoon to Edmund's home in Deeping St James, Lincolnshire, the opening part of the account reading:

> *The Return of Edmund Waterton, Esq., with his fair bride (after a wedding tour in the south of England), to his family domain at Waterton Hall, Deeping St. James, was honoured on Thursday week by a reception the like of which has probably never before been known in this parish. Mr. Waterton, during his residence here, has gained the respect and goodwill of a large portion of the parishioners and neighbours, by his courtesy and urbanity, his great but unostentatious liberality, his kindness and consideration to all parties and creeds. As soon as the day and hour of the arrival became known, neighbourly consultations took place, and quiet preparations began to be made for a suitable reception of their good and worthy friend and his bride, which publicly manifested itself a few hours before the arrival, at 2.30, at the approach to the Hall, by banners and flags, archways and mottoes, and a stream of well-wishers. The bride and bridegroom arrived at the Great Northern Station, Peterborough, about 1.30, and were met by a carriage and two pairs of handsome greys, with postillions, and were at once conveyed to Deeping. On the arrival of the carriage and its happy occupants, a few hundred yards from the bridge, they were met by a number of parishioners and a band of music, while some thirty or forty stalwart tillers of the soil, who knew and felt his worth, begged of him to allow them to remove the horses and draw the carriage themselves to his home. To this he consented: the horses were removed, and ropes attached, and the newly-wedded pair were thus conveyed to their home, amidst the rejoicings of the crowd. On the near approach to the bridge, a stream of flags waved over the road,*

and the first greeting in their ancient family county of Lincoln was in front of the "Bell" – a motto on canvass, in beautiful worked letters, "Long Life and Happiness." A few yards further on was the word "Welcome," prettily surrounded with flowers, evergreens, &c. Over the carriage entrance was a beautiful arch of evergreens and flowers, with the words "Thrice Welcome," in gilded letters. Over the carriage drive was another pretty design, with the words, "Bright and joyous be your Lives;" and under it, more beautiful still, were assembled the members of his family, to receive them home, also his maid servants dressed in neat attire to greet their master and new mistress to the Hall. At the entrance to the Hall was an elegant arch of evergreens, intermixed with flowers, &c., and bearing the emphatic words, "Welcome Home".

Ellen, now as Mrs Waterton, was about to embark on a new life as the 'lady of the manor'. Before alighting from their carriage, Ellen and Edmund were to receive an address from the gathered crowd of tradesmen and residents congratulating Edmund on his marriage and welcoming his bride, wishing their union to be long and happy. After a bouquet of flowers had been presented to Ellen, she and Edmund stepped from the carriage to enter the Hall wherein each were greeted with a kiss from family members, after which Edmund introduced the servants to Ellen according to their position in the household.

The newspaper account then continued, commenting upon Edmund and Ellen returning to the front of the Hall and Edmund thanking neighbours and friends for the very cordial and kind reception they had given to him and his wife. The account ended to describe the evening scene as celebrations continued:

At six o'clock, a large bonfire was lighted in the park, in front of the Hall, and many smaller ones throughout the park. A barrel of tar was used amongst the combustibles, to give greater effect; and the barrel itself was lighted and rolled round the park. The initials of Mr. and Mrs. Waterton, "E. E.," were affixed over the word "Welcome," in large letters of wire, covered with combustible material, and placed in front of the windows of the Hall: when lighted they were seen most distinctly for about ten minutes, and much admired from the rooms of the Hall, and by the large number of people assembled in the park. A band of music played during the evening and much enlivened the occasion.

With no family letters or personal diaries belonging to the Mercer family having been found, it is not possible to shed light on the lifestyle of Ellen Mercer during the years leading up to her marriage or when and how she first met her husband-to-be. It is not possible to say if their union was the result of a love match or if the marriage was to be a happy one. The facts were that Ellen, the future heiress to a considerable fortune had married a widower with a large family and who was old enough to be her father and had a history of debt problems having been declared a bankrupt at one period. Perhaps because he came from a Catholic family bearing an impressive pedigree and had attained prominent positions in the Catholic Church hierarchy, made him a suitable addition to the Mercer family. In some instances where a daughter might or was to inherit, a condition of the inheritance was that she kept the family name or added the family name to that of her husband. Such a condition was not to be with regard to Ellen Mercer.

In comparison to the Mercer family much more is known about the family Ellen had become a part of, such knowledge being due to three excellent publications on the Waterton family from which the following two chapters, albeit abridged versions, are based upon to a large degree, the publications being *Charles Waterton 1782–1865* by Julia Blackburn; *Squire Waterton* by Gilbert Phelps; and *Charles Waterton – A Biography* by Brian Edginton.

John Mercer must have known about the somewhat chequered history of the man his daughter was to marry, and any concerns regarding the suitability of him as a future son-in-law were probably outweighed by John Mercer's wish that a male child of the marriage, albeit a Waterton by name, would secure the future of Alston Hall. Fate and religion would decide otherwise.

Chapter six

The Watertons

Edmund Waterton's father had been the somewhat eccentric Charles Waterton born at Walton Hall near Wakefield in Yorkshire on 3 June 1782, the eldest son of Thomas and Anne Waterton, Anne being the daughter and heir of Edward Bedingfeld, the second son of Sir Henry A. Bedingfeld, third baronet of Oxburgh Hall in Norfolk. Thomas's father, another Charles and the 25th Lord of Walton Hall had married Anne, daughter of Christopher Cresacre More of Barnborough near Doncaster, sixth in line of descent from Sir Thomas More who had been Lord Chancellor to Henry VIII, and it was this Charles who was imprisoned at York because of loyalty to the Royal House of Stuart.

The pedigree of the Watertons went back before the Conquest but the eccentric Charles (born 1782) was not of a direct line but had descended from a second son, the Watertons of Walton being the progeny of John Waterton who had acquired the estate in 1453. Up to the reign of Henry VIII things had gone well for the Watertons but following the Reformation they became recusants after refusing to subscribe to the tenets of the Church of England, and were subjected to crippling fines and all kinds of other harassments. During the reign of Queen Mary, Thomas Waterton of Walton Hall had been appointed High Sheriff of York but this would be the last public commission to be held by the Watertons.

During the Civil War the fifth generation Thomas Waterton fought for the king at Marston Moor in 1614 to be one of 4,000 Royalists to die, and tradition has it that shortly after the battle Oliver Cromwell lay siege to Walton Hall when its drawbridge was destroyed. During these troubled times a swivel gun had been mounted on the Hall's gateway and in withstanding the siege the gun was used to fire a cannon ball across the lake fracturing the leg of a Cromwellian soldier. Some years later Charles's father found the cannon ball *nine inches deep under the sod* where the soldier was supposed to have been standing, and in 1857 when sludging work within the lake and close to the old gateway was in progress, Charles would describe … *we found an iron swivel-cannon, eight feet deep in the mud, and resting on the remains of the ancient bridge … The little iron ball … seems to have been cast to fit this gun.*

In 1745 Prince Charles, the Young Pretender and grandson of Charles II invaded Scotland in an attempt to restore the exiled house of Stuart to the throne. Walton Hall was to be searched for arms, when, at the suggestion of Charles, the gun was thrown into the lake, following which his grandfather *had the honour of being sent prisoner to York, a short time before the battle of Culloden, on account of his well-known attachment to the hereditary rights of kings.*

Charles Waterton (born 1782) would resent the way his ancestors had been treated and remained loyal to their religious convictions throughout his life, practising many acts of Christian charity irrespective of the religious standing of those on the receiving end. He resented the loss of opportunity to have had an active part in government, and in one of his many publications would write:

> *Had our religion not interfered with our politics, my early days would probably have been spent in the service of my country.*

With his rich Yorkshire accent Charles had no 'airs and graces' and was always willing to help those far less fortunate than himself. He enjoyed life to the full and was a gifted and enthusiastic pioneer of the science of natural history to which he made an enormous contribution to up to his untimely death in 1865. He was to have four brothers and two sisters – Thomas (1785–1854) who settled in France and died unmarried; Christopher (1787–1811) see this chapter; William (1794–52) who became a member of the Society of Jesus; Edward (1798–1845) who went to New Zealand and died at sea, unmarried; Isabel; and Helen who married Robert Carr (see later) and died in 1840.

In 1767 Charles's father, Thomas, as the 26th Lord of Walton, had inherited the family home at Walton near Wakefield in West Yorkshire, an Elizabethan Hall on an island surrounded by its lake within a vast estate of almost 300 acres. He was soon to have it demolished and replaced by one erected in the Classical style we see today. A visitor to Walton Hall (now a hotel) with an interest in heraldry might inquire as to why the shield of

Arms executed in stone albeit much weather worn and situated within the pediment high above the entrance to the Hall, depicts two coats of arms joined together.

This is an example of marshalling in heraldry using the method of impalement to denote some form of an alliance, in this particular case a marriage, not seemingly of Thomas who had the Hall built, but that of his eldest son Charles who inherited the Hall on the death of his father in 1805.

In 1829 Charles married Anne, the second daughter of Charles Edmonstone of Cardross Park, near Dumbarton (see below), Charles Edmonstone being 12th in male descent from Sir William Edmonstone who had married Princess Mary the daughter of Robert 111, and 13th in line from Sir John Edmonstone who married Princess Isabel the daughter of Robert 11 of Scotland. Anne Waterton died within the first year of her marriage to Charles Waterton.

Today looking up at the marshalled Arms, in the dexter half of the shield (left-hand half on observing the shield) we see the Waterton Arms, the blazon being *'Barry of six ermine and gules, over all three crescents sable'*, whilst in the sinister half are the Arms of Edmonstone *'Or, three crescents within a double tressure flory and counter-flory gules'*.

The double tressure (a double border inset from the edges of the shield) enriched with fleur-de-lis as displayed at Walton Hall, is known as the Royal tressure seen in the Scottish quarter of the Royal Arms. Over a period of time the Royal tressure was to descend by easy stages through all armigerous social ranks in the northern kingdom. It was accepted as being indicative of Royal ancestry no matter how remote on the female side of the family, hence its appearance at Walton where the marshalled shield is surmounted by the Waterton Crest, *'An otter passant, holding in its mouth a pike, all proper'*, whilst the motto is *'Better kinde frembd than kyen'*, which one source has re-worded to read *'Better kinde frende than strange kyne'* to mean – 'it is not always a good idea to trust one's relatives'.

During the building of the new Walton Hall, the water gate of the old Hall by which connection to and from the mainland by boat had been made and which in times past had provided some degree of security was saved from demolition. Today, musket ball marks within the structure present tangible evidence of a siege during the Civil War period, whilst the present-day cast iron bridge allowing access to the Hall on its island was a replacement for what had been a stone bridge.

Most of Thomas Waterton's relatives during the years of Catholic oppression after the Reformation had gone to live abroad; Southern Spain,

Belgium, South and North America, North Africa and even New Zealand were amongst the destinations. Educated abroad by English Jesuits, Thomas had an aunt, Mary Augustine More who in the closing decades of the eighteenth century was the Mother Superior in the English Convent in Bruges. The convent, its address today being 85 Carmersstraat, Bruges, had been started in 1629 by the Order of English Augustinian Canonesses who had fled England following the Reformation, the convent becoming a high-class finishing school for young Catholic ladies. Between 1736 and 1739 a church, seen today with its impressive dome was added, and in 1972 the convent ceased to be an educational institution following which it was to be used to house seminaries and pilgrims.

Whilst at the convent Mary Augustine More was in regular correspondence with Thomas Waterton from 1779 to 1791, one letter indicating a somewhat strange situation. In it she sent Thomas fond greetings from his 'wife' at the convent and enquired about the well being of his wife and young family in England. The 'wife' referred to in the convent was Eusebia Pickering of Portuguese-English decent who had arrived at the convent as a 20-year-old in 1758 with her two sisters. Apparently her 'marriage' to Thomas Waterton had never been solemnized in a church and it has been suggested that maybe the reason behind her entering the convent was so she could make no claims on Thomas. She was of a sensitive nature especially if contradicted when some might fear of her losing her senses as some of her family members had done when confronted with similar occasions.

Thomas's son Charles, after home tuition up to about ten years of age, was sent to a preparatory school at Tudhoe, near Durham, before eventually going to Stonyhurst College in 1796. This was a time when Roman Catholics were not allowed to send their sons for higher education to the established universities as the entrance examinations to them involved the signing of the Thirty-nine Articles of the Church of England. So it was at Stonyhurst, the Roman Catholic public school that Charles was to undergo his final educational studies.

From an early age Charles had shown a developing interest in natural history and soon after his time at Stonyhurst the opportunity arose for him to extend this interest onto a more professional level. This began in November 1804 when he sailed from Portsmouth on a six week voyage to British Guiana for the Demerara region on the northeast coast of South America to take charge of a sugar plantation his father had recently bought *for the benefit of his younger children*, a plantation to be named *Walton Hall*.

The other reason for his voyage to the coast of South America with its warm climate was to recover from an infection of the lungs brought on by a serious chill following the effects of yellow fever he had contacted in Malaga. Having completed his education at Stonyhurst in 1801, Charles in November of the following year along with his younger brother Christopher, had set sail during the Peace of Amiens period for Malaga in southern Spain where two of their maternal uncles had a house there as well as one near the foot of the Montes de Malaga. An epidemic of yellow fever hit Malaga in 1803 and having contacted the fever Charles was to become immune from it but whilst he was in Malaga the older of his two uncles died of the fever. After an earthquake hit Malaga, Charles along with Christopher decided to head for home leaving their surviving uncle who chose to stay and who died the following year in a fresh outbreak of yellow fever in the area. Whilst in Malaga, Christopher must have contacted the fever that would apparently lay latent in his blood stream, as he would eventually succumb to a fresh attack of the disease, its effects presumably contributing to or being the cause of his early death some years later.

On arrival back at Walton Hall from Malaga, Charles was in a poor state of health and was to face the rigours of a Yorkshire winter. Although he would recover to some degree, a journey to warmer European climes such as Italy or southern France to fully recuperate would be a good idea. But such a journey was out of the question because of the on-going war with France, and so South America seemed a sensible choice bearing in mind that his father's plantation there needed a superintendent from the family line.

Near the *Walton Hall* plantation were the two plantations partly owned by Charles's uncle Christopher, known as *La Jalousie* and *Fellowship*, the principal crop of one being coffee with no less than five hundred Negro slaves, the other producing sugar and coffee worked by three hundred slaves. Christopher had married a Mrs Anne Waddell who had been twice widowed and through whom he would acquire a part share in the two plantations she had inherited from her first husband. Christopher and his wife would return to England not long after his brother, Thomas, (Charles's father) had acquired the plantation in Demerara. So as well as *Walton Hall,* Charles was also to superintend *La Jalousie* and *Fellowship*.

Prior to his departure to South America, Charles would dine with Sir Joseph Banks, naturalist and explorer and a President of the Royal Society, and what the Guiana region had to offer in natural history naturally was a topic of conversation between the two men during their meeting following which they became lifelong friends. Sir Joseph would advise Charles to return to England or some other temperate climate every three years or so as the best way of keeping his health in the tropics. In the early nineteenth century health hazards in low swampy regions not only came from malaria and yellow fever but also from smallpox, typhoid and dysentery. Charles would say later that he *followed this admirable advice with great success.*

On 29 November 1804, Charles set out from Portsmouth to arrive in the Guiana capital of Georgetown in the following January to find a landscape upon which vast and well-kept sugar, coffee and cotton plantations stretched far into the distance before reaching a hinterland of rain forest rich in flora, insects, mammals etc. But such a tropical paradise had a sinister side – slavery.

The first shipment of Negro slaves from the coast of West Africa had arrived in the West Indies in the sixteenth century to be sold and put to work by Spanish colonists there. Soon the British became involved with this diabolical trade of human traffic, ships leaving British ports with cargoes of cheap manufactured goods to be exchanged for Negro men and women, many having been captured in tribal wars and who were then to suffer the appalling conditions of the voyage to the American colonies where they would live out their lives as slaves on plantation settlements. During the seventeenth century and the following one more settlements were established by the Dutch, French and the British in Guiana when the slave trade would increase at an alarming rate, a time when ownership of such settlements could suddenly change their nationality due to political agreement or take-overs following warfare. For example in 1781 British privateers captured the Dutch owned areas of Essequibo, Demerara and Berbice, and in the following year the French captured them and handed them back to the Dutch. The British again captured these three provinces in 1796 only to return them again at the Peace of Amiens in 1802 and then recapturing them in 1803 when the War with France was renewed, and so by the time Charles Waterton arrived in 1805 these provinces were under British rule.

Demerara was also the name of the river that flowed through this fertile region of sugar cane growing before entering the Atlantic at the Capital, Georgetown; brown Demerara sugar being looked upon as a sugar of very high quality and an important trade for the British economy. By 1830 the Demerara area plantations which also produced coffee and cotton had a workforce in the region of 100,000 Negro slaves managed by Britons many of high social status like the Watertons, who styled themselves as merchants, planters, etc., whilst discreetly avoiding the term slave-owners, and who back in Britain lived a life of sheer luxury from the profits of their plantations.

On his arrival in Demerara, Charles would encounter his first involvement with slave labour, and in his role as superintendent would travel about on the back of a mule. Not far away was the *Belle Vue* plantation (the name relating to a district of Wakefield in Yorkshire) of Michael Daly and his wife Anne, Charles's aunt. As a young man walking in Wakefield and home on holiday from Demerara, Daly had met Anne. Eventually they married and went to live on Daly's estate in Demerara where Charles would visit them on a regular basis during the spare time he had.

Charles Waterton's attitude to slavery was almost hostile, later writing:

> *Slavery can never be defended. He whose heart is not of iron can never wish to be able to defend it: while he heaves a sigh for the poor Negro in captivity, he wishes from his soul that the traffic had been stifled in its birth.*

But whilst Charles applauded the efforts of those against slavery, he insisted that the conditions of plantation slaves in British colonies was not as wretched as it had sometimes been depicted, but such insistence may well have been his way of easing his conscious because of his involvement with slave labour. Whilst the transportation of Negro slaves to British colonies was stopped in 1807, it would not be until 1833 when the Emancipation of Slaves in the British Empire came about.

There seems little doubt that on his arrival in Georgetown in 1805, Charles's interest would not be totally focused on the management of his family estates there, a vocation seen by him simply as a role of some responsibility. His main objective would be when he could find the time to venture into the hinterland of the region to explore and record its natural history. Such a scientific approach into the world of natural history was beginning to gain momentum in European academic circles and Charles would be amongst the first of many explorers associated with this new science.

Many of his first experiences on setting foot in Guiana would have been alien to him when one considers his upper-class upbringing followed by his education at Stonyhurst. James Rodway, an authority on the history of the Georgetown region would say of the 22-year-old Charles:

> *In Demerara he was looked upon by the rollocking boys of that age as not quite right in his mind. For, first of all, he was a teetotaller, when*

Fig. 6.1 Portrait of Charles Waterton in the National Portrait Gallery, London.

custom never excused a man from having a drink. We may also safely state that he would be out of place among the cock-fighting and card-playing gamblers, as well as those votaries of Venus then prominent in Georgetown.

Following the death of his father in 1805 Charles returned home in Yorkshire to accept his inheritance and an annual income of £700. His mother, strange as it may seem and according to Julia Blackburn in her publication of 1989, was to inherit one guinea and a very meagre yearly income, and seems to have left Walton Hall, nothing or very little being known about her until her death was signed at Park Place near Liverpool in 1819. Park Place is shown as a short road on a map of 1824 of the Toxteth district of Liverpool, one end of the road becoming Park Road, the other end St James' Place. On one side of Park Place is St Patrick's Roman Catholic Chapel built between 1821 and 1827, and also what appears to be a private enclosure with buildings at its Park Road end, whilst beyond is an expanse of open land. On the opposite side of Park Place is a long block of a building, and any of these buildings could well have been some sort of Catholic retreat where Charles's mother ended her days, but current researches have failed to establish such a retreat. In the absence of a Will of Thomas Waterton and a death certificate of his widow, it is not possible to say why Charles's mother left Walton Hall after the death of her husband or where she went and why Park Place was to be associated with her death.

Norman Moore (see later in this chapter), was to report that *according to the testimony of those who knew her*, she was, *a lady of more than ordinary dignity and judgment* and that:

> *She early and successfully taught her children high principles and scrupulous conduct. They retained, throughout their lives, a loving recollection of how much they were indebted to her; and to the end of his days her eldest son would speak of her and her deeds with affectionate reverence.*

Charles was back in Demerara in 1807 where in September he was made a lieutenant in the 2nd Regiment of the Demerara Militia, and on 2 August 1808 was commissioned by the British Governor to bear dispatches from the Commander of the Fleet, Admiral Collingwood, to the Spanish Captain-General of the Orinoco, Don Felipe de Ynciarte. Such a commission was to give Charles his first experience of the natural wonders of an area of primeval forest so bringing about the desire to arrange further exploration when time allowed.

On his return to Georgetown Charles continued to carry out his

Fig. 6.2 The Waterton shield of Arms. Blazon: Barry of six ermine and gules, over all three crescents sable.

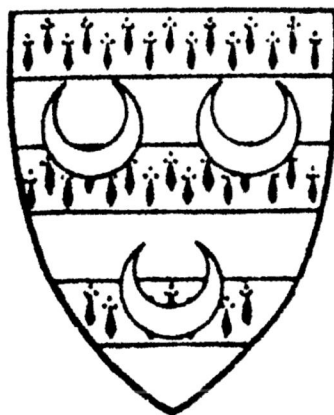

responsibilities on and off regarding the upkeep and management of the *Walton Hall* plantation, and in the Spring of 1812, now able to resign his role as plantation manager decided to set out to explore the unexplored wilds of Guiana for what he would refer to as his first *Wanderings*. Before the journey he would visit Warrows Place the home at Mibiri Creek, Demerara, of his friend Charles Edmonstone and his half-Indian wife Helen for the christening of their second child Anne Mary and for which he would be her godfather.

On 26 April 1812 Charles set out on his expedition of exploration venturing by canoe up the Demerara River accompanied by six Indians, a Negro slave and his friend Charles Edmonstone who would leave the party on reaching his home at Mibiri Creek. Soon Charles would have malaria and meet the Macusi Indians who would introduce him to their potent curare that they used in their blowpipe arrows for killing birds and animals, the main purpose of Charles's trip being to bring back a supply of the poison for medical experiments back in England.

Curare, an extract of bark and other ingredients killed quickly but did not poison the body but paralysed the respiratory muscles, the victim dying due to a lack of oxygen. However, if the lungs could be kept working the victim might eventually recover, unharmed. The first European to present an account on curare was Sir Walter Raleigh who referred to it by the name of ourari and by the time Charles Waterton was setting out for the jungles of Guiana in 1812, curare was known as wourali. By this time small doses of the poison was known to serve as a muscle relaxant, and its possible use for the treatment of spastic diseases such as tetanus and lock-jaw was now arousing interest in English medical circles. Fourteen months before Charles had set out on his journey in April 1812, Dr B. C. Brodie had read a paper before the Royal Society describing an experiment on a rabbit that had been inoculated by curare and then kept alive for almost an hour and a half by artificial respiration. More curare was needed for further experiments.

The preparation of curare (wourali) involved six basic ingredients: the bark of the wourali vine; a root of a bitter taste; glutinous juice from two kinds of a bulbous plant; triturated fangs of lancehead and bushmaster snakes; a pepper; and a few specimens of two species of stinging ant. The bark of the wourali vine and the root were scraped into shavings which were then placed into a colander of leaves that was held over an earthenware pot and water added, the resulting coffee-like liquor straining into the pot. The bulbous plants were then squeezed over the pot, their glutinous juice acting as a binding agent following which the crushed pepper, ants

VIEW OF WALTON HALL IN THE DISTANCE; OF THE ANCIENT RUIN; AND OF THE CAST-IRON BRIDGE.

Fig. 6.3 Walton Hall, near Wakefield, West Yorkshire.

and the ground snake fangs were added before the pot was placed over a slow burning fire. On boiling, more juice from the wourali vine was added, scum removed, and slow boiling continued until the mixture had turned into a thick syrup, deep brown in colour. After being tested and proved satisfactory it was pored into a calabash to dry, the top of the vessel being sealed by leaves over which a piece of deer skin was tied round it with a cord. A calabash was the name given to the shell of a large tree melon-like fruit grown in the tropic regions of America, and today a calabash can be seen along with a blowpipe and arrows in the Charles Waterton Exhibition at the Wakefield Museum in West Yorkshire.

Much of Charles's journey had been on foot amid the dangers from creatures of the jungle and even the weather would not be on his side with rain-swollen rivers. On the return journey negotiating the rapids of the river Essequibo his canoe was upset with the loss of the ingredients he had collected of which curare was made from, but fortunately the samples of curare were saved. The whole journey from Georgetown and back would take four months and during the return journey Charles would rest and receive care at the Portuguese fort at Sao Joachim. By August 1812 Charles now sick with malaria arrived back at Charles Edmonstone's home, Warrows Place at Mibiri Creek to be nursed back to a reasonable state of health by Edmonstone's wife before his return to Georgetown.

When he had first settled in Demerara, Charles Edmonstone had gone into partnership as a timber-cutter and merchant with a fellow Scot, William Reid who lived on the Camouni Creek and who had friendly relations with the neighbouring Arawaks, a local indigenous American group. The ancestors of the Arawaks had settled on the coastal area of Guiana eventually coming into contact with European invaders and settlers from whence their numbers declined due to disease, war, and slavery. Reid had married the daughter of one of their chiefs known as Princess Minda, her daughter by William Reid eventually becoming the wife of Charles Edmonstone and hence the mother of Anne Mary. As mentioned above, Anne would become the wife of Charles Waterton in 1829.

On his return to Georgetown Charles would be given a hero's welcome and attended a ball in his honour at Government House and was now entrusted to deliver in person official despatches to Lord Bathurst the Colonial Secretary in London. Charles was now a sick man suffering from attacks of malaria and the long voyage back to England had done nothing to improve his health so much so, that soon after his arrival at Liverpool in the spring of 1813 the despatches were sent to London by mail coach and the arranged meeting with Lord Bathurst cancelled. Charles would receive an official invitation to explore Madagascar but would refuse the invitation as he was still having bouts of malaria, and at Walton Hall would set about creating the world's first nature reserve on his estate.

In the meantime at the Veterinary College in London work had begun with the curare he had brought back from Guiana and among the experiments were those on four donkeys. Two were to die minutes after being inoculated with curare, a third revived but died three days later, whilst the fourth survived after an incision was made in its windpipe through which its lungs were regularly inflated for two hours with a pair of bellows. After such was discontinued the donkey relapsed following which the artificial respiration procedure was recommenced, the donkey eventually recovering. The animal was christened *Wouralia* and died almost twenty-five years later after a life on the pastures of Walton Hall.

Charles wanted to believe that curare as a muscle relaxant might turn out to be an effective treatment for hydrophobia, the unnatural dread of water and a symptom of the disease rabies in which paralysis comes about in the victim caused by the brain being over-stimulated, its cells dying. Charles was willing to supply the drug or administer it on any creature or human suffering rabies from the bite of a mad dog.

Soon after the donkey *Wouralia* had died of old age at Walton Hall in February 1839 Charles was called to Nottingham General Hospital by the surgeon Francis Sibson requesting Charles's assistance with a patient suffering from hydrophobia. A Nottingham policeman in attempting to rescue a trapped dog had been bitten by it on his lip and nose, and six or seven weeks later the policeman began to show symptoms of hydrophobia. Charles, with a supply of wax balls containing curare, rushed off to Nottingham but by the time he arrived the policeman had died.

A couple of days later Charles was demonstrating the effects of curare and of artificial respiration as its antidote to a large audience at

Fig. 6.4 The English Convent, Bruges.

the Nottingham Medical School. Two asses were inoculated with curare and artificial respiration administered, one dying three days later, the other making a full recovery. In recognition of Charles's association with the medical world the intensive care unit at the General Hospital in Nottingham was to be called the Waterton Ward.

As late as 1878 the medical journal *The Lancet* was still suggesting that hydrophobia could be treated with curare but that appears to have been the last time such a claim was made. It would not be until 1942 that curare-based drugs were first used clinically, and today in open-heart surgery, organ transplant surgery and delicate brain operations, derivatives of curare are considered almost essential as a muscle relaxant and shock absorber. During the coronavirus outbreak of 2020, curare-based drugs were given to patients in intensive care suffering from the virus who had to be placed in a state of relaxation before the somewhat traumatic and vital procedure of artificial ventilation.

After the death of his father in 1805, Charles between 1805 and 1812 worked 'at intervals' as the manager of the *Walton Hall* plantation until it seems that it was to be sold probably in 1812 or soon afterwards thus allowing Charles to begin his natural history pursuits into the Demerara hinterland. In January 1815 the *Walton Hall* plantation is mentioned in the *Demerary and Essequebo Royal Gazette* of Saturday 21 January 1815:

> At the Commissary-Court of the 6th of February, 1815, will be passed the following Transports and Mortgages; viz.
>
> 3. By J. M'Kirdy, Transport of Pl. Walton Hall, situated on the Aroabische or West Sea coast of Essequebo, together with a number of 81 slaves, the names thereof to be seen at this office, and further, with all the Buildings, Cultivation, and other appurtenances, thereto belonging – to Benjamin Kingston.
>
> 4. By Benjamin Kingston, a mortgage on the above Plantation Walton Hall, with a number of 81 slaves, and additional number of 76 slaves, the names thereof to be seen at this office – in favour of J. M'Kirdy.

On 19 March 1816 Charles boarded a ship at Liverpool and set sail for South America for what would be his second *Wanderings*, his intention to arrive in Brazil then cross the Amazon jungle to arrive back in British Guiana by the back door, a land and river journey of many miles, a part of which through dense tropical rain forest. His second *Wanderings* were to

Fig. 6.5 The English Convent, Bruges.

be a success and his thoughts turned once more to a homeward journey to England. With the tropical rains about to begin and a European summer to look forward to, he set sail in the early spring of 1817 with a huge collection of bird specimens.

On returning home he would finish and mount his specimens and after what was to be an idyllic summer at Walton Hall the middle of October found him setting out for a tour of Italy during which he would visit the Vatican. His intention was to deliver personally a letter to Pope Pius VII regarding the plight and state of religion among the Indians of South America. At the time anti-Jesuit feeling was still strong even though three years earlier the Pope had restored the Society of Jesus to favour, before which the Society had suffered more than two hundred years of suppression, and Charles's letter was in defence of the Order.

Unbelievable as it may seem it is said that with an old school friend of Tudhoe days, Charles climbed to the top of the dome of St Peter's both leaving their gloves on the tip of the lightning conductor. Needless to say the Pope would have been displeased and the audience with him was cancelled, the reason behind the cancellation may have been that Charles in having such an audience refused to wear black, wanting to appear in his royal blue uniform of his Jesuit school, Stonyhurst. However, another possible reason may have been the contents of the letter a part of which complained about moral degradation in the Catholic Church in South America that could be read as an a attack on Vatican policy. If the letter had to be read beforehand by someone such as the Cardinal Secretary, perhaps the decision was made that the Pope was not to receive the letter and a audience with Charles.

In February 1818 Charles was back in England after his Grand Tour of Italy and in February 1820 set sail from the Clyde for the third of his *Wanderings* prior to which he had visited his friend Charles Edmonstone and his family at Cardross Park, their Scottish home near Dumbarton. This old family estate had once been part of the dowry of one of Edmonstone's ancestors Princess Isabella of Scotland, daughter of King Robert II, first of the Stuarts, and after more than twenty years in Guiana, Edmonstone had returned to Scotland a wealthy man able to buy back the family mansion. Charles would arrange to use Edmonstone's old home Warrows Place in Demerara now uninhabited, as a base for the forthcoming expedition.

In the past Charles had made many visits to Edmonstone's home, Warrows Place, especially to recuperate from bouts of fever due to the tropical environment. During these visits he had established a firm friendship with a freed black slave who had worked for Edmonstone, who presumably had given him the name of John Edmonstone. John had a thorough knowledge of the South American forest regarding its animals and its wide range of fauna and flora, and the many years he had spent in the rain forest of Guiana had led him to develop with the help of Charles Waterton the skills of taxidermy.

Eventually Charles Edmonstone in returning to Scotland had taken John with him who later became a servant in the household of Dr Duncan, a medical lecturer at Edinburgh University. During the time when Charles Darwin was studying at the same university from October 1825 to April 1827, he had heard that John had been taught taxidermy by Charles Waterton and in consequence would employ John to give him lessons in such a skill. John would also sensitise Darwin to the boiling political and social problems of the day, not least of which were the evil institution of slavery and racism of which John was a victim. From then on Darwin spent the rest of his life as a committed anti-slavery activist. In Edinburgh John lived at 37 Lothian Street a few doors down from where Charles Darwin and his brother Erasmus lived.

In 1820 Charles Waterton's wife to be, Edmonstone's daughter Anne Mary, was 8 years old, Charles at this time having set his sights on marrying her when she reached a suitable age; after all she had two royal pedigrees, one being Indian Arawak, the other Scottish. On leaving the Edmonstones in that year for Guiana, weeks later he arrived in Georgetown to find the Capital in the middle of a yellow fever epidemic that had already claimed the lives of many of its older inhabitants as well as many of the slave population. After taking on supplies for his *Wanderings* into the interior, Charles set out for Warrows Place stopping on the way to receive hospitality at the home of Edmonstone's nephew Archibald Edmonstone. On arrival at Warrows Place he found the house almost derelict with collapsing roof, rooms now the abode of bats, and the rain forest closing in, all heralding a scene that had become commonplace about the region since the Abolition Law of 1807.

Charles would spend eleven months on his expedition, at one stage capturing a cayman (a crocodile) in the Essequibo River to dissect and preserve it as one of his prize specimens. Soon afterwards the main rain season began to set in so a decision was made to return to England, and in the spring of 1821 Charles arrived in Liverpool with a huge collection of his natural history specimens, a part of which included two hundred birds and the cayman. The Customs officer at the port was not satisfied with the amount of duty to be paid on the specimens that would remain at Liverpool for six weeks during which the matter was resolved ending with Charles paying the necessary amount.

Back at Walton Hall Charles had decided to build a wall round his estate to keep poachers and foxes out, work on it beginning in 1821; five years on it encircled the Walton parkland. Three miles in length and in places sixteen feet in height at a cost of £9,000, in today's money that would amount to around £2.5 million, it was to encompass the first nature reserve known at the time.

During this period Charles had become interested in a publication, *American Ornithology* by Alexander Wilson, an expatriate Scot who had lived the final years of his life in North America where he died in 1813 when the eighth of nine eventual volumes of his work was about to be printed. Charles decided that he must see the birds of North America and early on in 1824 set sail for New York.

He was impressed with the city and its people and after a month or so set out towards Albany on a Hudson River paddle steamer. After seeing

Niagara Falls he returned to New York before setting off to spend a few days in Canada visiting Quebec and Montreal. Back in North America he went to Philadelphia where he had his portrait painted (fig. 6.1) by the artist-cum-dentist Charles Willson Peale who in his younger years had begun a natural 'curiosities' collection and had superintended the recovery of bones of mammoths from a swamp in the Catskill Mountains.

On leaving Philadelphia Charles returned to New York before sailing southwards in 1824 across the equator, his intention to see Antigua then island-hop through the West Indies for a last visit to his beloved British Guiana. After a week in Antigua he boarded the mail boat for Guadeloupe and Dominica where in the primeval rain forest of the latter he found flying beetles larger than birds. From Dominica he sailed via Martinique, St Lucia and Barbados to eventually arrive in Demerara, and in January 1825 he would leave British Guiana for the last time, sailing for Southampton. On arrival in England he took the stage for Wakefield to arrive home cold and ill to a late and bleak winter countryside. At the end of August *The Times* had announced the publication of his book, *Wanderings in South America, the North-West of the United States, and the Antilles, in the Years 1812, 1816, 1820 and 1824, by Charles Waterton Esq., of Walton Hall, Wakefield.*

By 1827 Charles was back in Scotland visiting the Edmonstones at Cardross Park to find them unhappy and ill at ease at being so far away from their former home in Demerara, and Charles Edmonstone was now a sick man. Charles Waterton's thoughts had now turned to marriage; he needed an heir, and the purpose of his visit was to arrange his engagement to Edmonstone's daughter Anne, now 15 but not yet of marrying age.

Charles needed to marry a Catholic and Anne was a Protestant, so it was decided that Anne and her older sister Eliza would be sent to the English Convent in Bruges to complete their education. Charles's marriage to Anne was to take place in 1829, the year of the Catholic Emancipation Act that to some extent relaxed the constraints Catholics had been subjected to since the Reformation. Charles, knowing that he was marrying a person who had once been a Protestant and was now a Catholic, distrusted the established Church of England regarding the legal side of his marriage. To make sure that there were no legal complications he decided on two wedding ceremonies, a Catholic one in the English Convent in Bruges on 18 May, and a Protestant one on 20 December in St Helen's Church in the parish of Sandal Magna, near Wakefield. By the time of the December ceremony Anne was six months pregnant.

On Monday 18 May 1829, in the eighteenth-century chapel of the seventeenth-century nunnery in Bruges at the unearthly time of 5.30 in the morning, the barely 17-year-old granddaughter of 'Princess Minda' of Guiana walked down the isle in a gown of fine book muslin with white veil to marry her almost 47-year-old Squire of Walton Hall. Following the marriage ceremony the bride and groom had breakfast in the convent after which along with Anne's sister Eliza who was being chaperoned by John Gordon, a Scottish priest, who had officiated at the wedding, left by canal barge for Ghent before continuing their honeymoon in Belgium, France, Switzerland and Italy. Eliza in the meantime returned to England to stay in Wakefield for a while with Charles's sister Helen and her solicitor husband Robert Carr.

On her return from her honeymoon Anne settled in at Walton Hall with its vast collection of dead animals and reptiles etc., to live a lifestyle expected of her as the wife of the local 'squire', even though she was perhaps an unwilling partner in a marriage of convenience. Embroidery, writing letters, playing the piano, walks in the surrounding parkland, would be part of a daily routine for a 17-year-old who was missing her family and friends in Bruges and Scotland. Her father had died the previous year whilst her sister Eliza had returned to the Cardross Park family home where her mother was dependant upon laudanum, an opium based painkiller, which gave concern as to who should care for Eliza's youngest sister, Bethia; her other sister Helen having entered the convent in Bruges.

But all this day-to-day routine coupled with sadness of being so far away from her family and friends would soon come to an end for Anne. On 21 April 1830 her baby arrived, a boy to be named Edmund but six days later on 27 April, Anne died of puerperal sepsis – childbed fever and was interred three days later in the Waterton family vault at St Helen's Church in nearby Sandal Magna. Sadly, after Anne's burial the following was entered in the Sandal Magna Parish Register:

> Anne Waterton of Walton Hall, a Roman Catholic, was buried without a service by Vicar T Westmorland.

Overpowered by grief Charles blamed himself for her death, – bacteria he thought from his collection of dead specimens, and decided to live out his life in 'self-inflicted penance for her soul.' From then onwards he would never again sleep in his bed but on the floor with a hollowed-out block of wood for a pillow. Each year with his son Edmund, and his late wife's two sisters, Eliza and Helen, who were to live with him at Walton Hall, he would return to the English Convent in Bruges, spending an hour every day in meditation and prayer close to the altar where his marriage to Anne had taken place less than a year before her death.

In the back end of 1830 Charles made a brief pilgrimage to Bavaria to witness the recovery of a nun from an incurable disease, and during his time there bought a large collection of oil paintings, one in particular being a portrait of St Catherine which Charles considered to be a good likeness of Anne and which would be given pride of place over the mantelpiece at Walton Hall. There when finished at the Hall a chapel would be dedicated to St Catherine. On his way home Charles stopped at Bruges to visit what had been Anne's convent and its chapel where he had married her to find Bruges struggling with much unrest in a bid to become independent after fifteen years of Union with Holland.

Throughout the 1830s Charles was still very much involved in the new science of natural history and as usual, religious and current affairs. Anyone presenting thoughts on such matters that Charles might strongly disagree with would suffer the wrath of his anger by word of mouth, his pen or his printed word. The 1830s would witness much debate between those involved with the Catholic Church and the established Anglican one. Since the Reformation, cathedrals and churches, building wise, had sunk into various states of decay, and even the ways in which religious worship was being conducted in the Anglican sector was being seen by many to be in need of reform.

To the rescue came the newly formed Evangelical Movement that would offer examples of piety, morality and pastoral concern, all thought to be lacking within the doctrines of such places of worship. There were those who also supported anti-papist sentiments, and on 23 June 1836 Charles attended a meeting in Wakefield organised by a group of preachers called the Reformation Society where he would perform his share of heckling from the floor.

In July 1839 with his son Edmund now nine years of age and his sisters-in-law Eliza and Helen, Charles set out on a two-year pilgrimage to Italy leaving Hull by the steamship *Seahorse* for Rotterdam. From Rotterdam the party went onto The Hague, Leyden, Haarlem, Amsterdam, Antwerp, Bruges and Ghent, churches and museums being part of the itinerary. From Ghent their carriage headed towards Brussels through Liege to Aix-la-Chapelle with its religious relics and medicinal waters. As winter approached the time came to leave Aix-la-Chapelle to travel south to Freiberg where Charles and his party stayed for a few days before heading into Switzerland crossing the Alps for the descent into Italy and Milan. After a few days in Milan the party crossed the Lombard Plain to Bologna and on to Florence where a visit was made to the Zoological Museum. On arrival in Rome it was decided to stay for the Month of Mary following which the party would head for Naples, arriving at the cathedral on 19 September. After the festival of St Januarius and the Battle of St Elmo, Charles and his party continued to Reggio and on 24 September boarded a steamer for Sicily. On returning to Naples the Waterton party headed for Rome once again for another winter season where the young Edmund would spend time with certain dignitaries of the Catholic Church.

As midsummer approached and the heat of Rome with it, on 16 June 1841 the Waterton pilgrims headed for Civita Vecchia where the following day they boarded the paddle steamer *Pollux* for Livorno, leaving in the late afternoon to involve an overnight crossing. The weather was serene and the sea calm, suddenly those at sleep were awakened by a tremendous crash, the steamer *Monjibello* on route to Civita Vecchia had collided with the *Pollux*. Utter confusion broke out. On board the *Monjibello* was Charles Bonaparte, the nephew of Napoleon, and with the help of Charles Waterton the rescue of the stricken passengers from the *Pollux* that sank in less than 20 minutes was soon underway.

As the damaged *Monjibello* was able to limp back to Livorno where temporary hotel accommodation was available, the Waterton party decided to embark on board the *Monjibello* that was not as badly damaged as had been feared. At Livorno, Charles and his relatives had made new plans, taking the post-chaise back to Rome where they booked in for a month at the Palazzo di Gregorio in the Via Due Macelli. During this stay in Rome Charles would buy some young owls of the little owl kind hoping to introduce the species in England, and on 20 July along with twelve owls, the Waterton party left Rome to travel by sea to Genoa to stay the night at Nori between Genoa and Alessandria before crossing into Switzerland via the Gotthard Pass to Basle. From Basle the party went onto Aix-la-Chapelle before the rest of the journey home via Ostend and Dover.

Before heading for Yorkshire, Charles, now suffering from dysentery, called at Northumberland House in the Strand, London, the town house of the Duke of Northumberland to leave a letter for a mutual friend, the Archdeacon of Northumberland and rector of Howick. Not all the young owls would survive the long journey and on 10 May 1842 only five had survived to be released into the grotto at Walton Hall.

Whilst Charles would travel a great deal in Europe his thoughts must have been constantly back in the rain forest of Guiana where he had spent some of his happiest times. In his memoirs he would declare:

> *No country in the world can offer a more extensive and fertile field to the ornithologist, than our celebrated colony of Demerara.*

But all had not been well within the slave population of this region. A rebellion of slaves broke out in Guiana in 1823 with slaves downing tools, fields being torched and plantation owners imprisoned in their own houses. The militia would be called out, the ringleaders to be exported or executed. Even though the slave trade itself had been abolished in1807 it would take another twenty-six years to set the enslaved free. By the early 1830s slave owners were losing the battle to keep slavery and in 1832 the British Government drafted plans for the abolition of this scandalous and appalling system.

As to what would happen on the slave plantations once Parliament had abolished Negro slave labour throughout the British Empire in 1833, little regard if any was given to the plight of the slave, only the slave owner would benefit. In place of slavery a negotiated settlement was established whereby freed slaves were forced into a system of tied labour apprenticeship for fixed terms. But there would be another darker side to abolition. Those who had worked the slaves argued that the slaves had been their personal property, the loss of which therefore should amount to some financial compensation. The right of owning property went to the very heart of British law and in exploiting this the slave owners in Britain were to receive compensation.

The pay out was huge amounting to a total bill of twenty million pounds paid by the British taxpayer; in today's money it would amount to seventeen billion pounds. As well as aristocrats and landed gentry, among the slave owners in Britain were lawyers, doctors and vicars, all to benefit in some way or other from the handout. Any moral objection for receiving such was soon out-weighed by the greed for money, and at the time of this compensation scheme thirty-seven members of the House of Lords and more than eighty MPs had been slave owners.

Many of those on receiving the money bought shares in a variety of companies and new enterprises such as railways and projected institutions, whilst some of the landed gentry and members of the aristocracy were able to improve their estates, some building new mansions. Slavery had been a British way of life and now these investments were to influence Britain's future economy, and today much of modern Britain is based upon the outcome of this compensatory scheme.

Today, at the time of writing, a group of historians from the University of Central London are at the National Archives in Kew examining ledgers which have not seen the light of day for nearly two centuries that list those men and women who received such a pay out. The compensation claims, dated 30 November 1835 and now recorded on the UCL database for the *La Jalousie* and the *Fellowship* plantations in Guiana which had 292 slaves, amounted to £15,482 14*s*. 8*d*., the claimants being Robert, George, Henry and Agnes Waterton, Matilda Jermingham and others. In 1832, Robert Waterton had registered for himself and others, 79 enslaved persons on the *Fellowship* estate.

In connection with the *Walton Hall* plantation the following claim is recorded on the UCL database.

> British Guiana Claim No. 2426 (Walton Hall)
>
> Date 11th Jan 1836.
>
> No. of slaves 300.
>
> Claim amount £16,283 6*s*. 7*d*.

In September 1841 Charles's son Edmund, now eleven, entered Stonyhurst College where for the next nine years he would enjoy both its educational and social life, and by the spring of 1843 Charles was planning his next trip to Italy with Eliza and Helen, one that would come about in the following year. In the meantime Eliza's lung trouble had not improved, a source of anxiety that would turn out to be consumption, and in the autumn she and Helen went to stay in Hornsea on the Yorkshire coast to take in the bracing air, returning in November. Charles spent Christmas at Stonyhurst and whilst back at Walton in January was to have printed a poster condemning the pending closure of local common lands.

In the autumn of 1844 with son Edmund at Stonyhurst, Charles and his two sisters-in-law along with footman and maid set out for the Continent to arrive in Innsbruck, then Bolzano and finally on All Soul's Eve, Caldaro, where it was arranged to be introduced to the Holy Ecstatica of Caldaro, Fraulein Maria von Mori who was living out her days in prayer and dedication to her faith in the nearby Franciscan monastery. After Caldaro, Venice was reached, the Waterton party booking in at the Hotel d' Europe from where eventually a stay was made in Bologna before heading for Rome via Rimini, Pesaro, Ancona and Loretto. Charles and his pilgrims were to stay in Rome for about seven months, returning home via Civita Vecchia and Marseilles in June.

Eliza's lung trouble was worsening and it was agreed that the winter sunshine of Madeira and its warm Atlantic sea air might ease the problem, so in November she with Helen and Charles set out for the island. However in early January Charles had to leave his sisters-in-law, returning home to attend to the business of a pioneer nature reserve in Yorkshire. On the Walton Hall estate Charles found that during his absence poachers had played havoc with the pheasants and hares whilst his gamekeeper had been 'amusing himself in the alehouse', and soon afterwards Charles would promote the estate's mason to the post of gamekeeper.

The warm summer of 1846 at Walton Hall must have been ideal had it not been for the fumes and poisoned drainage water from a newly established soap boiling works on the northern boundary of the Hall's parkland contaminating the estate. The problem would continue throughout the rest of the 1840s during which time Charles would instigate legal action against the owner of the works (see next chapter). In the late summer of 1846 with a new keeper in charge of his estate Charles was confident enough to visit Belgium following which he would pay a visit to the zoological exhibits in the British Museum.

In 1850 Eliza and Helen were to travel to Bruges to see an Ascension Day procession, Charles intending to join them a short time later. On his arrival in Dover by night train from London he went in search of his boat for Calais that was moored in the darkness of the night and in his attempt to board it, fell into the water. After rescue he stayed overnight in the Dover Castle Hotel where he refused to see a doctor. The next day the afternoon boat took him to Calais from where he caught the overnight train to Flanders. Meeting up with Eliza and Helen in Bruges he began to suffer from a fever, cough and sneezes, the result of his harbour dip in Dover. Throughout his adult life he had performed on himself with lancet and bowl the age-old practice of blood letting which he considered the cure for all ills. So recovery came soon after he had extracted several ounces of blood from himself followed by a gentle dose of laxative made up of jalap and calomel.

Charles spent a month in Bruges during which time he saw the Ascension Day proceedings and also made the obligatory pilgrimage to the seventeenth-century chapel of the English nunnery there where he had married 21 years earlier. As the May observances ended he returned home and later in the summer went on holiday to Scarborough, the Yorkshire seaside resort that was fast becoming popular especially with the more well-to-do, Scarborough, Bruges and Aix-la-Chapelle being favourite holiday venues for Charles and his two sisters-in-law.

Edmund, now aged 20, was back at home at Walton Hall having completed his education at Stoneyhurst, and in April 1851 reached the age of 21, the church bells at Sandal Magna and Wakefield ringing out to mark the occasion. He had done well at Stonyhurst but father and son had become different in so many ways. Even though Edmund would inherit his father's generosity, in important matters where large amounts of money was concerned he would become irresponsible, money being no object especially when he had certain speculations in mind, an attitude that would soon lead him into debt. Not sharing his father's passion for natural history, soon after leaving Stonyhurst he had set off to Rome eventually becoming a member of Pope's X1's entourage and in 1857 became the Pope's Privy Chamberlain.

In the meantime Charles had visited the Great Exhibition in Hyde Park, London that had opened on May Day 1851 and needless to say Charles was not impressed with the taxidermy exhibits. The year before had seen Richard Owen who was preparing the natural history section for the exhibition, staying at Walton Hall with his wife, the possible underlying motive for his visit to inspect Charles's natural history specimens and arrange to borrow some for the exhibition. Following his stay Owen made the expected request but five mouths later Charles Waterton replied explaining as to why he did not want his work to be put on show. His specimens had been done upon a principle never before contemplated and would be looked at with a nod of approbation, and that would be all. After the exhibition Charles by a series of letters to the *Illustrated London News* criticised the appearance of preserved specimens that had been on show, the faults in preservation presenting *a mockery of nature*.

In the early autumn of 1851 Charles was off to Scarborough again with his sisters-in-law, autumn being the best time there when the crowds had gone and a log fire was always available at their place of accommodation which would either be number 1 on the Cliff or the Royal Hotel. By the late summer of 1854 Charles with Eliza and Helen was back on the Continent in Aix-la-Chapelle after originally planning to visit the south of France which had to be cancelled owing to a cholera epidemic in the towns en-route. From Aix-la-Chapell they went to Brussels then on to Ostend, arriving home in Yorkshire in late October where plans were made for a late autumn holiday in Scarborough.

The spring of 1856 saw Dr George Harley (Harley Street in London is named after one of his ancestors – the first Earl of Oxford) spending a few days at Walton Hall, the main purpose of his visit being to obtain fresh supplies of curare from Charles for experiments he was conducting into the properties of strychnine, a deadly poison that produces paralysis in its victims. Shortly afterwards he would claim to have discovered that curare was *'a true physiological antidote to strychnine'*. During his visit to the Hall he was shown Charles's preserved specimens following which Charles demonstrated to him the technique he used in taxidermy (see later).

The 1850s in the warmer months at Walton Hall saw large numbers of visitors being allowed by tickets of admission to enjoy its grounds, some having picnics, some made up of large groups including weddings parties who danced and often accompanied by one of the local brass bands. Each year a hundred or more patients from the West Riding Mental Hospital came with their own choir and band, Charles dancing with them, rowing them on the lake and joining them for dinner in the grotto before they left for Wakefield.

Christmas 1858 had seen Edmund home from a two-year appointment in Rome to spend the festive season with his father at Stonyhurst College. Whilst in Rome he had created upon himself a Knight of the Order of Christ, but as usual was still in debt, an on-going situation that would give his father some concern. Many of the religious honours Edmund gained would cost him dearly as the expenses involved included papal fees and the costs of the elaborate and expensive costumes he had to wear on certain occasions that he had to pay for himself.

Applications from those wishing to enjoy the grounds of Walton Hall during the summer months continued but English weather at times could be spiteful such as in July 1859 when a party of about 120 arrived to be subjected later in the day to a violent thunderstorm. Soon afterwards Charles and his sisters-in-law set out for Aix-la-Chapelle where they were to spend four weeks before returning home to set off again for five weeks this time in Scarborough out of season.

Edmund was to pursue a line of study and research eventually becoming a noted antiquary and a collector of finger-rings of the episcopal, cardinal, etc., type; the collection being mentioned in the *Illustrated London News* of 17 January 1863. The Holyrood Madonna of carved wood and probably of late sixteenth century in the Church of the Sacred Heart in Edinburgh was the gift of Edmund in 1869 from an auction at the London house of the 4th Earl of Abercorn, the relic alleging to have once been in Holyrood Palace. The partial remains of the Wakefield Cross now in the museum of St Mary's Abbey, York, was another religious relic rescued by Edmund. Apparently it had been erected in the churchyard at Wakefield, probably about the year A.D. 940 where it remained standing until the Reformation but in the age of religious intolerance that followed, the cross was to suffer mutilation. In 1862 what was left of it was discovered serving as a doorstep in a shop in Wakefield whence it was rescued by Edmund to be kept in the Walton Park estate and in 1870 the remains were removed to York.

In 1840 Charles Waterton's sister Helen had died childless to leave behind her solicitor husband Robert Carr who passed away in February 1853 and whom it is believed was the 'Yorkshire solicitor' who had lent Edmund £800. In his Will, Robert Carr left his estate in reversion to Edmund upon his marriage and in the meantime Edmund was to receive the income from the estate, that is, agricultural rents etc., but such a windfall seemingly did not arrest Edmund's lifestyle of high spending.

In 1853 Edmund was to receive from his father an annual settlement of £300 that Edmund quickly transformed it into a mortgage of £2,000. In September 1856 Edmund would mortgage his annuity from the Robert Carr estate and also the reversion of the Walton Hall estate for another £700. Two months later his aunt Eliza bought up the mortgage and advanced him £2,000, and by the middle of 1859 he owed her £5,000.

On 20 August 1862 Edmund married Josephine Margaret Alicia Ennis who provided him with a dowry of £13,300, Josephine being the second daughter of Sir John Ennis, baronet, of Ballinahown Court, County West Meath, Ireland, a millionaire who was to be a MP, Governor of the Bank of Ireland, High Sheriff of County West Meath and County Dublin, and Chairman of Ireland's Midland Great Western Railway. By the time of his marriage Edmund's debts had risen to £18,000 arising from a series of wild mortgages on his assets, and because of such a situation the relationship between father and son had become strained. Charles apparently was not to be told of the pending wedding and was several hundred miles away in Aix-la-Chapelle with his two sisters-in-law at the time of the ceremony. On marrying, Edmund bought a house near Bury St Edmunds where in June 1868 his first son, Charles was born.

When it came to obtaining money to satisfy his thirst for spending it Edmund could be unscrupulous. It seems that his father had received a large amount of money in allowing the construction of a railway line across a part of his land and had promised to give some of it to his son. Secretly with the aid of a London lawyer Edmund arranged for the entire sum considered by Edmund as his father's marriage settlement to be paid into his account, a transaction that was to stand as a legal document. After learning about this Charles Waterton in December 1863 redrafted his Will, not disinheriting his son but making his two sisters-in-law and the family solicitor into executors, the two sisters to be given a sum of £10,000. Charles did not possess such an amount and so it was to stand as a mortgage right on Walton Hall. Edmund now married and having received his wife's dowry of £13,300, would be in a position one would have thought to at least pay off the mortgage to release whatever would be left of his inheritance following the payment of debts, but on his father's death some eighteen months later the mortgage was still outstanding.

Charles spent Christmas of 1864 at his usual venue Stonyhurst College but on this occasion without Edmund who was with his new family in Ireland and planning to build some sort of Catholic seminary in Walton village. Although Charles was a most benevolent person he had mixed feelings regarding Edmund's planned seminar. Still very much concerned about his son's debt problems, on 11 January 1865 Charles wrote to Edmund, the opening paragraphs of the letter reading as follows:

> I shall be overjoyed, if the proposed religious establishment at Walton village can be effected without detriment to the worldly affairs of your family, which apparently will be numerous, and must be provided for.
>
> So soon as you shall have satisfied me that you are not in debt, and that no London lawyer (rot them) shall have anything to do, directly or indirectly with the affair, then and in that case, and only then, I will joyfully provide, from my Bark Quarry, every stone that may be necessary for the Building.

On his eighty-second birthday, 3 June 1864, Charles had rowed his two sisters-in-law Eliza and Helen to the northern end of Walton Hall lake to a spot not far from where his grandfather was buried, to show them an ancient cross between two oak trees and where he would express his wish to be buried there when his time came. Such a sad event would take place exactly one year later.

Charles had cemented a firm friendship with a young teenage student of taxidermy and natural history, Norman Moore, whom he treated him as another son in that Edmund did not share his father's interest in natural history. Moore had arrived unexpected at Walton Hall in 1863 from Manchester as a 16-year-old apprentice in a cotton factory by day and a student of natural history in the evening. Over the next two years he would continue to visit Walton Hall observing and making notes of Charles's way of working. He was to study at Cambridge and become Sir Norman Moore, a President of the Royal College of Physicians, and a doctor.

On the morning of 25 May 1865, Charles and Norman Moore, along with a carpenter, crossed the lake to the northern end of the park to supervise work that had to be done on some plank bridges near the stone cross between the two oak trees. On the way back to the boat Charles tripped over a bramble and fell heavily on his side. In much pain he managed to return to the Hall where in the drawing room he agreed, due to the distress shown by those present, not to go to his attic room but instead to rest in Eliza's sitting room nearer the ground floor. A surgeon arrived from Wakefield and administered leeches to Charles's skin with obviously no effect whatsoever, but it is said that although in great pain Charles watched this medical procedure with interest.

In the meantime a telegram had been sent to Edmund who was in Rome performing as Chamberlain to the Pope. The next morning Charles was a little better, the afternoon seeing a second visit by the surgeon, this time with another doctor who decided upon *Severe concussion of the liver* which years later was said by someone else as *Ruptured spleen*. That evening Charles's condition worsened, it was clear that the end was near and Canon Browne in Leeds was sent for to administer the last rites. As the ladies of the house gathered round the sofa in Eliza's room on which Charles lay, Charles gave his blessings to each in turn – to Eliza and Helen and to Lydia their niece who was now living at Walton Hall, then to his two infant grandchildren Charles and Mary Paula Pia, to Norman Moore, and a farewell message for Edmund. He then received the Last Sacraments, repeating all the responses. Charles composed himself to die, clasping in his hands a malachite and a bronze crucifix that had once belonged to the grandson of James II the last Roman Catholic king of England.

The end came in the early hours of the next morning with his faithful friend Moore by his side, who later in his journal would write:

> ... he died at twenty-seven minutes past two in the morning of May 27, 1865. The window was open. The sky was beginning to grow grey, a few rooks had cawed, the swallows were twittering, the land-rail was craking from the ox-close, and a favourite cock, which he used to call his morning gun, leaped out from some hollies, and gave his accustomed crow. The ear of his master was deaf to the call.

The funeral began at 9 am on 3 June 1865, Charles's 83rd birthday. After Requiem High Mass conducted by the Bishop of Beverley the oak coffin bearing the Waterton Arms was carried in procession to the water gate headed by the Bishop accompanied by priests carrying lighted tapers followed by Edmund with family members behind him. At the gate the coffin was lowered into the Walton Hall coal barge now converted into a floating bier that was to take its place behind the leading canal longboat containing the Bishop, four Monsignors and said to be thirteen priests. Four boats in formation carried the principal mourners whilst towed in the rear, empty and rigged with black bunting was Charles's boat *Percy*. As the funeral cortege headed serenely down the lake to the grave between the oak trees, tenants, servants, and other mourners, walked along both sides of the lake at the same pace as the flotilla. At the grave the Bishop, assisted by the priests, conducted the burial service that was brought to a conclusion with the chanting of the Benedictus.

Charles was laid to rest in the spot where the year before he had erected a stone cross that was to have an inscription in Latin, which translated read: *Pray for the soul of Charles Waterton whose weary bones lie close to this cross.* The grave lies in the woods a little way to the right of the red tree seen today on the 16th hole on the Waterton Park golf course.

With the passing of Squire Charles Waterton the world had lost a 'character' who had 'stood above the crowd' in many ways without fear of condemnation. When it was the fashion to sport a beard and a good mop of hair, he would always appear standing almost six feet in height, clean-shaven with short-cropped hair. His high jinks at Stonyhurst Christmas gatherings much to the embarrassment of Edmund, and the times when hosting dinner parties he spent the entire evening mimicking a wild animal moving on all fours, climbing over tables and hanging from pieces of furniture, although seemingly childlike were certainly never childish but a harmless presentation of his gentle character. There may have been some deep-seated reason behind such behaviour, but his peculiar brand of individualism helped to make him a great naturalist venturing into situations that would have been alien to most men, especially those from a similar background. It has been mentioned that his sensitive nature and fundamentally gentle soul made him particularly susceptible to the pressures of his traditions and upbringing, and that to some extent his absorption in exploration and natural history was a sort of compensation.

When Sir Robert Peel's Catholic Emancipation Act was introduced in 1829 to remove some of the restrictions Catholics had had to contend with since the Reformation of the 1530s, it would be on condition that Roman Catholics signed the oath: '*I do hereby disclaim, disavow and solemnly abjure any intention to subvert the present Church Establishment within this realm.*' Even though many Roman Catholics would sign, Charles Waterton would refuse thus debarring himself from such official positions as the Magistracy and the Deputy-Lieutenantship of his county that he could have taken had he signed.

He never owned a microscope and did not pursue scientifically the world of natural history like his friend Darwin did, who following the publication of his 'natural selection' theory, would turn his back on his church. Charles Waterton would never have done the latter and so as a naturalist it seems that he decided simply to enjoy exploring the natural world, publishing his observations and presenting his specimens of taxidermy.

Charles was a prolific writer of letters especially to certain 'authorities' criticising and outlining his concerns on specific issues of the day. His writings about his travels and experiences which he referred to as his *Wanderings* in the pursuit and recording of natural history would be an instant success such as his *Wanderings in South America, the North West of the United States, and the Antilles encompassing the years 1812, 1816, 1820, and 1824*, first published by J. Mawman & Co. (London) in 1825. Further editions by different publishers of this particular work appeared in the nineteenth century and throughout the twentieth century. The Waterton National Park in Western Canada covering thousands of acres of unspoilt wilderness is named after him.

Throughout his adult life and after death Charles Waterton was often referred to as the eccentric squire, a character trait seen by many as perhaps a manifestation of his uncompromising and individualistic nature. Dame Edith Sitwell would write of him:

> ––– *this noble, brave and beloved old man ... He was an eccentric only as all great gentlemen are eccentric, by which I mean that their gestures are not born to fit the conventions or the cowardice of the crowd.*

Yet at certain times such eccentric behaviour could manifest into what might be described as sheer madness as what must have happened when Charles Darwin met Charles at Walton in the 1840s.

In 1826 the 17-year-old Charles Darwin, wanting to learn the art of taxidermy, had met Charles briefly in Edinburgh. Twenty years later Darwin visited Charles at Walton Hall and following the visit Darwin was to say he had felt that he had been a guest at some sort of Mad Hatter's tea party. Such feelings may have been so near the truth in that Charles, one might suggest in the kindest possible way, may have been suffering from the effects of bichloride of mercury that he used extensively in preserving his natural history specimens. He had a hat that he never allowed to be brushed but soaked it in a solution of bichloride of mercury; he also applied this to the lining of his carriage.

Charles was proud of his new method of preservation that he had perfected by 1820, the year when he had set out to South America taking with him bottles of bichloride of mercury. In 1856 he was still using the mercury compound when in the spring of that year he had a visitor to see his specimens in his Yorkshire home, the London physician George Harley (mentioned above) who at first thought the specimens were stuffed. Charles was to inform him the specimens were not stuffed but hollow, devoid of bones, and then proceeded to work on a specimen explaining the processes involved and praising the virtues of his mercury compound. It is thought that Charles may have begun his particular method of preserving his specimens sometime between 1810 and 1813 the oldest dated specimen in his collection being a scarlet ibis labelled 1810.

Before Charles began his method of preservation and for well into the second half of the nineteenth century, taxidermy consisted of specimens usually stuffed with straw, their body shape kept rigid with a skeleton of wire, whilst the usual skin preservative was arsenical soap or less often, camphor. Very early specimens were stuffed with tobacco and spices, the bodies kept rigid with their own skeletons. Charles produced specimens that were hollow, the skins having been soaked in a solution of bichloride of mercury and alcohol (one teaspoonful of bichloride of mercury to a bottleful of alcohol) from three to four hours according to skin thickness, and then dried following which the skin was moulded into shape. The solution made the skins firm enough to support themselves and also made them anti-putrescent and a repellent to insects such as clothes moths; presumably why Charles applied the solution to the lining of his carriage. This method used by Charles involved a good deal of time and along with the costs of bichloride of mercury, was responsible for the method not being universally adopted although it was to be accepted as the best one for the purpose of preservation.

Any chemist will say that certain chemical compounds of mercury either inhaled or absorbed through the skin can be lethal to the complex working of the brain and can in some situations produce states of madness in the unfortunate victim. Some of the felt hat makers of Lancashire's Lune

Valley working in the eighteenth and nineteenth centuries with mercuric nitrate are a striking example as to the dangerous usage of mercury in its compound form, in this case allied to a particular process, the result of which throughout the hatting industry in general would sadly present the phrase, 'as mad as a hatter'. During one particular period in felt hat manufacture the combination of rabbit fur and wool was used, the rabbit fur being shorn off the skin and 'carrotted', a process in which the fur was treated with mercuric nitrate so rendering the fibres suitable for the felting process in which they were blended with the carded wool.

Due to mercuric poisoning a hatter could develop the shakes, and a number of hatters were admitted to the County Lunatic Asylum in Lancaster in the early nineteenth century as recorded in the Admissions Register of the Asylum for 1816–23, now in the Lancashire Archives in Preston.

Another way by which Charles could have absorbed mercury in its compound form was by taking doses of a mixture of jalap and calomel as a laxative as mentioned above. Jalap was a purgative drug obtained from the tuberous roots of a Mexican climbing plant, whilst calomel was a compound of mercury and chlorine (mercurous chloride) used in medicine as a laxative to purify the body. Charles's recipe for this mixture was ten grains of calomel well mixed up with twenty grains of jalap; such an amount could be made into four pills.

There is no doubt that during his adult life Charles did receive a considerable intake of mercury, a poison that once it enters the body never leaves it. But the suggestion that Charles's eccentric behaviour might have been due to his usage of mercury compounds and doses thereof, simply cannot be proven. He may well have shown such behavioural traits in his younger years long before he went to South America. Yet it was this eccentricity that his friend J. G. Wood would refer to in a most supporting and affectionate way in his fitting tribute to Charles. In the tribute, Thackeray was William Makepeace Thackeray the novelist.

> *It was perhaps eccentric to have a strong religious faith, and act upon it. It was eccentric, as Thackeray said "To dine upon a crust, live as chastely as a hermit, and give his all to the poor." It was eccentric to come into a large estate as a young man and to have lived to extreme old age without having wasted one hour or one shilling. It was eccentric to give bountifully and never allow his name to appear in a subscription-list. It was eccentric to be saturated with the love*

of nature. It might be eccentric never to give larger dinner parties, preferring to keep an always open house for his friends; but it was an agreeable kind of eccentricity. It was eccentric to be ever childlike but never childish. We might multiply instances of his eccentricity to any extent, and may safely say that the world would be much better than it is if such eccentricity were more common.

Like many Victorians, Charles was fascinated by freaks and produced several taxidermical jests, a notable one being a clever slur against the political establishment of the day. Entitled 'John Bull and the National debt', it showed the country as a porcupine with an almost human face supporting a tortoiseshell so weighed down by the National Debt of 800 million pounds, it was being overcome by six creatures depicted as devils. Sadly these taxidermical jests did nothing to support or enhance the reputation of Charles as a serious exponent of natural history, particularly amongst those at work in the professional circles of this new science, many of whom considered such *taxidermical arrangements* better suited to the freak shows of the Victorian fairgrounds.

After the death of Charles, Walton Hall went through a period of leasehold and by 1878 had been sold to Edward Simpson (see next chapter) the Hall remaining the Simpson family seat until after the Second World War during which it became a military hospital. After the war it became a maternity hospital (a civil annex to the Manygates maternity hospital run by the West Riding Health Authority). The Hall closed as a working hospital in December 1966 and then fell into a state of serious neglect for a number of years before being bought by a private owner who was to add leisure facilities to make the venue into a country club. Presumably these were the facilities built upon the mainland near the bridge, facilities to have six squash courts built in 1978, the club becoming national squash champions for three consecutive years in the early '80s.

Since the late 1970s the Hall has been a hotel and in June 1982 to celebrate the 200th anniversary of Charles Waterton's birthday, the Guild of Taxidermists held a day symposium at Walton Hall, with guest speakers, buffet lunch, grand celebration dinner, bird-mount competition and a visit to the Bi-centenary Exhibition at Wakefield Museum. Two days later, the Yorkshire Society of Anaesthetists held a similar symposium, and 15 April 1988 saw a permanent Charles Waterton Exhibition being officially opened at Wakefield Museum by the local MP David Hinchliffe.

Following the death of Charles Waterton in May 1865 income from the Walton Hall Estate was totally insufficient to meet the debts of Edmund who inherited his father's collection of specimens. Generous but showing no thrift whatsoever Edmund began to give away as presents to friends priceless family heirlooms, and in November 1865 his aunts Eliza and Helen arranged the sending of Charles's collection of specimens to St Cuthbert's College, Ushaw, for safe keeping. Eventually the collection arrived at Alston Hall as a gift to John Mercer from Edmund, entirely filling one room in the mansion. The *Preston Guardian* newspaper some years later on Saturday 9 January 1897 in mentioning the collection at Alston Hall wrote:

> One large room contains the collection of Charles Waterton, and here are displayed many fine examples of the fauna which he collected from dangerous expeditions in the miasma-haunted swamps and dense jungles of South America and other regions. There are gorgeous-plumed birds, many specimens of monkeys, strange-looking reptiles, a gigantic crocodile which, as he tells us in his "Wanderings", he once bestrode – curious groupings of birds, all labelled apparently by his own hand.

In the summer of 1908 Ellen Waterton sent the collection on loan to Stonyhurst College, and on 4 May 1915 Ellen's daughter Monica, then a nun, changed the loan into a gift. During the summer of 1967 the collection was transferred still on loan from Stonyhurst to Wakefield City Museum where some of it remains today on display, part of the collection having been returned to Stonyhurst to be displayed in its original setting in the Long Room.

Some years after the death of Charles Waterton, the grounds of Walton Hall very nearly saw the mining of coal (see next chapter). In 1890 a short distance from the nearby village of Walton, the construction of Walton Colliery, then known as Sharlston West, began. The colliery was to employ 1,285 men underground and 298 on the surface to produce 2,200 tonnes a day. In 1959 an underground explosion of methane gas occurred killing five people. December 1979 saw the closure of the mine leading to the loss of 550 jobs.

Chapter seven

Edmund Waterton

On the day before his father's funeral Edmund and his wife had arrived at Walton Hall laden with rings, pictures, marbles etc. from Rome, and a few days after the funeral Edmund had planned to build a chapel of mourning behind his father's grave. A larger chapel was planned on the island near the Hall to where his father's coffin it was decided would finally rest. The chapel never grew beyond two exterior walls.

In August 1865 sheriffs had arrived at Walton Hall to seize whatever goods they could find belonging to Edmund, and Eliza would intervene to buy back everything for Edmund. However, it would seem that he had began to prepare a legal case against his aunts Eliza and Helen to dispute their right to have inherited anything from his father. Preferring not to create a confrontation the aunts offered to leave Walton Hall if Edmund in turn would keep the Hall intact and unchanged, so in September the sisters bought themselves a house in Scarborough, Edmund and his wife Josephine moving into Walton Hall to officially name it Walton Castle.

During Edmund's short period at the Hall, bailiffs were constantly in the house and grounds, and to make money to pay for his pleasures and pay off his debts, Edmund would arrange shooting parties when water birds were shot off, game going the same way. To many these events about the parkland must have been seen as distasteful to say the least, considering that his father had spent years developing the park into the nation's first nature reserve. Edmund would also initiate a plan to sell land for building plots. By March 1866, Eliza, to whom Edmund still owed money, filed a formal Bill of Complaint against him in an attempt to restrain him from the felling of trees for timber on the Walton Estate and the digging for stone on the land and coal under its surface.

In 1868 Edmund received legal confirmation that he was the owner of everything that had once been his father's but in spite of this he was still in debt and decided to live along with his family on the Continent. It would seem that Edmund would live in one place until a lack of credit would force him to move on and quite often he ended up in whatever house his aunts were occupying at the time, whether in Brussels, Bruges or Ostend. In August 1870, the year she died, Eliza wrote to Norman Moore from Ostend:

> We have Edmund and all his family staying with us; the latter for some months, but we hope that they are leaving soon.

By 1869 Walton Hall had a new tenant, Charles George Fane, and then in 1871 the Hall and part of its parkland were leased to a solicitor, Edward Hailstone who had lived at Horton Hall near Bradford and who would reside at Walton Hall until his death twenty years later.

The year 1876 found Edmund owing gambling debts and declaring himself a bankrupt, and in 1877 was to sell Walton Hall and its 259 acres to Edward Simpson (1843–1914) the eldest son of the soap manufacturer Edward Thornhill Simpson who had died in 1873 and who had been Charles Waterton's old adversary in the days of a soap and vitriol works battle during the forties and early fifties.

During Charles's long tour of the Continent of 1839–41, a plot of land just outside the boundary of his Walton Hall estate had been sold to a local industrialist who was to build a soap-boiling and bleaching factory on it, land that had once belonged to the Waterton family and which Charles over a period of twenty years had tried to buy back. As the factory flourished its industrial processes discharged poisonous fumes and waste products into the surrounding area, and on the Walton estate soil and water were to be contaminated, trees becoming crippled and fish dying. Charles and his neighbour Sir William Pilkington, whose estate was also badly affected, would bring about an action for damages at the York Assizes. Charles won his case and was awarded £1,100 in costs, however the problem continued and Charles went to court again in August 1849 but this time Edward Thornhill Simpson, the owner of the factory, won the day.

In consequence Charles and his long-suffering sister-in-laws decided to buy a piece of riverside land at Thornes, four miles away that had navigation rights, wharf facilities and a residency, Thornes House, and offered it for sale at a knockdown price in the hope that Simpson would be attracted to the site, moving his factory there. Then in October 1849 they went to court for a third time and managed to get an injunction served on Simpson to close the Walton factory down and move it to the site at Thornes. Simpson procrastinated but by 1853 the Walton factory had ceased to manufacture soap whilst his business was to continue on the land at Thornes.

In 1877 having bought Walton Hall, Edward Thornhill Simpson's son Edward was unable to take up residence there until Edward Hailstone's lease ended in 1891 even though Hailstone had died in the meantime. The selling price for the Hall and its land came to the exceptional inflated figure of £114,000 due to a recent discovery of coal seams within the grounds that fortunately were never to be mined due to the coal being much broken. Had mining commenced, Walton would have become a mining village.

Shortly after selling Walton Hall Edmund bought what had been the Manor House in the small village of Deeping St James in Lincolnshire, about six miles north of Peterborough, renaming it Deeping Waterton Hall as he made himself believe that the house was of a more ancient possession of the Watertons than had been Walton Hall.

By now Edmund and his wife Josephine had five children. The first-born had been Charles Edmund Maria Joseph Aloysius, born on 10 June 1863, his birth being recorded in the district of Marylebone, London, whilst his unusual number of Catholic forenames indicated his parent's strong connections to the Catholic faith. To be known as Charlie, he would marry Josephine Mary Rock in 1890, the *Wells Journal* of 14 August reporting the marriage at the Roman Catholic Chapel at Shepton Mallet when the two bridesmaids were the bridegroom's sister Agnes Waterton and Princess Stephanie de Rohan. Charles and Josephine were to have three sons in the 1890s, Joseph born 1892 in London; Charles born 1894 in Biarritz, France; and Edmond (or Edmund) born 1896, also in Biarritz. In the last five years of life before dying in 1906 aged 44 Charles would father four sons.

Next to be born to Edmund and Josephine was Mary Paula Pia in December 1864 who was to become an Augustinian nun. Josephine's third child was Agnes Mary Pia born on 17 August 1866, who would marry Joseph Sutcliffe, their child being Inez Mary. Agnes died on 1 January 1949 in the Istituto Santa Giuliana Falconieri in Rome.

On 14 May 1868, Josephine gave birth to a daughter, Amabil who died some weeks later on 26 September and was buried in the family chapel at Walton Hall. Today at Walton Hall, now the Walton Park Hotel, the gravestone of Amabil can be seen mounted on the wall by the staircase marking the place where she was buried.

Josephine's fifth child was Josephine Mary Teresa Everilda Gabriella

Pia born in Brussels on 12 March 1871, who was to marry Alfred Harrison in 1890, (and later in 1934 married Major Charles Langdale) and died in 1947; the Harrisons having two children, Alfreda and Angela, the latter eventually marrying Hugh Crawford.

Edmund and Josephine's last child was Thomas More Mary Joseph Pius born on 8 July 1876 in Boulogne, France. He died a bachelor on 15 January 1922 in St Joseph's Hospital, Mount Street, Preston, in Lancashire.

Following the sale of Walton Hall Edmund's bankruptcy was annulled in 1879 when it was agreed he should pay 2s. in the pound in discharge of debts to his creditors. The year 1879 would seem a good one for Edmund buying the house in Deeping St James and the publication of his *Pietas Mariana Britannica*, a history of English devotion to the Virgin Mary with a catalogue of shrines, sanctuaries, offerings, bequests, and other memorials of the piety of our forefathers. However, the year ended in great sorrow with the death of his wife Josephine on Boxing Day in Cannes, France. At Deeping Waterton Hall Edmund would make arrangements for the conversion of a stable there into a private chapel into which the remains of Josephine were interred.

Edmund continued as Privy Chamberlain to the Pope as well as spending time in Lincolnshire with his children, the youngest being three-and-a-half-year-old Thomas, and also a new generation of debts. The Census of 1881 found Edmund at his home in Deeping St James with his two youngest children Josephine (10) and Thomas (4) who would have a

Fig. 7.1 Edmund Waterton wearing his official decorations of the Catholic Church.

governess-cum-teacher, the house being run by a housekeeper, cook, two housemaids, general servant, butler, and a groom. Then in the final quarter of the year came his marriage to Ellen Mercer, the future heiress of Alston Hall and its estate.

On 3 August 1884 Ellen gave birth to a daughter, Monica Mary Colette Paula, and on 5 June 1887 Ellen gave birth to another daughter, Ethelburga Mary Magdalene Pega, but sadly during the following month Edmund died of Bright's disease at the age of 57 at Deeping St James. For the past six years he had been a sufferer of the disease and prior to his death had spent the previous winter in Algiers returning in reasonable health but soon the disease would take a hold of him.

The death certificate in recording his death on 21 July 1887 at which his son Charles was present, mentions Edmund's occupation as having been 'Landed Proprietor' and cause of death as 'Chronic Nephritis 6 Years'. This was commonly known as Bright's disease when structural changes in the kidneys, usually chronic inflammation of the blood vessels in them, result in the presence of protein and specifically albumin in the urine. It would be the English physician Richard Bright (1789–1858) who it has been said with nothing more sophisticated than a candle and a silver spoon discovered protein in urine and in 1827 published his pioneering study of kidney disease.

Edmund was interred in his private chapel at Deeping Waterton Hall where the remains of his first wife Josephine lay at rest. Throughout his life Edmund had been a staunch supporter of the Catholic faith devoting years of research into its history, and was a Knight of the Supreme Order of Christ; a Knight of Malta; a Papal Privy Chamberlain; and a Fellow of the Society of Antiquaries, whilst at one stage in his career he had been a J.P. Today, a memorial of Charles Waterton and his wife Anne as well as Edmund and Josephine can be seen in the English Convent in Bruges (fig. 7.2).

From a certain age Edmund had become conscious of his darkish skin tones, the result of his mixed race parentage whilst his aunts Helen and Eliza because of the darkness of their skins, sadly were to be marked as outsiders. Edmund had been well built, a huge figure of a man standing at six feet and three inches in height, broad in the chest and in perfect proportion. In his younger days whilst at Stonyhurst he was known as Long Tom, there he was popular with masters and fellow pupils alike and excelled in sporting activities. In his adult life he was always dressed elegantly in the latest fashion of the day much adorned by jewellery, and in 1861 the year before his first marriage his bedroom at Walton Hall showed that he had a taste for ease and luxury. A room filled with expensive furnishings, costly chandelier, handsome bound books, and pipes and cigars in profusion; a room in stark contrast to his father's one opened to the rafters.

Yet there could be a different side to Edmund, a darker one he called his 'old enemy, hysteria', seen in his mood changes from a state of boredom to one of anxiety. Throughout his life he had a stammer and at times was a compulsive eater who liked his wine, an indulgence most probably responsible for him having gout early on.

In one of the rooms at Walton Hall during one period of Edmund's time there was a life-sized portrait of him dressed in what he described as the 'becoming costume' of the Italian Papal Order of the Cameriere Segreto, whilst in the adjacent drawing room was another portrait of him in full Highland dress, presumably an illusion to the Scottish side of his mother's ancestry.

It is so easy to condemn Edmund and look upon him as being the 'bad guy' in the saga of the Watertons, but such condemnation might appear to be unfair. In the 1860s Edmund wrote a letter to a friend declaring that he had given up drinking, gambling and debauching before continuing to write: –––*considering how I have been placed, and what I have had to put up with, it is well I have not done worse.*

Julia Blackburn in her brilliant portrayal of Edmund in her publication of 1989 mentions the mysterious reference to 'Little McDonnell' the young lad who was to be brought up for the Church and sent to Stonyhurst at Edmund's expense, presumably because he had reasons for feeling financially obliged to the child.

Always to remind Edmund was the dislocated family history on his mother's side whilst on his father's side centuries of a powerful lineage had drawn to a close. His father's indifference to dress and appearance along with his apparent immunity to the demands of his position in the social hierarchy was a marked annoyance to Edmund.

During Ellen's marriage to Edmund, her father and her step uncle Canon Taylor were to be invited to the Farmers and Tradesmen Annual Association Dinner to be held at the Bell Inn, Deeping St James on the Thursday evening of 26 January 1882 at which Edmund was to be chairman for the event. Reporting on the occasion shortly afterwards on 4 February the *Grantham Journal* wrote:

> *The chair was taken by Edmund Waterton, Esq., of Deeping Waterton Hall. Letters of apology for not being able to attend were received from John Mercer, Esq., J.P., of Alston Hall, Lancashire, and the Rev.*

Fig. 7.2 Memorial to the Waterton family in the English Convent, Bruges. Translated it reads:

JESUS MARIA JOSEPH
SACRED TO THE MEMORY
OF CHARLES WATERTON OF WALTON HALL, 1782–1865
RISEN FROM THE STOCK
OF HIS BLESSED MARTYR THOMAS MORE,
AND OF HIS WIFE ANNE EDMONSTONE, 1812–1830
WHO AMONG HER RELATIONS COUNTED THE HOLY QUEEN MARGARET,
WHO WERE JOINED IN MATRIMONY IN THIS CHURCH
AND TO THE MEMORY OF EDMUND MARY WATERTON
OF THE ROMAN ORDER OF KNIGHTS OF CHRIST
1830–1887
AND OF HIS WIFE
JOSEPHINE M. ALICIA ENNIS
1836–1879
GOOD LORD JESUS GIVE THEM REST

Canon Taylor, of St. Augustine's, Preston. The Right Rev. Dr. Riddell, Bishop of Northampton, had arrived that day at Deeping Waterton Hall, and his Lordship was pleased to accompany Mr. Waterton to the dinner, where he met with a most cordial reception. After the usual loyal toasts, Mr. Waterton begged to be allowed to propose the health of their illustrious guest and his old and valued friend, the Catholic Lord Bishop of Northampton. They had known each other from boyhood, and thus their friendship dated from early years.

After Edmund's death, Ellen with her two daughters was soon to leave Deeping Waterton Hall. How happy and successful Ellen's short marriage had been one cannot say as no letters nor dairies have been found. Probably there were times when Edmund's impulses to spend money may have given Ellen some cause for concern.

In 1891 Edmund's eldest son Charles sold Deeping Waterton Hall (known as the Manor House) and its land to the Marquess of Exeter, but the chapel remained the property of the Waterton family and continued to be used by the Roman Catholic community. In 1919 the Manor House was let to the Roman Catholic teaching order the Xaverian Brothers as a novitiate (a place housing religious novices), the Brothers buying the property in 1932.

The Xaverian Brothers community, a Roman Catholic society of educators from Bruges to be known as the Brothers of St Francis Xavier, was a society founded by Theodore James Ryken in 1839 in Bruges who had been born in the village of Elshout, North Brabant, Holland, on 30 August 1797 to middle class Catholic parents. Ryken was soon to be orphaned and then brought up by a saintly uncle who instilled in the young boy's character qualities of faith, zeal for souls, and devotion to duty that were to be associated with Ryken in his adult life. After training as a shoemaker, Ryken decided to devote his life to the Christian education of youth and at the age of 34 went to America to spend three years offering his services as a catechist (one who practices oral instruction allied to Christian principles using a question and answer technique) among the missionaries to the American natives.

During his second visit to America in 1837 he found that the city youth, especially the children of immigrants, were even more in need of instruction than the native Americans and consequently was encouraged by Bishop Rosati of St Louis to found a religious congregation of layman whose members would labour among all classes of American youth. On returning to Europe Ryken visited the Pope in Rome to receive his approval and blessing regarding his mission plan, eventually renting a house on Ezelstraat in Bruges where on 20 June 1839 with two companions, a tailor and a weaver who had promised to join him in his venture, Ryken was to establish the foundation of an institute of religious educators with worldwide missionary aspirations.

By 1841 the venture had grown to such an extent that a large estate allowing space for additional buildings was purchased in a neighbouring section of Bruges by the aid of a bank loan, a loan that would become a burden over the years to Ryken until, when in old age, he willingly turned over his office to a younger man in order to save his congregation from financial ruin. In 1869, by which time the debt had been cleared and the Brothers had grown to 133 in number, Ryken was present at the first General Chapter of his Order. He died aged 74 on 26 November 1871.

Candidates to become Brothers came from Germany, Holland, Belgium, England, Ireland and France, and in 1848 a colony of Brothers went to England to open schools in parishes in Bury and Manchester. At the invitation of Bishop Martin John Spalding of Louisville, Kentucky, Ryken's idea of sending Brothers to America came to fruition in 1854, 2004–5 marking the 150th anniversary of Xaverian Education in the United States.

In 1940 the Xaverian Brothers' preparatory school for boys at Foxhunt Manor in Sussex was evacuated to Deeping St James, and after a serious fire in the Manor House, the school was moved back to Sussex and the Manor House reverted to a novitiate. In 1952 a local businessman bought the house and grounds and it was agreed that some of the land should be reserved for a new and larger Catholic Church to be built at a later date. When the land was developed in the 1960s as the Manor Park Estate a site was allocated for the erection of the Catholic Church, Our Lady of Lincoln and St Guthlac. Eventually the stone font, the fourteenth-century wooden crucifix and the sixteenth-century wooden statue of Our Lady that Edmund had originally installed in his new chapel, were removed from the chapel to the new church. With the move to the new church, the Waterton Chapel was abandoned and fell into disrepair.

In 1988 the re-interment of the remains of Edmund and his first wife Josephine was to take place in the cemetery of Deeping St James' Priory Church when two of Edmund's direct descendants were in attendance. The old chapel and land were sold and the chapel re-developed into a house to leave the Waterton Arms public house as a prominent reminder of the Watertons in the village. Charles Alec Oliver Waterton born in 1947 the great grandson of Edmund's first-born son Charles was to continue the male line and live in Western Australia.

In October 1990 by a strange coincidence a group of students studying Bruges lace making at Alston Hall stayed at the English Convent in Bruges. Only a few weeks before the students left Alston for Bruges had they realised that Ellen Mercer had been the second wife of Edmund Waterton. At the convent Mrs Hazel Westray was shown and photographed the Waterton Memorial there.

Chapter eight

The wind of change at Alston

Having returned to Lancashire after Edmund's death, Ellen Waterton in 1889 had not taken up residency with her father and stepmother at Alston Hall but was living at 9 Ribblesdale Place, Preston, a select residential area immediately to the south of the town's Winckley Square. Close by in the Square was the Convent of the Holy Child Jesus that had opened in 1875 for the education of Catholic girls after nuns had bought number 23, formerly the home of Thomas Batty Addison, the Recorder of Preston for £2,000. In 1889 Ellen's eldest daughter Monica was of school age or approaching it (born in 1884), which leads one to suggest the reason for Ellen residing in Ribblesdale Place was for the education of Monica at the nearby convent.

The Taunton Commission of 1868 had found that girls' education was lacking in the basics, and teaching methods needed to be improved. The Order of the Holy Child Jesus founded in 1846 (see later) had recognised some years earlier this problem and had set out to provide the appropriate primary and secondary education in many areas of the country. On their arrival in Preston the nuns dressed as widows or servants to avoid anti-Catholic feeling set up a small convent school at St Walburge's in 1853. Following the Taunton Commission two more convent schools were formed in Preston in 1871, one at St Mary's Church, the other at English Martyrs Church, and in 1875 the three were brought together at 23 Winckley Square.

From its opening in 1875 the Winckley Square Convent School prospered, the nuns acquiring other property nearby. In 1909, the same year when the school was entering pupils for Senior Oxford Examinations, rooms were built specifically for chemistry and physics, the school having become a centre for science some years earlier in 1887. In 1978 with the re-organisation of secondary education, Winckley Square Convent School was absorbed into Newman College and three years later in 1981 the Winckley Square Convent closed following which the buildings were sold to be acquired for a different purpose other than the education of girls from the Catholic community.

Today 9 Ribblesdale Place is still very much a part of the Preston Winckley Square area that had developed from 1799 onwards to become the town's most fashionable area to live, the abode of many a leading Preston citizen where in the 1860s gates and gatekeepers were in use to keep out undesirable types.

Marion Roberts in her publication of 1988, *The Story of Winckley Square, Preston*, gives a brilliant illustration of what life was like in the Square

Fig. 8.1 John Mercer's estates in the township of Alston at the time of his death in 1893. (By kind permission of Alan G. Crosby)

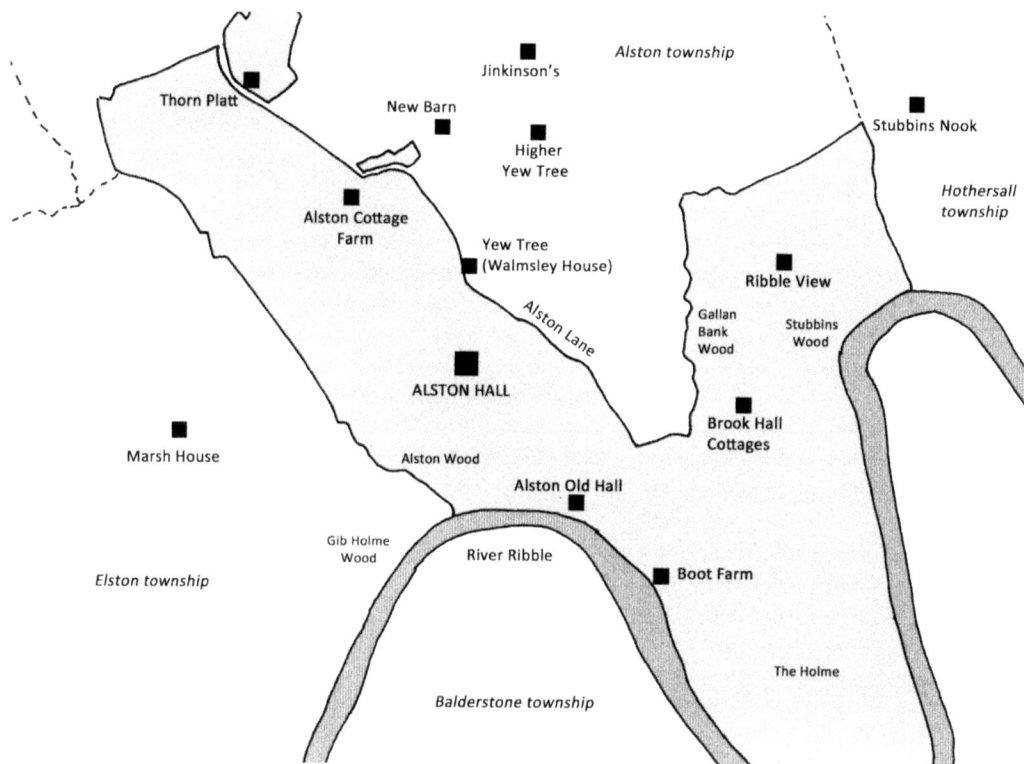

during the nineteenth century, the first paragraph of her introduction reading:

> *Towards the end of the 18th century, Mr William Cross, attorney and Deputy Prothonotary for the County of Lancaster, returned from completing his legal studies in London, and, inspired by the squares in that city, decided on a similar project of his own. To that end he purchased a considerable amount of land. From a fellow-attorney, Mr Thomas Winckley, he purchased Town End Field, and much of Winckley Square occupies that land.*

She mentions that the first house to be erected was for Cross himself in 1799 whilst the second house to appear was for Colonel Nicholas Grimshaw, who became Colonel of the Preston Royal Volunteers when the regiment was raised in 1797 in the face of a threat of invasion by the French. Grimshaw was Preston Guild Mayor in 1802 and in all was seven times the Mayor of Preston, including twice as the Guild Mayor. Amongst those who were to take up residency in the Square as the nineteenth century progressed were Thomas Batty Addison, Recorder of Preston and the advocate for the erection of the Union Workhouse in Fulwood. Other well-known residents were the Rev. Roger Carus Wilson, Vicar of Preston from 1817 to 1839; Thomas Miller of 'Horrockses, Miller and Co.', Preston textile manufacturers; Sir Charles Brown, doctor at Preston Royal Infirmary from 1870 to 1922; and Edward Garlick, resident engineer of the town's new dock, the largest in the country when opened in 1892.

Number 9 Ribblesdale Place was built as part of a 'semi' and would be the larger of the two houses, being double fronted in contrast to its single fronted neighbour, each having basement and dormer accommodation and a Georgian style columned entrance. The Census of 1891 found Ellen still in Ribblesdale Place with daughters Monica (6) now a scholar, and Ethelburga (3), and listed in the household that had four servants, was Ellen's cousin, Elizabeth Burrows (36). One of the servants, a 45-year-old widow Mary Dixon was a sick nurse, an indication that someone in the household suffered poor health that most probably was Ellen, as later on there seems to be evidence that throughout her years she had a heart weakness.

Preston of the 1890s was not a place to live if one had a heart condition or respiratory problems. Sulphur-laden smoke from what seemed countless factory chimneys and domestic grates sounded the death knell for many, especially during the winter months, but Ribblesdale Place was most conveniently placed for the Winckley Square Convent School.

Obviously Ribblesdale Place would only be a temporary address for Ellen who soon after the Census of 1891 moved to Lytham with its clean seaside air, her address in 1892 being 'Ferndale', 3 West Beach, Lytham, a desirable residence fronting the estuary of the River Ribble where she remained for a number of years and was still there in 1904. As to what had happened to her two daughters following Ellen's move to Lytham, it is presumed that they were sent as boarders to a school in Carlisle where they were being educated in 1901 (see later). In Lytham, Ellen would still be within a convenient distance from Alston Hall where her father was not in good health.

Marion Roberts writing about Winckley Square in the 1980s, and who would later write about the history of Alston Hall, mentions the Rayner family who were to reside at 9 Ribblesdale Place after Ellen Waterton had left the house. The Preston Directory for Guild Year 1922 tells us that number 9 was the home of Dr Arthur Rayner, the first director of Preston Royal Infirmary's X-Ray Department that opened in 1904. Dr Rayner's daughter was to be Phoebe Hesketh who would write a poem about times past in the Square entitled *The Ghost of Ribblesdale Place, Preston*. A part of the poem read:

> *But what about our house, solid Number Nine*
> *with my father's name half rubbed away in brass,*
> *where X-rays sparked and crackled, and we two,*
> *the noisy ones, were banished to the garden ?*
> *I see my younger sister in the grass*
> *threading a daisy-chain*
> *while I, impatient, spur the horse-on-wheels*
> *down to the cherry tree*
> *inside the high wall topped with jagged glass.*

The wall is still there overlooking Avenham Park and the river Ribble beyond. Phoebe Hesketh was the niece of Edith Rigby the Preston suffragette who was born Edith Rayner and the sister of Dr Arthur Rayner. In 1893 just before her twenty-first birthday Edith married Dr Charles Rigby and the couple set up home at number 28 Winckley Square next door to Dr Brown. Always concerned about the plight of the under-dog she would inquire into the working conditions of housemaids to the annoyance of her Winckley Square neighbours, and in 1899 founded an evening school and recreation club for working girls in St Peter's school

ALSTON HALL HOME FARM, near Grimsargh Station, on the Longridge Railway.

HIGHLY IMPORTANT SALE of 72 Head of CATTLE, six Shire and other Horses, Fat Lambs, Implements, &c.

MR. E. G. HOTERSALL is honoured with instructions from the Exors. of the late John Mercer, Esq. (on account of the above farm being let) to offer for Sale by Auction, on WEDNESDAY, May 17th, 1893, at One o'clock prompt, the following FARM STOCK, Horses, Implements, &c.: One present Calving Heifer, one Gelt Cow in full milk, seven back-end Calving Cows, 10 grand Autumn Calving Heifers, two Fat Heifers, 20 capital Bulling Heifers, 15 very smart Back-end and this Spring Calves, 12 Scots, very fresh, two prime Scot Fat Calves, one capital fat two-year-old Bull, 12 three-parts bred Fat Lambs.

The HORSES consist of bay Cart Mare, aged, with foal at foot, quiet, and a good worker. Black mare, Moonbeam, five years old (Vol. 12), sire Maharajah, dam Honest Maid ; bred by T. H. Miller, Esq. ; quiet and a good worker ; served by Lancashire Lad. Brown Mare, Myra, three years ; sire Cressy, dam Sir John Falstaff ; a capital mover and quiet in all gear. Capital strong bay Yearling Gelding, by Blythe Echo. Brown half-bred Horse, aged ; quiet and a capital worker.

The IMPLEMENTS consist of Spring Lurry, in capital condition ; Horse Hay Rake, in good condition ; one-horse power Bone Sowing Machine, nearly new ; one Turnip Sower ; one double-furrow Plough ; Albion 2-horse Mowing Machine, in grand condition ; capital Bone Mill for steam power, nearly new, by Picksley, Sims, and Co. ; one 4-horse power Vertical Engine and Boiler, with Shafting, Pulleys, and all complete, nearly new ; Barrel Churn, for hand or steam power ; Butter Worker. Cream Separator, all in good condition, and supplied by the Aylesbury Dairy Co.

The Auctioneer has great pleasure in recommending the above Stock as being well bred, full of quality, hair, and condition, nearly all roans, and well worthy the attention of buyers of good stock. The late owner spared neither pains nor money in securing the best stock he could get.

For further particulars, apply to the FARM BAILIFF, or to the AUCTIONEER, Lightfoot House, Broughton.

Waggonettes will leave Mr. Potter's yard at 11 o'clock on the morning of sale.

Fig. 8.2 The *Preston Guardian*'s advertisement, Saturday 6 May, 1893 for the sale by auction of animals, implements etc. of Alston Hall Home Farm to be held on Wednesday 17 May.

in Brook Street. The Preston Directories for 1892 and 1895 lists Misses Hannah, Agnes, and Jane Wearing living at 9 Ribblesdale Place whilst for 1904 and 1910 only Hannah is listed.

A copy of the Will of Ellen's late husband was not to be found during researches so it is not possible to say if Ellen was to benefit money-wise or in any way after his death. Edmund's first-born son, Charles, who was to sell Deeping Waterton Hall in 1891, would have been the main benefactor because of his position as head of the family.

As to the path taken by Edmund's two youngest children of his former marriage Josephine and Thomas when Ellen left Deeping Waterton Hall, Josephine was in Preston in 1890 staying with Ellen in Ribblesdale Place in preparation for her marriage to Alfred Henry Harrison (of South Kensington) in St Wilfrid's Church in nearby Chapel Street. The wedding was to take place on 10 April of that year and the next day the *Preston*

Fig. 8.3 Alston Hall in about 1896 or soon afterwards. Sitting on the terrace are Ellen Mercer and her two daughters. At the open window of the rose bedroom is most probably the caretaker Elizabeth Pendlebury. (By kind permission of Longridge Town Archives)

Alston Hall Nr Longridge

Fig. 8.4 Number 9 Ribblesdale Place (the one for sale), Preston. This was the temporary home of Ellen Waterton in 1889 presumably whilst her two young daughters were being educated at the Catholic Convent in nearby Winckley Square.

Herald in publishing its report on the event would mention that owing to a celebration the marriage could not be solemnised at the high altar but took place at the altar of the Sacred Heart, beautifully draped and decorated with choice plants and flowers, a carpet being laid from the entrance of the church to the altar steps. The Rev. Father Payne performed the ceremony, the bridesmaids being Miss Agnes Waterton, Miss Harrison, Miss B. Harrison, Miss F. Harrison and Miss Monica Waterton, whilst the best man was Mr L. Harrison, cousin of the groom. Members of the wedding party were conveyed afterwards to the home of the bride in Ribblesdale Place.

In 1901 Josephine and Alfred were living at 20 Lansdowne Road, Wimbledon, with their daughter Angela (6) when Alfred was living on his own means. Alfred had been born at Felton, Sussex in 1866, the son of Daniel Alfred Harrison born in Grays Inn Road, London in 1835 and Mary Jane (nee Hardcastle) born in Australia in 1841. The Census of 1871, the year when Daniel was an owner of property and would become a bankrupt, found the Harrisons living at The Folly Lea House, Luton Road, Wheathampstead, near St Albans, Hertfordshire. With Daniel and his wife were their four daughters; Catherine (11), Emma (10), Mary J. (7), Mary A. (1), and three sons; Alfred (5), Herbert (4), and Reginald (2). Also listed was Arthur W. Kidd an assistant secretary; Mary A. Jones an assistant governess; two male servants of which one was eleven years of age; and three female servants, cook, nursemaid, and nurse.

November 1891 would find Alfred and Josephine at the County Ball in Bury St Edmunds at which the Duke of Clarence and his brother George the Prince of Wales attended. The large number of guests had been listed in groups to be in descending order, the foremost one listing those such as the Earl and Countess of Cadogan, Lady Emily Cadogan, Lady Sophia Cadogan who was making her debut, Lady Edith Ward, Lady Gertrude Molyneux, Lord Chelsea etc. Alfred and Josephine were to be listed in a group from The Hill, Stowmarket within which were Mr L. Harrison, Miss Agnes Waterton, Miss Mary Scrope, Miss Hammond, and Mr H. Scrope, the latter being a member of a family in which Ethelburga Waterton would become a part of in 1912 by marriage.

It seems that the marriage of Alfred and Josephine was not to be a happy one even though they were to have a daughter and a son, as by 1911 they were living apart. In that year whilst Josephine was with her daughter then sixteen and Ethelburga Waterton at Billing Hall in Northamptonshire (see later), Alfred was at Pathmore, in a two-room apartment accommodation in St John's Road, Hampton Wick, Surrey. He died years later in 1933 at Elm Dean, St Martin's Hill, Surbiton, not far from Wimbledon Common, his residential address at the time being Woodlands, Crooked Billet, Wimbledon Common. In his Will, Alfred was not to mention Josephine and as his son Alfreda had died, daughter Angela was to be the beneficiary of Alfred's Will.

In 1934 Josephine married retired army officer Major Charles Stourton Langdale at the Oratory in London, the wedding being reported as follows on 5 March:

> A service will be held on Thursday morning at the Brompton Oratory which will join in marriage two of the oldest families of England.

They are both Yorkshire, both Roman Catholic. For their beginnings we must go back, in the bridegroom's case to 1005, when the heiress of Sir Thomas Houghton brought Houghton to Patrick de Langdale; and, in the bride's, to Crusading days.

Cousin of Colonel Philip Langdale, the bridegroom, Major Charles Stourton Langdale, is also a relative of Lord Mowbray and Stourton, the premier baron. He is a grandson of the Hon. Charles Stourton, whose mother was a Langdale, and to whom a cousin, Mr. Philip Langdale, the then head of the Langdale family, left his estates and his surname.

Since the War, when he served with the West Riding Regiment and was badly wounded, losing a leg, Major Langdale has lived abroad mostly. His bride is Mrs Alfred Harrison, who before her marriage in 1890, at the age of nineteen, was Miss Josephine Everilda Waterton, of Walton Hall, Wakefield, and Deeping Waterton, Lincolnshire.

Fig. 8.5 St Wilfrid's Church, Chapel Street, Preston.

Mr. Edmund Waterton, her father, was Privy Chamberlain to Pope Pius 1X, and named all the children of his first marriage either Pius or Pia. His mother was descended from the Edmonstones who twice married into the Scottish Royal family, and one of his own daughters, half-sister to Major Langdale's bride, became a Scrope of Danby.

In 1946, the year before her death, Josephine made her Will whilst a resident in St George's Retreat (St Mary's care home), Burgess Hill, Ditchling Common, East Sussex. She would leave a mere £377. Her younger brother Thomas never married and in 1891 when 14 years of age was a boarder at Stonyhurst College. Ten years later he was 'living on his own means', the Census of 1901 finding him at the Whitewell Hotel not far from Stonyhurst whilst the next Census lists him as a boarder still living on his own means, at 3 Walton Parade, Preston. For his Will his address had been Burton Hill, Petworth, Sussex, and following his death on 15 January 1922 in the hospice of St Joseph's Hospital, Mount Street, Preston, probate amounted to £2,581 14s. 10d.

Josephine's sister Agnes Waterton who had been with her at the County Ball in Bury St Edmunds in November 1891, married Joseph George Sutcliffe in the following year. Joseph who had been to Clare College, Cambridge was a widower who had been born in Halifax, Yorkshire in 1854. In 1877 he had married Katherine Emma Georgina Willis in Great Yarmouth who died in 1890 aged 37, the third daughter of the Rev. H. M. Willis, the rector at Trimley St Mary near Felixstowe.

For the 1891 Census Joseph is residing at The Hollies, Ipswich Street, Stowmarket, with a young family of six; George A. W. (11) who died in 1901, Joseph W. G. (9), Mary Milgitta (7), Mary Monica (5), Edmund J. (4), and Mary Cuthberge M. (2). In the household were a cook domestic and two nurse domestics. Joseph's father, Joseph senior had married Mary Ellen Furness in Preston, Lancashire in 1853, the daughter of John Furness a flax spinner who lived at Spring Bank, Fishergate Hill, Preston. In 1861, the year he died, John (73) then a widower was residing at 4 Camden Place off Winckley Square in Preston.

On 13 March 1893, Ellen Waterton's father, John Mercer died aged 73 years at Alston Hall. For the past two years he had suffered from heart trouble and a year before his death this had developed into angina pectoris. Among those present at the death were his wife, daughter Ellen, Canon Taylor and Dr Taylor (nephew of John's wife). Shortly afterwards on 18 March the *Preston Chronicle* published John Mercer's obituary.

Fig. 8.6 Number 187 Queen's Gate (centre one in a terrace of three) Kensington, London, the home of Ellen Waterton and where she died in 1909.

Universal regret will be expressed at the loss which the community has sustained through the death of Mr. John Mercer, J.P, C.C., of Alston Hall, which occurred on Monday evening at his residence. The deceased gentleman was widely known, and held in very high esteem by all who were acquainted with him for his genial and benevolent

Fig. 8.7 The Brompton Oratory, London.

disposition. His health had been failing for about two years, but until a comparatively recent date he had been able to attend to business, and he was present at the County Council meeting in February. Within the past few weeks, however, his health broke down entirely, and the services of Dr. Hammond and Dr. Taylor had to be called in. Towards the close of last week his condition became critical, and he succumbed on Monday evening. Mr. Mercer was born at Elm Grove, St. Helens, on December 23rd, 1820, and was trained to his father's profession, that of a mining surveyor. Amongst the principal works of his earlier years was the laying out of a portion of the Caledonian line in Scotland. Returning to Lancashire he became associated with Mr. Wright, of Wigan, in the ownership of a colliery, and later, in conjunction with Mr. Evans and other gentlemen, he engaged in extensive colliery operations at Park-Lane, High Brook and other places in the neighbourhood of Wigan, and also in South Wales. Energetic, persevering, and clear-headed, he was wonderfully successful in business, and soon attained to a position of comparative affluence. Twenty-one years ago he purchased the Alston Hall estate, and built the fine mansion which now adorns it. He has continued to reside there since, and he took a warm interest in local affairs. Mr. Mercer was placed on the Commission of the Peace for the County on May 27th, 1869, and he has been for a number of years one of the most regular attenders on the magisterial bench at Preston. On the passing of the Local Government Act, 1888, he was chosen as representative of the Ashton-in-Makerfield division on the Lancashire County Council, a position which he continued to hold down to the time of his death. He was associated with several important committees, and rendered valuable services to the county in many ways. Mr. Mercer was twice married. His first wife (Miss Grove, of St. Helens), by whom he has issue one daughter (the widow of the late Edmund Waterton, son of the eminent naturalist), died some years ago. His second wife was Miss Taylor, sister of the Very Rev. Canon Taylor, of Lytham, formerly of Preston, and her two sons died a few years ago. She survives her husband, whom she nursed through his illness with loving solicitude. The funeral took place at the Alston Lane Catholic Church, on Thursday. Prior to the ceremony Requiem Mass was said in the beautiful domestic chapel of the Hall by the Very Rev. Canon Taylor, of Lytham, brother-in-law of the deceased. The cortège left the house for the church at 12 30. The Rev. Father Walton officiated at the graveside. Amongst those present at the last rites were the Very Rev. Canon Taylor, Very Rev. Dean Pyke, Rev. Father Gordon, and Rev. J. Taylor; Messrs H. Fairclough, W. Maybow, A. F. Evans, Edward Pyke, J.P., C. J.Clarke, Jackson, W. Ponthern, J. D. Swift, T. N. Thornton, W. F. Anderton, J.P., Dr. Taylor, Dr. Hammond, J.P., A. J. Speeden, H. Darlington, and H. J. Bromslow. Wreaths were sent by Dr. G. Taylor, Mr. W. F. Anderton, Mr. and Mrs. C. Brown, Mr. and Mrs. Thornton and family, Master John Taylor, Mr. and Mrs. Clarke, Mr. Nicholas Cockshutt, by loving nieces, Lytham, the men-servants at Alston Hall, Mr. Joseph Brown, the officials of the Garswood Coal and Iron Company, Mr. John Spencer, the officials and workmen from the colliery at Earlstown, the members of the Burtonwood Social

Club, and others. The arrangements were efficiently carried out by Messrs. W. Gray and Co., of Preston.

Four days later on 22 March the *Wigan Observer* would also publish an obituary similar to the Preston newspaper and to mention John and Helen Mercer's two sons:

––– who, to the profound grief of the parents, died early.

The Alston Hall estate was bought 21 years ago, and it is a fact worthy of record that had the eldest son lived he would have attained his majority this week. –––

–––. On the death of the boy, Mr. Mercer, who had spent large sums in improving the property, ceased to take any interest in extending the estate.

The Wigan report was also to mention the work John Mercer had done in connection with Lancashire's asylums:

He sat on the bench regularly at Preston, and he attended the meetings of the County Council when well; but his best work was on those committees on which he was elected, especially that controlling the county Asylums in the northern district.

This mention of John Mercer's involvement with county asylums in the northern district led to investigations to reveal that at one of these asylums, Whittingham, a short distance from Alston Hall, John Mercer in 1884 would instigate the building of a railway from the Preston and Longridge line to the mental hospital.

As industrialisation got underway in towns and cities during the first half of the nineteenth century, the appalling working and living conditions along with high birth rates that had a high percentage of illegitimacy would bring about considerable mental health problems among the working class populace.

At the beginning of the century Parliament had turned its attention to the question of pauper and criminal lunatics; the Lunatics (Paupers and Criminals) Act of 1808 giving local Justices the power to raise local rates to build asylums for housing both criminal lunatics detained 'during His Majesty's Pleasure' and pauper lunatics who could be transferred from poor houses. Unfortunately the Act was permissive and local Justices were usually loath to raise the rates 'unnecessarily'. Only nine authorities would

Fig. 8.8 Number 69 Grosvenor Street, Mayfair, London. At the time of Ellen Waterton's death this was the home of her stepdaughter Josephine Harrison.

take the opportunity to build asylums, one being Lancashire with the building of Lancaster Moor where the decision to build had been taken in 1809, the hospital opening in 1816.

More Acts would follow such as The Regulation, Care and Treatment of Lunatics Act of 1845 that required the provision of asylums for the care of pauper lunatics, and in 1853 legislation prohibiting restraining devices on lunatics in workhouses would lead to further calls for the mentally ill to be institutionalised.

Preston had erected a workhouse in its Deepdale district in 1778 as a replacement for one established in 1674 in the Avenham area, and by the 1860s the Deepdale workhouse could accommodate 480 and had a school for infants. It was a grim place having an inner yard where those fit enough were allowed to meet, truly a 'Bastille' of the poor. Conditions within were to be the subject of severe criticism following an inspection by Poor Law Inspector R. B. Cane in November 1866 who reported:

> This workhouse is old, ill arranged, and unsuitable in every respect for the purposes for which it is used, namely, the reception of all classes of poor.–––.

> Ventilation, in the proper sense of the term, can hardly be said to exist in any of the wards.

> The wards are for the most part dark, low, close, gloomy, and unhealthy; they are dangerously crowded with inmates, especially in the infirm and sick wards.

> Many of the infirm people, men as well as women, are sleeping together two in a bed. The sick have not all of them a separate bed to lie upon.

> In the "venereal ward" the patients affected with syphilis are sleeping together two in a bed.

> Two women, owing to a want of room, have lately been placed together in the same bed in the lying-in ward, both having just been confined.

> Four patients, two men and two boys, were lately sleeping together in the same bed in the "itch ward".

> Six men occupied two beds in this ward to-day,–––.

The "itch" he mentions was then the popular name for scabies, a contagious skin disease caused by a mite. Soon after Cane's visit in 1866 the workhouse was to be replaced by a new one erected in Watling Street Road, its foundation stone having been laid in 1869. This was the year that saw the building of an asylum at Whittingham, the asylum opening on 1 April 1873. It had been built in response to a growing shortage in space at the existing County Asylums at Lancaster, Prestwich near Manchester, and Rainhill near St Helens. These mental hospitals admitted patients from all over the county, so quite a number of patients were sent to Whittingham from the Manchester area, Liverpool area and Lancaster rather than to their own local asylums. Lancaster would build the Royal Albert, opened in 1870 as a hospital for children between the ages of 6 and 15 who had learning difficulties as distinct from the insane, and founded on the belief that after nine years of training and education these children would be able to leave and become active and useful members of society.

Fig. 8.9 The Mercer grave in the churchyard of the Catholic Church of Our Lady and St Michael, Alston, near Longridge.

The Whittingham asylum had 1,260 patients at the beginning of 1882 and 1,347 in the following year. By 1884 this had increased to 1,647, the year when John Mercer was a member of The Committee of Visitors at the asylum and in the minutes of the committee meeting held at the asylum on 25 June 1884 can be read:

> *Mr. Mercer laid before the Committee a plan for a proposed Railway Communication between the Asylum and the Grimsargh Railway Station.*

At this period, provisions for the asylum and coal for its gas works and boiler house were arriving by road transport. The conveyance of such provisions and coal by a railway would lower transport costs, and following John Mercer's idea for a railway it was:

> *Resolved that the further consideration of the Plan be deferred until the next meeting and that Mr. Mercer, Mr. Anderton, and Mr. Whittaker be appointed a Committee to consider the practicability and the expense of carrying it into effect.*

The committee mentioned was to be a four-man sub committee of which John Mercer with his past expertise and experience in railway construction was to be a member, this sub committee becoming known as the Tramway Sub Committee. It seems that the original idea of a railway line was to be changed to a horse-drawn tramway most probably due to the costs involved, as when the idea of a railway was first conceived there was much wrangling between the four-man committee and the hospital's finance and general purpose committee. Preston at this period had been operating horse-drawn trams for public transport for a number of years, but such a system would not appear on the Whittingham line.

Grimsargh Station mentioned was on the Preston & Longridge Railway line that had opened on May Day 1840, its primary function to transport stone from the quarries in Longridge to a deport at Ribbleton in Preston although it would be a passenger line as well. It was to be horse-drawn until 1848 when a steam locomotive was introduced, before which the loaded wagons descended from the quarries by gravity controlled by a brakeman. On reaching a suitable level from Longridge, the horses that had travelled with the train of wagons then provided the traction to Preston, and on Wednesdays and Saturdays two horse-drawn passenger trains ran each way. Intermittently the railway was seen as a key element in a number of schemes to link Fleetwood and Preston with Yorkshire and the North East but such schemes were not to materialise, and in 1866 the railway came under the joint ownership of the London & North Western Railway and the Lancashire & Yorkshire Railway.

When the four-man committee at Whittingham was established it had been calculated that the cost of the 2,863 yard standard gauge hospital line at £12,000 (to be reduced later to £9,000) would give an annual saving of £1,050 over road haulage. But this was conditional upon the London & North Western Railway and the Lancashire & Yorkshire Railway working the service to Whittingham who declined, but instead granted junction facilities with their main line at Grimsargh. On October 1st 1884, an application was made for a siding to connect the proposed Whittingham hospital line to Grimsargh station and it would be the alteration of the plans for the construction of the junction facilities at Grimsargh that would lead to the resignation of John Mercer as a member of the Tramway Sub Committee.

On Thursday the first day of April 1886, John Mercer was the chairman of a special meeting of the Committee of Visitors of the Whittingham Asylum held at the County Offices in Preston. At the meeting he reported the negotiations that had taken place between the Sub Committee and the owners and tenants of the lands required for the purposes of the new tramway from which it appeared that a general settlement could be affected without resort to Parliament.

A little over a year later on Wednesday 25 May 1887, the Committee of Visitors of the Whittingham Asylum met at the asylum at which John Mercer was present. Minutes of the meeting now in the Lancashire Archives, show that John Mercer would state that in consequence of the alteration of the plans for the construction of the junction of the tramway at Grimsargh Station whereby his rights as a neighbouring land owner would be seriously affected, he had decided to tender his resignation as a member of the Tramway Sub Committee.

It was resolved that his resignation be reluctantly accepted.

By 1888 the £9,000 allotted for the line had been almost spent and an application to the finance committee for £5,000 was made to complete the works and also to provide a locomotive and rolling stock to avoid the need for horse traction. Extra funding was provided and in March 1889 the permanent way was finished and traffic began running on the line in the following June. The first locomotive for the line was a new 0–4–0 wheel gauge saddle tank type engine purchased in 1888 from Andrew Barclay and Sons of Kilmarnock, at the same time two goods vans were ordered to make up its train. In 1889 the first four-wheel passenger carriage was purchased from the Lancaster Carriage and Wagon Company.

After the Second World War a direct bus service was provided to the Whittingham hospital leading to a reduction of passengers on its line that closed in 1957. Passenger services on the Preston to Longridge line had closed in 1930 and in 1967 its section from the Courtauld factory branch line at Redscar to Longridge was closed. Following the closure of Courtaulds in 1980 the line from Deepdale to the exchange sidings at Redscar was abandoned, and in 1994 the closure of the section from Maudland to Deepdale (opened in 1850) brought about the complete closure of the Preston to Longridge line. The Whittingham hospital closed in March 1995.

John Mercer would leave a considerable fortune, his estate being valued at a little over £129,000 (about £9 million today) as well as a number of legacies and annuities, but six days before his death he had made a codicil to drastically reduced the majority of them because of the depressed state of the coal industry where most of his investments lay, though his trustees were authorised to restore the original amounts if trade revived.

A few weeks after John's death, what had been his Alston Hall Home Farm (the Alston old Hall farm), its animals and implements were to be sold by auction on the instructions of the executors of John's Will, details appearing in the *Preston Guardian* newspaper of 6 May 1893. Behind the decision to sell the farm's animals and implements was given in the newspaper's advertisement (see fig. 8.2) as *on account of the above farm being let.*

By the terms of John Mercer's Will, the executors being Canon James Taylor of Lytham, Edward Pyke of Southport, and solicitor John Shaw Darlington of Wigan, Alston Hall was devised to his trustees to enable his widow Helen to live there if she so desired until her death, after which his daughter Ellen Waterton was to live there if she so wished until her death. John hoped that Ellen would remarry and have a son, but failing that, Alston Hall was to pass to *the first daughter of my said daughter Ellen, according to seniority by her late or any future husband.* An article in the *Morning Post* of 12 June 1893 in mentioning John Mercer's charitable bequests made interesting reading ending with the following:

The Alston Hall estate is settled upon Mrs. Mercer for her life and upon Mrs. Waterton for her life, and upon her first son who may attain the age of 21 years, or if there be no son who attains the age of 21 years, upon her daughter who first attains that age, and, on failure of these trusts, upon like trusts in favour of Mr. Mercer's niece, Mrs. Burrows, and her issue, and the residuary personal estate is to accumulate in trust for all the testator's grandchildren, or as the case may be, for all Mrs. Burrows's children on the succession of one of them to the Alston estate. If there should be no such successor the residue is bequeathed to the Roman Catholic Bishop of the diocese which includes Preston, for religious and charitable purposes.

Mrs Burrows mentioned above was Miss Burrows, the daughter of John Mercer's sister, Elizabeth Birch Mercer who in 1851 had married Henry Wilson Burrows, the wedding taking place on 9 August in Christ Church, Prescot. In 1871 Henry Burrows, a teacher of music was living in Booth Street, North Meols with his wife and two daughters, Mary J. (18) who died in that year and Elizabeth Frances (16). In the household run by three servants was also Henry's niece Martha (6). Ten years on Henry's wife was a widow, still living in Booth Street with daughter Elizabeth Frances and Henry's niece Martha.

In John Mercer's Will the bequests to the Roman Catholic Church were considerable. Canon Taylor who had been his brother-in-law was to receive £5,000 for the education of students for the priesthood, and £5,000 was to be given for religious and charitable purposes in connection with the Roman Catholic Church north of the river Ribble. However, if the diocese of the Roman Catholic Bishop of Liverpool should be divided, one third of the latter sum was to be applied for objects south of the Ribble and two thirds of it north of that river.

John Mercer was to bequeath to his wife Helen his horses and carriages and consumable stores, and the use and enjoyment for her life of his furniture and household effects along with the collection of preserved birds, animals and curiosities formerly belonging to Charles Waterton and given to John Mercer by his son-in-law, the late Edmund Waterton. Subject to Helen Mercer's life interest the contents of the Alston mansion were bequeathed to her stepdaughter Ellen for her life, and on her death to follow the trust of the settled real estate. Helen and Ellen were each to receive £1,000 reduced by a codicil to £500 as well as life annuities of £2,000 each reduced by the codicil to £1,500.

Canon Taylor and John Mercer's sister Mrs Mary Lupton along with John's niece Miss Elizabeth Frances Burrows were each to receive a life annuity amounting to £250 to be reduced to £200 by the codicil, but if Miss Burrows should become a tenant for life of the Alston estate her annuity was to be £2,000, reduced by the codicil to £1,500. John Mercer bequeathed to his cousin John Mercer, £100; to John Pendlebury who had been his coachman at 'The Woodlands', £50; to his domestic servants, £10 each; and to Edward Pyke and John Shaw Darlington for the trusteeship, £100 a year each.

By November 1895 Helen Mercer was seriously ill with diabetes, and her brother, Canon Taylor had cause to write a letter from Lytham to the Bishop of Liverpool requesting permission for her to have Holy Communion at Alston Hall.

Dated the 2nd of November, it begins with the mention of an oratory at Alston Hall, a document for the erection of which was hung up in the sacristy, and also a list of priests who were authorized to say Mass at the oratory if they so wished. The list did not mention permission for Holy Communion being given to members of the family or the domestics living at the Hall, so Canon Taylor therefore presumed that Holy Communion was not allowed at the Hall without permission from the Bishop.

The letter mentions that John Mercer was ill for a considerable time, and that the late Bishop had given permission for him to receive Holy Communion either in the Mass or after the Mass if he could not come down to the oratory, a time when Canon Taylor had given John Mercer Holy Communion. The letter was now asking for the same permission for Mrs Mercer who had been ill for some months and was now confined to her bedroom where she was expected to remain for some time.

Considering the difficulty in giving Helen Holy Communion during her sickness, Canon Taylor asked to be allowed to give her Communion as he had given it to her late husband. The letter continued, requesting if Dean Pike could do the same in case he went there when Canon Taylor was unable to, and the same for Dr O'Donoghue in case Canon Taylor asked him to.

It seems that permission was granted two days later on the 4th of November.

On 4 February 1896, Ellen's stepmother, Helen Mercer died aged 55 from diabetes and on the following Saturday the 8th, the *Preston Guardian* began Helen's obituary by saying:

> The news of the death of Mrs. Mercer, of Alston Hall, which occurred on Tuesday, will be received with great regret in the district, where she was well-known and highly respected as a benefactress of local charities.

On Friday 7 February at 11am the funeral cortège left Alston Hall, the hearse being the carriage of the undertakers, Messrs. Gray and Co., Fishergate, Preston. At the funeral service in Alston Lane Roman Catholic Church in which there were numerous and exquisite floral tributes, Mass was said by the Rev. Father Walton following which Helen's remains were laid to rest in the Mercer family grave.

Helen Mercer left effects amounting to precisely £2,039 5s., and would leave her diamond cross and earrings and her four best rings to Ellen who decided not to take up residence in Alston Hall but continued to live in Lytham. In the meantime the fully furnished Hall would have a caretaker and be frequently visited by Helen's brother, Canon James Taylor who had helped John Mercer in running the Alston estate.

John Mercer had been appointed as a county magistrate in May 1860 and would be a regular member of the Preston bench. When the first Lancashire County Council was elected at the end of 1888 he became the councillor for the Ashton-in-Makerfield ward in south Lancashire. His support for charitable causes was well known and in August 1910 the community of Downall Green near Ashton-in-Makerfield celebrated the outcome of one. Under the heading NEW CATHOLIC CHURCH AT DOWNALL GREEN, the *Wigan Observer* on the 24th of that month published the following:

> In the presence of 2,000 persons, Dr. Whiteside the Roman Catholic Bishop of Liverpool, on Sunday afternoon laid the foundation stone of a new Catholic Church at Downall Green, which is to be erected in memory of the late Mr. John Mercer, J.P., of Alston Hall, near Preston, founder of the Park Lane Collieries. A procession, numbering several hundred scholars, proceeded to the site of the new edifice, a large number of the clergy being in attendance. Among those present in addition to the Bishop were: Dean Sommer, St. Patrick's, Wigan; Dean Powell, Birchley; the Revs. Dr. Bennett and Father

O'Mears, Ashton-in-Makerfield; the Revs. Fathers Newsham and Swarbrick, Liverpool; the Rev. Dr. Kenny, Wigan; the Rev. Father Kelly, Blackbrook; the Rev. Father Walmesley, Haydock; the Rev. Father Smith, Pemberton; the Rev. Father Morgan, St. Helens; and the Rev. Father James Smith, Downall Green. In his address, Dr. Whiteside referred to the success which had attended the mission in a brief number of years, and stated that the late Mr. John Mercer, who had made his wealth in the district as a colliery proprietor, had left £6,000 towards the erection of the church. The building, with a presbytery, would cost something like £10,000, and he appealed to Roman Catholics in the district to give generously in order that the remaining £4,000 might soon be obtained by their priest.

In 1901 Ellen Waterton was still at 3 West Beach, Lytham, enjoying the clean air of this elegant seaside town, and with her were her cousin Elizabeth Frances Burrows, Evelyn Mary Kathleen Power a companion, and six servants, one being described as a lady's maid. At Alston Hall Elizabeth Pendlebury, the widow of John Mercer's coachman, was in residence as caretaker with her three teenage children. This was the year when Ellen's two daughters Monica and Ethelburga, now teenagers, were boarders being educated in the Catholic school belonging to the religious Community of the Sacred Heart at Stanwix, Carlisle, Cumberland, founded in the nineteenth century.

Unfortunately only two photographs of Ellen have come to light in researches, the one of her on the terrace at Alston Hall soon after the mansion had been built with her father, stepmother and step grandmother (fig. 2.2), and the one with her daughters Ethelburga and Monica sitting alongside the same terrace years later, probably in c.1896 following the death of her stepmother (fig. 8.3).

Monica would shortly extend her education with the nuns of the Sacred Heart at Haywards Heath in Sussex, and in 1905 at the age of 21 entered Holy Orders to become a nun at the Convent of the Holy Child Jesus, Mayfield, in East Sussex, and was professed (to be received into the religious Order) on 14 September 1907.

The Society of the Holy Child Jesus was an international community of Roman Catholic nuns founded in England in 1846 by American born (Philadelphia) Cornelia Connelly who had converted to Catholicism in 1835. Since the beginning of the Reformation period in the first half of the sixteenth century there had been a ban on Roman Catholic convents until the passing of the Catholic Reformation Act of 1829 that brought about a much awaited programme of new convent building of which the Society of the Holy Child Jesus would be much associated with.

One of the priorities of the Society was the education of girls and in 1846 Cornelia Connelly escorted a small group of them from the Society's school in St Leonard's-on-Sea to the idyllic village of Mayfield which lay fourteen miles away to the northeast where they apparently had a picnic beside the derelict remains of a building known as the 'Old Palace'. During the fourteenth and fifteenth centuries this had been the holiday retreat of the Archbishops of Canterbury, and following the Reformation Henry VIII had given it to his leading noblemen of the day. Eventually the Old Palace building came under the ownership of the Baker family who were in the local iron industry, and following the decline of this industry along with the fortunes of the Bakers, the Old Palace had become abandoned by the mid eighteenth century to remain derelict.

During her visit to the 'Old Palace' buildings and its estate Cornelia Connelly was to be impressed by the site in that it would make an ideal location for a new convent and school. Soon afterwards the Duchess of Leeds would purchase the buildings and estate land, eventually presenting them to Connelly's Society of the Holy Child Jesus, and on 28 May 1863 Mother Cornelia Connelly formed a school for her Society there and November saw Mass being celebrated on the site for the first time since the Reformation of the sixteenth century. New building began in 1864 and by 1866 a part of the buildings had been designed as a school for girls by the Catholic architect Edward Welby Pugin, son of A. W. N. Pugin, 1872 witnessing young girls from the school in St Leonard's been brought over to Mayfield to continue their education. The development of the school at Mayfield continued and in order to meet the needs of a growing number of pupils another school was added in 1897. In 1953 the school at Mayfield and the one in St Leonard's merged to form St Leonard's–Mayfield School with pupils up to the age of 13 remaining in St Leonard's before being transferred to Mayfield to continue their education until 18.

Soon after being professed in September 1907, Monica had decided or perhaps had been advised to become a teacher within her Order. Following a Report of 1895 of a Secondary Education Commission, it was seen that Catholic high schools needed to operate on efficient lines, and therefore it was necessary for teachers in these schools to have gained a teaching diploma. The outcome of the Report was the establishment of a Catholic Teacher Training College in Cavendish Square, London in which Monica would be based; her first post as a student teacher being at her Order's school in St Leonard's in 1908.

In about 1907 Monica's mother, Ellen Waterton had moved to London most probably to be near her daughter's teacher training college whereby she could offer Monica support towards her new venture. At 8 Embankment Gardens, Chelsea on 31 January 1908 shortly after the death of her step uncle Canon Taylor at Alston Hall in the same month, Ellen signed her Will in the presence of her parlour maid Mary Josephine Cullen and her house maid Annie McAree, appointing Nicholas Cockshutt, Barrister-at-Law of Preston and Joseph Pyke of Southport, corn merchant, as her trustees and executors.

Embankment Gardens was in a prestigious area of residences, presumably available on a leasehold arrangement and situated immediately off the Chelsea Embankment of the Thames between Battersea Bridge and Albert Bridge. A little to the west on the river's embankment was Swan House of 1876 by Richard Norman Shaw, the well-known architect of the period, the two 'swans' on its entrance door still to be seen today.

Soon afterwards Ellen would move again this time to the South Kensington area of London to reside at 187 Queen's Gate close to the Royal Albert Hall and nearer to Cavendish Square. This particular area of Kensington had been developed from the 1850s onwards to create a cultural centre for the arts and sciences of which Prince Albert, the husband of Queen Victoria would be the instigator before his premature death in 1861. From some of the profits of the Great Exhibition of 1851 held in nearby Hyde Park, a Royal Commission had purchased eighty-seven acres of the Gore Estate that was southwest of the park for the proposed scheme. Soon upper-class housing began to appear on three sides of a rectangle bounded on the west by Queen's Gate, on the east by what would become Exhibition Road, and Cromwell Road to the south; the area to be known as 'Albertopolis'. Following the death of Prince Albert a memorial to him would be erected in Kensington Gardens off Kensington Gore whilst within the rectangle mentioned above, the Royal Albert Hall was to be built between 1867–71, the Natural History Museum between 1873–81, followed by the Imperial Institute of 1887–93 which unfortunately save for its impressive tower was demolished from 1956 onwards to be replaced by the Imperial College of Science and Technology.

A visit to Queen's Gate on 21 August 2016 to locate number 187 found the house being the middle one of three making up a short terrace between Bremner Road and Prince Consort Road, number 187 being the

Embassy of the Republic of Bulgaria. Erected in the Italianate style and stucco clad, each dwelling was to have a basement with six floors above, the uppermost one presumably at one time offering attic accommodation for servants. When built in the nineteenth century and perhaps the time when Ellen was in residence, the first two floors of each dwelling would have accommodated reception rooms whilst the occupancy of the building would be available on what was known as the London leasehold system.

London houses of this type were to be erected on lands once owned by the monasteries, lands that following the Reformation passed into the ownership of the aristocracy, and to preserve the family inheritance houses built on these settled estates in the Victorian period were subjected to this leasehold arrangement. The Grosvenor Estate for example, which had large areas of land east of Park Lane and where Mayfair and Knightsbridge would come under housing development, had a policy of locating large family homes there whereby the incoming nouveaux-riches of the 1850s onwards could compete with the aristocracy for such prime sites.

Queen's Gate where Ellen lived for a short time was to be South Kensington's grand boulevard created in the 1850s with the co-operation of the 1851 Commissioners, H. B. Alexander and the 5th Earl of Harrington. All the important Victorian architects and builders were involved, the southern section being added in the 1870s. Like number 187 many of these grand houses were Italianate in style clad in white or cream stucco, but the demand for such palatial family multi-storey homes began to fall off and by the late 1870s a number lay unoccupied, some to be converted into flats, hotels, schools and embassies

Ellen Waterton died on 10 January 1909 aged 53 at her Queen's Gate home after having contacted influenza that brought on pneumonia then heart failure, the name of Josephine Harrison, Ellen's stepdaughter of 69 Grosvenor Street, Mayfair, being on the death certificate registered on 13 January. Ellen's body was conveyed to the nearby Brompton Oratory on the Monday evening where it reposed for the night prior to its journey to Preston the following morning and then to Alston. Such an arrangement was appropriate in recognition to what had been Ellen's strong allegiance to the Roman Catholic Church and the widow of a Privy Chamberlain to the Pope.

Following Requiem Mass at the Oratory, Ellen's remains left London in a special saloon attached to the ten o'clock train from Euston, her daughter Ethelburga, cousin Elizabeth Burrows, Misses Power, who would be the sisters Eva and Augusta, (see later), and stepdaughter Josephine, being amongst the group accompanying the body on its journey to Lancashire. Ellen's remains arrived at 2.41pm in Preston to be received at the station by Dean O'Reilly (Lytham), Fr Almond also of Lytham, Rev. Dr O'Donoghue (Wigan), Fr Prescott (St Augustine's, Preston), Fr Taylor (St Thomas of Canterbury and English Martyr's, Preston), Mr Joseph Cockshutt (Ellen's solicitor), Mr Cuthbert Pyke (of Lostock Hall), Mr Titus Thorp, and others.

Later that afternoon at the burial service at the Catholic Church in Alston, the rector, Fr Bridges conducted the last rites following which Ellen was interred in the grave of her father and stepmother. On the same day the *Lancashire Evening Post* was to pay a tribute to Ellen, part of the tribute reading:

> *Mrs. Waterton, who was the owner of the Alston Hall estate, has lived a retired life, and is known chiefly by her numerous benefactions in this and other parts of the country. She has contributed largely to various charitable objects that appealed to her, and in this diocese she has been the means of establishing two new missions.*

On 15 April 1909 Ellen's Will went to probate, her trustees and executors still being Nicholas Cockshutt, Barrister-at-Law of 23 West Cliff, Preston, and Joseph Pyke of 'Merton Bank', Southport, the Will showing that the gross value of the estate amounted to £56,962 12*s*. Ellen was to leave £500 to the Superioress for the time being of Oulton Abbey, *in return for the kindness shewn to me when at the said Convent.*

Initially Oulton Abbey had been Oulton House in 1720 built for Thomas Dent a solicitor. The house was added to in 1822 and in the 1830s was occupied by the Duke of Sutherland while Trentham Hall was under construction. In 1838 Oulton House became a private asylum until 1853 following which the house was acquired by an Order of Benedictine nuns.

The Order had been founded in Brussels in 1597 and would be re-established in Ghent in 1624 for English nuns. In 1797 the nuns were forced to flee the Continent and initially settled in Preston before moving to Caverswall Castle near Oulton in 1811. There, A. W. N. Pugin was consulted to design a church for the Order but the moated site proved too small and the nuns moved to Oulton House in 1853, where the Abbess Lady Juliana Forster commissioned A. W. N. Pugin's son, Edward Welby Pugin, then aged just nineteen, to design a church for the new abbey. It was to be one of his first commissions, the church opening in 1854 and consecrated in 1856. During the nineteenth and twentieth centuries the nuns ran a small boarding girls' school in the house, and after this closed in

1968 the house was a retreat centre until 1989 when the house became Our Lady and St Benedict's Nursing and Residential Home.

In September 2018 a letter was sent to Oulton Abbey enquiring when and why Ellen Mercer had been there. A reply dated 8 April 2019 came from Geoffrey Scott the archivist of Douai Abbey, Upper Woolhampton, Reading, who in apologising for the delay in replying to my letter explained that the archives of the English Benedictine nuns of Oulton Abbey had recently been deposited in the Douai Abbey library when he was handed my letter. He explained that the records of the Oulton Abbey School that the nuns had run were not extensive but did include registers and in one he had found a reference to Ellen Mercer. Someone had cut out a part of the reference as indicated below, the comments in brackets being those of Mr Scott.

> *Ellen Mercer September 1864 (presumably entry date), daughter of John Mercer of Alston Hall, Lancs. Charles Waterton, her father-in-law, was nephew of Lady (entry cut, but it might be a nun of Oulton – Abbesses were addressed as 'Lady', a Lady in her own right), –––.*

If Ellen did enter the convent school in September 1864 it would be a sad and traumatic time for her, especially as a minor, the date being the same month and year when her uncle and mother died. As mentioned earlier in chapter one, her father married again in 1866, and in 1871 aged fifteen Ellen was one of seventy nine girls boarding at the Convent of Notre Dame on the side of Clapham Common, London. Nothing has been found to say if she would ever experience a long-term residency at Alston Hall in a happy family environment.

In Ellen's Will, (see below) Mrs Elizabeth Pendlebury a widow with three children and the caretaker at Alston Hall during the Census of 1901 is mentioned. She had married Peers (or Piers) Pendlebury who had been the coachman at Alston Hall in 1881 and coachman and groom in 1898. He died in 1900 and was the son of John Pendlebury who had been John Mercer's coachman at the 'The Woodlands'. Three servants, Maria Healey, widow; Margaret Austin, spinster; and Mary Dixon, widow, were also to be mentioned.

When Ellen had made her Will in January 1908 at 8 Embankment Gardens, Chelsea, the spinster sisters Eva Mary Kathleen Power and Augusta Mary Catherine Power were living with her. Both were to be mentioned in the Will. Little has been found regarding the early life of the two sisters except that in 1881 when Eva was 6 and Augusta 4 they were with their brother Arthur K. (7) and widowed mother Catherine J. (41) living on an income in Norton Road, Hove, near Brighton where two servants were employed. In 1911 the two sisters were residing at 7 Alexandra Square, Kensington, the Census of that year recording them as lodgers.

The Will was to be presented in the usual jargon of solicitors and devoid of punctuation for which one has included to make easy reading, and following the introductory part it read:

> ---. I give, devise, and bequeath all my real and personal estate and effects whatsoever and wheresoever, and of what nature or kind soever unto my said Trustees upon the trusts hereinafter expressed that is to say, to pay the following legacies namely: To the Roman Catholic Bishop of the Diocese of Liverpool the sum of five thousand pounds for such uses in the said Diocese as he may think fit and the sum of two thousand pounds to the said Roman Catholic Bishop in addition for uses for poor Missions in the said Diocese at his discretion. To my stepdaughter Agnes Mary Sutcliffe one thousand pounds. To my stepdaughter Josephine Mary Harrison one thousand pounds. To the Superioress for the time being of Oulton Abbey five hundred pounds in return for the kindness shewn to me when at the said Convent. To the Superioress for the time being of the following Institutions namely Saint Josephs Orphanage, Theatre Street, Preston, aforesaid five hundred pounds. To the Little Sisters of the Poor, Fulwood, Preston, aforesaid one hundred pounds. To the Convent of the Sisters of Nazareth, Lancaster, one hundred pounds. To the Treasurer of the Lancashire Secular Infirm Clergy Fund, twenty five pounds. To Frances Burrows late of Lytham, Spinster, five hundred pounds. To my old Servants: Mrs Pendlebury, Widow, one hundred pounds, and if she predeceases me I direct my Trustees to pay this sum equally to all her children or if they or any of them be infants to apply the same or such portion thereof as they may think fit for the maintenance or benefit of such infant children. To Maria Healey, Widow, fifty pounds. To Margaret Austin, Spinster, fifty pounds, and to Mary Dixon, Widow, the sum of fifty pounds. As to the sum of five thousand pounds I direct my Trustees to pay the income thereof to Eva Mary Kathleen Power, now residing with me, Spinster, during her life free of duty, and as to the sum of one thousand pounds I direct my Trustees to pay the income thereof to Augusta Mary Catherine Power now residing with

me, Spinster, during her life free of duty such sums of five thousand and one thousand pounds to form part of my residuary estate at their respective deaths. As to the rest, residue and remainder of my real and personal estate, I direct my Trustees to divide the same into two equal parts or shares and to pay the income of such equal parts or shares equally (subject as hereinafter mentioned) to each of my daughters Monica and Ethelburga during their lives, or to the survivor of them if one be dead for the life of such survivor, and if my said daughters or either of them shall die leaving issue in trust, to hold her equal part or share for such issue in equal shares as tenants in common as well as the share of such other daughter who shall die without issue, and if both of my said daughters shall die without issue, then the residue shall be paid to the said Bishop for the said Diocese of Liverpool for such uses in his said Diocese as he may think fit, and I hereby direct that if either of my said daughters should have become or hereafter become a professed nun, I direct my Trustees to pay to the Superioress of her Order the sum of five thousand pounds and thereafter the income of such daughter so becoming a professed nun shall be paid to the daughter who may not be a professed nun for her life or until she also becomes a professed nun, and if both my said daughters should have become of hereafter become professed nuns I direct my Trustees to pay the income of my residuary estate to the said Bishop of the said Diocese for uses in the said Diocese as he may decide whilst they be nuns, but if either or both of my said daughters should through ill health or any other cause leave the convent I direct my Trustees to pay the income of my residuary estate in the same manner as they would have done had my daughter or daughters respectively not become professed nuns namely to both daughters equally if they should leave as aforesaid or to one daughter only if she should leave as aforesaid if the other should remain a nun and whilst such other daughter so remain a nun.

The Will then mentioned that all moneys to be invested under the Will were to be invested in Public Stocks or Funds or Government securities including any railway or other limited company, and securities of any municipal Corporation, such investments to be at the discretion of the Trustees. As to Ellen's furniture, jewels, articles of personal use or adornment, or other effects in or about her home at the time of her death or stored in any other place by her, the Will was to state:

I direct my Trustees to deal with such in any way my said daughters may in writing request including the right and power to give the same or any part or parts thereof to my said daughters or either of them if requested as aforesaid.

On 5 November 1909 some seven months after the probate proceedings of Ellen's Will, an article appeared in the *Manchester Courier* with a main heading PRESTON LAWSUIT SETTLED under which was the heading ALL IMPUTATIONS WITHDRAWN to read as follows:

In the Chancery Division, on Tuesday, Mr. Justice Parker had before him an action brought with reference to a settlement executed by Ethelburga Mary Pega Waterton, of Alston Hall, near Preston. On the case being called, Mr. Clauson, representing the plaintiff, said he was happy to say that his Lordship would not be troubled, as the plaintiff and defendant had taken the advice of their respective counsel, and had arranged terms of settlement. Mr. Grant, K.C., Mr. Methold, and Mr. Lindon Riley represented the defendant, and they proposed to take an order in the terms that had been agreed between counsel. He desired to say as little about the matter as possible, but it was necessary to state that the action arose out of the execution of a settlement by a young lady. It was a voluntary settlement, and was executed shortly after she attained 21.

Mr. Grant said that terms had been come to, and his client was perfectly willing to carry out his part of them.

Mr. Clauson said that it was necessary for him to state publicly that on behalf of his client he unconditionally withdrew all charges or imputations that might have been made against the defendant in the pleadings, and he wished to state most emphatically that there was no suggestion of any dishonesty whatsoever against the defendant, as that was absolutely in accordance with the facts. He had no difficulty whatever in taking that course.

His Lordship made an order staying all proceedings in accordance with the terms of the schedule.

We will probably never know the details of the lawsuit. A visit to the old and the new law courts in Preston to see if a transcript of the lawsuit was available for inspection proved unsuccessful. I was informed that if such had been saved and stored it eventually would have been destroyed after a certain time span had elapsed.

Clearly the lawsuit had been about Ethelburga who having been denied a fortune due to 'order of birth' was unhappy with a part of her mother's Will. With regard to the terms that had been agreed in the lawsuit, Mr. Grant's client who *was perfectly willing to carry out his part of them* presumably was a trustee of the Will. It would seem that the issue that had been raised possibly bore reference to the part of the Will that stated:

> *––– I hereby direct that if either of my said daughters should have become or hereafter become a professed nun, I direct my Trustees to pay to the Superioress of her Order the sum of five thousand pounds and thereafter the income of such daughter so becoming a professed nun shall be paid to the daughter who may not be a professed nun for her life or until she also becomes a professed nun, –––*

As Monica's sister Ethelburga had not become a nun, then as the Will clearly outlined, the Trustees were to pay five thousand pounds to the Superioress of Monica's Order, following which what would have been Monica's income had she not become a professed nun, Ethelburga was now to receive.

Some years later in 1917 when Alston Hall and the land and farms on its estate came up for sale, Ethelburga was mentioned in part 14 of the Special Conditions of Sale as a tenant for life under a trust or power of sale in a certain Indenture of Settlement. Was this the Settlement mentioned in the lawsuit? A portion of part 14 of the Special Conditions of Sale of 1917 written in legal terms and therefore devoid in places of punctuation is presented below, Lot 2 being Alston Hall.

> *As to Lot 2 Miss Monica Mary Collette Paula Waterton is entitled in fee simple and as to the remainder of the property Miss Monica Collette Paula Waterton is entitled in fee simple to one undivided moiety thereof and Messrs. Cuthbert Pyke, Titus Thorp and Edward Joseph Blackett are entitled in fee simple to the other undivided moiety thereof as Trustees of a certain Indenture of Settlement and are selling the same with the consent of Mrs. Ethelburga Mary Magdalen Pega Scrope the tenant for life under a trust or power of sale in the said Settlement. By an Agreement dated the Fifth day of July, 1917, made between the said Monica Collette Paula Waterton of the 1st part the said Ethelburga Mary Magdalen Pega Scrope of the 2nd part and the said Cuthbert*

Pyke, Titus Thorp and Edward Joseph Blackett of the third 3rd part it has been agreed that Lot 2 and the rest of the property shall be sold together and that if the property shall be sold in one lot the purchase money and the cost of the sale shall be apportioned between Lot 2 and the rest of the property in the proportions which the reserve fixed for Lot 2 in the case of a sale in several lots and the aggregate of the reserve prices fixed for the rest of the property respectively bear to the whole of the purchase money. A copy of the said Agreement can be inspected by appointment at the office of Messrs. Titus Thorp & Ainsworth aforesaid a week before the sale. The Purchaser shall be deemed to have full notice of the contents of the said Agreement.–––

In July 1917 Alston Hall and its estate were sold to William Birtwistle, a local cotton manufacturer, for £23,000 (see chapter 14).

Today the Mercer memorial in the graveyard of Alston Catholic Church bears the inscription:

OF YOUR CHARITY
PRAY FOR THE SOUL OF
JOHN MERCER
OF ALSTON HALL
WHO DEPARTED THIS LIFE 13th MARCH 1893
AGED SEVENTY TWO YEARS
ON WHOSE SOUL SWEET JESUS HAVE MERCY
R.I.P.

HELEN MERCER
WHO DEPARTED THIS LIFE FEBRUARY 4th 1896
ON WHOSE SOUL SWEET JESUS HAVE MERCY
R.I.P.

OF YOUR CHARITY
PRAY FOR
THE REPOSE OF THE SOUL OF
ELLEN WATERTON
DAUGHTER OF
JOHN MERCER
WHO DIED JANUARY 10th 1909
AGED 53 YEARS
ON WHOSE SOUL SWEET JESUS HAVE MERCY
R.I.P.

Chapter nine

Canon James Taylor

After the death of Helen Mercer at Alston Hall, her brother, Canon James Taylor, who in 1901 was living at 2 Clifton Street, the Presbytery of St Peter's R.C. Church in Lytham, would occasionally stay at the Hall, but eventually suffering acutely from gout would take up permanent residency, dying there suddenly on 3 January 1908. He was buried in the cemetery he had founded at Lytham on land given by the Clifton family, and in his Will, left £21,815. When Marion Roberts was researching her book on Alston Hall during the early 1990s, old local residents could remember him shooting game on the Alston estate at the back end of the year.

The day after his death the *Lancashire Evening Post* in mentioning his passing paid a tribute to him, commenting that although formerly of St Peter's, Lytham, he owing to indisposition and inability to continue priestly office had been living in retirement at Alston Hall. He had been the *fidus Achates* of Dr Bilsborrow the Bishop of Salford, and both as lovers of the pedigree shire horse had attended exhibitions in London and large provincial shows. Also mentioned was that Monsignor Taylor was best known as an administrator and his pulpit addresses were remarkable for brusque admonition in plain Lancashire phrase. A few months later on 9 July the same newspaper would mention the sale of the shire horses at stud farm, Alston.

James Taylor and John Mercer had been good friends. During one period John Mercer would undertake a tour of America taking James Taylor with him and on their return James would give lectures about the trip illustrated with 'limelight' views of the principal sights. James as a Fylde man coming from an old family of farmers, would help John Mercer to become involved with the breeding of shire horses of which the Alston stud would win many honours not only locally but nationally. In Lancashire the breeding of the shire horse, initially referred to as the cart horse was pioneered by the third Earl of Ellesmere at Worsley Hall near Manchester in 1869, who was to be behind the founding of the English Cart Horse Society in 1878.

By this time the breeding of cart horses had become a popular and in some cases a necessary venture on many country house estates, a time when agriculture was in a depressive state. One of the causes of the depression was the import of cheap priced wheat grown on the vast prairie lands of North America to be sold in Britain at prices well below that at which British-grown corn could be marketed. Many British farmers became bankrupt and buying prices for agricultural land would fall at an alarming rate. This is why James Taylor with his farming background would encourage John Mercer to buy land in Alston at a time when such was going cheap, thereby increasing the acreage of the Hall's estate. Mother nature would also take a hand in damaging British agriculture at this time with rains and bad harvests, 1879 being the wettest year on record. Adding to this were outbreaks of foot and mouth disease and also liver-rot in sheep.

The breeding of cart horses not only for farm work but also for urban duties suddenly became a profitable enterprise for those farms and country estates that were to survive the depression. At Alston Hall what had presumably had been a sideline the breeding programme began in earnest when James Taylor would bring in Robert Singleton, a gifted and dedicated horseman as farm bailiff. A number of pedigree horses were purchased as foundation stock for the breeding programme, one being 'Cambridge Sally' bred in the Fens and to be sired by 'Scylax' owned by Thomas Shaw of Winmarleigh. In 1890 the mare gave birth to 'Alston Sally' the Hall's first home-bred foal. After John Mercer's death, James Taylor and Robert Singleton continued with the breeding tradition at Alston selling a mare called 'Alston Rose' to Lord Rothschild of Tring Park, a horse that was to be declared champion mare at the London Shire Horse Show of 1901 and 1902. Kept for many years at Alston Hall was a silver cup that had been awarded at the Garstang Agricultural Show to the executors of John Mercer for 'the Best Yearling Filly in "Alston Violet", 1898'. The cup was returned to the committee of the Show in 2017.

At 14 years of age James Taylor had begun his studies for the priesthood at Ushaw College, Durham, being ordained in 1858. In December 1863 he was appointed to establish the mission of St Thomas of Canterbury and English Martyrs in Preston, and on 21 May 1866, the church's foundation stone was laid, an event that saw a crowd of ten thousand attending. The church (to be known locally as 'English Martyrs') was erected in what was to become a heavily populated and poor area well to the north of the town centre, and after a mammoth fund-raising campaign, the Rev. James Taylor opened it in December 1867. A tall tower planned to stand on the southwest corner of the site, unfortunately was not to be built.

During the 1830s and 1840s as the textile industry in Preston expanded, a massive development of terraced house building gradually spread northwards from the St Peter's area north of the town centre down to the bottom of the Moor Brook valley along which Aqueduct Street would be constructed. Today, buildings of the University of Central Lancashire have long since been erected upon the sites of these working class homes that existed amid streets such as Nelson Street, Victoria Street, Gordon Street etc. By the 1850s plans for further housing development were underway on land north of the Moor Brook, the area under consideration amounting to about one hundred and seventy acres belonging to Henry Myres of Buckinghamshire, land enough for 1,800 homes. Many of these

Fig. 9.1 Church of St Thomas of Canterbury and English Martyrs, Preston.

houses would be 'two up and two downers' (two bedrooms upstairs and a sitting room and a kitchen downstairs) with the smallest of rear yards possible under building regulations. By the 1860s this area of once open land had been transformed into a grid pattern of terraced streets such as Barlow Street, Hammond Street, Havelock Street, etc. It was with the large Catholic populace of this area in mind that the Bishop, the Rev. George Gillow, asked the Rev. James Taylor to establish the Church of St Thomas of Canterbury and English Martyrs.

Erected on the corner of St George's Road and Garstang Road, the church was designed by Edward Welby Pugin (1834–1875), the son of A. W. N. Pugin mentioned in chapter three. After the death of his father, Edward continued with many of his father's commissions, one being for Ushaw College. During his studies at Ushaw, James Taylor would have admired the work there of Edward W. Pugin and this is probably why Edward was chosen to be the architect of the Preston church.

Edward was to have an office in Liverpool as well as the one in London and would design more than seventy churches in England and Scotland and in addition, schools, convents and presbyteries. He would also have an Irish practice. Amongst his notable works in the North West were to be All Saints Church, Barton-upon-Irwell, Manchester and Gorton Monastery, Manchester.

In Ramsgate where his father had designed the 'Grange', Edward was to undertake a number of architectural commissions for the expanding town. In 1867, along with others interested in a good business proposition, he purchased land for the erection of a commodious row of terraced homes, the following year seeing the beginning of their conversion into what was to be known as the Granville Hotel. Although a success for the town, the building of the hotel was to be the immediate cause for Edward's bankruptcy in 1872. Not long afterwards he went to the United States where he was to have a number of commissions. Even though he was engaged three times, Edward never married and died in London in 1875 and was interred in the tomb of his farther in St Augustine's Church, Ramsgate.

Edward's father married three times. His first wife Anne Garnet (or Garnett) died after giving birth to a daughter, Anne. His second wife Louisa Burton who died of rheumatic fever had five children, Edward, Agnes, Cuthbert, Catherine and Mary. Soon after the death of Louisa, A. W. N. Pugin married Jane Knill who gave birth to Margaret followed by Edmund Peter, later known as Peter Paul who became Edward's practice partner before Edward's unexpected death in 1875.

Fig. 9.2 Canon James Taylor outside St Peter's Church, Lytham.

After Edward's death, Peter Paul and Edward's brother, Cuthbert Welby Pugin represented the firm of Pugin & Pugin until 1880 when Cuthbert retired to become a 'sleeping partner'. Peter Paul continued the practice on his own still under the name of 'Pugin & Pugin' until his death in 1904, during which time he had been the architect of several churches in the North West including the Church of Our Lady of 1880 in Higher Walton Road, Walton-le-Dale near Preston. In 1888 he added transepts and an apse to Edward's Church of St Thomas of Canterbury and English Martyrs in Preston, and in 1894 enlarged Edward's Church of the Sacred Heart of 1857 in Talbot Road, Blackpool, with the addition of a crossing at the east end with its impressive octagonal lantern. After 1904 the firm of 'Pugin & Pugin' and its connection with the North West continued in the hands of Sebastian Pugin Powell (1866–1949), (the son of Anne Pugin and John Hardman Powell) and his cousin Charles Henry Cuthbert Purcell (1874–1958).

The Rev. James Taylor became a Canon in 1873 and was sent as Rector to St Augustine's R.C. Church, Preston. In recognition for the work he had done in establishing the Church of St Thomas of Canterbury and English Martyrs in Preston, he was presented during the evening of Tuesday 7 April 1874 with an illuminated address and a gold chalice before a congregation of about 1,500 in the Preston Corn Exchange in Lune Street, which became the Public Hall in the 1880s. The illuminated address was the work of H. Rielly, lithographer of Fenwick Street, Liverpool, whilst the chalice was the work of goldsmith Mr Thomason of Birmingham.

An account of this presentation evening mentions Canon Taylor having been given the task of establishing a Catholic mission in the north of Preston in the stable of a cottage a little to the north of where the new Church of St Thomas of Canterbury and English Martyrs was to be erected. The cottage was presumably the one shown on the town map of the 1840s, on the corner of Garstang Road with what would be eventually Ripon Street. Opposite the little Catholic mission would be the entrance lodge of the newly formed Moor Park on land that had previously been a part of Fulwood Moor where the last horse races had taken place in 1833, land to be enclosed in 1834 for the new park. Opening day for the mission church was 22 January 1865, a time when Preston was still in the dreadful grips of the Cotton Famine. Two services were held, one during the day then the evening, the total collection amounting to £33 10s.

There is no doubt that during his work in the Cotton Famine years to establish his mission church, James Taylor would have seen at first hand the appalling conditions the working class population of Preston had to suffer. In fact the Preston Guild of 1862 was the most controversial of all the guilds to date, much condemnation being focused on the lavished celebrations planned for the town's well-off minority while the majority of its citizens were unemployed and destitute. Such experiences must have spurred James Taylor on towards his goal at a time when the town's Catholics were beginning to re-establish and present themselves to be accepted as rightful and respected citizens after four centuries of persecution.

Even after the Catholic Emancipation Act had become law in 1829 thus allowing Roman Catholics to sit in Parliament and to hold all offices under the Crown except those of Lord Chancellor and Viceroy of Ireland, up to 1835 the exclusively Anglican Corporation of Preston had avoided to recognise the existence of a large and growing Roman Catholic population in the town. It would be in Preston Guild week 1842 that the Roman Catholic Church for the first time was to have an official involvement in Guild festivities, when a morning concert of sacred music was held in St Wilfrid's Roman Catholic Chapel in Chapel Street.

The Relief Act of 1791 abolishing the double land tax on Catholics also permitted the celebration of Catholic worship in public places, but it was not until the Act of 1829 became law that Catholic chapels were allowed a peal of bells and a spire. The Church of St John the Evangelist at Kirkham of 1845 by A. W. N. Pugin and to be known as The Willows was the first Catholic church in the Fylde area of Lancashire to have a spire and a peal of bells said to be the first to ring out in a Catholic church since the Reformation.

In 1835 there were only three Catholic places of worship in Preston; St Mary's, St Wilfrid's, and St Ignatius'. St Mary's Chapel had been erected in 1761 to be behind shop frontages in Friargate, a time when the building of Catholic chapels especially in towns were to be situated 'out of sight, out of mind', St Mary's being no exception.

By 1793 St Wilfrid's Roman Catholic Church had been established in Chapel Street. Built in brick in a plain architectural style, the building was to undergo a re-build (estimated cost being £10,000) internally and externally in 1879–80 by Ignatius Scoles and S. J. Nicholl when galleries were removed and massive Shap granite columns installed to support a tunnel-vault roof with penetrations. Outside, new red brick and terracotta cladding with its exuberant ornamentation were to present the impressive North Italian style we see today.

A number of years were to pass in the town before the building of the next Catholic Church, St Ignatius' of 1833 in Meadow Street near the town centre and the first church in Preston to have a spire. Designed by S. S. Scoles (1798–1863) of London, the church would undergo later extensions in 1858 by Joseph Aloysius Hansom (1803–82) of Hansom cab fame, much to the dismay of Scoles. Recently the church has become Preston's Catholic Cathedral.

After St Ignatius' came St Augustine's by A. Tuach, a pupil of Scoles and built 1838–1840 in St Austin's Place southeast of the town centre. Erected in the Classical style with its four-columned portico having pediment and Ionic capitals it was to be much enlarged. The apse was to be of 1878 but most of the enlargement was due to a campaign in 1890 by Sinnott, Sinnott & Powell from which two corner towers with cupolas in Italian Renaissance style would come about as well as the aisle-less interior with its giant pilasters and coffered segmental tunnel-vault.

However, the town's crowning glory in church building arrived with the building of Joseph Aloysius Hansom's R.C. Church of St Walburge, Pedder Street, its doors opening for Mass on 3 August 1854. Money amounting to a little over £8,000 towards its building had been raised by door-to-door collection and bazaars between 1847 and 1852. Inside, a magnificent hammer beam arrangement would support a roof to eradicate the need for obstructive pillars, whilst outside buttresses dealt with side thrust forces exerted on the two side walls. A large rose window was added to the west end in 1863 followed in 1866 by the completion of a limestone tower and spire surmounted by a 15 foot high cross. The 309-feet high spire is reputed to be the third highest spire in Britain, the one on Salisbury Cathedral being the highest followed by the one at Norwich Cathedral. After the opening of the Church of St Thomas of Canterbury and English Martyrs in 1867, the next new Catholic Church to appear in Preston was St Joseph's of 1873–4 by J. O'Byrne, in Skeffington Road.

Preston Guild week September 1882 saw the Catholic population of the town making an impressive contribution to the celebrations. On the first morning six bishops celebrated High Mass simultaneously; the Bishop of Clifton in St Wilfrid's; the Bishops of Liverpool, Salford, and Leeds in St Augustine's where Canon Taylor had been sent as Rector; the Bishop of Shrewsbury in St Walburge's; and the Bishop of Middlesbrough in St Thomas of Canterbury and English Martyrs.

Cardinal Manning, who had performed the wedding ceremony of Ellen Mercer and Edmund Waterton during the previous year in London, would also be in Preston for the Guild. The presence of six Roman Catholic

Bishops and a Cardinal were to be seen by the Catholic populace as a welcome and important element in the Guild's celebrations.

Years before in 1850, a plan had been announced by Pope Pius IX to re-establish Roman Catholic archbishoprics and bishoprics in England that led to an outcry from most Anglican bishops. The following year the Ecclesiastical Title Act was passed decreeing that no other clergy could hold titles already in use by Anglican clergy, but the Roman Catholics had chosen their bishoprics in places to which no Anglican bishops were attached, and so in 1851 the Act was repealed.

The 1882 Preston Guild was when the Catholic churches and their attached Sunday and elementary day schools would march in procession with the Anglicans like they had done in the Guild of 1862. But now in 1882 it was decided that in addition, all the Catholics would join in their own special procession, that of the Catholic Guilds which marched on the Thursday. In 1838–9 St Wilfrid's Guild, a friendly society had been established to provide medical care, sickness benefits, death grants, as well as organising events and social gatherings for its members, a guild that had marched with the friendly societies in the 1842 Guild. Attached to St Ignatius' Church a women's guild was founded in 1839 to be followed by others, some for boys and girls.

The Catholic Guilds procession of 1882 was made up of well over five thousand members whilst at the rear came members of the United Catholic Brethren. The journalist Anthony Hewitson in his *History of Preston* would give an eyewitness account of the procession, part of which would read:

> – a gigantic and magnificent demonstration. Never before was there such a muster, such a march of Roman Catholics in Preston. For this Guild they exercised all their spectacular skill, and aggregated all their available processional forces.

When the procession ended many of the marchers went to Lark Hill Convent near Canon Taylor's Church of St Augustine's to be addressed by dignitaries of the Roman Catholic Church including the Bishops of Liverpool, Salford, and Leeds, led by Cardinal Manning, when all expressed their admiration for the procession.

In 1883, Canon Taylor went to St Joseph's, Birkdale (built 1865–7 having been designed by Edward Welby Pugin) before finally going to St Peter's, Lytham in 1885, the church of his brother, Roger, who had died during the same year, As one of the trustees of John Mercer's Will and a considerable beneficiary of such, Canon Taylor would use his inheritance to enrich St Peter's Church where there is a memorial to him. Also in the church is the altar to St Joseph that John Mercer had placed there in 1877.

In nearby St Annes-on-Sea, Canon Taylor arranged the building of the Church of Our Lady Star of the Sea of 1890–1, by the firm of 'Pugin & Pugin', and with the help of Ellen Waterton organised the building of the Church of the Sacred Heart of 1899 at Thornton-le-Fylde (also by 'Pugin & Pugin') as well as its presbytery and school.

September 1914 saw the official opening of St Joseph's R.C. Church in Ansdell. Designed by 'Pugin & Pugin' of London & Liverpool, it had been erected in the memory of Monsignor James Taylor and his brother, Father Roger Taylor, their legacy having paid for the new church which had cost £12,000, Yorkshire stone having been used in the building of the church, presbytery, and hall.

Chapter ten

End of the Mercers at Alston

Following the death of Ellen Waterton in 1909 and in accordance with John Mercer's Will, the new owner of Alston Hall was Ellen's first-born daughter Monica Mary Colette Paula Waterton, now a nun by the name of Mother Mary Borgia in the Convent of the Holy Child Jesus, Mayfield, East Sussex.

In 1911 Monica was still a trainee teacher and was at the school belonging to the Convent of the Holy Child Jesus, Layton Hill, Blackpool, in Lancashire. Most probably she would have requested this particular posting to be near her trustees to deal with legal matters regarding her inheritance that at this time presumably would still be under discussion.

In 1856 the Roman Catholic Bishop of Liverpool had invited the Sisters of the Society of the Holy Child Jesus to send out a branch from their house in Liverpool to teach in a Poor School on Talbot Road, Blackpool. They arrived with twelve girl boarders and after four years of success, a school for girls was founded in 1860 to be located in Raikes Hall, Blackpool. In 1870 a move was made to a site at Layton Hill that the Sisters already owned and where an imposing convent building had been erected that is still extant and part of the present day school, St Mary's Catholic Academy in St Walburga's Road. The new convent school of 1870 was admitting boy pupils by 1880 but in 1900 they were separated out to go to St Joseph's College in Park Road.

In 1910 Monica's teacher training college address, Cavendish Square, London, is quoted on a legal document or indenture relating to a transfer of a mortgage on property at Stalmine, near Blackpool for which Monica would be involved. Seemingly a John Woodhouse had borrowed various

Fig. 10.1 Convent of the Holy Child Jesus, Layton Hill, Blackpool.

sums on the security of this property over the period 1839–1862 amounting in total to £1,400. The mortgage was to be transferred between several lenders, and in 1908 it was transferred to the following three persons, Edward Pyke of Southport, Cuthbert Pyke of Lostock Hall, near Preston, and Nicholas Cockshutt, Barrister-at-Law of Preston, who were to hold it jointly. As mentioned above, Edward Pyke of Southport had been one of the Trustees of John Mercer's Will, and Nicholas Cockshutt a Trustee of Ellen Waterton's Will.

The purpose of the indenture was to transfer the mortgage to three other parties, namely Monica Mary Colette Paula Waterton, spinster of Cavendish Square, London; Alice Worsley, spinster of Cherwell Edge, Oxford; and Emma Frewen, spinster of 22 Winckley Square, Preston, this last address being the Convent of the Holy Child Jesus, where, in the following year Emma then aged twenty five is a boarder and an assistant teacher.

Without examining the contents of the indenture one assumes that the transfer mentioned above would be a way of re-investing money by the trustees of Alston Hall and its estate for the future benefit of Monica's inheritance, their power to do so having been stipulated in her mother's Will. Yet events were to take place shortly afterwards that were to present a totally different perspective on Monica's inheritance and that of the future of Alston Hall and its estate.

Having taken a vow of poverty, Monica Mary on inheriting Alston Hall and its estate, ceded the administration of the Hall to her religious Order, very much wanting the nuns to make use of the mansion for religious purposes. However the Order felt it was not in a position as far as personnel, finance, or apostolic work was concerned to fully accept the offer of the Hall and its estate. One reliable source of information mentions that the Hall was considered to be a holiday retreat for the nuns.

Fig. 10.2 Monica Mary Colette Paula Waterton as Sister Mary Borgia. (By kind permission of the Society of the Holy Child Jesus Archives, Oxford)

S.M.Borgia

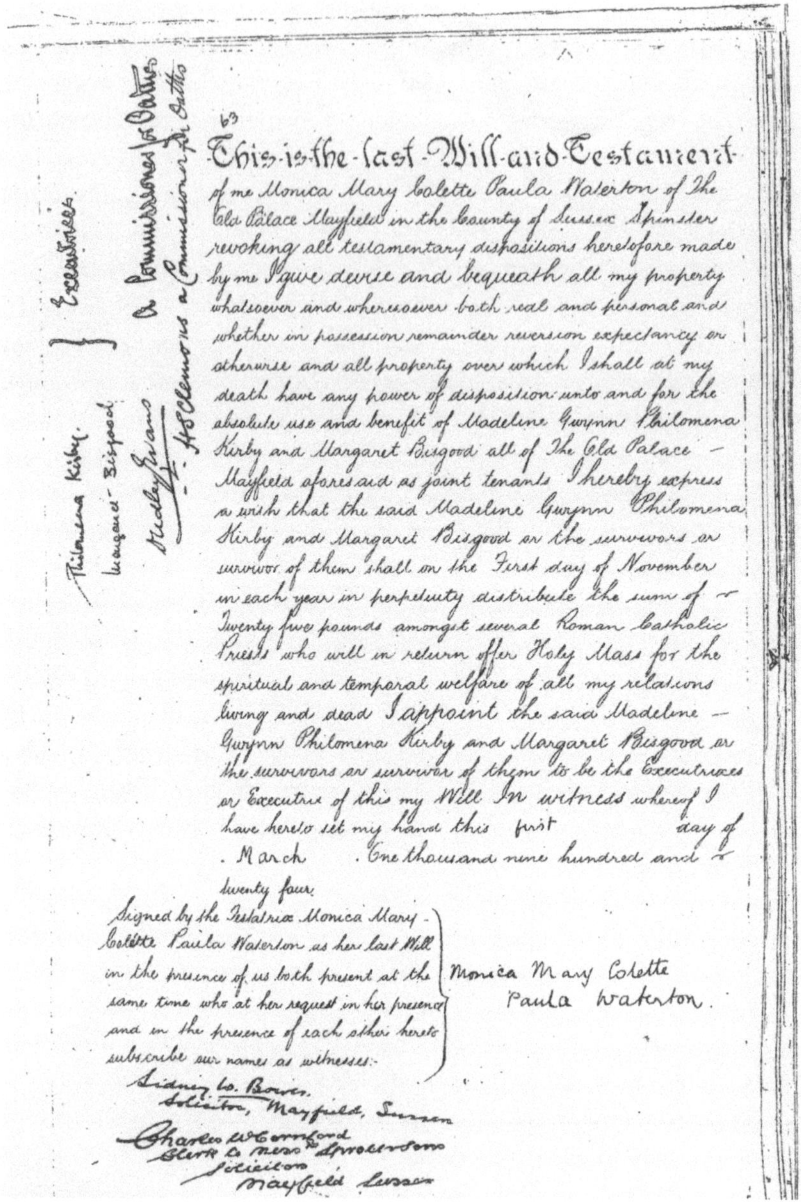

This is the last Will and Testament of me Monica Mary Colette Paula Waterton of The Old Palace Mayfield in the County of Sussex Spinster revoking all testamentary dispositions heretofore made by me I give devise and bequeath all my property whatsoever and wheresoever both real and personal and whether in possession remainder reversion expectancy or otherwise and all property over which I shall at my death have any power of disposition unto and for the absolute use and benefit of Madeline Gwynn Philomena Kirby and Margaret Bisgood all of The Old Palace — Mayfield aforesaid as joint tenants I hereby express a wish that the said Madeline Gwynn Philomena Kirby and Margaret Bisgood or the survivors or survivor of them shall on the First day of November in each year in perpetuity distribute the sum of Twenty five pounds amongst several Roman Catholic Priests who will in return offer Holy Mass for the spiritual and temporal welfare of all my relations living and dead I appoint the said Madeline — Gwynn Philomena Kirby and Margaret Bisgood or the survivors or survivor of them to be the Executrices or Executrix of this my Will In witness whereof I have hereto set my hand this first day of March One thousand nine hundred and twenty four.

Signed by the Testatrix Monica Mary Colette Paula Waterton as her last Will in the presence of us both present at the same time who at her request in her presence and in the presence of each other hereto subscribe our names as witnesses:-

Monica Mary Colette Paula Waterton.

Sidney W. Bowes. Solicitor, Mayfield, Sussex

Charles W. Cranford Clerk to Messrs Sprocerson Solicitors Mayfield Sussex

[left margin, vertical:]
Executors:
Philomena Kirby.
Margaret Bisgood.
Madeline Gwynn

A Commissioner for Oaths
A Commissioner for Oaths

Fig. 10.3 Last Will and Testament of Monica Mary Colette Paula Waterton.

In the meantime Monica continued with her teacher training to qualify in 1914, the Teachers' Registration Council Register of that year giving her residential address as St Leonard's-on-Sea, a possible indication that for the final stage of her teacher training she had returned to her Order's school on the Sussex coast.

Monica was to do much work in helping the poor and is remembered for the work she did in the Holy Child Jesus Settlement at Poplar in the East London docklands area where she devoted all her spare time in making things for the Settlement Bazaar in aid of funds. One admires Monica's dedication to her faith and the way she showed it in her many religious commitments, especially in the poverty-stricken areas of London, the very city where she could have joined polite society. Instead she turned her back on a considerable fortune and devoted her life to those in dire need of help and comfort.

Through the Waterton family she was a descendant of Saint Thomas More at whose canonisation in 1936 in Rome she attended. She took pride in the lifestyle of her Yorkshire grandfather Charles Waterton from whom she inherited many characteristics, including a unique interest in the wonders of the animal world and an ingenuity that in her case was directed to the fashioning of novelties for bazaars from fish bones and similar unexpected materials. She loved to make tiny things, an unusual trait in one unusually tall of stature. The use of oddments that others would have discarded was indicative of another marked feature of her personality, namely her great love of holy poverty.

Monica would most likely have been told long before her teenage years the many stories surrounding the life of grandfather Waterton, listening to his many acts of kindness to those less fortunate, such as the times when his poorer neighbours became ill and could not afford a doctor, when he would send his own physician at his own expense and supply the necessary medicine and essential food. Maybe she listened to the tale of Charles as a schoolboy walking up a lane and meeting an old lady who asked him for charity. Without a single coin on his person he gave her a fine darning needle that was of the greatest value to him in blowing eggs.

On 1 March 1924 Monica made her Will in which her sister Ethelburga is not mentioned (see fig. 10.3). Madeline Gwynn Philomena Kirby and Margaret Bisgood mentioned in the Will were also to be mentioned in the 1932 Will of Agnes Swarbrick, of 22 Winckley Square, Preston, this address being the Convent of the Holy Child Jesus.

Shortly before Christmas 1943 Monica underwent a serious operation in London, but the doctors held out no hope of recovery and she was henceforth compelled to lead the life of an invalid, her suffering in her final months being aggravated by the flying bombs which roared almost ceaselessly over Mayfield from June to September. Monica died aged 60 from cancer of the colon on 7 October 1944 at the Mayfield Convent where for many years she had held the office of Sacristan, and was laid to rest in the cemetery there.

Monica's Will went to probate on 26 April 1945 at Llandudno when the administration of all her estate was granted to:

> *Philomena Kirby and Margaret Bisgood both of The Old Palace aforesaid Spinsters two of the executrixes named in the said Will – Power reserved to the other executrix.*

The Probate Register continued:

> *And it is hereby certified that an Affidavit for Inland Revenue has been delivered wherein it is shewn that the gross value of the said Estate in Great Britain (exclusive of what the said deceased may have been possessed of or entitled to as a Trustee and not beneficially) amounts to £57541. 0. 1. and that the net value of the personal estate amounts to £56311. 11. 10. And it is further certified that it appears by a Receipt signed by an Inland Revenue Officer on the said Affidavit that £12080. 14. 9. on account of Estate Duty and interest on such duty has been paid.*

Chapter eleven

Ethelburga Waterton

In 1911 whilst Monica was preparing for a life of religious sacrifice and dedication, her sister Ethelburga was living a contrasting lifestyle amongst the Catholic wealthy elite, and for the Census for 1911, the year before her London wedding to London solicitor Stephen Francis Eustace Scrope she was living at Billing Hall, Great Billing, near Northampton.

Billing Hall was the home of Gervase Henry Elwes, the celebrated English tenor whose brother Dudley Cary Elwes was to become the Roman Catholic Bishop of Northampton. At Billing Hall Ethelburga was a tenant, a situation most likely having been arranged by her future husband who was related to Gervase Henry Elwes's wife Lady Winifride (nee Feilding).

Gervase Henry Elwes had been born at Billing Hall in 1866, the eldest son of Valentine Dudley Henry Cary Elwes and his second wife Alice Ward, the family converting to Roman Catholicism during a visit to Nice in France in 1874. Gervase attended two Roman Catholic Schools, the Oratory, Edgbaston (1877–81), and Woburn Park (1881–5), where he studied music and sang in school choirs, and from 1885 to 1888 read law at Christ Church, Oxford.

On 11 May 1889 Gervase Elwes married Winifride Mary Elizabeth Feilding, the daughter of the 8th Earl of Denbigh, and in that year decided to enter the diplomatic service, moving to Munich to study for the Foreign Office examination that he did not actually sit for. In 1891 he accepted a post as an honorary attaché in Vienna followed by a post in Brussels in 1892.

Returning to England in 1895 to reside at Brigg Manor, the family manor in Lincolnshire, he continued to study singing and in December 1902 was to undertake his first professional engagement in Paris. In 1904 he sang the title role of Elgar's 'The Dream of Gerontius', Edward Elgar being a close friend, and in 1909 on the death of his father, Gervase Elwes succeeded to the family estate. However regarding money his inheritance was somewhat dubious, but soon afterwards he had Billing Hall considerably improved, letting it out to Ethelburga Waterton who was to be an ideal tenant. Elwes and his wife would spend long periods away from Billing during Gervase's career as a singer and in her biography of her husband, Lady Winifride describes with real feeling in leaving Billing for several years. The return was made in 1913, the year after Ethelburga had married Stephen Scrope in London's Roman Catholic Cathedral.

Gervase Elwes, who was involved with upper-class music making, also worked with charitable organisations and during the First World War visited the front line on three occasions to entertain the troops. It was while on tour in the United States in January 1921 that he fell between the

Fig. 11.1 The *Tatler*'s published photograph of Ethelburga Waterton to announce her engagement to Stephen Scrope.

Fig. 11.2 *The Sketch*'s photograph (published 17 July 1912) of Ethelburga, seemingly in her travelling attire following her wedding of the previous day.

The Sketch 17 July 1912

DAUGHTER OF A POPE'S PRIVY CHAMBER-LAIN: MISS ETHELBURGA WATERTON, WHOSE MARRIAGE TO MR. STEPHEN SCROPE WAS FIXED TO TAKE PLACE AT WESTMINSTER CATHEDRAL ON JULY 16.

Miss Waterton is the daughter of the late Mr. Edmund Waterton, of Deeping Waterton, Lincolnshire, who was Privy Chamberlain to Pope Pius IX. Mr. Stephen Scrope is the younger son of the late Mr. Simon Scrope, of Danby Hall, Middleham, Yorkshire.

Photograph by Keturah Collings.

train and platform at Back Bay station, Boston, Massachusetts and died a few hours later that day. He was buried at Billing, Northamptonshire.

During her stay at Billing Hall, Ethelburga would have occupied a great deal of her time planning her wedding that must have been one of the highlights in London's social calendar for 1912. With Ethelburga at Billing Hall for the Census of 1911 were her stepsister Josephine Harrison, Charles Langdale, Cecilia Langdale, Josephine's 16-year-old daughter Angela, and two visitors Gertrude Dalmesky and Percy Bramley. Josephine Harrison and Charles Langdale would take the role as witnesses at the forthcoming wedding. As to the household staff at Billing Hall in 1911 the Census shows there were twelve members: a governess; footman; scullery maid; cook; kitchen maid; three housemaids; two ladies maid; butler; and a housekeeper.

Stephen Scrope's ancestors had been of high aristocratic status in

England for centuries, and in the 1380s the Scrope name was to become prominent in the Court of Chivalry in a suit regarding an armorial controversy between Sir Richard Scrope and Sir Robert Grosvenor. The story behind this controversy briefly outlined below might appear to the reader as being far removed from the history of Alston Hall, but it serves to illustrate how Ethelburga after marrying Steven Scrope became part of a family so prominent in the annals of England's history.

In 1385 Sir Richard, first Baron Scrope of Bolton in the county of Lancashire, was inspecting Richard II's army ready for its campaign against Scotland, when he noticed a knight, Sir Robert Grosvenor from the county of Cheshire with his men gathered about a banner bearing the same Arms of Scrope, 'Azure, a bend Or'. Lord Scrope angrily insisted that Sir Robert was infringing the Scrope Arms, Sir Robert arguing that it was Scrope who was bearing the Arms of Grosvenor. This was a period when the heralds had not yet established one's right to bear Arms, and earlier Scrope had met a Cornishman named Carminow who bore the same Arms, the matter being referred to a committee of six knights who decided that both men were entitled to the same Arms. As Cornwall was so far away the knights may have considered it to be all but a foreign country and this could have had some bearing on their decision, one which Scrope probably most reluctantly had to accept, but now in 1385 the same problem had arisen again with someone else, so he decided to approach a military court with his complaint against Grosvenor.

It was clear from the evidence that had been collected by specially appointed commissions by May 1389, that both parties had a right to the disputed Arms, but Scrope had been Lord Treasurer, Steward of the King's Household, and Chancellor of England, whilst Grosvenor was but a provincial knight. Finally, the Duke of Gloucester, Constable of England awarded the Arms, 'Azure, a bend Or' to Scrope and granted the same but with a plain bordure argent for difference to Grosvenor, but that was not the end of the matter.

Grosvenor appealed and on 27 May 1390, the case came before the King who declared that the plain bordure argent was a mark of cadency, perfectly sufficient as a difference between cousin and cousin in blood, but not a sufficient difference in Arms between two strangers in blood in one kingdom. The king therefore cancelled and annulled the sentence given by the Court of Chivalry and so Grosvenor having lost his appeal adopted the Arms, 'Azure, a garb Or'. In 1888 Grosvenor the Duke of Westminster won the Derby with a horse named Bend Or.

In 1881 Stephen Scrope at the age of eight was in his family home, Danby Hall, Thornton-Steward, Leyburn, in Yorkshire, where thirteen servants were in employment. Stephen's father, Simon Thomas Scrope had married Emily Jane Berkeley in 1855, the daughter of Robert Berkeley of Spetchley Park in Worcestershire, her sister Mary becoming the Countess of Denbigh following her marriage in 1857 to Rudolph William Basil Percy Feilding who in 1865 became the 8th Earl of Denbigh and who also became a convert to the Roman Catholic faith.

Burke, in his *Peerage, Baronetage & Knightage* of 1890 tells us that Rudolph who died in 1892, was born in April 1823, and on 1 June 1846 married Louisa the only child of David Pennant junior and Lady Emma Pennant of Downing, Flint. Louisa died in Naples on 1 May 1853, and on 29 September 1857 Rudolph married Mary the fourth daughter of Robert Berkeley of Spetchley Park in Worcestershire. By Mary, Rudolph had the following issue (males being listed first whilst birth dates in brackets are from the Census of 1891):

1) Rudolph Robert Basil Aloysius Augustine, Viscount Feilding, late captain of the R.H.A., born 26 May 1859, married on 23 September 1884, the Hon. Cecilia Mary Clifford, daughter of Charles Hugh, 8th Lord Clifford.

2) Francis Henry Everard Joseph, born 6 March 1867, late R.N.

3) Basil George Edward Vincent, born 13 July 1873.

4) Philip, born and died of 5 December 1877.

5) Clara Mary Henrietta. (1861)

6) Edith Mary Frances, became a nun.

7) Hilda, died an infant on the 14 April 1866.

8) Winifride Mary Elizabeth, married Gervase Henry Elwes in May 1889.

9) Agnes Mary. (1871)

Amongst the titles bestowed upon the Earl was that of Count of Hapsburg by which he was a Count of the Holy Roman Empire, thus having the right to have a double-headed eagle displayed behind his shield of Arms and Crest. In German heraldry it is not unusual to see Arms and Crest depicted in front of an eagle displayed either single-headed or double-headed, an arrangement that for centuries has been accepted as meaning, or as indicative of, princely rank or other honours of the Holy Roman Empire. With reference to the eagle displayed in this manner,

Arthur Charles Fox-Davies, compiling his *A Complete Guide to Heraldry*, published in 1929 wrote:

> *The Earl of Denbigh and several members of the Feilding family have often made use of it with their arms, in token of their supposed descent from the Counts of Hapsburg, which, if correct, would apparently confer the right upon them. This descent, however, has been much questioned, and in late years the claim thereto would seem to have been practically dropped.*

For the Census of 1891, Simon Thomas Scrope (68) and his daughters Mary (22) and Margaret (30) are visitors to Newnham Paddox Hall, the home of the 8th Earl and his wife Mary the Countess. Amongst those listed for the household are the Earl's son Viscount Feilding and his wife with their four infant children, and the Earl's daughters Clare and Agnes, and son Basil.

At the time of the 1891 Census Simon Scrope's wife Emily is at Danby Hall with three of her sons and three daughters, her son Stephen being at school in Eckington, Derbyshire. During the following year whilst out with the Bedale Hunt near Eastby Abbey, Stephen was to have a life changing accident when his horse came down. Suffering from spinal injury he was bedfast for several years and afterwards unable to ride to hounds or shoot.

By the time the Census of 1901 was taken, Stephen's mother, Emily, was a widow and head of the household at 47 Campden House Court, Kensington, London, where a nurse, lady's maid, parlour maid, house maid, cook, and kitchen maid were in domestic service. With her were her son Stephen (28) single and a solicitor's clerk, and four daughters all single and living on their own means, Mabel (41) who died in Brighton in 1914, Cecily (36) who died in Kensington in 1950, Ursula (36) and Mary (32).

On 16 July 1912, within the impressive setting of London's Roman Catholic Cathedral, Stephen Francis Eustace Scrope now aged 40 and a solicitor, married Ethelburga Mary Magdalen Pega Waterton aged 25, the service being conducted by the Bishop of Northampton assisted by the Rev. Father Browne and the Rev. Father Ketters in the presence of the witnesses Captain Charles Stourton Langdale (who was also best man), Emily Scrope and Josephine E. Harrison. The bride was to be given away by her nephew Mr Waterton, and at the time of the marriage the bridegroom was in residence at 3 Duke Street, Manchester Square, London, whilst the bride was staying at the Coburg Hotel, Mayfair, where the wedding reception was to be held. Ethelburga's stepsister Josephine had organised the reception from where subsequently the married couple left for Scotland.

The following day the *Yorkshire Post and Leeds Intelligencer* reported the wedding giving a detailed description of Ethelburga's wedding dress and the attire of her six bridesmaids and two pages, all of which were in a style of the seventeenth century. Ethelburga's dress was to be a copy of the one seen in Van Dyck's 1632 painting of 'Henriette von Frankreich' who was the Catholic Princess Henriette Maria (1609–69), the youngest daughter of Henry IV of France who married Charles I of England in 1625. Etheburga's wedding robe was of rich ivory satin embroidered with blister pearls and trimmed with Venetian point lace, her long train being lined with silver tissue and lace, whilst her plain tulle veil was arranged over a little cap of satin edged with pearls and orange blossom.

The bridesmaids were Miss R. Harrison, Miss E. Walmesley, Miss Gertrude Walmesley, the Hon. Dorothy Mostyn, Miss Winefride Acton and Miss Dorothy McCote, who wore dresses embroidered with pearls, each having large collars, two in pale blue satin, two in pink, and two in green. Each bridesmaid wore a lace and pearl cap and carried an ostrich feather fan. They also had crystal pendants with the bride and groom's initials in diamonds supported by enamel and pearl chains, the gifts of the bridegroom. The bridegroom's two little nephews, the Masters Scrope, acted as pages and were dressed in seventeenth-century suits of palest daffodil yellow satin. Ethelburga's travelling dress was of ivory cloth trimmed with coarse lace and a sash of deep blue satin with a floating panel of purple chiffon. Her large white hat was covered with ostrich feathers and lined underneath with blue silk, whilst her travelling cloak was of the same cloth and lace as her gown.

The day after the wedding *The Sketch*, a weekly journal on Royalty and the aristocracy, published a photograph of Ethelburga (fig. 11.2) seemingly in her travelling attire mentioned above, whilst some time before, the *Tackler*, a magazine of London life focusing on society and drama news, had published a photograph (fig. 11.1) of Ethelburga to announce her engagement.

In 1919 Stephen's mother Emily Scrope died and in 1923 Stephen was a shareholder and an executive in the Great Western Railway. In 1935 he and Ethelburga attended the canonisation in Rome of Ethelburga's distant relative Sir Thomas More. The following year Stephen Scrope died, the *Yorkshire Post and Leeds Intelligencer* of 17 December reporting his death at the age of 64 at 71 The Drive, Hove, Sussex, and to mention that he had been an authority on the history of racing in Yorkshire and had lived at Harrogate before he went to Hove. A Requiem was to be held at the Catholic Church, Norton Road, Hove, at 10am the next day.

During her marriage to Stephen, Ethelburga was to bear nine children of which a son, Edmund John, born in 1921 died two weeks later, the surviving children being;

1) Conyers Stephen Scrope, born February 1913, died 1993. Became a Lieutenant Colonel and married Lady Mary Egerton in 1945 in Westminster, the couple having six children.

2) Charles Waterton Scrope, born June 1914, died 1976. Married Catherine Mary Youngs in 1939 to have two daughters.

3) Rosamund Mary Scrope, born 13 July 1915, died 1994. Married Sir Noel Percy Hugh Dryden, 10th Baronet, in 1941 to have one son.

4) Adela Mary Millicent Scrope, born July 1916, died 1999. Married Major Charles Arthur O'Connor to have one son.

5) Mary Monica Elizabeth Scrope, born 28 July 1917, died 1991. Married Alexander Murray Stephen in 1947.

6) John Henry Francis Scrope, born 1919, died 1943. Killed in a flying accident at Hatfield whilst engaged in operations as a flight test observer. He often visited his uncle, Henry Scrope of Danby Hall, Middleham, for shooting and fishing.

7) Geoffrey Thomas Scrope, born 1920, died 1982. Became a Lieutenant Colonel, married Jean T. Kingston in 1967 in Chelsea.

8) Hugh Everard Scrope, born July 1923. Married Betty Patricia Wilkinson in 1952 to have three daughters.

Hugh Everard Scrope would be the last survivor of Ethelburga's children, who on 12 July 2010 at almost 87 years of age, wrote from his home in Rock, North Cornwall, a letter to the then Principal of Alston Hall College, Graham Wilkinson, to mention that he had a mallet presented by Alfred Darbyshire to John Mercer junior and also a trowel presented to Master John by Isaac Wilkinson and James Kirby, contractors for the Hall.

Ethelburga is listed in the Register for 1939 as being in Norwich at 26 Ipswich Road with her two daughters, Rosamond, single and a floral decorator; Mary, single who is doing unpaid domestic duties; and son Geoffrey, single and a student. Also in the household were a female nurse (born 1882) and a general maid (born 1922). The presence of a nurse is a strong indication that all was not well regarding the health of someone in the household, presumably Ethelburga, as some years later she would die of heart failure that had been associated with the death of her mother and grandfather.

On 1 November 1973, at 24 Harrington Road, Brighton, Ethelburga died aged 86, the cause of death being congestive cardiac failure brought on by mitral stenosis and rheumatic heart disease. Her son Hugh Everard was the informant for the death certificate upon which was recorded Ethelburga's date of birth and place (5th of June 1887 at Deeping St James) and her usual address as having been Burwood Lodge Cottage, London Road, Datchet, Bucks, the same address as her son Hugh Everard.

Chapter twelve

A lessee at the Hall

By the time of the 1911 Census, Elizabeth Pendlebury, who had been the caretaker at Alston Hall prior to the death of Ellen Waterton in London in January 1909, had left the Hall and was living at 46 Shuttleworth Road in Preston with her two daughters and son. As the summer of 1912 approached, the nuns of Monica's Order, having expressed that they had no wish to accept the Hall on a permanent basis, plans would be in place to receive William Eccles as a lessee for the next fourteen years, a term that would be cut short, as on 15 November 1915 the *Lancashire Post* would mention his bankruptcy examination at Preston.

At the time of this examination William Eccles had formerly been a partner with a brother in the family textile firm of Messrs Joseph Eccles and Co. of Steam Mill, Preston, and Winewall Mill (demolished in *c*.1972) at Cotton Tree in the parish of Trawden, near Coln.

Steam Mill on the northern side of Fylde Road, Preston was a manufactory (weaving establishment), its name having been taken from a steam-driven corn mill that had once operated on its site along with a flax-spinning mill. John Swainson had 350 looms there in 1862, but there is no mention of the manufactory in 1869 so probably it had been a victim of the Cotton Famine of 1862–5. By 1870 it was under the new ownership of Joseph Eccles & Co., cotton manufacturers, and years later before its final closure the manufactory would be listed in the Preston Trade Directory of 1936 for Joseph Eccles & Co. Ltd. Today, Joseph Eccles's initials and the date 1870 can still be seen in the splendid monogram executed in terracotta on the front of the Preston mill.

The building of Winewall Mill in Cotton Tree probably began in 1847 and by 1854 a loomage of 640 looms had been installed operating on steam power. In 1884 Joseph Eccles of Steam Mill in Preston, purchased Winewall Mill. After the First World War Winewall Mill manufactured artificial silk fancies and cloth to be exported to China, India and South America. In the early thirties the business was registered as Joseph Eccles & Company Limited and in August 1939 it went into voluntary liquidation.

The Census of 1871 found Joseph Eccles who had been born in Accrington in 1831 residing in Victoria Parade, Preston with his wife Alice (40) and a family of seven children, Mary (14), Margaret (10), Alice (3), Thomas (12), Joseph (7), William (5), and Robert (1). Mother-in-law Mary Westwell (72), and a servant, Jane Bell (20) are also listed.

In 1881 the family are living at 'Fairfield', Long Lane, Lea, Preston when Joseph is employing 300 hands as a cotton manufacturer and of his sons Joseph junior (17) is now a cotton manufacturer apprentice, whilst William (15) and Robert (11) are at school. Thomas is not listed nor is he mentioned in the probate of his father's Will in the 1890s.

Fig. 12.1 A diesel engine unit that would have been similar to the type installed at Alston Hall *c*.1913–14 to produce electricity.

In 1891 Joseph senior is still at 'Fairfield' but now a widower living with daughter Alice; sons William and Robert; two granddaughters Alice J. Kirkland (8) and Margaret Kirkland (9); and four servants. Joseph's cotton manufacturer son, Joseph junior, at this time when the Census was taken, was at a hotel in St Anne's Road West, St Anne's, near Lytham.

Joseph Eccles senior died in 1896 the probate of his Will mentioning a sum of £29,715 to his sons, Joseph, William and Robert. By 1901, the three Eccles brothers had been married for some time and had families of their own. Joseph had married Jessie Hawkins in 1894, and in 1901 was living at 29 Ribblesdale Place, Preston, with his wife and their two children and three servants. Robert, who had married Edith Alice Ainsworth in 1893, was now residing at Black Brook Hall, Gregson Lane, Walton-le-Dale with Edith and their young daughter Margaret, where they employed a cook and a housemaid. William in 1901 was living at 'The Grange' in Colne with his wife Emily (nee Ainsworth, whom he had married in 1897), and their two daughters, Kathryn (4) and Emily Eileen who was not yet one year old.

Emily Eccles was the sister of Edith Alice, their father Hargreaves Ainsworth having been born in Darwen in 1840. For the Census of 1871 he is listed as living with his wife Margaret Jane at 'Ingol House' near Preston with his three daughters, Sarah Jane (8); Emily (1); Edith Alice (not yet 1); his son William Haughton (5); and a female servant. Another son, Charles would be born in 1874.

The 1891 Census finds Hargreaves Ainsworth as a retired farmer and commission agent, living on his own means at 'Mill Bank', Cadley Lane, Fulwood, Preston, with his wife and some members of his family, and a female general domestic servant. Shortly afterwards Hargreaves Ainsworth moved to Windermere, and on 16 September 1897 William Eccles, who had been born in Accrington in 1866, married Ainsworth's daughter, Emily. In 1911 Hargreaves Ainsworth, now 71 and described as a retired farmer and also retired dealer in cotton yarns, was living at 'The Larches' in Windermere where he died on 29 September 1925, the net value of his personal estate at his death amounting to just under £4,000.

In 1911 prior to his move to Alston Hall, William Eccles and his wife, now with four daughters, twins Joyce and Gladys having been born in 1904, were residing at 'West Bank', a house with twenty rooms in Clifton Drive, Lytham. The number of servants in the house amounted to seven; a cook; two housemaids; a maid; a kitchen maid; a footman; and a butler; such an array indicating a lifestyle of some affluence.

At this time his brother Robert (41) had retired from cotton

Fig. 12.2 The low position of brass fingerplate and doorknob on a mahogany door installed *c*.1913–14 for what had originally been the smoking room or study. (June 2015). Bottom right on the floor of the entrance hall is a connection nozzle for a vacuum cleaning system also installed in *c*.1913–14.

manufacturing and living at 'Greyrigg', near Broughton to the north of Preston, with his wife Edith and 14-year-old daughter Margaret and two servants. In 1911 William's older brother Joseph (47) was still at work in the family cotton weaving business, and living with his wife in Whinfield Lane, Ashton, Preston, where he employed four servants. During this year his daughter Jessie would be a boarder at 'The Grange' in Buxton, whilst her brother Roger would be undertaking his education in Rugby.

When in partnership with his brother in 1905, William Eccles had a capital of nearly £2,700, but by 1912 when he had taken on the lease of Alston Hall he was already overdrawn at the bank even though he had received more than £22,750 from his brother. By 30 November 1914 his capital had all gone and he had entered a new partnership with his brother, selling the whole of his joint properties to him and receiving from him a salary of £780 a year.

At William Eccles's bankruptcy examination in September 1915, the official receiver ordered him to furnish a full account of the sums of money he had spent in the last three years. Eccles attributed the cause of his failure to the *cost of furnishing and fitting up Alston Hall*, and was to say, *"If I had known what the cost of Alston Hall was going to be I would never have taken it"*, but the official receiver would press him about his wanton extravagance. Pressed by his creditors, some of whom he paid off by instalments, Eccles had become involved with moneylenders and when asked how many thousands he had spent on Alston Hall, he said, *"It must have been over £10,000"*.

Obviously William Eccles must have had permission to carry out the alterations from Monica Waterton or her trustees, or whoever was responsible for the upkeep of the mansion and its appointments. But one wonders why permission was given for the drastic alterations to the windows on the Hall's southeast-facing façade as mentioned in chapter three.

Eccles was to employ E. J. Andrew of Winckley Square, Preston, as his architect for the various alterations, and at the enquiry Eccles contended that there was a lot of work done at the Hall by the architect, which went beyond his orders. He persisted in this contention and it became a major issue. For his part, Andrew told the enquiry that he had frequently called Mr Eccles's attention to the high cost of these alterations; that sometimes the work was carried out twice, even three times, at Eccles's request.

Whilst at Alston Hall, William had employed three to five gardeners, five indoor servants, and a chauffeur, and with his wife had ordered exotic furnishings and antiques, including a carpet costing 300 guineas. Furniture had been bought amounting to £10,000 on a higher purchase agreement of which £4,000 was still outstanding, and over a period of three years he had spent more than £3,000 on clothing for himself and his family. At one stage when hard pressed for money he had pawned his wife's rings and furs.

In connection with Eccles's bankruptcy, a remarkable case would arise at Manchester Assizes and tried by a Mr Shearman without a jury. It was brought by Mr Joseph Philip Garnett, chartered accountant, of Manchester, against James Todd, chartered accountant of Preston who was the trustee under Eccles's bankruptcy.

The following is taken from a report of the case that appeared under the heading 'Litigation at Manchester Assizes'.

> *Mr. Acton, who, with Mr. Jordan, appeared for the plaintiff, explained that the dispute was as to the rights of the plaintiff under the assignment of a hire purchase agreement and power of attorney.*

He claimed under these documents to be entitled to a large quantity of furniture in respect of which he had actually paid £3,620.

In substance the defence was that the plaintiff could not recover either the furniture or its value under the documents in question, because the hire purchase agreement which was the foundation of the whole transaction was void as being an unregistered bill of sale.

The Judge asked whether it was suggested that the hire purchase agreement was not genuine.

Mr. Acton replied that he did not think that could be pleaded for one moment. Mr. Garnett was beyond controversy a gentleman of the highest standing and position in Manchester, and there could be no suggestion that there was any sort of sham or disguise about what had taken place.

The hire purchase agreement and power of attorney had been given by Mr. Eccles to Messrs. Goodall, Heighway, and Lamb, of Manchester, who had carried out the decorations and supplied the furniture at Alston Hall, and had been assigned by that firm to the plaintiff, who provided Messrs. Goodall, Heighway, and Lamb with the money representing the value of the furniture specified in the agreement. It was his extravagance in regard to the decoration and furnishing of Alston Hall, said Mr. Acton, combined with other extravagance, which had led to Mr. Eccles's failure. In 1912, however, he was generally believed to be a person of great wealth whose solvency was beyond question.

In July last, however, Mr. Eccles, whose extravagance had in the meantime brought about his downfall, filed his own petition in bankruptcy, and when plaintiff claimed the furniture under the assignment and power of attorney the point was taken that the hire-purchase agreement was a bill of sale, and that it was void owing to the want of registration.

The plaintiff and Mr. Drury, secretary of Messrs. Goodall, Heighway, and Lamb when these transactions took place, having given evidence as to the circumstances in which the hire-purchase agreement was made, Mr. Acton argued that the agreement could not be considered to be a bill of sale.

> *Mr. Rigby Swift, K.C., M.P., who, with Mr. Glover, represented the defendant, in reply quoted authorities in support of the contention that the document was a bill of sale – that it was a cloak to secure repayment of a loan.*

> *The Judge agreed, and gave judgment for the defendant.*

On 13 March 1913 when being pressurised by his creditors and when his finances were in a very precarious condition, Eccles had paid £76 10s. for a Grant of Arms, an act that later was referred to by the examiner at Eccles's bankruptcy hearing as *nonsense of this sort*.

An enquiry to the College of Arms in London in October 2016 confirmed that the Arms had been granted on 13 March 1913. In the text of the patent, William Eccles is described as of Alston Hall in the parish of Longridge, in the County Palatine of Lancaster, gentleman, the grant being made to him and his descendants (College of Arms Ms: Grants 82/91), the blazon of Arms and Crest being;

Arms: Or, two halberts in saltire proper between three roses gules barbed and seeded also proper, two in fess and one in base.

Crest: On a wreath of the colours (Or and gules), the head of a halbert proper between two wings Or.

No motto was shown on the grant. As for the halbert (or halberd) mentioned in the above blazon, this is sometimes referred to as a pole-axe, a battle-axe in form, mounted on a long pole with which a foot soldier was equipped. Such an axe was provided with a shank (or socket) to fit on the end of the pole, the upward extension of the axe being in the form of a sharp spike.

Eccles is a name frequently associated with commoner and privileged person alike, and for those who bear Arms in the name of Eccles although unrelated to the above William Eccles, the use of two halberds in saltire is quite a common charge or feature on their shields. For example the Arms of John Stewart Eccles, D.L. of Ecclesville, Fintona, in County Tyrone, who was born on 6 October 1847, has the blazon; 'Argent, two halberds saltierwise azure' as seen in *Burke's Landed Gentry* of 1879.

However, during researches one found in *Burke's Landed Gentry* of 1937 a reference to Joseph Eccles of Halston Hall, Whittington, Oswestry, Salop, a J.P. (1931), born on 15 July 1878 and educated at Repton, who on 14 May 1921 married Alice Dorothy Patience, widow of Major Vere de Hoghton. Joseph and Alice were to have a son, David John, born in 1922 and educated at Winchester. Listed are the blazons of Joseph's Arms, Crest, and motto:

> Arms: Azure, two battleaxes in saltire between as many esquire's helmets in pale, all Or.

> Crest: A cubit arm in armour, holding in the hand a broken battleaxe in bend sinister, all proper.

> Motto: *Se defendendo.*

Surprisingly this entry for 1937 also bears reference to Joseph Eccles being the son of Joseph Eccles of Myerscough House, Garstang. The house, a few miles north of Preston and not far from Alston Hall, is mentioned in *Northward*, published in 1900 having been written by Anthony Hewitson who in his account regarding Myerscough House wrote:

> *In 1883 the whole of the estate, including the House, was sold by auction to Mr Leeming, of Lancaster, for £48,000. Directly afterwards he sold the property: it was bought by or on behalf of Mr. Joseph Eccles, cotton spinner and manufacturer, Preston, who in a short time went to reside at Myerscough House, where he is still living, and at which he has made many improvements. It has an antique, serenely-pleasant appearance, and from a pretty, octo-gabled structure, with central tower, which surmounts the general building, a very good view of the surrounding country can be obtained. Myerscough House has for some years been fitted up with the electric light; it was one of the earliest country residences in North Lancashire – if not actually the very first – supplied with this luminant.*

It was this last sentence that caught one's attention in that perhaps William Eccles was a frequent visitor at Myerscough House where he admired its electric lighting and had it firmly in mind on his arrival at Alston Hall just when the Edwardian period (1901–11) had ended. As already mentioned above this was a period which saw the introduction of new technology for the country house in general such as electricity, and in modernising Alston Hall in the way he did, Eccles simply followed a national trend.

A short distance away to the south of Preston is Cuerden Hall that Reginald Arthur Tatton was to inherit following which between 1907–9 he would make extensive repairs and improvements that included the installation of electric lighting and a telephone. The stables were also converted to accommodate his motorcars. William Eccles may well have installed a telephone at Alston Hall.

During his period of bankruptcy William Eccles made an application for bankruptcy discharge that would be heard at the Preston County Court when the official receiver would say the case was one of 1915, and was in many respects quite out of the ordinary. Proofs for dividend had amounted to £13,681, and a dividend of 7s. in the pound had been paid on those proofs. At the hearing Eccles said he felt justified in taking Alston Hall because he thought he could live there for £2,000 to £2,500 a year, and was also to say that he was anxious to get into business again as early as possible as he felt he could make money. The application was adjourned to a later date with the probability of an earlier hearing with Eccles being advised to obtain legal assistance.

But for all his 'wanton extravagance' and financial downturns, it has to be said that William Eccles gave Alston Hall a new lease of life. Had it not been for his modernisation schemes, the building might have remained empty and unwanted to deteriorate to such a degree that after the First World War its demolition might well have been under consideration.

After leaving Alston Hall Eccles went to Rigg's Hotel in Windermere where he was in March 1915 staying for 25 days at £4 per day, at the same time borrowing money from moneylenders whilst overdrawn at the bank. On 19 March 1926 William Eccles died of a cerebral haemorrhage at Rose Cottage, Bonningate, Kendal, his daughter Kathryn being present at his death, following which he was interred in St Oswald's churchyard, Burneside.

Chapter thirteen

The 1916 sale of the Hall's contents

By the beginning of April 1916 thoughts of selling the Hall had become a reality. It again was unoccupied with a vast and expensive array of furniture, carpets, fittings, china, silverware, etc., a large proportion of which presumably had accumulated during the time of the Mercers as no mention has been found of a furniture sale at the Hall before 1916. Part of this array of furniture and appointments was bankrupt stock left over by William Eccles and plans would be already in place for the Hall's contents to be sold by public auction in the second half of the month.

One interesting item that was not to be on sale and which may have been purchased by John Mercer was a reed and pipe organ in the chapel. If the instrument was in situ at the time of the sale it was probably considered to be a 'permanent fixture', hence its omission.

Most of the rooms were well furnished, some over-furnished, and the incredible number of items in the sale seemed to be well beyond the number that one person alone such as Eccles could accumulate in his extremely short residency at the Hall even though a part of the title page of the sale catalogue read – *Comprising the Whole of the Contents of the above Mansion, recently supplied, principally by Messrs. Goodall's, and remarkable for its luxurious character and completeness.*

Much of the furniture would be the genuine article relating back to the age of the Adam Brothers, Hepplewhite and Sheraton whilst a large percentage must have been mass produced copies of such styles of furniture, especially the items that had been supplied by Goodall's. In 1890 the *Furniture Gazette* had observed that:

> *It would considerable astonish the Brothers Adam ... to find that the chimney-pieces, overdoors, and glass frames designed for them in 1790, are still in stock and still the latest fashion ... Off and on during the past thirty years, the "Adams" style has never been quite "dead".*

In the years leading to the end of the Victorian period, imitation eighteenth-century furniture would account by far the largest demand for new furniture. Large factories employing hundreds of workers were devoting all their efforts in producing these styles of furniture. Furniture shops were to be full of new copies of Sheraton and Chippendale for it was these pieces that the English public desired, and by the beginning of the Edwardian era it was recognised that there was a fitness in using certain styles for certain rooms in the country house. H. J. Jennings, author of *Our Homes and How to Beautify Them (1902)*, considered that:

> *For the dining room, you may have it Italian Renaissance, Francois Premier, Elizabethan, Jacobean, eighteenth-century English, or modern English Renaissance. French styles may be put on one side for an English dining room; so may the Gothique Anglais ... For the drawing room there are available the whole range of the French styles, from Louis XIV to Empire, also the English Chippendale to Adam period, and, if these give not scope enough, the English Renaissance as practised by the English School. A breakfast or morning room ... is essentially of the national character.*

Perhaps William Eccles in 1912 had been advised on the above before re-decorating and furnishing Alston Hall. The sale of April 1916 would involve a total of 1,545 lots being disposed by auction over a period of six days, the sale being by the order of the trustee of Eccles's bankruptcy, his accountant Mr J. Todd. The 14th and 15th April between 10am and 4.30pm had been designated the viewing days pending the sale of this exotic collection arranged for the 17th to the 19th and the 26th to the 28th of April.

A motor char-à-banc was to run on view and sale days every hour from 9.30am to 2.30pm from the salerooms of the auctioneers E. J. Reed & Sons of 47 Fishergate, Preston who had issued a catalogue of the furniture and appointments, the return fares being one shilling and six pence. Train times had been given from Preston to Grimsargh Station and a field had been reserved at the Hall for the parking of cars.

It was not a good time to sell, the First World War was continuing with

• ALSTON HALL, NEAR PRESTON. •

By Order of the Trustee.— In Bankruptcy, *Re* WM. ECCLES.

CATALOGUE

OF THE

COSTLY, : ARTISTIC, : AND : USEFUL

Furniture & Appointments

Comprising the Whole of the Contents of the above Mansion, recently supplied, principally by Messrs. Goodall's, and remarkable for its luxurious character and completeness.

Boudoir and Upright Grand Pianofortes, by Brinsmead, Schiedmayer, and Chappell.

Rare Antique ADAM SIDEBOARD.

Suites of Shield-back Chippendale Chairs. Old Carved Oak Court Cupboard.

Chests, Gate-leg Tables, EARLY ENGLISH WALNUT FURNITURE, of Queen Anne, and William and Mary Periods. Tall Case Clocks.

1,500ozs. of STERLING SILVER,

Including many Fine Pieces of George II., George III., and Early Victorian

OLD SHEFFIELD AND ELECTRO-PLATE. Valuable OLD CHINA, embracing Specimens from the CHELSEA, DERBY, WORCESTER, SPODE, SÈVRES, DRESDEN, and other Factories.

Oil Paintings and Water-Colour Drawings,

By J. W. Oakes, R.A., Conrad Keisel, Wm. Watson, Tom Mostyn, Frank Mason, E. Richardson, &c.

A few Choice ARTIST PROOF ETCHINGS, after Meissonier and Dendy Sadler.

Superb Suites of RICHLY-CUT GLASS and Table Appointments.

Costly Oriental, Persian, and Axminster CARPETS.

A Complete Equipment of HOUSEHOLD LINEN of the Finest Quality.

Expensive Electric Light Fittings, Electric Motor Vacuum Cleaning Machine, and other Effects,

Which will be Sold by Auction

BY

∴ E. J. REED AND SON ∴

Pursuant with Instructions from JAS. TODD, Esq., the Trustee,

On Monday, Tuesday, and Wednesday, April 17th, 18th, and 19th;

ALSO ON

Wednesday, Thursday, and Friday April 26th, 27th, & 28th, 1916,

COMMENCING AT ELEVEN O'CLOCK EACH DAY.

VIEW DAYS.—Admission by Catalogue only (Price 1/-), FRIDAY and SATURDAY, APRIL 14TH and 15TH, from 10 a.m. to 4 30 p.m.

Mather Bros., Printers, Preston.

Fig. 13.1 Title page of the catalogue for the 1916 sale.

Lot 482.　　　　Lot 481.

Charles I. Oak Table—Lot 685.
Oak Chest—Lot 687.

Fig. 13.2 Lots 685, 687, 482 and 481 illustrated in the 1916 sale catalogue. Lot 685, a Charles I oak table with date 1635. Lot 687, an antique oak chest. Lot 482, a Grecian-shaped Derby vase with dolphin handles and a garden scene. Lot 481, a pair of Crown Derby vases having panels with landscapes, each vase fitted in a loose circular base with double handles.

no end in sight, and money to spend on luxurious items was becoming less and less available. At the opening of hostilities in 1914 stock exchanges round the world had crashed as insurance premiums rose, and investors seeking to liquidate their assets would be responsible for bond and stock prices falling. Income tax at the start of the war had been 6 per cent and super tax 8 per cent. By November 1914 these figures had doubled, and in 1918 income tax would be at 30 per cent and super tax at over 50 per cent.

The sale would highlight what had been an almost unbelievable lifestyle of sheer luxury at the Alston mansion, and to many members of the public, the timing of the sale may well have been looked upon as being

Fig. 13.3 Lots 688, 686, 695, 404 and 403 illustrated in the 1916 sale catalogue. Lot 688, an antique oak armchair dated 1688. Lot 686, an early English oak court cupboard that had been purchased from the sale of the collection of the late Paul Catterall, Lytham. Lot 695, a dinner gong of Burmese bronze. Lot 404, a pair of bronze statuettes. Lot 403, rare and valuable antique bracket clock with Cambridge and Westminster chimes.

Lot 404.   Lot 403.

Lot 688.

Lot 686.
COURT CUPBOARD.

Lot 695.

inappropriate, considering what was happening in nearby Preston and further afield on the battlefields of Flanders and Northern France.

Being a garrison town and a major railway centre, Preston at the beginning of the war in August 1914 had become a base for mobilisation. The 5 August had seen the 1st Battalion of the Loyal North Lancashire Regiment assemble on Preston's market square to see the Mayor Harry Cartmel take possession of one of the Regiment's colours for safe keeping. Within weeks the regiment had suffered appalling casualties during the first Battle of Mons.

On 7 September 1914 on the same Preston market square the newly formed 'Preston Pals' – 'D' Company of the 7th Battalion, Loyal North Lancashire Regiment had assembled before embarkation for training on Salisbury Plain following which they left for the Western Front in June 1915 to take part in the battle of Loos that began at 6.30am on 25 September. Poison gas was to be used for the first time and as British troops went over the top to the sound of bagpipes, in places their own gas blew back onto them and everywhere they were cut down by machine gun fire.

In January 1915 it was reported that some 5,000 men were stationed in Preston, the town's barracks in Fulwood being full and overflowing. One thousand men were to be billeted in the Public Hall; 500 in the pavilion on Faringdon Park; 400 in private houses; and another 400 in the town's 'licensed houses'.

On the first day of sale at Alston Hall the contents of bedrooms 1 to 7; bachelor's bedroom; bedrooms 9 and 10; tower room; top landing and stairs; and drawing room, were to be auctioned as well as a huge collection of china. Bedrooms 1 to 7 would be for servants on the second floor, each one being different with regard to furnishings and amount of contents. For example, amongst the items listed for bedroom number 3 was a satin walnut chest of drawers; two bedroom chairs; and an iron 3ft combination bedstead fitted with a woven wire spring mattress having a curled hair mattress, complete with feather bolster and pillow. There were also a towel rail; a toilet glass in a birch frame; a soiled-linen basket; and a bracket clock, whilst on the floor was linoleum of Indian straw pattern, and an Axminster carpet strip.

In contrast to bedroom number 3, bedroom number 5 had a fireplace with a 3ft 6in. black and polished iron kerb fender, the main furniture being a white enamelled wardrobe; a pair of white enamelled toilet tables; a dressing table having a bevelled and landscaped mirror; and a wash stand having a tiled top and back. The brass-mounted 3ft 6in. French bedstead

Lot 691.

Lot 655.

Lot 690.

Lot 656.

Lot 684- Queen Anne Table.

Fig. 13.4 Lots 691, 655, 656, 684 and 690 illustrated in the 1916 sale catalogue. Lot 691, a bracket clock having a chased dial with enamelled numerals, the case ornamented with scroll mouldings, with bracket to match; total height 4ft. 6in. Lot 655, a rare antique Chippendale tallboy chest of drawers. Lot 656, a pair of antique walnut Queen Anne chairs. Lot 684, a rare antique walnut Queen Anne table. Lot 690, a Florentine bronze group by Clodion.

Lot 714.

Fig. 13.5 Lot 714, Grandfather clock by J. Fisher of Preston. This was a superb clock with an eight-day movement and a brass and silvered arched dial showing the phases of the moon and days of the month. The mahogany case had panels inlaid with floral and fine lines of brass, the head having Doric columns entwined with brass stringing supporting a moulded arch cornice with a centre vase ornament.

with two pillars was fitted with a woven wire spring mattress complete with a thick curled hair mattress and a feather bolster and pillow. There were also a rush-seated chair; two alarm clocks; a white enamelled towel rail; a wall mirror, and a soiled-linen basket. At the window was a linen blind whilst on the floor was linoleum of Indian straw pattern, a Kidderminster carpet square and a linoleum mat. The room also had an electric light pendant; clearly this had been a room designated for someone in a high position in the servant hierarchy.

For some of the lots in the photocopied version of the sale catalogue in the Hall's archives, their prices had been written in pencil. Whether these were the starting price or the selling price one is unable to say, as for example the grandfather clock by J. Fisher of Preston has the price of £26, although Marion Roberts in her publication of 1994 says the clock was sold for £21. However, the prices in the following text are those written in the photocopied version of the sale catalogue.

The sale on the second day, Tuesday 18 April dealt with the contents of the housemaid's room; sewing room and linen store; a bathroom; small green bedroom; green bedroom; dining room; and the music room.

The small green bedroom as a guest room was well appointed with furniture including two identical Adam style bedroom suites in mahogany decorated with ivory white enamel and oval green medallions, each comprised of a wardrobe, dressing chest, washstand, and a 3ft 6in. brass bedstead. There were also three chairs *en suite*; a stand table *en suite*; and a double toilet service having 2 jugs, 2 basins, 2 soap boxes 2 sponge trays, 2 brush vases, 2 chamber pots and a slop pail. As well as bedding and mattresses, a box Ottoman and a cane corner linen basket were also amongst the lots on sale. Two Holland blinds; a pair of Swiss lace curtains having a floral trellis pattern on fine Brussels net; and a pair of green linen tapestry curtains with fadeless linings made up the window appointments. The fireplace had a 4ft 6in. satin brass kerb fender, three fire implements, extra cinder tongs, and a coal vase *en suite*, whilst the floor was covered in linoleum upon which was an Axminster carpet and a Persian hearth rug.

Next door, the green bedroom had similar style furniture and appointments as the small green bedroom but being a larger room had extra furniture by way of a pillar wardrobe; a four-fold draught screen 6ft high and 7ft wide, and a mahogany chest of drawers. As in the small green bedroom, the window appointments, the hearth suite, and floor covering in the green bedroom were more or less the same, but the latter did not have a double toilet service, instead a mahogany night commode was listed. Electric lighting was provided by a satin brass three-light electrolier with pendant chain, lamps and cut glass shades; a satin brass two-light pulley pendant over the dressing table; and three table lamps each having a green silk shade and flexible connection.

As to be expected the furniture and appointments of the dining room were most luxurious. One impressive feature was the fireplace (fig. 4.19) whilst at the window facing the dell area were three Holland blinds with spring rollers and three lots of Swiss lace full floral pattern curtains on fine Brussels net, the main curtains being dark green plush trimmed with silver metallic braid, each with cord and tassel loop. This array of costly drapery had a double pelmet to match.

One assumes that this window had been re-modelled during William Eccles's time at the Hall to allow more natural light to enter the room when a single centrally placed mullion built-up of stone blocks was installed to present two large windows as seen in fig. 3.17, as the three Holland blinds listed in 1916 for the window could well be an indication that originally the window had two mullions with transoms. It seems that Holland blinds had been fitted in the private rooms of the Hall soon after it had been built,

740   Old French Empire Stand, containing Ten Tea Spoons, Tongs and Tea Strainer

741   Pair of Salad Servers

742   Pair of Antique Sugar Tongs, pierced and engraved

743   Six Tea Knives and Forks, with engraved electro-plated blades, silver ferrules, and Mother o' Pearl handles

744   14in. Circular SALVER, with engraved centre, shell and scroll border, on four scroll leaf feet, 1843   —43 oz.

745   14in. Circular SALVER, with gadrooned border, on three club feet, initialled " J.T.M." Geo. III., 1768   —46½oz.

746   9in. Circular Salver, engraved centre, with foliate scroll border on claw feet. Geo. II., 1743   —22½oz.

747   6in. Circular Salver, engraved Centre, crushed bead edge, on claw and ball feet, 1783   —4 oz., 14 dwts.

748   6½in. Plain Chippendale Waiter, Geo. II, 1737   —8 oz. 6 dwts

749   6in. Circular Waiter, with beaded edge, on claw and ball feet, Geo. III, 1782   —7 oz. 6 dwts

750   Two Geo. II. Circular PLATES, 10in., with gardooned borders and crest, 1765   —30 oz.

751   Pear Shaped TEA AND COFFEE SERVICE, richly embossed with roses and scroll design, initialled " W. E." comprising :—Coffee Pot, Tea Pot, Sugar Bowl, Cream Ewer, Hot Water Jug and Hot Milk Jug   —102 oz.

752   24in. Oblong TEA TRAY, engraved centre, with gadrooned and shell border, initialled " W.E."   —151 oz., 6 dwt.

753   Handsome Oblong TEA POT, engraved with vine leaves and birds, Geo. III, 1811   —17 oz., 10 dwts

754   Geo. III. Oval TEA SERVICE, whorl flute pattern, with gadrooned border, and leaf handles, initialled " T," comprising :—Tea Pot, Sugar Bowl, and Cream Jug   —40 oz.

755   Geo. III. Pear shaped COFFEE POT, beautifully embossed and engraved with foliage, flower and scroll designs, 1776   —27 oz.

756   Geo. III. Cylindrical COFFEE POT, plain, with narrow gadroon border, 1808   —12 oz.

757   Geo. IV. SMALL TEA POT, bordered in relief, with convolvulus leaves and flowers, 1829   —13 oz.

758   Set of Four Geo. III., plain Oval Salts, with gadrooned borders, on shell and club feet, with loose blue glass linings, 1763   —11ozs.

759   Two   do.   initialled on bottom " S. W."   —5 oz., 10 dwts

760   Six Geo. III, engraved Salt Spoons

761   Pair of Plain Geo. III Circular Salts, on club feet

762   Pair of Circular Sweetmeat Dishes, with gadroon borders, each fitted with richly cut glass bowl, Geo. III, 1810   —6 oz.

763   Helmet Shaped Sugar Basket, with pierced border and engraved bands, reeded handle and oval foot, fitted with a blue glass lining, 1789   —6 ozs.

Fig. 13.6 A page from the 1916 sale catalogue listing some of the items of silver.

fig. 8.3 showing them in *c.*1896. In 1916 when Eccles had left the Hall presumably the same blinds were still in situ as seen in fig. 3.2.

For the 1916 sale the doorway from the dining room into the conservatory had a similar pair of curtains with pelmet and loops to those at the dining room window. For electric lighting the room had a set of five, cut and frosted dome lights with oxidized copper mounts. Amongst the furniture was a Spanish mahogany dining table with 'D' ends forming a 5ft circular table when closed, and fitted with three extra leaves so enabling it to be extended to 11ft 3in. Other tables included four Spanish mahogany circular tables *en suite*; a mahogany Chippendale side table (60 guineas);

Fig 13.7 Lot 808, Old Sheffield Plate epergne illustrated in the 1916 sale catalogue. This was of foliate scroll design having four branches each fitted with a cut glass circular dish, the centre coronae supporting an 11 inch diameter cut glass dish to match. All was set on an 18 inch diameter mirror base that had a raised floral border with shell and claw feet. An extra set of sconces was available for converting the epergne to candelabra.

Lot 808.

and three coffee tables, whilst the Adam style sideboard (90 guineas) was of figured mahogany.

Chairs amounted to two suites of mahogany shield back chairs, one comprised of two armchairs and four singles (£9 each), their seats covered in green Morocco leather, the other suite having six chairs upholstered *en suite*. Also on sale were three mahogany knife boxes; a mahogany garde-vin fitted with loose metal lining, and of sarcophagus design on carved claw feet; three Japanese bronze jardinières, two of which were a pair; three pairs of circular hassocks covered in dark green velvet; a pair of Florentine bronze statuettes 16 inches high, on rouge marble plinths; and an antique bracket clock by William Meris of Westminster, which had full Cambridge and Westminster chimes.

Adding to this luxurious array of items for auction were a number of picture engravings, a pair of coloured ones being Fore's stable scenes – 'Thoroughbreds' and the 'Mail Change' by J. Harris after J. F. Herring. There were also oil paintings, one being 'Group of Highland Sheep' (30 guineas) by William Watson (1881). Other lots in the room included the satin brass hearth suite of Adam design with 5ft kerb fender, three fire implements, extra cinder tongs, and two oviform coal vases *en suite*. Lot 431 was a Royal Axminster carpet of light ground with interlaced design of Oriental flowers and foliage in rich subdued colours and with border to match. Lot 432 was its underlay whilst lot 433 was a Persian hearth rug.

Lots 434–501 amounted to an impressive collection of Old China and decorative ware representative of names such as Dresden; Coalport; Caughley; Worcester; Spode; Rockingham; Derby; Chelsea-Derby; Coalbrookdale; Oriental; Sevres; Crown Derby; Capo di Monti, and Wedgwood. Within the collection was an ironstone pot-pourri jar decorated in Oriental style; a Viennese enamel timepiece; three carved ivory figures, and a Japanese bronze figure.

The mention of a music room in the sale's catalogue would present some thought as to its location as this was the first time a reference to such had been presented. However, the sale's catalogue listed a Chesterfield settee having been fitted within the bay of the room. Taking into account that the Hall had five rooms, each with a bay, that is the morning room, drawing room, rose bedroom, boudoir, and the chapel, the latter was the only one absent by name in the sale's catalogue, thus leading one to conclude that the chapel had been converted into a music room.

In the summer of 1912 the new Catholic Chapel of St Mary Magdalen in Penwortham near Preston that was to open at the end of September, received as a gift the altar from the chapel at Alston Hall, the altar to be later extended and furnished with a tabernacle and baldacchino executed in Caen stone and marble. Presumably this would be the time when the chapel at Alston Hall was deconsecrated thus allowing William Eccles to use it as a music room.

Among the contents of the music room for the 1916 sale were: a three light electrolier on a suspension chain; an antique mahogany mule chest; a pianoforte by Chappell & Co.; a Chippendale mahogany cabinet fitted out with a 'His Master's Voice' gramophone and storage for records; two card tables; an afternoon tea stand; two coffee tables; an occasional table; and two armchairs. On the floor was a costly Persian centre carpet, 12ft by 8ft 6in. in rich crimson, blue and fawn colours. Also in the room was an oxidized brass Grecian-shaped coal vase on a tripod stand, and a mahogany framed fire screen with plate glass centre panel and glazed side panels. These latter two items would have been for a hearth suite, but knowing that the chapel (then listed as the music room) was not to have a fireplace, one came to the conclusion that the coal vase and fire screen had been placed in the room whilst the sale was in progress. Also in the room was lot 531 described as *Bunting Union Jack, 12ft. by 6ft.*, (15 shillings).

At the time of the 1916 sale there may well have been the reed and pipe organ mentioned above in the music room even though the instrument is not listed. Whether or not John Mercer had purchased it for religious use one is unable to say, only that the first reference to be found for the organ was in the 1940 inventory for the contents of the chapel when a description of the instrument was presented.

It had been made by W. Bell & Co. of Guelph, Ontario, Canada, and was a two manual 23 stop, reed and pipe organ of 5 octaves, having pedals for one row of reeds. Provided with a hand side blower and double foot blowers with wind indicator, it was presented in a mahogany casing on an oak bench.

The Bell Piano and Organ Co., an instrument manufacturing firm, had been established in 1864 in Guelph by brothers William and Robert Bell with a staff of three, the firm producing 25 four-legged 'Diploma' melodeons in the first year. In 1871 W. Bell & Co. opened a factory on Market Square, and by 1881 nearly 200 employees produced annually over 1200 melodeons and reed organs, some of which were exported as far as Australia. In 1884, for which the firm claimed to have produced 26,000 instruments, Bell formed a partnership with his son W. J. Bell (1863–1925), Mrs W. B. Kennedy, and A. W. Alexander. The younger Bell in 1888 sold the firm to an English syndicate at which time the name was changed to the Bell Organ and Piano Co. Ltd., and the manufacture of pianos on a grand scale began. The organ at Alston Hall would remain in the chapel until the Hall's contents sale of February 1949 when it was then sold including its seat for a mere £21.

Although music played a significant part in the entertainment environment of many a Victorian country house, presumably this was not to be a common event at Alston Hall where John Mercer and his wife lived a rather reserved and quite lifestyle. In some instances where music did play a significant part in the lifestyle of a country house, women sang or played the piano in the drawing room whilst men would sing and play an organ in another room to be known as the music room. Perhaps William Eccles had this in mind when he converted the chapel into a music room.

One popular type of organ was the Aeolian Pipe Organ, considered as the ultimate status symbol of the Edwardian country house. It worked off a roll similar to that for a pianola but its organ pipes could achieve a wider range of effects than piano strings and its stirring music was accompanied by drums and cymbals. Played on the same principle as the pianola, the Aeolian enabled anyone to command the impressive tones of a pipe organ, and a booklet about it was available at The Orchestrelle Company, Aeolian Hall, 135–6–7, New Bond Street, London, W.

It would be in the chapel at Alston Hall during a visit of 2 January 2019, that one would discover yet another hidden decorative gem of the mansion's Victorian past. Due to water damage during the fire, wallpaper was peeling from one of its walls to expose an originally plastered and green painted surface upon which stencilled lines had been applied to represent mortar joints in a mock wall of ashlar stone blocks. Also on the wall and well above dado level was a stencilled decorative narrow frieze as shown in fig. 16.8.

Such was a type of wall decoration common in many a building of some importance during the Victorian era, the stencilled joints being part of an art technique known as *trompe l'oeil,* 'to deceive the eye', that presented realistic imagery to create the optical illusion that the depicted object existed in three dimensions. The technique can still be seen in stage scenery and Alfred Darbyshire most probably would have applied it when designing scenery in the theatre. William Burges was to adopt the technique with good effect as seen today at Cardiff Castle and not far away at Castell Coch for the 3rd Marquess of Bute.

Presumably the papering of the chapel walls at Alston Hall came about during the time when William Eccles was converting the room into a music room. Unfortunately due to the magnitude of the water damage to this design feature it would not become a part of the new scheme of decoration following post-fire restoration.

The third day of the 1916 auction sale at Alston Hall dealt with the contents of the pink suite's bedroom, dressing room, and bathroom; the boudoir; main landing and stairs; the hall; the main lounge; and the sale of Sterling silver.

As would be expected the pink bedroom represented luxury almost beyond belief. Holland blinds on spring rollers were fitted at the windows, the main window and the side one having curtains in soft pink with cream patterns, draped valances and fadeless linings. Electric light fittings in the room consisted of a satin brass three-light electrolier on a pendant chain; a two-light pulley pendant over the dressing table; two satin brass electric light brackets to match over the mantelpiece, and two satin brass electric light table lamps. The bedroom suite of figured dark Spanish mahogany with inlaid satinwood was comprised of a 7ft wardrobe; dressing table with mirror, and a 5ft bedstead in satin brass of Adam design, its head and foot having oval panels containing cross rails with foliate centre rosettes and square rail extensions beneath. Fitted over the bedstead was a canopy of pink satin curtains lined with cream silk, whilst the pink satin cover of the bed's eiderdown quilt matched the window draperies. With its panels covered *en suite* with the room in pink satin with floral devices was a four-fold screen.

Amongst the rest of the furniture were three chairs upholstered in floral pale green silk tapestry; a mahogany stand table with under tray; a gentleman's dressing table; a writing table, and an Ottoman couch. Also present in the room was a washstand; a Bisto china double toilet service having two basins; two ewers (large jugs); a brush vase; a soap dish; two chamber pots, and a slop pail. The hearth suite in satin brass was comprised of fender, three fire implements, pokerette, and cinder tongs, and there was an urn-shaped coal vase to match. The floor was covered with linoleum upon which had been laid carpet felt for the Persian carpet (£65) that had a Wilton carpet surround. There was also a Persian rug and a jewel safe 26in. by 20in. by 20in., its interior fitted with a mahogany nest of drawers.

The main landing and stairs had been well equipped with electric light fittings, lot 647 amounting to three pendants of an antique brass lantern pattern with suspension chains, lamps and frosted glass shades, lot 648 being the same, whilst lot 649 was a single pendant with lamp and English cut glass shade. Lot 654 must have been the most impressive, comprised of brass chain pendant electrolier with a double cluster of lights, one with six scroll arms, the other with four arms, fitted with lamps and ten English cut glass shades (10 guineas).

The items of furniture on the landing included a rare antique Chippendale mahogany tallboy (39 guineas); a pair of Queen Anne chairs in English walnut (£10); an antique tallboy chest of six drawers in black mahogany (£10 10s.); a dwarf chest of drawers inlaid with satinwood fine lines and banded with rosewood fluted columns (£12); an antique wall mirror (£7 10s.); an antique tall cased clock with Whittington and Westminster chimes (£45); and a Leveson's Patent Lounge Chair de Luxe in walnut and fitted with adjusting movements and wheel castors. Leveson and Sons of Lawrence Street, London had been founded in 1849 and specialised in furniture for invalids and babies. There was also a valuable oil painting 'Leaving Home' 28in. by 34in. (£27), artist unknown and depicting a young woman standing at a stile taking a parting look at her country home with a distant view of London in the background.

On the floor of the landing and its west and east corridors was an Axminster carpet of crimson ground with arabesque pattern in soft green and dark shades. For the sale this had been divided into the following lots;

Lot 663. 54 yards on west corridor, from small green bedroom and bathroom to main landing entrance, with best hygienic underfelt as fitted.

Lot 664. 47 yards on main landing and small vestibule to rose suite, with the best hygienic underfelt as fitted.

Lot 665. 31 yards on east corridor to boudoir and pink suite, from entrance to main landing, also on top landing near bachelor's bedroom, with the best hygienic underfelt as fitted.

On sale were also nine yards of bordered stair carpet 22in. in width with patent thick felt stair pads on the staircase leading to the bachelor's bedroom. Indian straw pattern linoleum had been laid before carpeting on the two corridors and main landing, whilst on the main staircase were 15 yards of 46 in. in width Axminster stair carpet to match the one on the landing, secured by twenty-four satin brass triangular stair rods.

The impressive collection of Sterling silver was represented by lots 732–820, one of the most attractive items being lot 808 shown in fig. 13.7, an Old Sheffield plate (silver on copper) epergne; a centrepiece for the dining room table especially on special occasions. Representing foliated scroll work in design it had four branches each fitted with a cut glass circular dish, whilst the centre coronae supported a cut glass dish of eleven inches in diameter to match. This superb piece of craftsmanship stood on a circular plateau having a raised floral border and a mirror eighteen inches in diameter, the plateau supported on feet of a shell and claw design. A set of sconces for converting to candelabra was also available.

A week later, Wednesday 26 April, the fourth day's sale presented the contents of the oak sitting room; the blue bedroom; the rose suite's bedroom, dressing room and bathroom; and the morning room.

Like the music room, the oak sitting room was mentioned for the first time by this name in the existing archives of the Hall via the sales catalogue of 1916, the room having been the servants' hall erected shortly after the arrival of William Eccles in 1912. With a servants' hall Eccles could employ more servants at the Hall to enjoy the lifestyle of a country squire. The Edwardian era (1901–11) had seen country houses in general being the venue for those arriving in their new motorcars to spend weekends shooting and making merry; perhaps Eccles had such in mind for Alston Hall.

The contents of the oak sitting room as listed give a clear indication that the room had originally been furnished as the servants' hall. At the window were a blue linen blind and a green baize curtain and the furniture was somewhat plain in appearance, the kerb fender of the fireplace being of black polished iron. The room could be lit by a satin brass three-light electrolier having a pendant chain and three frosted glass globes and lamps.

In the room in keeping with its new title of the oak sitting room, were several items of oak furniture including a brown oak 6ft sideboard of early English design and a brown oak telescopic dining table 3ft 3in. wide by 8ft, its two loose leaves enabling it to be extended to 12ft. Perhaps William Eccles had a vision of his household staff seated around the table, butler at one end, housekeeper at the other, male members down one side, females opposite. Lot 832 was for six brown oak chairs with shaped seats and square rail backs, whilst lot 833 was a stained walnut side table with drawer. Lot 826 represented a bracket clock with a twenty-one day movement in a brown oak case.

Being a recent addition to the Hall and presumably furnished at a time when William Eccles was about to become bankrupt, the servants' hall at Alston probably was never used as such, or if it did it would be only for a short time. In the years leading up to the First World War servants' halls were already in decline brought about by a changing social and economic climate. Domestic service as an occupation, especially for women was losing its popularity as opportunities in new kinds of work offering better pay and conditions increased. At the time of the 1916 sale many male domestic servants were fighting the war in Europe, and the status symbol of having a servants' hall in many a country house had become far less attractive. It is probably with such thoughts in mind that the person or persons responsible for the contents sale at Alston decided to list the servants' hall as a sitting room. Yet just over a year later when the Hall and its estate were to be sold by auction the oak sitting room and the music room were listed respectively as the servants' hall and the chapel.

For the 1916 sale, the morning room contained stunning furniture including a Sheraton telescopic dining table of Spanish mahogany; Chippendale and Sheraton display cabinets; a revolving bookcase and a 7ft library bookcase; an upright grand pianoforte by John Brinsmead & Sons, with stool; a 6ft Chesterfield settee covered in green woollen repp with chair to match; a suite of six Chippendale shield back chairs; a child's armchair in Sheraton style; and two armchairs, one upholstered in old rose striped velour velvet, the other in floral pattern silk tapestry.

Also in the room was a great deal of Oriental china including a 52-piece Canton china tea and coffee service, and some Wedgwood. The room with a fitted Axminster carpet was lit by a five-light electrolier and a standard floor lamp, and before the fireplace was a satin brass hearth suite and a lynx-skin rug. There were numerous sets of cut table glass and also china including a Royal Worcester dinner service; a Royal Worcester breakfast and tea service; and a Royal Worcester dessert service.

The following day was the sale of items in kitchen number 1 and kitchen number 2, (one of these being the scullery); the butler's pantry; the study; and the flower room. Lots appertaining to items of silver and electro plate were also available on auction.

As to the electric lighting that had recently been installed, this was being supplied by a self-contained power plant in a lean-to building on the stable end of the stable block, a power plant consisting of a diesel engine driving a dynamo to produce electricity to be stored in accumulators. The mention of electricity at the Hall would be in the memoirs (1991) of Dr F. L. Mitchell who with his wife had attended a weekend course at Alston Hall in 1986, and who as a child had lived with his parents from 1923 to 1938 at 'Alston Villa' a short distance from the entrance gates of the Hall.

Dr Mitchell would recall electricity in the Hall being supplied by a room full of glass accumulators situated *in a building near the garage in the stable yard,* the accumulators being charged once per week by a single cylinder diesel engine with dynamo in another room behind. Firing about twice every second, the engine used an old oil drum as a silencer, the noise being heard easily from 'Alston Villa' nearby and much further away.

Dr Mitchell's description fits perfectly with the type of power used during the Edwardian period to provide electricity in large country houses, a diesel engine driving a dynamo, the electricity produced being stored until needed in accumulators. One recalls a different power technology to produce electricity to be stored in a similar way for the Scorton mansion (Wyresdale Hall, today known as Wyresdale Park) of Peter Ormrod mentioned in chapter three. Instead of a diesel engine a waterwheel (replaced later by a water turbine) in the cotton mill in the village there powered a generator to feed electricity into accumulators some distance away in the Home Farm of the Hall. Part of the sale particulars when the Hall was for sale in 1922 read:

> The house is lighted by electric light generated by means of a water wheel and dynamo at Scorton Mill, being conveyed thence by overhead cable to storage batteries at the Home Farm. The wheel and dynamo belong to Mr John Battersby who, by verbal agreement, supplies the necessary current, for an annual payment of £50.

The Scorton waterwheel was large, made of iron and a breast type of 30 feet in diameter with rim gearing. It was dismantled in the 1930s when presumably the water turbine arrived to drive the dynamo.

At Alston Hall no waterpower for producing electricity was available and so the diesel engine would be the ideal form of power technology, a type of engine that had been the invention of the German engineer (born in Paris) Rudolf Diesel (1858–1913) in 1895. By the end of the Edwardian period, compact diesel engine units were seen as ideal for the generation of electric lighting in country mansions, as even though in some towns and cities the first electric generating companies were operating on steam power, their distribution network was limited due to a number of circumstances. It would not be until the 1930s and 1940s that outlying districts such as Alston would be supplied by electricity following the extension of the National Grid, a network of distribution first introduced in the twenties.

As used in the country house environment, the diesel engine was set into motion by rotating its flywheel whereby the engine's piston then compressed the oxygen in the cylinder to create an extremely high temperature that was to ignite the incoming vaporised diesel oil to produce the power stroke.

Lesley Lewis in her book *The Private Life of a Country House* first published in 1980, writes about her early years living with her parents in

Pilgrims' Hall, a house between Bury St Edmunds and Canterbury. She presents a delightful description of how Albert Murrant, the person in charge of the diesel engine that ran a dynamo to charge a row of batteries for the Hall's electricity system, started the engine.

> To start the engine, which ran on oil, he would prime it by means of a blowlamp. When it got suitably hot he would swing the big flywheel which drove the belt, and the spokes of the bright brass governor would cease to stand distinct, blurring as the speed mounted. It worked beautifully and may be working still, as we sold it after getting on to mains electricity just before the 1939 war. It was a substantial piece of machinery, bedded solidly in concrete, and it gleamed from polishing and its slight film of oil. Apart from light and, in summer, the refrigerator, it could power only one plated breakfast heater for the dining-room, used on Saturdays and Sundays when we might be late.

During the time of John Mercer at Alston Hall and for some time afterwards the Hall was lit by oil lamps and candles only, as the mansion would never have a supply of gas. From the late Victorian period to the end of the Edwardian one, the Hall remained closed for long periods except on those occasions when Canon Taylor was in residence, who in his remaining years most probably never contemplated modernising the Hall's lighting arrangements.

Any property remaining empty for a long time can soon deteriorate and Alston Hall may well have been no exception, and with the arrival of William Eccles in 1912 one can appreciate that a considerable amount of restoration work could well have been called for with oil lamps to be replaced by electroliers and possibly an update of a solid fuel fired central heating system. Therefore there is no doubt whatsoever that it was William Eccles who in the process of 'fitting up Alston Hall' as mentioned at his bankruptcy hearing, as well as installing the electric lighting system and possibly updated an ageing central heating system, gave the mansion a new lease of life.

The early electric lighting system at Alston Hall would have been looked upon with some degree of jubilation, whereby the electroliers supporting new type light bulbs would illuminate rooms with a clear and dirt-free light after replacing the poor lighting of oil lamps and candles whose contaminating residue had for years soiled furnishings, walls and ceilings.

These new light bulbs of the period had been the invention of Joseph Swan, a Newcastle chemist and inventor who on 18 December 1878 demonstrated to the Newcastle-on-Tyne Chemical Society that a carbon filament in a glass globe evacuated of air would glow when an electric current was passed through it. Two years later in December 1880 Sir William Armstrong installed these lamps in his home 'Cragside' in Northumberland, powering them from a generator driven by a water turbine. From June 1881 the House of Commons was lit by these incandescent lamps, and towards the end of the same year Swan type lamps had been installed to illuminate the Savoy Theatre in London.

The first application of electric lighting had appeared in the late 1850s in the public sector using arc lights formed by an electric arc between two carbon rods that gave an intense light, ideal for public spaces, steam engines providing the power for the generators. By 1878 the Gaiety Theatre in London was lit by arc lighting and the following year Blackpool inaugurated its seaside illuminations using arc lights. However the large intense beam of the arc light was most unsuitable for domestic use; the solution was the introduction of the incandescent Swan lamp.

It seems that during his brief stay at Alston Hall, William Eccles not only had electric lighting installed but also had a piped vacuum cleaning system fitted with connection points, the system being mentioned when the mansion came up for sale by auction on 25 July 1917. The operation of the system was simple in that the electricity supplied by the diesel engine and dynamo set activated an electric motor in the cellar to operate an air pump that vacated air within a network of pipes about the mansion. Fixed to this network were connecting points to which a sweeper could be connected, the vacuum in the pipeline thus sucking away silently the dust and dirt to a discharge point somewhere in the system. Fig. 12.2 shows the remains of one connecting nozzle in the entrance hall near the door of what had originally been the smoking room or study.

Probably the first large country house in Britain to have a similar system was Minterne Magna in Dorset, the house having been built in 1903–7. Its centralised system had a large pump in the basement to which was connected a series of tubes to the major rooms where outlets covered by brass flaps and situated in the skirting boards enabled housemaids to plug in the hoses of the vacuum sweepers. Such a system had been patented in 1903 to be known as the 'Silent Dustman'. Sennowe Park in Norfolk also had this technology and new country houses were still being built with centralised vacuum cleaning systems prior to the Second World War, two examples being Eltham Palace (1936) and Charters (1938).

On a much larger city scale, evolving as late as 1910, was the 'Silent

Dustman' system of A. and P. Stevens within the London Hydraulic Power Company's network of high-pressure water mains, the Company having been formed in 1884 to provide hydraulic water pressure for use in hotel lifts, offices, warehouses etc., and eventually the docklands. In the 'Silent Dustman' system of the Company, mains water was used in a jet pump to produce a vacuum in a pipe in which the system was to be fitted. Along the pipe were a number of nozzles to which sweepers could be fixed, the dirt from the sweepers being drawn into a hydraulic pipe and carried away to the drains.

The Liverpool Hydraulic Power Company formed in 1887 to provide hydraulic power in warehouses and commercial premises, cranes and hoists etc., was also to have a 'Silent Dustman' system. In 1924 the Company claimed that the vacuum cleaners were noiseless and gave the highest vacuums, with no working parts to 'get out of order'.

The history of municipal hydraulic power systems and how they operated is a fascinating part of our industrial heritage and deserves a mention, albeit a brief one.

The London Hydraulic Power Company's first pumping station was at Falcon Wharf east of Blackfriars Bridge where four steam engines pumped water to two accumulators each having a vertically placed ram of 20 inches diameter and a stroke of 23 feet, the top of each ram weighted by a load of 106 tons. Each ram would rise to its stroke height of 23 feet as water was pumped to it, the immense weight of 106 tons thus creating a final water pressure of 750 pounds per square inch. As water began to be used in the city's system the ram would descend and once half down an electric bell signalled the engineer in charge to stand by and if necessary start up an additional set of pumping engines. Other pumping stations were subsequently built within the network and in 1953 the Company began to replace its steam engines with electric motors to drive the pumps. Pumping finally ceased in 1977 and in 1985 Mercury purchased the Company to obtain over 150 miles of its ducts for carrying telecommunication cables.

The public distribution of hydraulic power had been pioneered by Hull in 1877. Its system would continue until extensive damage was done to it by enemy aerial bombardment during the Second World War that led to the winding up of the Company. Manchester was to open its municipal supply in 1894 followed by Glasgow in 1895, and like many dock enterprises throughout Britain, Preston Dock that opened in 1892 had its own hydraulic power system for which steam engines pumped to one accumulator.

As to when solid fuel central heating was installed at Alston Hall, most likely it would be on the completion of the mansion in the second half of the 1870s as this most welcome technological innovation along with bathrooms and water closets had become a common addition in large country houses by then. A plan of the Hall on the first edition (1893) of the Ordnance Survey map shows the boiler house alongside the stable yard.

One of the duties of Ann Hirst (later Ann Lightfoot, see chapter 15) as Deputy Warden of the residential college at the Hall in the 1960s was to stoke up the central heating boiler at 11pm to make sure that there would be a plentiful supply of hot water in the morning. In her reminiscences she would write:

> I hated that job as it meant going outside, climbing down a small ladder into the boiler house, and shovelling coke to fill the boiler, coming out to breathe out the fumes and to brush off the dust.

After the Hall's contents sale of April 1916, fifteen months were to pass before the Hall and its estate would come up for sale. Why it should have remained empty for such a period, particularly at a time when a large number of country houses had been converted into hospitals for war casualties remains unknown, unless those responsible for selling it were advised to await awhile until house prices reached a suitable level as 1916 was not a good time for selling country houses.

Alston Hall would have made an ideal hospital for war wounded after its contents sale of April 1916 when its rooms could have easily been converted into wards. Situated in its peaceful environment and with the help of Monica's Order of nuns it could have easily become a convalescent hospital for the many war-stricken men that at the time were arriving back from the horrors of war in France and Belgium. At one period during the war, the Whittingham Asylum Hospital near Alston Hall would receive soldiers stricken by the conflict.

On 1 July 1916, only a few weeks after the Alston Hall contents sale, 100,000 British troops would climb from their trenches and walk across No Man's Land. At the end of the day almost 60,000 of them had been either killed or wounded. Later in the same month on the same battlefield, the 'Preston Pals' Company saw action resulting in 10 officers and 213 of other ranks killed, just 50 men managing to return to the British lines. By August the 'Preston Pals' had virtually ceased to exist.

By May 1915 over 600 men had passed through a hospital for war wounded in a pavilion erected on the north end of Preston's Moor Park.

This pavilion of the Royal Lancashire Agricultural Society had arrived from Blackburn and when complete it had 174 beds. Preston's Royal Infirmary was to provide 100 beds for the wounded and the hospital in Mount Street was to make available 15 beds.

During the war more than two million British and Empire soldiers were wounded resulting in general hospitals being overwhelmed, hence the requisition of many a country house for hospital accommodation, and in some of these houses it was not uncommon for a room to become an operating theatre. A number of smaller country house hospitals catered for convalescent patients rather than those more seriously wounded. 'Broadleys' the house of 1899–1900 by architect C. F. A. Voysey (1857–1941) at the side of Lake Windermere in the Lake District was one. Built for Arthur Currer Briggs, the son of a colliery owner, the house was turned into a convalescent hospital by his wife Helen who provided the funds with herself as matron. Her son Reginald was among the patients having been invalided out with shell shock.

Chapter fourteen

Sale of the Hall and its estate in 1917

In July 1917 Alston Hall stood empty of furniture except for a few pieces left over from the sale of the previous year. A decision had been made to sell the Hall and its estate by auction that was to take place on Wednesday 25 July 1917 at 3 pm by Messrs. E. J. Reed & Son at their saleroom, 47 Fishergate, Preston. Messrs. Titus Thorp & Ainsworth, chartered accountants of 11 Winckley Street, Preston, were to be among the auctioneers for the sale, the other three being Messrs. J. W. Fair & Rea, land agents and surveyors of 8 Winckley Preston; Messrs. B. & F. Tolhurst, solicitors of Gravesend; and Messrs. Hammond & Richards of 26 Lincoln's Inn Fields, London, W.C.

On the almost 475 acre estate which included about 26 acres of half of the river Ribble, were six stock and dairy farms and four cottages. The farms were being occupied on a yearly tenancy and in view of the sale the tenants had been given notice to determine their tenancies by February next. In addition to the fishing and other rights attached to the river frontage, the possibilities of using the water for power for electric current, not only for lighting purposes but also for driving agricultural and other machinery on any part of the estate and in many other ways, was mentioned as being very considerable and of special value. The estate was first to be offered as a whole in one lot and if this was not possible it was to be sold in lots that amounted to twelve in number, and on examining the particulars for each lot it was interesting to note their water supply.

Lot 1 was the stock and dairy farm known as Woodfold Farm, situated about two thirds of a mile from Grimsargh and one and a half miles from Longridge railway station, the lot having a frontage of about 140 yards to the Preston and Longridge main road near the railway station at Grimsargh. Because the water pipes from the Thirlmere reservoir in the Lake District to Manchester passed through lot 1, the sale of this lot was to be subjected *to the conditions of an Indenture dated 8th October 1885, between John Mercer, Esq., and the Mayor, Aldermen and Citizens of the City of Manchester.*

Lot 2 was the Hall and its immediate grounds that included the Shamrock Pit, a field, another pit known as the Dairy Pit, and an embankment. The particulars for the Hall would list its vestibule and entrance hall, lounge, morning room, study, drawing room, winter garden (this would be the conservatory), dining room, strong room with iron safe and shelving for silver, kitchen, scullery, larder, storeroom, butler's pantry, servants' hall, 18 bedrooms (among which would be the principal bedrooms), dressing rooms, 5 bathrooms, lavatories, drying room, housemaid's room, tower rooms, excellent cellars, and a hand-worked hoist from the ground to the first floor. Mentioned was the electric lighting fitted throughout being supplied by a self-contained plant, and also the connections throughout the house for an electric motor vacuum-cleaning machine. The water supply was from the Preston Corporation reservoirs and the sale of this lot was

Fig. 14.1 William Birtwistle.

Fig. 14.2 John Marsden.

subject to the terms of the Agreement with the Corporation, dated 19 June 1912, the Agreement having been made with Monica Waterton following which the stables and outbuildings, Croft and bungalow cottage, were also to be supplied with water from the Corporation. The Hall was fitted with hot and cold water, supplying modern baths and lavatories throughout, whilst the outside boiler house provided heat to radiators in the entrance hall and ground floor rooms.

Mentioned are the conservatories adjoined the mansion and also a peach house, a melon house, a tomato house, potting sheds, tool house etc., whilst the front garden and grounds contained well laid out plantations and walks, rockeries, fishponds, and specimen trees. The two main outbuildings were the stable block accommodating a four-stalled stable, harness room with living rooms and lofts above, and a coach house having been converted into a motorcar garage above which was a large room suitable for use as a billiard room, play room, or museum.

Near the entrance gates were the two brick and stone built and slated cottages each containing a sitting room, kitchen, pantry, bathroom and three bedrooms, each cottage being lit by electric light, as was also the drive to the Hall.

Lot 3 was a dairy and stock farm called Alston Cottage Farm, the house and premises being supplied with water from the Preston Corporation main through a meter whilst there was also a plentiful supply from wells near the house.

Lot 4 was a small holding comprised of a stone built and slated house with out buildings, the water main to Alston Hall running in the road past the house and co-extensive with the land. Outbuildings and yard were being supplied with water by a pump from an underground tank in Alston Cottage Farm yard, the water to which was being brought in iron pipes from a pond in a nearby field.

Lot 5 was a meadow and arable field on the northeasterly side of Alston Lane and with frontage to it and also to Thorn Lane, whilst lot 6 was a meadow.

Alston Old Hall Farm (the Home Farm to Alston Hall) was lot 7, the farmhouse having been the original Alston Hall. Situated on the bank of the river Ribble the farmhouse still had its old banqueting hall with

Fig. 14.3 An event on the terrace at Alston Hall in about 1931. This was probably a garden party in aid of a charity. (By kind permission of Lancashire Archives)

Fig. 14.4 Ribble View House. (By kind permission of Diane Robinson)

open and timbered roof and flagged floor, then being used as a working dairy. There was a plentiful supply of good water from a well for domestic purposes, and in addition the farmyard was supplied from a reservoir in a nearby field and also a spring in another field, the water being conveyed in iron pipes that also fed a trough in a field. This water supply continued past the farm to supply the premises of Boght Farm that was lot 10. Lot 8 was a meadow and lot 9 a pasture field.

Boght Farm (or Boot Farm) was a stock and dairy mixed farm, its homestead standing in a beautiful situation on the bank of the river Ribble, whilst its extensive outbuildings catered for pigs, cattle and horses. Water supply for domestic purposes was from a well, and there was a good supply to the farmyard, washhouse and dairy brought in iron pipes from the reservoir in the field in lot 7. Water for a concrete trough in a nearby field was also supplied from these pipes, whilst the fishing in the river Ribble extended about one and a half miles round the lot.

Lot 11 was a stock and dairy farm called Ribble View containing the house where John Mercer had occupied for a short while during the building of Alston Hall. Outbuildings contained a shippon, provender house, stables, pig boxes etc., whilst the stone built house with cement rendered walls and slated roofs was recorded as containing *2 excellent front Sitting Rooms with large bay windows, Hall, Kitchen, Back Kitchen, Dairy, Pantry, Washhouse, and W.C. on ground floor, with six large Bedrooms, Bathroom, Lavatory, with hot and cold water and W.C. on first floor.* Roof water from the house led into a large tank and a supply of water was also obtained from a large underground tank from which the water was pumped by a force pump to the cisterns and cylinder inside the house. Water could also be pumped from this tank into the farmyard to supply the troughs.

Lot 12 consisted of two brick built and slated cottages with gardens known as Brookhall Cottages. Water was obtained from a well in a field immediately behind the cottages

On Saturday 28 July 1917, the *Preston Guardian* was to report the sale of the Hall and its entire estate for £23,000, the purchaser being William Birtwistle the well-known cotton manufacturer who was to have mills in nearby Blackburn and Preston. The nuns at the Mayfield Convent in East Sussex were to breathe a sigh of relief following the sale and were to note in their annals:

> Alston Hall, near Preston, the property of M. M. Borgia Waterton, which had been a great anxiety to the Society, was sold very satisfactorily. D. G. (dei gratia by the Grace of God).

William Birtwistle (1855–1936) was the second son of Micah Birtwistle (1830–98) whose father, William, (1808–67) of Blackburn had been the founder of what would be the Birtwistle dynasty of cotton manufacturers. In 1877 William married Susannah Holden of Blackburn; the couple were to have two sons and three daughters. When his father, Micah who had Stanley Street Mill in Blackburn retired in 1881, William entered into partnership with Richard Thompson (who had been an overlooker at the mill) to take over the Blackburn mill. Business success soon followed and in 1883 the partnership took over Woodfield Mill of 532 looms in Darwen, and in 1889 Nova Scotia Mill, Blackburn, a combined mill of 30,000 spindles and 450 looms.

The partnership ended in 1895, William keeping the Stanley Street and

Woodfold Mills, and over the next ten years William was to take control of a number of large spinning and weaving mills; Lower Darwen Mill with its small settlement of about 100 houses; the mill at Abbey Village near Withnell and its 100 homes; the Albion Cotton Works at Livesey near Blackburn; the Greenbank Mills of John Hawkins and Sons, Preston; the controlling interest in John Fish and Sons Ltd., Waterfall Mill, Blackburn, which included the nearby Primrose Mill of 600 looms; and finally, Hartford Mill in Preston. During this period William had also erected a new mill of 1889 at Whalley New road, Blackburn to be named 'Florence' after his second daughter and leased to his cousins, Samuel and Herbert Slater, the brothers operating the mill until 1925 when it was returned to the Birtwistle group of mills.

William's next stage in building his cotton manufacturing empire was to establish an office in Manchester from which he would sell the products of his mills under his own name. Needing a good right-hand man to carry out the day to day running of his mills he found such a person in John Marsden who as a young man in the preparation department of the Woodfold Mill, Darwen, had shown exceptional ability. It would be John Marsden as William Birtwistle's Managing Director who would reside at Alston Hall after the First World War.

William Birtwistle would purchase a number of houses, one being 'Billinge Scar' on the outskirts of Blackburn that had been the home of Daniel Thwaites of the Blackburn brewing family. In 1900 William acquired a house in the Lake District where he would have a steam launch on Lake Windermere and in 1910 he purchased his first steam yacht *The Norseman* that was kept on the Clyde for golfing holidays in the Western Isles. In January 1918, the tank 'Egbert' was in Preston for a fund raising scheme for the 'War Loan' fund, William's contribution being £116,000, and shortly afterwards the tank arrived in Blackburn when William gave £100,000.

William and Susannah's eldest son Arthur was to return from the War with the rank of Brigadier General having served in the Gallipoli and Near East Campaigns and France. In 1915 he was awarded the C.M.G. (Order of St Michael and St George), and in 1918 the D.S.O. and C.B. (Companion of the Bath). He died suddenly aged 59 on 19 May 1937, the year after his father's death and a few days before he should have attended the Coronation of King George VI in Westminster Abbey. He had lived at 'Billinge Scar' where in the 1930s his wife Alice had organised garden parties there for the Girl Guides and St John Ambulance Brigade. After his death Alice continued to live at 'Billinge Scar' but the house was too large for her and she moved to 'Westmead', a smaller and attractive house in Meins Road, Blackburn. During the Second World War 'Billinge Scar' was used by the Post Office as a training centre for telephonists. Released from such after the cessation of hostilities, the house would never again become a family home and was demolished in 1948.

Arthur Birtwistle left a son, Arthur Hillmen Birtwistle (Hillmen being his mother's maiden name), and a married daughter, Violet. Following the death of his father, Arthur Hillmen Birtwistle (Peter) (1913–86) began to take an active part in the management of the spinning side of the mills before joining the army at the outbreak of war. The Census of 1939 finds him residing at Ribble View House when he is described as an Estate Manager, Dairy Farmer, and Cotton Spinner and Manufacturer. On 1 March 1939, he was granted a shield of Arms and Crest, the latter complete with motto seen today executed in stone over the doorway of Ribble View House (fig. 14.5). The pair of eagles at the bottom of the steps leading up to the doorway (see fig. 14.4) would be a later addition by the present owners and have no heraldic connection with Arthur Hillmen Birtwistle.

The grant of Arms, (105/200) in the College of Arms, London, was made to him and to his descendants, the blazon being as follows:

> Arms: Sable, a chevron erminois between in chief two weasels statant argent and in base a birt naiant argent. (A birt being a type of fish)

> Crest: Upon a wreath Or and gules, a demi-weasel argent supporting a branch of the cotton plant flowered and fructed proper.

> Motto: SPE ET PERSEVERANTIA

It seems that the Arms granted were partly based upon the Arms of a Birtwistle at Huncoat Hall, near Blackburn, mentioned in William Flower's *Visitation of Lancashire* in 1567, because of the name connection only, the blazon of the Arms of Birtwistle of Huncoat Hall (fig14.6) being 'Sable, a chevron ermine between three weasels statant argent' whilst the Crest is a dolphin (turbot) proper.

As mentioned in chapter two above, Arms relating to different persons cannot be exactly alike so to 'difference' the new Arms of Arthur Hillmen Birtwistle with those of Birtwistle of Huncoat Hall, the chevron ermine (white fur with black spots and tails) on the latter Arms was presented on

Fig. 14.5 Crest of Arthur Hillmen Birtwistle over the doorway of Ribble View House. The Crest was most appropriate for one associated with the Lancashire textile industry, the blazon being: *Upon a wreath Or and gules, a demi-weasel argent supporting a branch of the cotton plant flowered and fructed proper.*

the Arms of A. H. Birtwistle as a chevron erminois (yellow fur with black spots and tails) and the weasel at the base of the shield changed to a birt. The birt on the Arms of A. H. Birtwistle is seen in heraldry as a pun or play on the name of the bearer, in this case the first four letters of the name Birtwistle. As for A. H. Birtwistle's Crest (fig. 14.5), this is the upper half of a weasel holding most appropriately because of Birtwistle's involvement with the cotton industry, a sprig of the cotton plant with a ball of cotton.

The early 1920s had seen William Birtwistle beginning to slow down in his business activities leaving more of such in the hands of his sons and managers, when he began to take an interest in the farming side of his recently acquired Alston Hall Estate. On buying the estate it is believed that he lived for a period in the Hall and then 'Ribble View'. There is also the mention of William Birtwistle after living for a time at 'Ribble View' moving for a period to one of the semi-detached cottages outside the main gates of Alston Hall, the adjacent cottage then occupied by William's

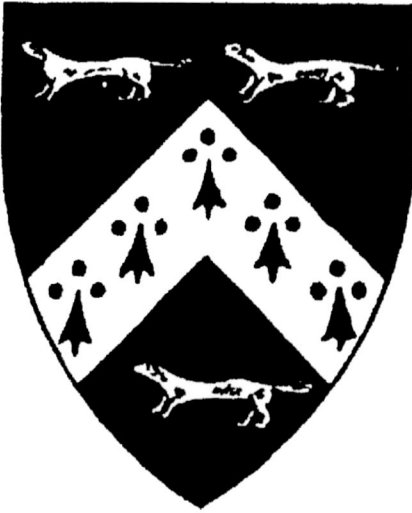

Fig. 14.6 Arms of Birtwistle of Huncoat Hall near Blackburn as mentioned in the 'Visitation of Lancashire' by William Flower, 1567. Blazon: Sable, a chevron ermine, between three weasels statant argent. (By kind permission of Lancashire Archives)

gardener Mr Crowcroft who had arrived in Alston from Witton Hall, Blackburn, in 1923.

On 10 December 1924 when his address was 'Ribble View', Alston, William Birtwistle founded the Alston Property & Investment Company Limited of which he was the chairman, the Company to be privately owned by the Birtwistle family. This enabled him to extend his Alston estate by purchasing farms and land in Alston, Elston, and Grimsargh, and early in 1925 he conveyed to the Company the following: Boght Farm; Ribble View Farm; Brookhall Cottage Farm; Woodfold Farm; Alston Cottage Farm; Alston Old Hall Farm; Farm in Alston Lane; Brookhall Cottage; Alston Cottage (Mrs Keighley, tenant); Alston Cottage (Frank Crowcroft, tenant); Alston Hall; Marsh House Farm; Charity Farm; Land (J. T. Hacking, tenant); Land (J. A. Graham, tenant); Land (Thomas Bolton, tenant); Land (Mr. Birtwistle, tenant); Cottage (Miss I. Field, tenant); Woods; Fir Trees Farm; all at Alston, Elston, and Grimsargh, at a value of £40,605.

The records of the Company for 26 February 1925 show that John Marsden, then the Managing Director of the Birtwistle Group of mills, would by agreement between him and the Company, be allowed to live in Alston Hall for the term of five years at the yearly rent of one peppercorn if demanded. The five-year term would extend up to the closing years of the 1940s when John Marsden retired.

John Marsden and his family were to move into Alston Hall in 1924, the following diary entry of 21 January of that year made by Mrs Nancy Clegg of Lower Yew Tree, Alston, (near the entrance gates of the Hall) stating:

> Alice went and arranged to clean the Hall ready for the Marsdens' to move in. Mr. Birtwistle has gone to Ribble View.

William Birtwistle was to establish a shop above the garage at Alston Hall for the sale of lengths of cotton cloth to local people and in her diary Nancy would write for August 1922 near the time of Preston Guild:

> ––– It was very close and hot today. Kept busy all week making ready for Guild Festivities. Alice went to Clark's Thursday. Cousin Mary came down this afternoon. We went to shop at Alston Hall –––.

John Marsden had been born in Darwen near Blackburn on 13 November 1874, and in 1886 at the age of twelve years began work at William Birtwistle's mill as a half-timer on a wage of 1 shilling and six pence per week. Soon after his fortieth birthday he married Mary Alice Wilkinson on Christmas Eve 1914, who was ten years younger than him.

Mary had been born in Darwen and was an excellent business woman having helped her cotton manufacturing father Thomas Wilkinson in the running of his two mills who on 22 May 1922 when he was a J.P., was presented with a painting by William Hunt (1790–1864) entitled 'Too Hot' by members of the Darwen Manufacturers Association in recognition of his valuable service as Chairman of the Association over a long period of years. It was said that when Mary and her sister were young their father lost everything in a slump just when he was starting up his mills, the family then moving to a cottage in Grindelton, near Clitheroe. Working hard at anything he could find for five years, Thomas at the end of that time would receive £200 from his wife enabling him to gradually re-establish himself into the cotton industry.

After their marriage, John and Mary Marsden lived at 'High Lawn' in Darwen, and were to have a daughter Mollie and a son Frank. About the time the family moved to Alston Hall, Mollie developed meningitis and almost died but brain damaged had occurred, and mentally, although never certifiable, she had permanent problems that were not always too obvious. Mollie then contacted polio from which she survived but tragically once again damage had been done, the young child being moved about the Hall lying flat in a wheel chair for a while before making a physical recovery.

Over the years amongst the many rumours or explanations as to why the handles on the doors at Alston Hall were placed in such a low position has been the one mentioning the movement about the Hall of an invalided infant. But the low positioning of the door handles was for the convenience of William Eccles's young twin daughters. When Eccles had the mahogany doors fitted to match a Georgian style décor, their door knobs and finger plates were placed in the same position as seen in 2015 when there would be no evidence on the doors that any re-positioning of knobs and plates had taken place.

John Marsden, tall and a keen and regular supporter of Preston North End football club where he had a seat in the Directors' Stand, was a great raconteur of mill tacklers' tales and enjoyed his Buick car. He also enjoyed dancing and would attend local balls and enjoyed parties and dinners on the Birtwistle yacht on Windermere before and after his marriage. Eventually his son Frank was sent to a boarding school in Silcoates near Wakefield, and later when able to, daughter Mollie was sent to a boarding school in Southport. Frank eventually entered employment within the Birtwistle grouping of mills.

The Marsdens did have some holidays in Britain but John apparently was not a great lover of holidays, liking his work so much. For some years he would take private rooms in a small hotel near St Anne's for a few weeks in August from where he could commute to his mill whenever he wished. It was at the hotel on 18 August 1936 that John's wife Mary became ill and died later that night at the age of 52.

Just a few weeks earlier on 13 June, John Marden's long-standing friend and employer William Birtwistle had died. His funeral service at Preston Parish Church had attracted large crowds of mourners in Church Street whilst inside the church mill operatives had filled the gallery to capacity. He had been one of the largest employers of labour in Lancashire textiles and ranked among the wealthiest men in the trade. Years before in September 1928 his wife had died, and ten months later at the age of 74 he would announce his engagement to his typist, 20-year-old Edith Stevenson. Two months later the couple were married in a secret early morning ceremony at St Thomas' Church in Preston following which they caught the train to Euston. Wherever the honeymoon was spent it lasted only over the weekend as William was back in his mill office at 8am on the Monday morning; the new home for William and his wife being 11 Moor Park Avenue, Preston, a convenient distance from his Preston mills.

In his memoirs of his happy years (1923–38) living near Alston Hall (mentioned above in chapter 13), Dr F. L. Mitchell recalls having Christmas dinner at Alston Hall with the Marsden family and also the times he had played with Molly who was about his age in the playroom over the garage, a room also used for storing fruit. He would also write about the time when he and Molly would gorge themselves eating peaches in one of the greenhouses, and the occasions in the billiard room when he would score for John Marsden's son Frank and his school friend, both then boarders at Wakefield Grammar School. The head gardener Mr Crowcroft, and his family who lived at the gardener's cottage just outside the Hall's gates would be mentioned as well as the Mardens' two cars, one the large Buick for going to the mill in Preston, the other thought to be a 'sit up and beg' Morris used by Mrs Marsden.

Dr Mitchell remembered the early 1920s when Alston Lane was not macadamised, the Council every few years going a little further with tar and chippings until the whole lane was covered with the help of a steamroller. He would remember the days when all the farms in the district were fully functional with mixed stock, and the times of catching fish in the old marl ponds and transferring them to other ponds. He would also mention the annual arrival of the machine to thresh the corn in the fields of Bamber's farm, a machine that was part of a 'train' made up of steam traction engine, thresher, baler, and finally the caravan in which members of the threshing team lived whilst undertaking their work.

Soon after the outbreak of the Second World War a 16-year-old girl arrived to stay for a short time at Alston Hall at the invitation of John Marsden. Her name was Gwen and she had been staying with relatives near St Helens safe from the dangers of wartime London where she had been living with her parents in Barnet where her father ran a subsidiary business of the St Helens glass firm of Pilkingtons. As the war developed, her parents had refused her for her own safety to return to London. John Marsden heard about this, he knew her family well having met them on holiday just prior to the outbreak of the war, and so following parental approval Gwen arrived at Alston Hall where she would be company for Mollie. She stayed for about nine months during which she celebrated her 17th birthday, her stay being longer than expected as it would be almost a year before her parents returned to St Helens. Years later in 1946 she married John Mercer's son Frank, and in November 2000 Gwen presented some of the memories of her time at Alston Hall with the Marsden family.

John Marsden when talking about his wife would sometimes mention their early years at Alston Hall when more staff was employed. On his return from the mills his bath would be prepared and his dinner suit brought out, and before he and his wife went to dinner, nanny would bring in their children Mollie and Frank to say goodnight.

John's wife Mary enjoyed giving garden parties for charities and in Mary's recipe book Gwen would note the provisions for 200 people amounting to 28lbs of bread, 6lbs of butter, 6lbs of sugar, 6 dozen tea cakes, 20 dozen sweet cakes, 2lbs of tea, 6lbs of beef paste, 8 quarts of milk, 1 dozen tins of fruit and 1 quart of whipped cream. Apparently two tins of each kinds of fruit would make a fruit salad and prices were listed; paste sandwiches (one round of bread) 2d., buttered tea cakes 3d., etc. Fig. 14.3 is a copy of a photocopy of a photograph of c.1931 (the photocopy now in the Lancashire Archives, Preston) of what presumably would have been one of a number of garden parties held at Alston Hall in the early 1930s.

During the time Gwen was at Alston Hall John Marsden had three indoor staff made up of Mrs Abba the housekeeper, her husband Frank the butler and general factotum, and Miss Moore who was an elderly aunt of Mrs Abba. Occasionally other staff came in, whilst outside, Frank Crowcroft who lived with his family in the gardener's cottage was still the gardener. Walking, playing tennis or croquet, table tennis in the smoking room, and snooker in the drawing room were amongst the leisure activities, especially when members of the Marsden family from Blackburn visited the Hall. Gwen would at times be helpful about the Hall and garden.

> I was happy to help with the housework when needed, as was Mollie, although she was far from thorough! I remember helping Mrs Abba to spring clean the furniture. One heavy item was on the landing. We rubbed them down with vinegar and water and then applied the new polish.
>
> I was allowed to help in the kitchen – quite an honour – after it was discovered that I was reliable.
>
> I discovered an interest and aptitude for mowing – with a large motor machine. Eventually I was sometimes turned loose on the front lawns, and even had the honour of doing the slopes. For that operation another person had to hang on with a rope.

Early on in the war a small group of young evacuees with one adult arrived at the Hall from Manchester and were housed on the top floor, but their residency would be short lived. Gwen Marsden in recalling her memories of that time would say about the young evacuees:

> I remember Mollie and I playing in the garden with one or two – and taking them for walks – but they didn't last long. It was far too remote

a spot for Manchester children and not fair on Mrs. Abba either. I think they felt they were at the end of the world!

Gwen Marsden would remember the winter at Alston when snow was level with the tops of hedges and when she and Mollie on their way back to Alston Hall from the post office at Grimsargh, being offered a lift by Peter Birtwistle (Arthur Hillmen Birtwistle) on his way to 'Ribble View' in his horse-drawn sledge. She also recalls skating with Frank on the large pond (presumably the shamrock pond) near the walled garden.

In November 1940 Richard Hoyle & Son, Valuers of 4 St Ann's Square, Manchester, produced an inventory and valuation of the household goods and personal effects at Alston Hall for fire insurance purposes in case of a bombing raid. It lists a number of beds in the cellar, John Marsden having decided to use the Hall's cellar as a refuge for his family and staff in the event of such a raid. It also lists an air-raid shelter with a reinforced concrete roof that had been constructed just inside the entrance to the walled garden. In April 1941 three bombs exploded close to the Hall and were probably jettisoned from an aircraft after its pilot/crew had failed to find the target, most likely the nearby aircraft works at Samlesbury. One bomb exploded in a wooden gully on the Hall's eastern boundary and two others in a spinney a little distance further down. Sadly, a cow was to be a casualty. A piece of shrapnel from one of these bombs was on display in the Hall when it had later become a college.

Electricity from an outside source had arrived during the 1930s, and in 1940 the Hall had a transformer house and switch room outside in the stable yard area, the equipment listed as being the property of the suppliers and containing a Metropolitan Vickers Transformer, 5KVA, 400volt/210, three sets of fuses, meter, 2 switches, and a distribution board. In the garage was a D.C. electric motor generator with belt-driven pulley to produce 100/150 amps at 1,200 r.p.m. In the cellar was a 25 HP electric motor to run at 950 r.p.m., and a Simplex iron-clad starter for the vacuum system.

In her reminiscences of wartime Alston Hall, Gwen Marsden would mention all the downstairs rooms being used, the main living room being the morning room that had a 'Steinway' piano whilst meals were taken in the dining room. During this period the presence of a billiard table in the drawing room must have been seen to be at odds with the room's elegant décor and its impressive furniture and appointments. Of the two principal bedrooms, the pink bedroom and the rose bedroom, the pink one was John Marsden's favourite although sometimes he used the rose one. Daughter

Mollie slept with Gwen in the blue bedroom whilst the green bedroom was Frank's bedroom before he joined the army. The small green bedroom was the housekeeper's bedroom. In many areas of the Hall at this time, particularly about the empty second floor rooms, there must have been a feeling of sadness, it was the dark days of war and thoughts were probably focusing on the future use of the Hall.

The inventory of 1940 shows that some of the furniture and appointments that had been in the 1916 sale were still in the Hall such as the two manual pipe and reed organ by W. Bell and Co.; a dark oak sideboard; an old oak court cupboard, and the grandfather clock by J. Fisher of Preston.

The inventory began with what was referred to as the entrance porch as having a large copper pitcher, and then listed the contents of the main corridor and the hall lounge (that was the entrance hall), both areas being well furnished with furniture and appointments. Amongst the many items to be listed would be an antique carved oak cupboard; a 6ft Chesterfield and two armchairs; an antique dark oak hall cabinet cupboard; various small tables and stands; a brass dinner gong; jardineires and vases; umbrella stand; hall seat; wall barometer and thermometer; mounted stag's head on oak shield; mounted stag's head and antlers on oak shield; a set of six black and white artist proof steel engravings – 'Hunting Scenes' by Thomas Blinks, 1890–2, and a water colour – 'A Bit of Old Blackburn' by Claude Strachan. On the floor of the entrance hall was an Axminster carpet, 13ft 6in. by 10ft 3in., whilst on the main corridor was a bordered Axminster carpet, 54ft in length and 4ft 5in. in width. One prominent feature amid this array of furniture and appointments was a white marble sculptured figure 'The Maiden' by R. J. Fecit of Rome. Five feet in height, it stood on a marble base 2ft 9in. in height.

Off the entrance hall, the open arched entrance to what was really the hall lounge and simply referred to in the inventory as the lounge, had green valour and lined curtains that were also at the room's window, whilst on the floor was a green Wilton carpet 18ft by 17ft. It would appear that the room had been set out as a library as it had a large Jacobean design bookcase containing various books and novels including thirteen volumes of Dickens and six volumes of Harmsworth's Household Encyclopedia. There were also a Jacobean design bookstand and a 6ft Chesterfield with two easy chairs. Among the various ornaments were bronze figures and ivory carvings, and also pictures by way of black and white etchings and artist-proof steel engravings. At its fireplace were an oxidised brass kerb, a three-piece companion set, and a wire spark guard.

The contents of the telephone room directly off the lounge were listed, as were the contents of the cloakroom and toilet situated off the vestibule.

The two windows of the morning room had braided blue velour curtains with pelmets to match. On the floor was a red and blue Axminster carpet, 22ft 9in. by 14ft, whilst among the main pieces of furniture was a Jacobean style bureau; a writing chair; a three-piece hide suite comprising a 6ft Chesterfield and two easy chairs; a single easy chair; an oak Jacobean style smokers' cabinet (listed were 2000 various cigars, cigarettes and tobacco); an oval gate legged table, and a carved panelled sideboard. Also present in the room was a Newhome U.S.A. treadle sewing machine in an oak cabinet; a Steinway Welte upright electric player piano in a Sheraton black mahogany case, and a silver electric table lamp, part of a set of four, the other three similar in design being stored in the strong room.

It would seem that the Marsdens had a passion for watercolours, the morning room having ten in moulded gilt frames and gilt slips, among them the two by William Hunt – 'Preparing for the Soiree' and 'A Rustic Beauty', and the two companion pictures – 'Game' by Archibald Thorburn (1916).

For the smoke room next door, referred to as the study in 1916, twelve watercolours were listed of which two – 'Moorland Scene' and 'Haymaking Time' were by Vicat Cole, R A. Considering the somewhat small dimensions of the room it was well furnished in having an oak extending table; a suite of five single chairs and one armchair with carved vine ornamentation, their seats and backs upholstered in hide; a single armchair with side head rests; other chairs; stools; nest of coffee tables, and a grandmother clock was also present. About the fireplace with its oxidised curb were a wire spark guard and a copper oxidised coal vase, and also listed was a two-bar Magicoal electric fire with cable connection and plug. Lino surrounded the floor upon which lay a red and blue Axminster carpet, 20ft 3in. by 13ft whilst at the window overlooking the view of the Ribble Valley were braided blue velour curtains with pelmet to match. The room was also to have an electric radio/gramophone that at the time of the inventory was out for repair.

Next came what had been the drawing room, now the billiard room with its billiard table by Orme and Sons Ltd. About the room were items of fine furniture amongst which were a Chesterfield and easy chair; a mahogany bureau; a mahogany bookcase; and the grandfather clock by J. Fisher of Preston. There was also a mantel clock with Westminster chimes by Kienzle Uhren; a Decca portable gramophone; and for the impressive fireplace with its oxidised curb and companion set, were an oxidised brass coal vase, and a brass twisted pillar smokers' companion. Fitted to the floor was an Axminster carpet and at the window were braided velour curtains with pelmet to match. Like the morning room and the smoke room, the billiard room had a number of watercolours, eighteen, among which were three by Albert Goodwin R.W.S., 'Bridge of Sighs, St John's, Cambridge'; 'Cambridge'; and 'Hereford (Maytime)'. One of the watercolours was 'Too Hot' by William Hunt (1790–1864), the painting that had been presented to Thomas Wilkinson J.P. the father of John Marsden's wife Mary Alice in 1922. Insurance value for the contents of the room amounted to £1,169 19s.

For the inventory, the music room is listed as the chapel, among its contents being the organ by W. Bell and Co. The room was now partly a store for sports and leisure equipment among which was a regulation size table tennis table with trestle supports. Other items included a walnut and mahogany bookcase with 225 various books and novels; a leather bound bible; three large coloured earthenware jardinières and another one whose companion was in the billiard room, and two oil paintings, 'The Discovery of Guy Fawkes' by I. Stieneer, and 'French Cottage Scene' by an artist whose name was represented by the initials E. G. D.

In what had been the flower room was a dog's sleeping box – John Mercer had an Irish terrier, and in the entrance porch to the conservatory blackout curtains had been fitted, whilst in the conservatory the white marble sculpture 'Pipes of Pan' was still there among gardening equipment and four large jardinières.

The dining room whose contents at this time had an insurance value of £1,407 15s. was still fulfilling the role it had originally been designed for. Amongst its furniture were an impressive 6ft 6in. sideboard; a mahogany extending dining table; a set of six mahogany chairs and a pair of carvers armchairs of Chippendale design with hide upholstered seats; a mahogany oval occasional table; a mahogany service table; a service tray on oak trestles; a small mahogany sideboard, and a mahogany brass bound wine cooler with lion head ring handles, on a mahogany stand. At the window were braided green velour and lined curtains with pelmet to match, and fitted to the floor was a rose coloured Wilton carpet 27ft 6in. by 23ft 6in. The fireplace had its oxidised brass fire curb and coal vase, and there was also a 1–3 bar and 3 kilowatt 'Magicoal' chromium plated electric fire (listed as radiator). In the room were jardiniers, vases, and fifteen oil paintings mounted in heavy moulded and gilt frames, one being 'My love to you' by W. Dendy Sadler, the painting that Gwen Marsden mentions in her reminiscences of October 2000:

——— is now in the possession of my middle, and local, son David. Apparently the twin to it went out to America – the wife toasting the husband. A pity – they would have made a lovely pair and, I suppose, would have been valuable.

The kitchen with its blackout curtains, presumably still had its original fireplace-cum-oven, its 6ft iron curb being listed, as were two painted dressers, one with store cupboard above, the other with a sycamore top, having five drawers and two cupboards. Among the modern day items were a Singer drop head sewing machine; a Murphy all mains wireless set; a two-bar electric fire; a Revo Maxima cooker that was on hire, and an electric iron.

In the adjacent scullery that presumably had its original fireplace, its 5ft iron curb listed, were drying racks; two pitch pine tables with drawers; cupboards, and a tiled sink. Of the modern items were a Servis electric washer, a Prestcold refrigerator on hire, and a galvanised iron electric washing boiler, also on hire. About the kitchen and scullery were a huge collection of utensils including crockery, pans, cake tins etc., and a cream-making machine.

In what had been designated the butler's pantry was now what appeared to be a general store room for an assortment of items including a 9-stave ladder and household cleaning equipment such as buckets, floor polishers etc. Around the walls were cupboards and there was also a service bench and sink.

The servants' hall next door was still laid out as a sitting room with what seemed to be inexpensive furniture, although one item was a grandfather clock in an inlaid mahogany case by Mason of Blackburn.

Back in the entrance hall, the main staircase had Axminster stair carpeting 47ft 6in. in length by 3ft in width, whilst the landing and passages that had Axminster carpeting in 1916, now had Wilton carpeting cut in various lengths and widths. The landing furniture included a mahogany Chippendale design long case clock; several chests of drawers, two of which had a cupboard on top; and a wardrobe. There were several artist-proof steel engravings, one being 'Squirrels' by Samuel Cousins, after Landseer. Among the list of engravings is mentioned a pair of artist-proof colour gravures, 'Blind man's buff' and 'Playing soldiers'; a gravure sometimes referred to as a photogravure whereby a photographic negative was transferred onto a metal plate and by the use of acid the photograph was etched into the plate to produce an engraving.

The boudoir in the entrance tower had four pairs of cretonne curtains at its windows, and a fitted Wilton carpet with an Axminster rug. The room had changed from the luxurious room it had been in 1916 to become a store place for items once associated with children, presumably those of John Marsden. Most likely it had been their playroom / nursery as the room had a quantity of toys and a child's model toy house with contents, and in a small storeroom under the nearby stairs was a small toy billiard table. The furniture in the boudoir amounted to three carved oak single chairs upholstered in brown velvet; a child's fireside chair; two 2ft 6in. single bedsteads; a box Ottoman and a small dark oak occasional table. There was also a porcelain flower vase.

At the window of the bathroom belonging to the pink suite were black-out curtains made up of blue umbrella cloth whilst in the adjoining dressing room the window had pink velour lined curtains with pelmet to match. The dressing room furniture was comprised of an inlaid mahogany wardrobe with full size centre mirrored door; an inlaid mahogany dressing table with oval swing mirror; a mahogany pedestal cupboard; an oak rocking chair with rush seat and back; a single inlaid mahogany rush seated chair, and a 3ft oak bedstead. Among the appointments part of which was a 3ft 6in. fireplace curb, was a 30-hour chromium bedroom clock.

At the main window and the side window of the pink bedroom were pink velour lined curtains with pelmets to match whilst fitted on the floor was a pink Wilton carpet 23ft 3in. by 19ft. The room's inlaid mahogany bedroom suite was comprised of a 4ft 6in. bedstead; a wardrobe with an oval full length mirror; a dressing table with oval and centre swing mirror; a washstand, and three single chairs upholstered in tapestry. Among other items about the room were a mahogany armchair; a small mahogany occasional table; and a china toilet set with two washbowls, water jugs, sponge bowl, soap bowl, brush vase, and pail. There was also a portable electric bed light with shade and cable connections, and at the fireplace were a 4ft 6in. curb and a gilt lacquered coal vase with lid. The insurance value of the room's contents amounted to £308.

Next door the blue bedroom appropriately had a fitted blue Wilton carpet, and at the window were velour and lined curtains with pelmet to match. The walnut bedroom suite consisted of wardrobe; dressing table; washstand, and a 4ft 6in bow-fronted bedstead. Other items of furniture consisted of three single chairs; an oak oval bedside table and shelf, and a dark oak dressing table with two medium sized drawers and two small trinket drawers. The attractive fireplace surround had a 4ft 6in. oxidised brass curb, and in the room were a pair of artist proof colour gravures, 'Ladies' after Richard Smythe and 'Children' after Arthur A. Brook, and a watercolour painting 'Alston Hall' by C. H. Hooley.

Next to be listed in the inventory and valuation of 1940 for fire insurance purposes was the rose bedroom, its contents of impressive furniture and accessories having an insurance value of precisely £300 12*s.* 6*d.* At its window were green velour and lined curtains with pelmets to match. Axminster carpeting covered the floor, and the mahogany bedroom suite had a wardrobe with a full length mirrored door, and a dressing table with centre square swing mirror. Part of the suite was a washstand with marbled top and back; pedestal cabinet with claw and ball feet; three single chairs upholstered in tapestry, on cabriole legs with claw and ball feet, and a 5ft bow fronted bedstead. Also in the room was a mahogany bedside table with under shelf, and a mahogany armchair upholstered in pink tapestry with loose cretonne covers and cushions to match. The fireplace had a 4ft 3in. curb and an oxidised copper coal vase with covered seat. There was also a Losol Ware Chusan Crown china toilet set with two washbowls and jugs, sponge bowl, soap bowl, brush vase, chamber pot, and pail. Four artist-proof colour engraves were in the room, one of them being of a French street scene after F. Marriott, 1922. An electric bed warmer with cable connections was also listed.

The rose suite's adjacent dressing room was well appointed with furniture, ornaments, and appropriate items such as cut glass powder bowls, silver mounted scent bottle, silver brush tray, etc. Green velour and lined curtains with pelmet to match presented window decoration whilst a black and rose carpet 15ft by 10ft had been fitted to the floor upon which was as small tapestry rug. In mahogany were a dressing table; a circular folding table; a chest of drawers; an armchair, and a single chair. In the room were three artist-proof steel engravings, 'Horses', 'Highland cattle', and 'Deer and young' after Rosa Bonheur, and at its corner fireplace was a 4ft guilt lacquered curb.

In the dressing room's adjoining bathroom the floor was covered in lino (25 square yards) upon which was an Axminster carpet 9ft 4in. by 4ft 5in, with two tapestry mats and a black wool doormat. Present were a washstand; a small occasional table; an oak single chair with rush seat; a wicker type soiled linen basket, and two personal weighing machines, whilst at the window were umbrella cloth blackout curtains.

Next came the green bedroom, one of its windows overlooking the conservatory. Blue and white linen curtains were at the windows whilst on the floor was a blue flowered design Axminster carpet fitted to the floor, 23ft 6in. by 21ft upon which were two reversible rugs. The mahogany bedroom suite was comprised of a 6ft 6in. wardrobe; dressing table; washstand and folding towel airer, and a 4ft 8in. bedstead. The room also had a carved mahogany single chair upholstered in moquette, and two mahogany single chairs upholstered in tapestry. There was also a carved kneehole secretaire, and for the fireplace a 4ft 6in. copper curb and a steel, brass bound coal cauldron. In addition to the room which had vases, electric bed light, framed photographs, and an artist-proof steel engraving 'Cherry Ripe' by Samuel Cousins, after J. Everett Millais, was a Royal Doulton crown china toilet set comprising two wash bowls and jugs, sponge bowl, soap bowl, brush vase, chamber pot and pail.

Next door in the small green bedroom were velour lined window curtains with pelmet to match, whilst on the floor was a Wilton carpet. The bedstead was of mahogany and the wardrobe like the dressing table and also the washstand was of inlaid mahogany. Among other items of furniture were three chairs upholstered in tapestry, and for the fireplace were a 5ft curb and a brass oxidised coal vase. Also present was a two-bar electric radiator with cable connection, and a photograph of the personnel of Silcoates School, 1931, the school of John Marsden's son, Frank.

The bathroom adjoining the small green bedroom had blue umbrella cloth as blackout curtains at its window whilst next to be listed in the inventory was what had been the boot and sundries store room, now a store for travelling cases; a Gladstone bag; a cabin trunk etc., as well as two electric table lamps, tennis rackets and sundries. The airing room with 3 square yards of lino had two bedroom chairs and a stool. Next on the list was the housemaid's pantry with its corner fireplace and 4ft cast iron curb, the window of the room overlooking the kitchen service yard and the stable yard. It was still a storeroom for household cleaning items and sundries such as carpet sweepers, buckets, brushes, etc., and also contained a wood bench with wood vice, and there were tool racks.

At the end of the corridor leading to the front end of the Hall was what had once been the school room now a bedroom well endowed with furniture comprising a 3ft oak bedstead; two wardrobes; three dressing tables; a chest of drawers; three bedroom chairs; and a washstand. An Axminster carpet 20ft by 16ft 6in, with the usual underfelt had been laid to have a lino surround, and about the room were various rugs, vases, three oil paintings of which two made up a pair, and various framed colour gravures and photographs.

The rooms on the second floor must have presented a somewhat forlorn scene in November 1940, a time when the war was not going well for Britain and her allies. Initially planned for servants' accommodation many of these rooms were empty. For this second floor level the inventory for insurance purposes began by listing the entrance tower room having lino, a wire and steel fireguard and a framed steel engraving. Next came two empty bedrooms, a servants' bathroom and a small bedroom adjoining it. As to the exact position of these rooms it is not possible to say as no plans have been found for the 1940s period, and fig. 4.30 shows the plan for this second floor level following reconstruction of rooms for residential college purposes.

However, it seems that the rooms listed above immediately after the tower room had been in the area shown on the 1950s plan (fig. 4.30) as dormitory 5, as the 1940s inventory would then continue with a bedroom, its position stated as *At other side of Tower Staircase* that was empty except for three oxidised fireplace curbs, 2ft 3in., 2ft 6in., and 2ft 9in. in length.

Adjoining this bedroom was another bedroom that had a variety of items; two lots of lino; two 4ft steel fireplace curbs; a painted, grained and varnished wardrobe; two rocking chairs; oak washstand that was part of the school room suite; a child's play cot; and three steel engravings 'Road to Ruin' series. These rooms were now near the entrance to the roof.

Next was a bedroom (probably what had been the bachelor's bedroom) now having 32 square yards of lino; an oak combination dressing table and wardrobe; a painted, grained and varnished wardrobe; two rush seated bedroom chairs; 4ft steel fireplace curb; and two steel engravings.

After this bedroom was the water tower's tank room with an adjoining small and empty room, and then a sundries store room having two shopping baskets; a steel fireplace curb; a model yacht; a quantity of toys; and a number of brass curtain rods and blind fittings.

The inventory of 1940 then listed the contents of an adjoining dark room with its array of bottles, test tubes, etc., used by Frank Marsden for developing his photographs before he joined the Armed Forces. As mentioned in chapter 4, next came a bathroom with lavatory, then a W.C.

Outside in the Hall's boiler house two boilers were listed in the inventory, one a Robin Hood Senior sectional hot water boiler, the other a Baxendale sectional one, and there was also a hot water tank and firing tools.

The inventory also contained a detailed lists of contents for the various small buildings associated with garden and grounds maintenance as well as the contents of the extensive array of glasshouses made up of a peach house, vine house, green house, carnation house number 1, carnation house number 2, and a tomato house. Listed for the peach house were six cast iron diamond grids 4ft by 2ft each; three wood lattice stillages; 150 earthenware plant pots, and three degging cans. In the vine house was a lattice four-tier plant stillage 46ft by 9in., and 60 earthenware plant pots. What would be within or near the greenhouse was a heating apparatus chamber consisting of boiler, pipe connections and firing tools, whilst more heating apparatus with a boiler was to be near or within the tomato house.

Amongst the contents of the coal and mower shed were three lawn mowers, two of which were Atco motor types, the third being a J.P. Super one. There was also a garden roller; tennis marker; long ladders and 10 tons of coal.

The ground floor of the old coach house was still a garage among its contents being typical items such as grease guns, oil cans, various tools, an Empire fire extinguisher, two foot pumps, a stock of old tyres etc. The floor above was listed as the games room and had nine blackout screens at its windows and was a store for garden equipment such as swing supports, hammock supports, a 7ft garden seat, garden table etc., as well as a complete set of tennis nets with posts and cast iron feet to support them. There was also a canvas screen and string for forming a golf practice course.

Across the stable yard in the old stable block, what had been the chauffeur's bungalow cottage was now empty of its contents except for lino on the floors and electric fittings. Its loft had become a general store for a large variety of objects including 17 hen coops; corrugated iron sheets; timber; mule pack horsepanier; creel rails; 300 earthenware plant pots; 2 large revolving blinds; 8 rolls of wire netting; quantity of wood stakes; 2 doors, and 2 wash hand basins.

In 1948 John Marsden, now well into his seventies, decided to retire from his position as a Director and General Manager in the Birtwistle group of mills, and on 5 August of that year married Mrs Annie Budd who had been a good friend of his late wife. After their marriage John left Alston Hall whilst Annie had left her home in nearby Grimsargh, the couple moving to 4 Myrtle Bank, Grimsargh.

Sadly, Mollie could still be a problem apparently taking herself off in the early fifties to Blackpool where in a gale force wind was hit by a flying hoarding that blinded her. Nothing medically could be done for her to retrieve her sight and she would spend some time at a blind home near

Leatherhead. Eventually she married Edgar who was also blind and who lived with twin sisters in Callow, near Hereford, Edgar doing market gardening on the family land there. Mollie had a bungalow built at the lower end of the land facing the Welsh hills and became a super cook as well as having green fingers in their huge garden.

During the Second World War many a country house had been requisitioned by the government for what was to be a variety of military and wartime needs such as training establishments, hospitals, schools, etc., many of the requisitioned houses providing accommodation for British and American troops. Bearing in mind the tremendous debt we still owe to these servicemen, many of whom would give their lives to secure our freedom, it has been said that the way country houses and their settings were wantonly abused by servicemen was a national disgrace. Some of the houses that had been mutilated never recovered and were to be returned in an unusable condition, and with the shortage of building materials for repair work at this particular period and a gloomy financial economic outlook, demolition became the order of the day in a number of cases.

By the early 1950s this holocaust of country house demolition was still continuing, one example coming to mind being Ribbleton Hall, sited a short distance southwest of Alston Hall. Built for Thomas Birchall a Preston solicitor in c.1865, his widow lived there for about twenty years until her death following which the Hall was let. In 1926 it was converted into flats and during the Second World War the government commissioned the Hall for billeting American troops. Preston Corporation bought it in 1949 and in the early fifties it was derelict, vandalised and a ruin. By 1955 it had been demolished, its site to become part of Grange Park for a new council house estate where today the outline of the Hall's foundations can be seen.

In the fifties and sixties the Victorian Society made tremendous efforts to save our Victorian architectural heritage, many of the Society's attempts being successful, some unfortunately not. The 1950s saw the start of a difficult period for Victorian architecture in general many seeing it as hideous and not in keeping with what hopefully would be a new look Britain, and such opinions were to gain momentum by the property development boom of the sixties.

Preston Town Hall for example having been partially destroyed by fire soon after the war was to succumb to the new building boom in the early sixties. Built in 1862–67 in the French Gothic style, its architect had been George Gilbert Scott and like his Midland Grand Hotel at St

Pancras Station in London, Preston Town Hall had an impressive corner clock tower, its hour bell being audible seven miles away. The building was gutted by fire in the early hours of 14 March 1947 following a police ball, and despite £140,000 of insurance money being available no serious attempt was made to restore the building that would stand partially as a ruin throughout the fifties and the beginning of the sixties. In the face of public protest the town council gave the order to demolish the remains and the site was cleared in 1962 to make way for the erection of an office block with shops at ground level to be known as Crystal House, a building many saw as having little architectural merit or character.

Following the retirement of John Marsden in 1948 the Birtwistle family would have no need for Alston Hall. Arthur Hillmen (Peter) Birtwistle was to become Chairman and Managing Director of all the operations allied to the Birtwistle Group of mills and was to have an operations office at his home in Mitton Hall near Whalley. Now the future role of Alston Hall must have seemed questionable to many with perhaps the possibility of it becoming a type of institution. Such a role would not be far away.

Chapter fifteen

A new life

Soon after John Marsden had left Alston, the Hall came up for sale but first the contents of its rooms had to be sold for which the days of 2 and 3 February 1949 were to be allocated. At the first day's sale the contents of the hall lounge, morning room, billiard room (the original drawing room), dining room, hall, and the chapel were disposed of. They included paintings, books, vases, clocks, furniture, carpets of the Brussels, Axminster, and Turkey types, the full-sized billiard table by Orme & Sons, and the organ by Bell and Co., together with its organ seat. Also there was much valuable china, glass, electro-plate and silver ware, whilst some of the furniture included items not having been sold during the 1916 sale or purchased then to remain in the Hall. One item to remain after the 1916 sale was the antique grandfather clock by J. Fisher of Preston, which in 1916 had brought £21 as mentioned in chapter 13. In the 1949 sale it would sell for a mere £8. The second day sale saw the contents sale of bedrooms, dressing rooms, bathrooms, linen room, kitchen and scullery, servants' hall, butler's pantry, greenhouses, garage, and outbuildings.

A few weeks later on Wednesday 30 March, the Hall was for sale by public auction starting at 2.30 pm at the Bull and Royal Hotel, Fishergate, Preston, figs 15.1 to and including fig. 15.8 being the particulars of the sale. However, the sale failed to find a purchaser and just over four months later on 9 August, Mr W. R. Tuson, the Chief Education Officer for the County Borough of Preston together with the Education Development Committee viewed the hall and decided in principle to acquire the property:

> ----- *for use as a Day Continuation School and County College, at which certain of the students will be boarders.*

Then on Saturday 3 December 1949 under the heading of 'Country mansion may become Preston college', a newspaper was to report:

> Subject to the approval of the Minister of Education, Preston Corporation are to buy Alston Hall, near Longridge, for £5,000. They plan to convert it eventually into a residential college for further education. In the meantime it is proposed, the Hall will be used to house the Education Committee's day continuation college.
>
> Alston Hall is considered ideal for educational purposes. It is estimated that it will cost £1,000 for conversion into a day continuation college, and about 3,000 to set it up as a residential college.
>
> At Preston Town Council meeting on Thursday, Alderman Mrs. A. M. Pimblett, chairman of the Education Committee, described the acquisition of the Hall as an important development in further education in Preston.

The newspaper report then under a sub heading, 'VARIED ACTIVITIES', continued:

> Mrs. Pimblett told the "Guardian" that Alston Hall would probably be one of the first residential colleges of its kind in the area. Other authorities might be granted facilities to use the college, and it would be of great benefit to youth organisations and all forms of further education.
>
> It would be the ideal place for all sorts of activities – week-end rallies, short courses for youth leaders and teachers, and many branches of adult education on a wide range of subjects. It was also probable that voluntary organisations would be allowed to use the Hall for week-end courses.
>
> She said that until it was possible to adapt it as a residential college it would serve another important purpose. The day continuation college, for young people who are released by the employers for educational purposes one day a week would be transferred temporarily to Alston Hall. This college which opened in February had been housed in the Avenham Institute, but the rooms were now required for other purposes.

The report then concluded by giving a short history of Alston Hall.

LANCASHIRE

In the Beautiful Ribble Valley.   **6 miles North-East of Preston.**

ILLUSTRATED PARTICULARS, CONDITIONS OF SALE AND PLAN

of the

Substantial Well-Situated Freehold Country Residence

with 9½ Acres

ALSTON HALL

Near LONGRIDGE

Entrance, Staircase and Lounge Halls, 4 Reception Rooms

Private Chapel

19 Bed and Dressing Rooms (including Two Suites), 5 Bathrooms.

Main Water and Electricity ; Part Central Heating ; Septic Tank Drainage.

Garages for 8 cars.   **Bungalow Cottage.**

DELIGHTFUL GARDENS AND GROUNDS

Fine walled Kitchen Garden, extensive Greenhouses.

COTTAGE.

VACANT POSSESSION ON COMPLETION OF THE PURCHASE.

HAMPTON & SONS

in conjunction with

SANDLAND & CO.

Have been instructed to submit the above for Sale by Auction as a whole or in
Two Lots (unless sold privately meanwhile)

At The Bull & Royal Hotel, Fishergate, Preston
On WEDNESDAY, 30th MARCH, 1949
At 2.30 p.m.

Solicitors : Messrs. CARTER & HOWARTH, 2, Shear Bank Road, Blackburn.

Joint Auctioneers :

SANDLAND & CO.,
4, Limbrick, Sudell Cross,
Blackburn.
(Tel. : Blackburn 44277).

HAMPTON & SONS, Ltd.,
6, Arlington Street, St. James's,
London, S.W.1.
(Tel. : Regent 8222).
Branches at Wimbledon and Bishop's
Stortford.

Fig. 15.1 Title page of the 1949 sale.

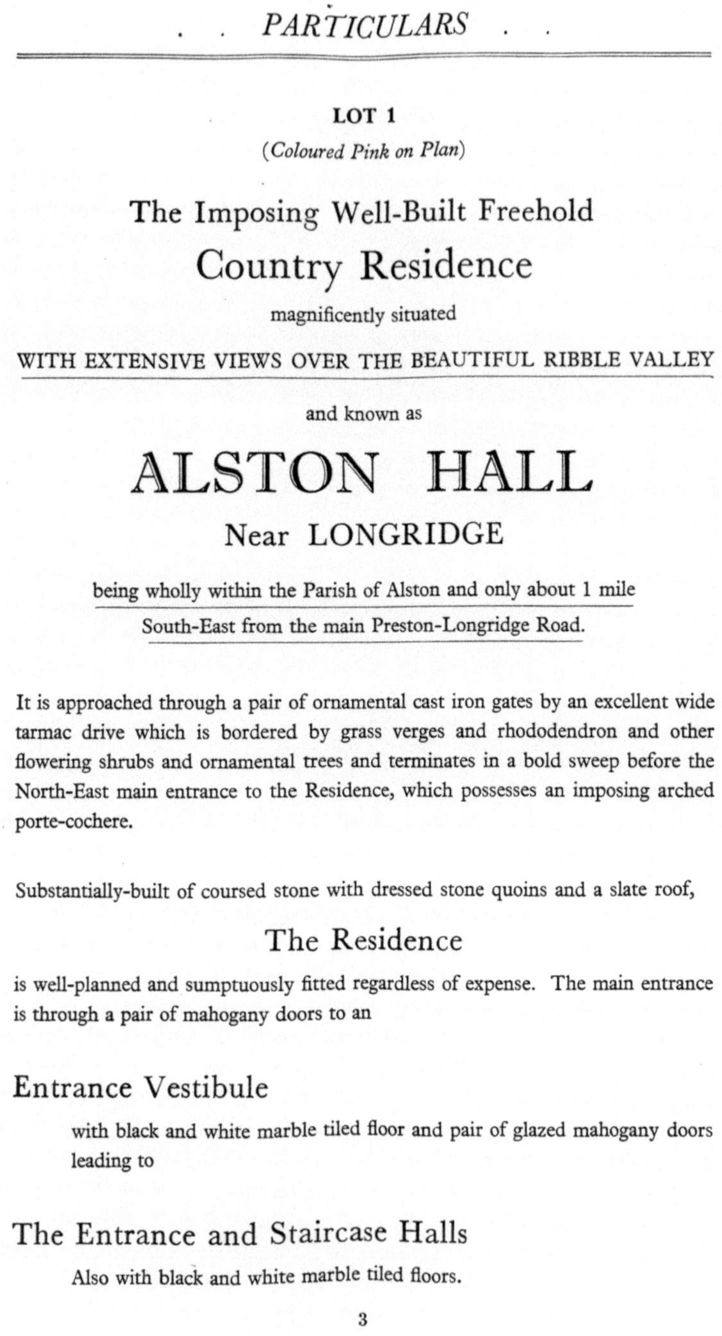

LOT 1

(Coloured Pink on Plan)

The Imposing Well-Built Freehold
Country Residence
magnificently situated

WITH EXTENSIVE VIEWS OVER THE BEAUTIFUL RIBBLE VALLEY

and known as

ALSTON HALL
Near LONGRIDGE

being wholly within the Parish of Alston and only about 1 mile
South-East from the main Preston-Longridge Road.

It is approached through a pair of ornamental cast iron gates by an excellent wide tarmac drive which is bordered by grass verges and rhododendron and other flowering shrubs and ornamental trees and terminates in a bold sweep before the North-East main entrance to the Residence, which possesses an imposing arched porte-cochere.

Substantially-built of coursed stone with dressed stone quoins and a slate roof,

The Residence

is well-planned and sumptuously fitted regardless of expense. The main entrance is through a pair of mahogany doors to an

Entrance Vestibule

with black and white marble tiled floor and pair of glazed mahogany doors leading to

The Entrance and Staircase Halls

Also with black and white marble tiled floors.

3

Fig. 15.2 Particulars of the 1949 sale (Lot 1 page 3).

CLOAKROOM

with black and white marble tiled floor and partly white tiled walls, marble topped wash-basin, W.C., etc., **Telephone Room.**

With direct access from the Entrance Hall is

A Fine Suite of Reception Rooms

comprising :

The Lounge Hall

facing North-East and measuring about 19ft. 6in. by 17ft. 4in., with a steel and bronzed canopied fireplace with marble surround and hearth, and carved mahogany mantel.

Morning Room

(North-East and South-East), about 23ft. 8in. (excluding bay) by 19ft. 9in., with "Baxi" patent fire in polished steel fireplace, having tiled cheeks and hearth, marble lining and handsome carved mahogany mantel.

Smoke Room

(South-East), about 19ft. 10in. by 16ft. 3in. with polished steel fireplace having tiled lining and hearth, marble lining and richly moulded Adam style white painted mantel.

Drawing Room

(South-East), about 28ft. 7in. by 18ft. 9in., excluding a square bay, 13ft. 9in. by 5ft. 5in., with a handsome "Anac" canopied fireplace having rich marble linings and hearth and heavily moulded mantel and a heavy mirror plate fitted to an alcove recess with flower box at foot. The walls of this apartment are divided into panels whilst the ceiling and cornices are richly decorated with moulding.

Dining Room

(South-East and South-West), about 27ft. 10in. by 23ft. 9in., with brass canopied fireplace, marble surround and hearth and richly moulded Adam style mantel and door to conservatory.

4

Fig. 15.3 Particulars of the 1949 sale (Lot 1 page 4).

There is a

PRIVATE CHAPEL

measuring about 17ft. square with lofty ceiling, marble tiled floor and an arched chancel, supported by marble pillars and lighted by three leaded light windows.

At the rear of the Entrance Hall is a Fine CONSERVATORY with black and white tiled floor, oak trellis work screen, etc., a FLOWER ROOM with sinks and draining boards and a teak falling leaf.

THE FIRST FLOOR:

is approached by wide, easy and handsome staircase with newels, turned balusters and handrail in mahogany and leading out on to a ·

GALLERIED LANDING

surmounted by a coved ceiling and lantern light. From this Landing the whole of the First Floor accommodation is approached. This comprises :—

Two Principal Suites

The Pink Suite

consists of **BEDROOM** (S.E. & N.E.), 23ft. 9in. by 19ft. 5in. with gilt fireplace having pink marble lining and hearth and Adam style mantel, marble-topped wash-basin on plated stand and with marble back and plated fittings. **DRESSING ROOM** with corner fireplace and radiator. **BATHROOM,** fitted with heavy roll-top porcelain enamelled bath, marble-topped wash-basin on plated stand, and marble back with plated fittings and swing mirror, chromium plated heated towel rail; **Separate W.C.** and **Boudoir** (N.E. & S.E.), 16ft. 1in. by 14ft. 7in., with attractive corner fireplace.

The Rose Suite

comprises **BEDROOM** (South-East), 19ft. 10in. by 17ft. 3in. (excluding large bay) with fireplace in tiled surround, marble lining and Adam style mantel; **DRESSING ROOM** with fireplace, marble-topped wash-basin with marble splash-back and plated fittings; **BATHROOM** with white tiled walls, fitted with heavy roll-top porcelain enamelled bath, marble-topped wash-basin, marble splashback and plated fittings; W.C.

5

Fig. 15.4 Particulars of the 1949 sale (Lot 1 page 5).

Between these Two Suites and communicating with the Bedroom of the former is the

Blue Room

facing South-East, 20ft. by 16ft. 5in. with fireplace having tiled surround and hearth, marble lining and painted mantel.

Three Guest Bedrooms:—

THE GREEN ROOM (S.W.), 24ft. by 21ft. 6in. with canopied fireplace, tiled surround, marble lining and Adam style mantel; **SMALL GREEN ROOM** (S.W.), 22ft. by 17ft. with fireplace in Adam style mantel, marble-topped wash-basin on plated stand with marble splashback and plated fittings; **BEDROOM**, 24ft. 4in. by 18ft. with fireplace and radiator.

Bathroom No. 3

partly white tiled to dado and fitted with heavy roll-top porcelain enamelled bath, marble-topped wash-basin and marble splashback with plated fittings, plated heated towel rail and W.C.

Also on the First Floor Landings are extensive ranges of cupboards, heated linen room, housemaid's pantry (well fitted).

ON THE SECOND FLOOR:

there are **NINE BEDROOMS,** four having fireplaces, **TWO BATHROOMS,** Boxroom, whilst above is the **TOWER ROOM** and staircase on to the flat roof of the Tower.

The First and Second Floors are each approached by two staircases.

6

Fig. 15.5 Particulars of the 1949 sale (Lot 1 page 6).

At Ground Floor Level are the

Domestic Quarters

which comprise a **Service Room** with hatch from Kitchen; **Strong Room** with steel door and inner grille, and fitted with a steel safe and long range of baize-lined shelves; wine and three other Cellars; a **Luggage Lift** to the First Floor; **Butler's Pantry,** 23ft. 10in. by 17ft. 7in. with extensive range of china, glass and plate cupboards and drawers, sink with white tiled splashback and heated towel rail; whilst on the far side of a baize-covered door are : **Kitchen** with range and "Sentry" boiler providing an auxiliary supply for domestic hot water, point for electric cooker; **Scullery,** white tiled to dado, fitted with 3 sinks, "Allgood" range and Larder with slate and marble shelving; **Servants' Hall,** 18ft. 5in. by 12ft. 3in. with fireplace, 4 Larders, one with gauze-panelled door, Servants' Cloakroom with corner wash-basin, W.C., and Housemaid's sink.

OUTSIDE and arranged round an enclosed flag paved yard are Fruit Room, Fuel Store, Wood Store, Two W.C.'s and Stokehole, housing a "Robin Hood"—New "Senior"-boiler for the central heating, Greenhouses and Garage, and an "Ideal" boiler for the domestic hot water supply. (Another boiler of smaller capacity as an auxiliary supply is located in the Kitchen).

Adjacent to the residence on the North-West and approached by a branch from the main drive are the

Garage Premises

arranged round a wall enclosed yard. They are principally constructed of brick, stone and slate and comprise **GARAGE FOR UP TO 6 CARS** (30ft. long by 25ft. 6in. wide), with inspection pit, hot water pipes, electric light and having two sets of double doors, with a large glass-covered washdown in front. **GARAGE FOR 2 CARS** with roll-up steel shutter door, large Storeroom adjoining; the last two named having a floor above suitable for a **DANCE FLOOR.** In the same building is a

Bungalow Cottage

comprising Living Room, Kitchen, Bathroom and Two Bedrooms with outside Wash-house and Coal Shed and large Loft above, where further rooms could be made with little difficulty if required.

A small Outhouse in this block is in the occupation of the Preston Corporation Electricity Department who maintain a Sub-station therein, and the property is sold subject to the continuance of this occupation and user, and the offer of vacant possession shall not apply to this portion.

7

Fig. 15.6 Particulars of the 1949 sale (Lot 1 page 7) The garage mentioned for up to six cars was in the old coach house whilst the one for two cars was in the old stable block as was the bungalow cottage (chauffeur's cottage).

THE GARDENS AND GROUNDS

form a perfect setting for the residence but are particularly inexpensive to maintain. For the most part they comprise natural beech woodland, much of which on the South-West is in a dell with steps and woodland paths leading down to an ornamental pool and series of small waterfalls.

On the South-East front of the residence is a

Broad Terrace

with stone steps down to

Terraced Lawns

from both of which magnificent open views are enjoyed over the beautiful well-timbered Ribble Valley, with glimpses of the river itself.

Adjacent to the Garage Premises is a

Fine Walled Kitchen Garden

intersected by concrete paths and well-planted with pear and plum wall-trained trees and cooking and dessert apple bush trees, as well as soft fruit bushes, etc.

There is also an extensive

Range of Greenhouses

comprising single-span melon and cucumber house; two double-span carnation houses; peach house with 4 peach and 1 nectarine trees; vinery with black Hamburgh vine, a second vinery or tomato house and a small plant house. Range of cold frames with 14 lights; potting and barrow sheds.

———————————

This lot extends to an area of nearly

$9\frac{1}{2}$ Acres

(Fencing and Fences—See General Remark No. 10).

8

Fig. 15.7 Particulars of the 1949 sale (Lot 1 page 8).

LOT 2

(Coloured Green on Plan)

The Semi-Detached Cottage

situate near the main entrance gates to Alston Hall, constructed of brick with a slate roof, and containing : **Small Entrance Hall; Sitting Room** with modern tiled fireplace and walnut mantel; **Living Room** with range (back boiler for domestic hot water) and corner cupboard; **Scullery** with sink and "copper," **Pantry;** and above, **Three Bedrooms,** one being fitted with bath (h. & c.), wash-basin (h. & c.) and cupboard. Outside is a small yard with W.C. and Coal Shed, and a small garden, together with a strip of plantation, the whole lot extending to an area of about

35 Poles

Main Water and Electricity (light and power). Septic Tank Drainage.

The Cottage is occupied by a Service Tenant and

VACANT POSSESSION

will be given on Completion.

This lot is sold subject to and with the benefit of such easements as are necessary to ensure the continuance of all rights of water, and electric supply, drainage and rights of way as at present, the Purchaser of this lot bearing a due proportion of the cost of repair and maintenance of any joint service.

Fig. 15.8 Particulars of the 1949 sale (Lot 2).

LANCASHIRE . . . *Mainly Five Miles from Preston*

Within easy reach by road and rail of Blackpool, Southport, Liverpool, Warrington, Manchester, Halifax, Burnley and many other Important Towns

FREEHOLD   IN LOTS

The Fine Agricultural Estate

well known as

THE ALSTON ESTATE

comprising

Twenty-two Well Equipped Dairy Farms and Holdings

(*Virtually all up to Attested Standard with superior Houses and Main Water and Electricity*)

Let to an established Tenantry

Accommodation Lands and Sites

Nine Substantial Cottages

Valuable Well Timbered Woodlands

and

Over 4⅓rd Miles (Single Bank) of Salmon and other Fishing in the River Ribble

In All About 1,570 Acres

GROSS INCOME   **£4,139**   PER ANNUM

For Sale by Auction in Lots (unless sold privately meanwhile) by Messrs.

JOHN D. WOOD & CO.

At The Bull and Royal Hotel, Preston

On FRIDAY, 7th OCTOBER, 1955, at 2 p.m.

Solicitors: Messrs. PEARSONS & WARD, 1, New Street, York. (*Tel.:* York 3661 and 4454.)

And at Malton, Yorkshire. (*Tel.:* Malton 247/8).

Land Agent: NORMAN WEIGHTS, F.A.I., 12, Chapel Street, Preston. (*Tel.:* Preston 2998.)

Auctioneers' Offices: 23, Berkeley Square, London, W.1. (*Tel.:* MAYfair 6341.)

Fig. 15.9 Title page of the Alston Estate sale of 1955.

Lot No.	Description	Area	Gross Income (Per annum)	

THE ALSTON PORTION (Plan No. 2)

Lot No.	Description	Area	£ s. d.	£ s. d.
1	Wood Farm, Grimsargh	17.849	98 2 0	
2	Marsh House Farm, Elston	133.070	321 8 0	
3	Chapel House Farm, Elston	88.149	255 11 0 Appd.	
4	Elston Old Hall Farm	122.423	252 14 6	
5	Useful Accommodation Grass Field	6.736	7 0 0 Appd.	
6	Elston New Hall Farm	124.668	288 10 0	
7	A Useful Woodland Area	26.380	—	
8	Nab Wood	18.780	—	
9	Place House Farm	89.969	243 0 0	
10	Elston Bottoms	15.478	69 16 0	
11	Useful Accommodation Grass Field	5.248	5 10 0 Appd.	
12	Charity Farm, Elston	45.579	91 6 0 Appd.	
13	Attractive Detached Cottage	.636	46 7 4	
14	A Valuable Grass Field	11.183	12 0 0	
15	Big Wood	24.782	—	
16	Berry's Farm, Elston	43.849	92 7 0 Appd.	
17	Ribble View House and Farmery	75.123	340 8 0 Appd.	
18	Alston Old Hall Farm	97.466	290 0 0	
19	Boot Farm	146.561	300 8 0	
20	Gib Holme Wood and Alston Wood	61.449	—	
21	Brook Hall Cottage Farm	14.932	58 10 0	
22	Brook Hall Cottage	.077	7 16 0 Appd.	
23	A Useful Grass Field	2.840	4 0 0 Appd.	
24	Lower Yew Tree Farm, Alston	43.909	114 6 0	
25	Alston Cottage Farm	50.504	160 4 0	
26	Alston Lane Farm	12.632	64 7 0 Appd.	
27	Alston Hall Cottage	.098	7 16 0 Appd.	
28	The Adjoining Cottage	.190	35 4 2	
29	A Valuable Accommodation Grass Field	3.325	9 0 0 Appd.	
30	Attractive Small Grass Paddock	.424	1 0 0 Appd.	
31	The Fishing Rights in the River Ribble	54.021	45 0 0	
32	No. 1 Kitchen Terrace	.060	38 2 8	
33	No. 2 Kitchen Terrace	.025	32 18 8	
34	No. 3 Kitchen Terrace	.048	40 14 8	
35	No. 4 Kitchen Terrace	.127	34 8 8	
36	No. 5 Kitchen Terrace	.068	37 9 8	
37	Valuable Plot	.040	5 0 0	
38	Fir Tree Farm	19.521	109 0 0 Appd.	
39	A Valuable Site at Grimsargh	.700	1 0 0 Appd.	
40	Another Valuable Site at Grimsargh	1.180	2 0 0 Appd.	
41	Accommodation Grass Field, Grimsargh	3.874	8 0 0 Appd.	
42	Accommodation Grass Field, Grimsargh	4.565	15 0 0	
				£3,545 5 4

THE WITHNELL PORTION (Plan No. 3)

Lot No.	Description	Area	£ s. d.	£ s. d.
43	Lower Close House Farm	48.034	140 0 0	
44	Abbeystead Farm	42.484	132 5 0	
45	Red Lee Farm	37.710	84 19 0	
46	Bensons Farm	11.511	34 0 0	
				£391 4 0

THE CHIPPING PORTION (Plan No. 1)

Lot No.	Description	Area	£ s. d.	£ s. d.
47	Clark House Farm, Chipping	62.100	—	£187 10 0
	Wayleaves (Whole Estate) G.P.O.		1 12 0	
	N. West Electricity Board		13 10 0	
				£15 2 0
	TOTAL	1,570.377 Acres		£4,139 1 4

Fig. 15.10 Summary schedule of the Alston Estate sale of 1955.

The Avenham Institute mentioned had been opened in 1850 to face Bushell Place and Avenham Walk and was known as the Institute for the Diffusion of Useful Knowledge, its principal function being the provision of education and instruction to working class people. By 1882 it was short of money and decaying physically, rescue arriving with a sum of £40,000 from an endowment from the trustees of the late Edmund R. Harris, the Preston benefactor. Extensions were made and science laboratories installed, and with its schools of technology, science and art, the building was known as the Harris Institute and was to be the forerunner of technical education in Preston. On 6 July 1895, William Ascroft J.P. President of the Harris Institute laid the foundation stone of the Harris Institute Victoria Technical School in Corporation Street.

The opening of a day continuation college by Preston Education Committee at the Harris Institute building in Avenham in February 1949 was from a direct request from Messrs. Courtaulds Ltd., a large factory that had been erected in the 1930s on the old Red Scar estate at Ribbleton on the outskirts of Preston for the production of viscose yarn that had begun in early 1939. At the Harris Institute building in Avenham known in 1949 as the Avenham Institute School of Art, the day continuation college had only two members of staff and had been given notice to move out of its inadequate accommodation by 1 November of that year. Suitable premises would have to provide a boys' craft room, girls' domestic science room, students' common room, dining room, and staff room. No suitable premises were to be found in Preston and to build a new building was out of the question when considering the austerity conditions and the shortage of building materials that prevailed in the years immediately following the ending of the war. Therefore Alston Hall appeared to be the answer to the college's needs.

First, permission had to be obtained for the change of use of Alston Hall from a house to one of a day continuation college. This involved Longridge Urban District Council; the Minister of Health (under the Town and Country Planning Act of 1947); the Divisional Planning Office in Blackpool; and Lancashire County Council Planning Department. Consent was obtained on 15 March 1950 following which a loan sanction for the borrowing of the purchase price from central government was applied for. On 9 August following a formal consent had been given the ownership of Alston Hall was to be conveyed by the Alston Property & Investment Company Limited to the Mayor, Aldermen, and Burgesses of the County Borough of Preston, the purchase price having been £5,000 but with the expenses of the sale the final sum was £5,259 3s.

The day continuation college at Alston Hall was to open in September 1950, James Shemilt having been appointed as Principal, its statutory purpose as a continuation college being to provide a liberal education for those young people who had left school at 15 or 16 years of age and entered full-time employment thereby being denied opportunity for higher education. Students were to attend on a voluntary basis on one or two days per week until they reached 18 years of age. There were to be no fees and students would travel by private bus to the Hall where a mid-day meal cooked in the college kitchen would be provided in the refectory at a charge of one shilling. Soon the college began to attract students from a wide range of employers, Messrs. Courtaulds, as to be expected, being foremost among these, whilst among the others were the GPO, Health Service, Local Government, Co-op, Gas and Electricity Boards, Civil Service, and high street banks.

A large range of subjects would be available such as book-keeping, handicrafts, botany, history, biology, homecraft, current affairs, local and central government, economics, mathematics, French, English language, English literature, nursery nursing, physical education, pre-nursing, general science, shop practice and commodities, geography, and social studies, whilst for some of these subjects examinations could be taken. Mornings would be devoted to academic work, afternoons to art and crafts, games, physical training, fieldwork, first aid, and the reading of books from the comprehensive library.

Following a visit to the new college at Alston Hall, Mr D. B. Sharp, an education officer from Courtaulds, would write a most appreciative appraisal of his visit in the February 1951 edition of *The Rayoner*, a Courtaulds magazine, a part of which read:

> *And as we travelled the seven miles from Preston to the Hall, we began to feel that the Local Education Authority had the right vision when it took over this imposing mansion, built in modern-Gothic style, for use as a headquarters for further education.*
>
> *There is no doubt that they realised, as so many educationalists before them, that environment can mean so much in the training of youth. In this was "Proud Preston's" own particular approach to the problem – a beautiful building in the most beautiful surroundings.*
>
> *We, ourselves, felt a thrill as we drew up at the front entrance, under the square tower which is the main feature of the Hall. And, before*

entering, we were attracted to the magnificent view which stretched from the front lawn. Wooded slopes stretch down from the bank on which the Hall stands to the valley of the Ribble, whilst the slopes on the other side of the river rise to the bare crests which are part of the Pennine Chain.

The quiet of the scene is only disturbed by the music of running water from the various rivulets making their way to the main river. An ideal spot for the field work in geology and geography in which the students revel!

The house itself provides a variety of accommodation – spacious rooms for classwork that have little similarity with the usual school classrooms, a large dining room with access to a well-equipped kitchen, a conservatory which makes an ideal meeting place for the tea break, an upper floor which it is hoped to use for accommodation for week-end conferences, outbuildings which make excellent rooms for craft work and indoor games, hot-houses where the resident gardener, Mr Crowcroft, delights in the growing of flowers, grapes, peaches, and nectarines.

Separate from the Hall and its immediate grounds was the Alston Estate, comprising about 1,570 acres of land supporting farms, cottages, timbered woodlands, fishing rights on the river Ribble etc., that came under the Alston Property & Investment Company Limited which had been formed by William Birtwistle in December 1924. Now with twenty-two and well-equipped dairy farms and holdings under a tenantry, the estate was to be sold by auction unless sold privately, by Messrs. John D. Wood & Co. at the Bull and Royal Hotel, Preston, on Friday 7 October 1955 at 2 pm. The huge estate was to be sold in lots, all freehold and amounting to forty-seven in number and figs 15.9 and 15.10 are from the catalogue drawn up for the sale.

As to the residential college section at the Hall, such was to receive its first students in early June 1956, almost six years after the start of the day continuation college, the long delay due to the considerable internal alterations that had to take place before the Hall could have a duel purpose of day continuation and residential college. The official opening of the college took place on 20 September 1956 by General Sir Robert Forbes Adam, the President of the National Institute of Adult Education.

Mr J. W. Lightfoot had been appointed as the Head of the Residential

Fig. 15.11 James Shemilt (1908–2000), the first Principal of Alston Hall Day Continuation College.

College, a post referred to as Warden, the word being seen at the time as being applicable to heads of such colleges as in Warden of All Souls, Oxford, and others in Oxford and Cambridge. Jack Whitley Lightfoot who had a B.A. from Manchester, had taught history for nineteen years in schools, followed by six years in adult education as assistant warden at Grantley Hall, near Ripon before arriving at Alston. In his new post he set about visiting various groups such as townswomen's guilds, men's societies etc., as well as those in industry to explain what Alston Hall could offer both residentially and to those who wanted to come for a day or an evening course.

Accommodating 400 young people each week the day continuation college continued on the ground floor whilst the residential college housed on two upper floors had accommodation for 34 students, the sleeping arrangements being mainly composed of small, curtained cubicles with bed, chair, dressing table and wardrobe.

The first students and lecturers to arrive at the residential college were from various organisations, the first course for canoeing followed by a class of civil engineering students from Manchester University who stayed twelve days doing fieldwork, as mentioned in chapter 4. Next came a party of trade unionists to discuss prophetically automation and possible redundancies. At this time there was much emphasis on youth, so five courses on youth leadership were organised and overseas visitors arrived to study the British way of life whilst a series of courses for the officers of young farmers' clubs were made available. Soon, courses were open to the general public in literature, music, local history, and biology.

In 1962 Miss Ann Hirst came to Alston Hall as Deputy Warden of the residential college. A former pupil of Lancaster Girls' Grammar School where she had been head girl, she had a degree in psychology from University College, London and had formerly held a management post in industry. In 1965 she and Jack Lightfoot were married, but only eight months later on Friday 21 January 1966 Jack was killed in a car accident in Alston Lane.

In a tribute to Jack Lightfoot's work the Chief Education Officer for Preston, Mr W. R. Tuson would say:

> *Everyone associated with the educational service will be terribly grieved at his death. His contribution to the educational life of Preston and district, through his work at Alston Hall, has been unsurpassed. He will be greatly missed and we grieve very much for his wife.*

The Preston architect Mr N. Keith Scott also paid tribute, part of which read:

> *From a scratch start in a huge Victorian mansion, tucked away in a fold of the Ribble Valley, Jack worked patiently and brilliantly, gathering round him gifted men and women in every branch of arts and sciences to present a constant panoply of instruction and entertainment which has been the wonder of notable visitors from all parts of the world. ---- his Sunday evenings were a constant revelation to mature intellectuals, as he spoke on sociology, art, literature or music.----Whatever plans the authority may have for his replacement, it is certain that Alston Hall will never be the same.*

In succession to her husband, Ann Lightfoot was officially appointed Warden of Alston Hall on 1 April 1966, the title of this position later to be renamed as Principal. Ann was someone who believed passionately in the work of residential adult education and during her time at Alston Hall was to make a monumental contribution in the further development of the residential college.

For twenty years or so Alston Hall was Ann's home; she truly was a residential college Principal. Alston for so long was her life and she thought it part of her purpose to make everybody feel welcome and at home during his or her time at the Hall. She was always in the entrance to welcome people with a cheery greeting and saw them again later in the day as she helped to serve coffee and tea. Tutors were often taken to her sitting room for a glass of sherry before dinner. She had the ability to choose tutors who were not only expert in their subject but also embodied the philosophy that she lived by example in the college. She died peacefully during the morning of 24 September 2007, just 20 years after she had announced her intention to retire following 26 years of service to Alston Hall College.

The year 1974 saw the reorganisation of local government leading to the responsibility for further education passing from Preston Borough Council to Lancashire County Council. Developments in further education in turn led to new premises being built for the W. R. Tuson College in St Vincent's road, Preston, and in 1981 all remaining work of the day continuation college at Alston Hall was transferred to these premises. Even though Lancashire County Council had completed the building of a new

Fig. 15.12 Jack W. Lightfoot (1908–1966), the first Warden of Alston Hall Residential College.

Fig. 15.13 Ann Lightfoot (1927–2007), the second Warden and then the first Principal of Alston Hall Residential College.

residential college for adult education at Chorley in 1975, it continued to maintain, support, and develop the work at Alston Hall, where re-wiring of the building, re-ordering of the dormitories into single and twin-bedded rooms, and the conversion of the science laboratories on the ground floor to form additional bedrooms, was to be undertaken.

Following the retirement of Ann Lightfoot after more than 22 years as Principal, Brian Leighton arrived at Alston Hall as her replacement in May 1988 to develop the residential college further, most particularly through the extension of the day course programme into the weekends. The leaded skylight high above the entrance hall was restored to its original glory; the old coach house was extended (as mentioned in chapter three); a modern electric lift for student use replaced the hand-operated luggage/laundry lift; the old and much loved Blüthner grand piano was replaced by a new Grotrian-Steinweg; the pottery room in the stable block was converted into three additional bedrooms with en-suite facilities; whilst in the main house seven rooms were to have en-suite toilet and bath/shower.

During Brian's time at the Hall the production of vegetables in the walled garden came to an end and some of the decaying greenhouses had to be removed, and in sympathy with such measures Brian would write in his 'Reminiscences 1988–1997' ----- *it gave me no pleasure to stop producing vegetables in the walled garden and to have the decaying greenhouses removed. These were economic necessities, but a sad break with the original purposes of the Hall and its grounds.*

In 1989 under Brian's leadership the 'Friends of Alston Hall' was established to add further support to the college. On Brian's retirement,

Fig. 15.14 Brian Leighton, the second Principal of Alston Hall Residential College.

Graham Wilkinson became College Principal in 1997 under whose professional and helpful leadership I continued my work at Alston Hall to present new courses in the history of Victorian and Edwardian architecture with much support from the ever-efficient courses manager, Dorothy Little. She and Graham would arrange the college's special jubilee programme 'Fifty Golden Years of Learning' in September 2000. Amongst the contributors would be Ann Lightfoot, Brian Leighton, Norman Duerden, Mike Pattinson, Joan Burns MBE, and Peter Gellhorn. Peter whose association with the college had been as a music tutor was an ex-conductor at Covent Garden and Glyndebourne, and an ex-Director of the BBC Chorus, and would unveil a new stained glass window (fig. 15.22) in the Hall's chapel to commemorate 50 years of learning at the Hall.

In 2,000 more than 1,300 visitors attended the combined Garden Fair and Open Day, all eager to see the various features, displays and demonstrations, whilst the days leading up to Christmas in that year would see almost one thousand enrolments on the 'Alston's Twelve Days of Christmas' programme. A popular event was to be the Sunday Alston Evening programme, each session beginning with a 3-course meal followed by a musical recital or an illustrated talk. Personally, it was a delight and a privilege to present an illustrated talk at some of those Sunday evening sessions.

One of Graham Wilkinson's disappointments during his time at Alston as Principal was his unsuccessful bid to convert the dilapidated greenhouse into a combined ground floor art studio and a venue for live musical and other performances. Graham was about to face a changing world of adult learning as pressure began to build on Councils to save money and to focus their resources on areas where they had a statutory responsibility. Such led to many Authorities ceasing to provide adult learning directly. For the time being adult education at Alston Hall was safe as senior officers and elected County Councillors continued to support the Alston College as well as the Lancashire College near Southport and the Adult College in Lancaster. Floor plans of Alston Hall figs 15.26 to and including 15.31 drawn up by Lancashire County Council and dated 15 December 2003 illustrate the immense amount of work that had been undertaken throughout the years in modernising the Hall into a successful residential college.

By 2008 the Lancashire Adult Learning Service was recognising the need to position itself to respond to the continually evolving government priorities with regard to adult education whilst at the same time being able to retain its colleges and the type of adult learning that had formed its roots. For Alston Hall this meant ensuring that through both its adult learning and its business activity, its college was able to operate effectively without government subsidy, generating all its income from fees charged. Strategies were put into place to attract new types of business to ensure the college could generate sufficient income to sustain its long-term viability, and with this in mind the college was to host weddings.

In the meantime, maintenance work on the buildings and programmes of interior refurbishment would be ongoing but changes allied to the general ambience of the college would be on the horizon. Escalating paperwork brought about by a spiralling quality of Ofsted inspecting demands presented a new approach in the administration of courses, and following the retirement of Graham Wilkinson as Principal in 2004 it seemed the stage was set for a new phrase at the college, one to be so very different to the one enjoyed by so many in Ann Lightfoot's day.

On 4 August 2014 Lesley Hinchcliffe took up her appointment as Business and Curriculum Manager at Alston Hall, her initial aim to present a customer service ensuring that tutors and presenters were delivering sessions in line with the current requirements of the Adult Education and Training sector. An increase in business revenue was much needed. A new course brochure for the Spring/Summer of 2015 was presented containing many new tutors and a huge variety of courses, but by now the costs of courses had risen to such a degree that many were being cancelled due to insufficient enrolment.

It seemed the writing was on the wall in connection with pending closure and as the courses' brochure for the September/December 2015 session came out, rumours regarding closure were already gaining momentum. On 29 July 2015 a correspondence from the Development Assistant at Alston Hall (who was taking voluntary redundancy) to Lesley Hinchcliffe indicated that the Alston Autumn/ Winter 2015/16 programme had been slimmed down and the brochure would contain only courses until the end of December. I would perform my last presentation on Sunday afternoon of 18 October 2015 on 'The Colleges of Oxford and Cambridge' following which the last courses continued, the final ones in the run-up to Christmas being part of the 'Twelve Days of Christmas' programme. At the end of December Alston Hall College had closed having been in an atmosphere of Council cut backs, a decline in course attendances and income, and in need of an estimated £900,000 to be spent on building maintenance.

Months later the *Lancashire Evening Post* of Thursday 26 May 2016, under the heading 'Education centre is to be private home again' would

Fig. 15.15 Graham Wilkinson, the third Principal of Alston Hall Residential College.

comment to say that Lancashire County Council was then able to confirm that it had accepted an offer for the nineteenth-century Gothic style country mansion and its 9.6 acre site with river views, a council spokesman having said: *After an extensive marketing exercise which created a lot of interest and led to eight bids, we have agreed an offer for Alston Hall which will be sold as a residential dwelling. We are now in the process of exchanging contracts.*

The newspaper article would also mention Jess Mortimer, Chair of the soon to be disbanded 'Friends of Alston Hall' who was to say that it was better that the Hall was sold rather than become derelict, and commenting; *It started life as a family home and hopefully that's what's going to happen now. But what is sad is that of course people from Preston and Lancashire will no longer have access to the beautiful grounds and situation.*

Fig. 15.16 Day Continuation College students in the chapel.

Fig. 15.17 The conservatory.

Fig. 15.18 Dining room in college days.

Fig. 15.19 Pink bedroom in college days. Shown is the doorway into a corridor that once presented access to the bedroom's dressing room and bathroom see fig. 4.25.

Fig. 15.20 Blue bedroom in college days. The plain appearance of the window area is the result of removing transoms and mullions in *c*.1912–14.

Fig. 15.21 Art tutor John Selby (left) with members of his art class in the upper room of the old coach house.

Fig. 15.22 The '50th Anniversary' window in the chapel. Designed by art tutor, John Selby; created by glass tutor, Bill Davis; and financed by the 'Friends of Alston Hall'; the window was unveiled in 2000 by Peter Gellhorn (ex-music tutor) to commemorate fifty years of learning at the Hall.

Fig. 15.23 Staff of Alston Hall Residential College (2000).

Fig. 15.24 Fine example of quilting on the entrance hall's landing. The three members of staff in the centre of the group are from the left; Sheila Grindley, Dot Little and Val Huxton.

Fig. 15.25 The final College Christmas (2015) in the entrance hall's reception area. Busy at work is receptionist Diane Robinson.

A few months later on Thursday 24 November the *Lancashire Evening Post* was to publish an article under the heading, '*Alston Hall's new future as a mansion – new owner seeks to turn site into country estate*'. The article by Fiona Finch began in capital letters to emphasise the next life of the mansion and read:

> *THE NEXT chapter in the history of landmark Lancashire building and former college Alston Hall has begun.*
>
> *Several months after the county council revealed it had accepted an offer for the Gothic style hall, which until it closed in December 2015 was a further education college offering day, evening and residential classes, the purchase has been finalised.*

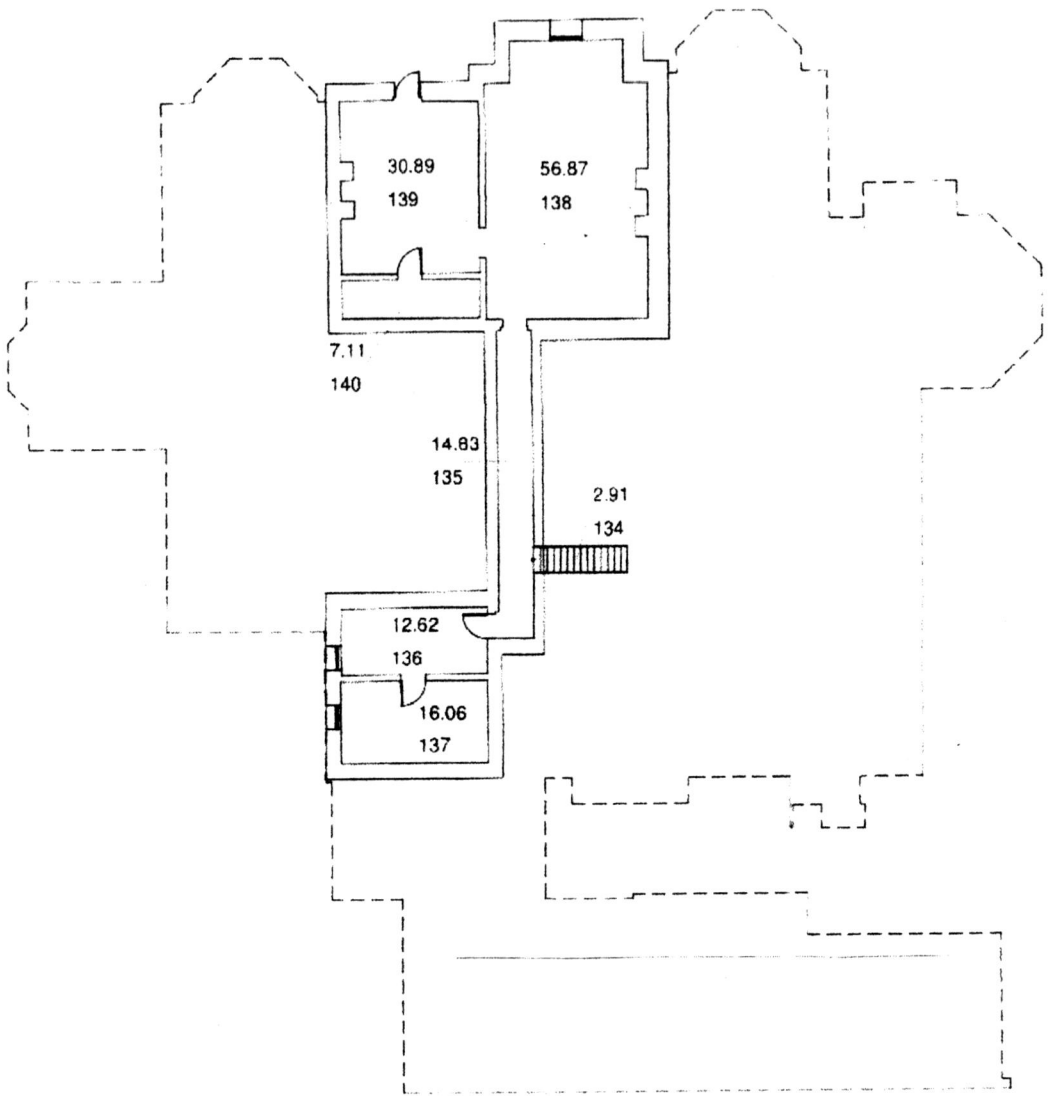

Fig. 15.26 Floor plan of the Hall's basement (2003). Of the two numbers shown for each room or area, the upper one is the area in square metres, the lower one the number for the plan.

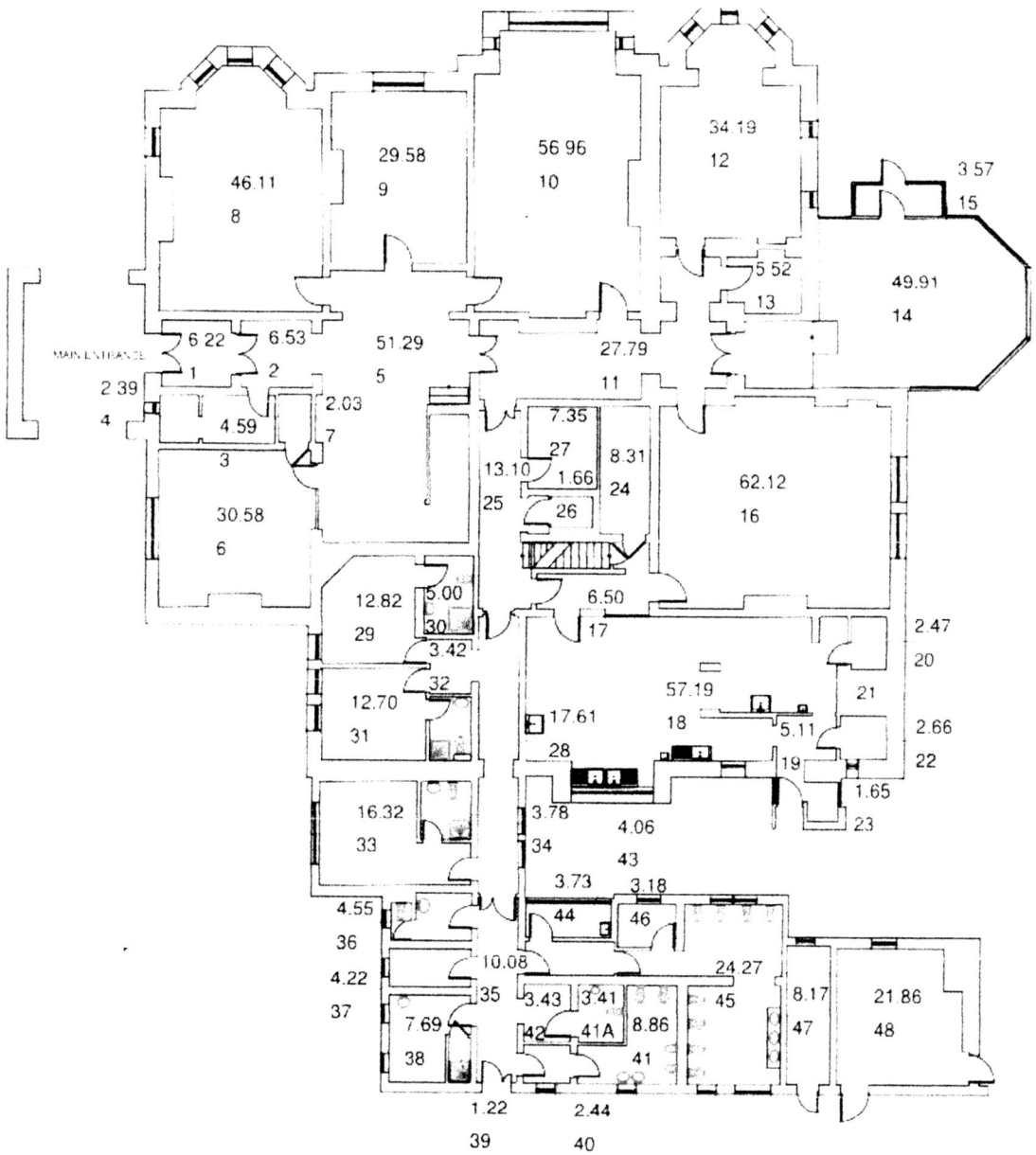

Fig. 15.27 Floor plan of the Hall's ground floor (2003).

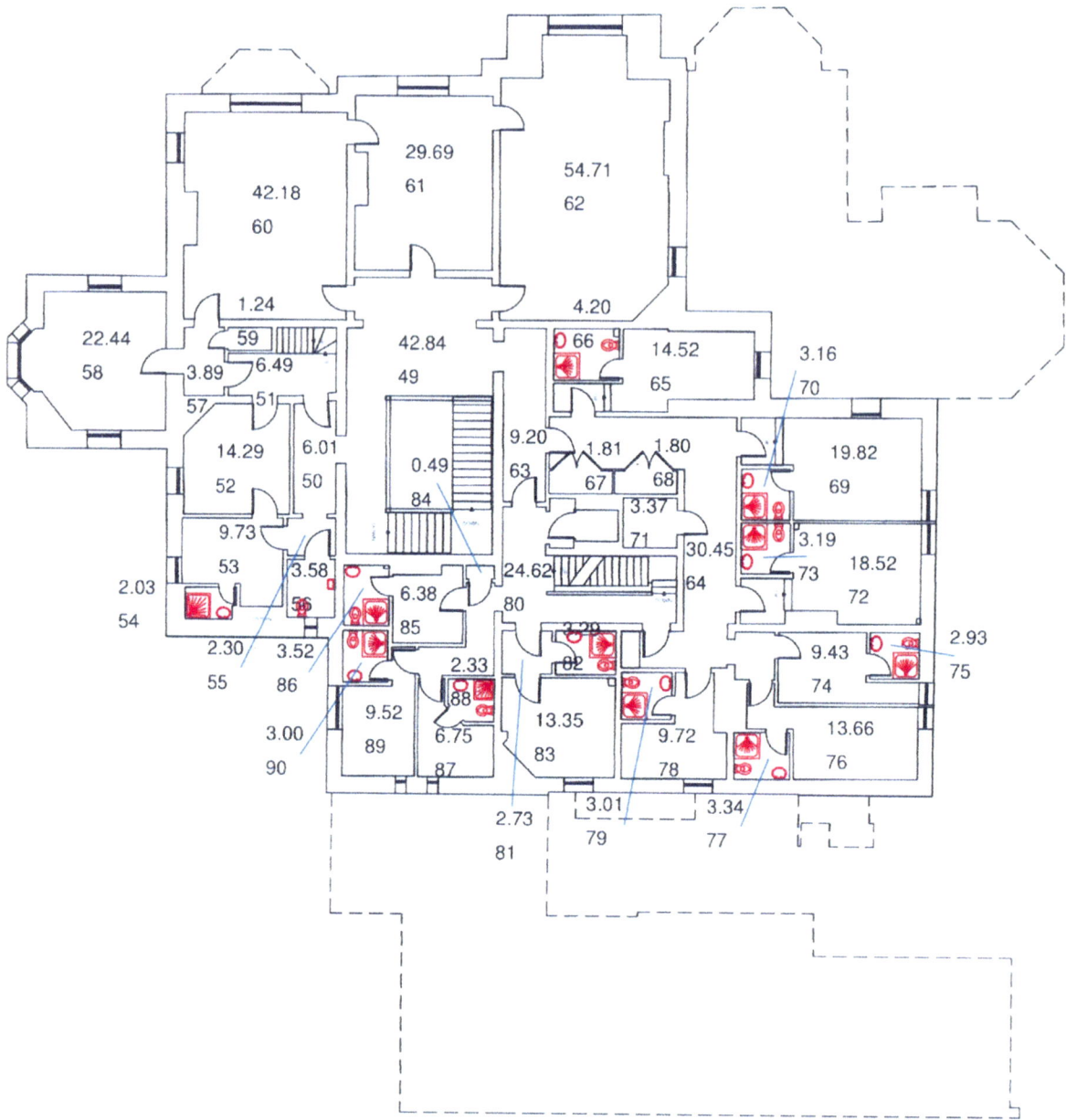

Fig. 15.28 Floor plan of the Hall's first floor (2003).

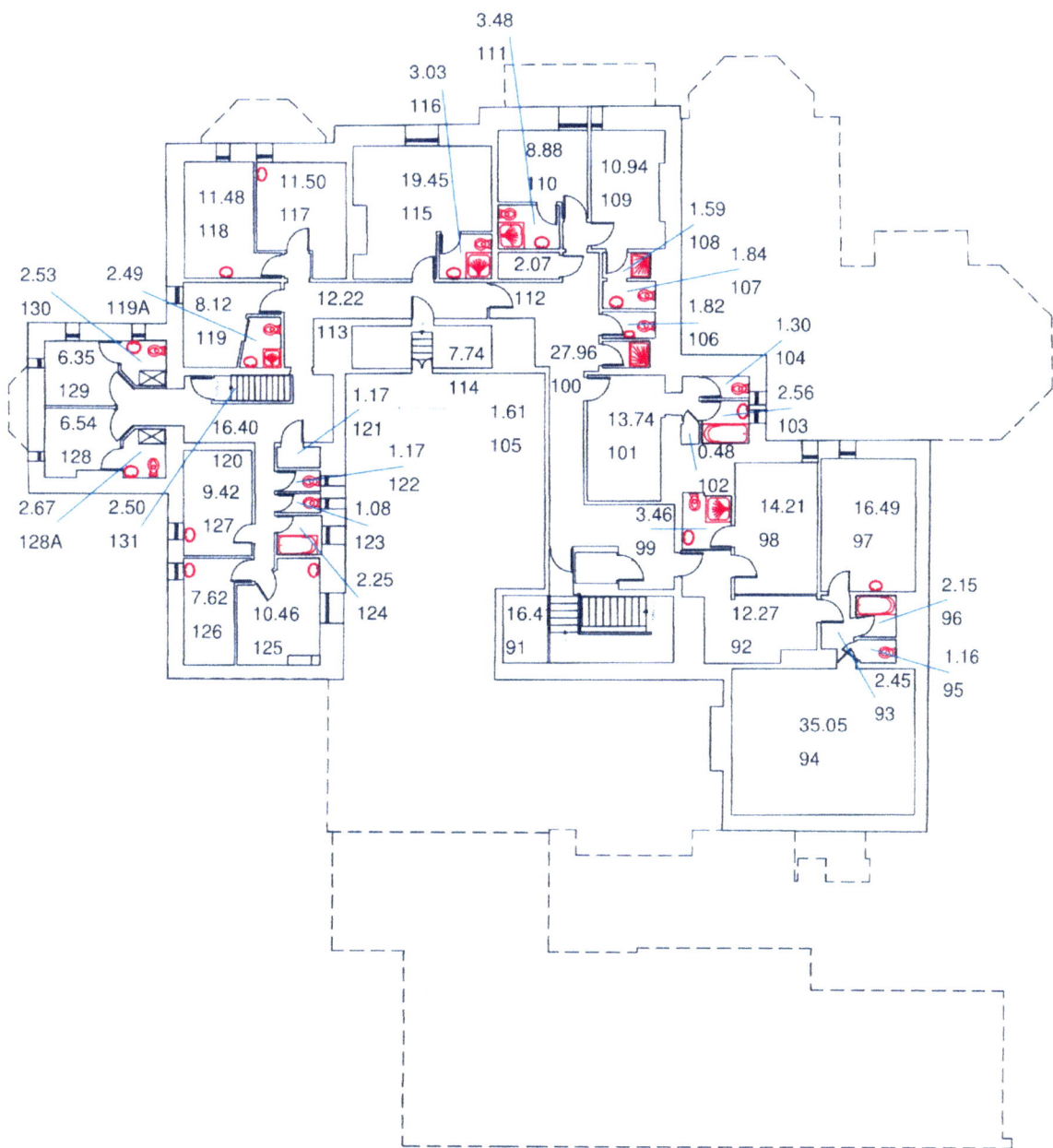

Fig. 15.29 Floor plan of the Hall's second floor (2003).

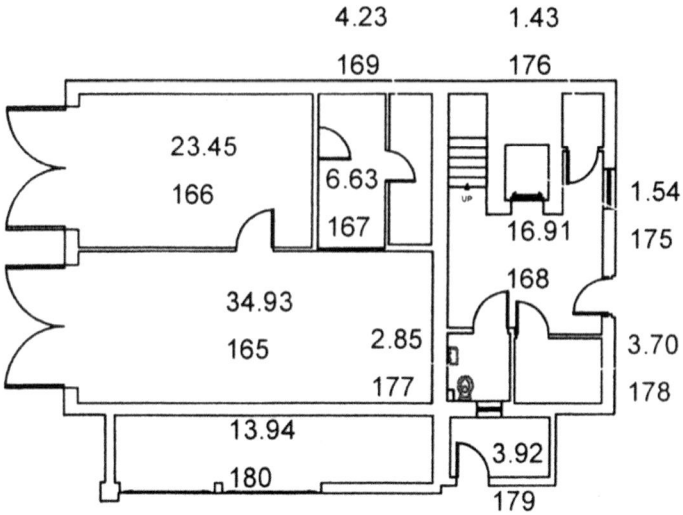

GROUND FLOOR PLAN:

4.23
169

1.43
176

23.45
166

6.63
167

UP

1.54
175

16.91
168

34.93
165

2.85
177

3.70
178

13.94
180

3.92
179

FIRST FLOOR PLAN:

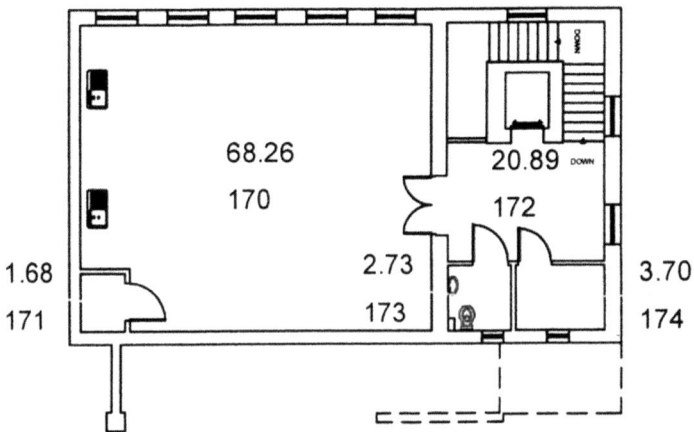

DOWN

68.26
170

20.89
172

DOWN

1.68
171

2.73
173

3.70
174

Fig. 15.30 Floor plans of the garden block (old coach house) (2003).

GROUND FLOOR PLAN:

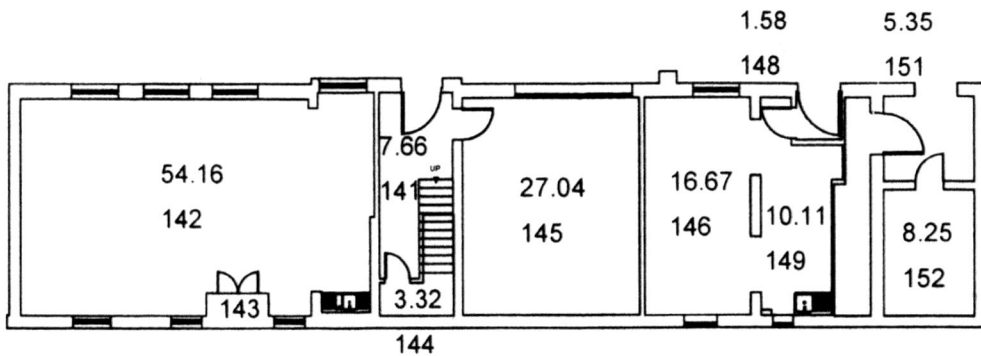

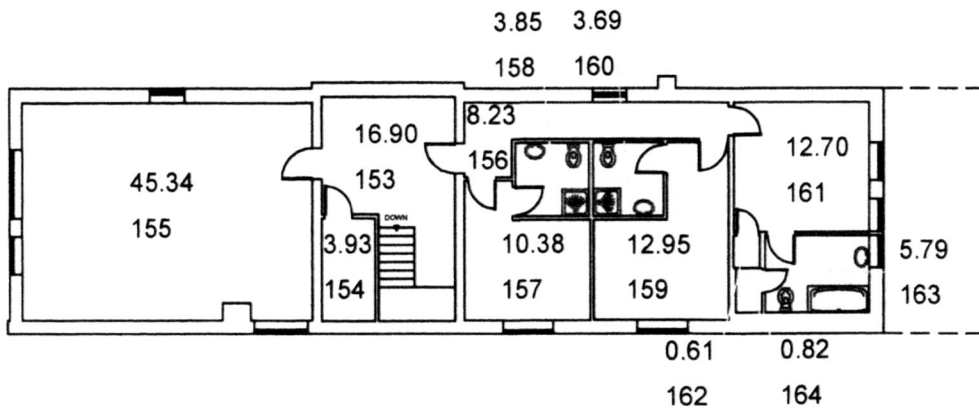

FIRST FLOOR PLAN:

Fig. 15.31 Floor plans of the stable block (2003).

Since it went on the market the 19th century former colliery owner's and later cotton magnate's home on Alston Lane, on the outskirts of Longridge, had gained Grade II listed status.

Agents CBRE revealed the new owner now wants to create a "high end" country estate.

Nick Huddleston, Associate Director at CBRE Manchester, said:

We understand the purchaser is proposing to convert and renovate the property back into a high end residential dwelling and country estate, which is fitting given its uninterrupted views of the surrounding Ribble Valley.

It's known the local purchaser paid in excess of 1.5m for the property which includes 35 en suite bedrooms, conference rooms, bar restaurant, a commercial kitchen, chapel, and conservatory. In addition the 9.6 acre site, which boasts mature gardens and woodland, has two separate outbuildings with classrooms and bedrooms.

The Hall had also operated as an events venue and was licensed for weddings

Mr Huddleston added: "We were inundated with interest for the property from a number of individual and corporate buyers with proposed uses ranging from conversion to a single residential dwelling, elderly care home uses, boutique hotel and wedding venue."

Architects Cassidy and Ashton recently submitted an application to Ribble Valley Council for permission for change of use from college to a residential dwelling on behalf of a Mr I. Patel.

Soon after this newspaper report was published work would begin on converting the mansion back to a family home, scaffolding beginning to shroud the building as work got underway to clean the external walls.

Chapter sixteen

Ordeal by fire

On Wednesday 15 March 2017 at around 10.30 pm a devastating fire broke out in the Hall. Two astronomers in the University of Central Lancashire's observatory 150 metres from the Hall were viewing the planet Jupiter at the time when they noticed that something was wrong when smoke began drifting across the telescope. UCLan researcher Dr Dan Holdsworth was later to say:

> *Quite a lot of smoke was causing us problems, so one of us stepped outside to see what it was and noticed there was an orange glow coming from the Hall and getting progressively brighter. We rang the fire brigade and as we stood there watching and waiting, at least three people came out of one of the outhouses next to the Hall. They were shouting and running around quite frantically with fire extinguishers and I assumed they were workers who had been working on the building.*

Fire crews from across Lancashire raced to the Hall and at the height of the blaze seventy-five fire fighters were at the scene where ten appliances, two aerial ladder platforms, and a mobile command centre would be in operation. A specialist drone team was also called in to survey the damage from above.

Later, Incident Commander Shaun Walton was to comment to the *Lancashire Evening Post*:

> *When our crews arrived there was a significant fire involving the roof space and the first floor of the building. With it being such a large building and with the extent of the fire, we felt it more appropriate to deal with it overhead from two aerial ladder platforms to make it*

a safer working environment for our firefighters. Because it was well established, it wasn't a case of firefighting, it was a case of containing it. Our crews did very well to prevent it spreading to the remainder of the building. The significant heat caused columns and beams to collapse and there was a lot of structural instability of chimneys and gable ends. We couldn't commit our staff into the building or its immediate perimeter because there was concern the structure was unstable and could collapse. The cause is under investigation.

Another brigade spokesman would say:

The fire investigation will have to wait until it is safe enough to go in. We don't know how long that is going to take, but it could be several weeks, even months. With the dangerous state of the building our main concern now is making sure everyone is safe. There is a structural engineer down there and he will decide whether it needs to be shored up before anyone can go inside

Former Alston Hall Principal, Graham Wilkinson's first words after hearing about the fire were: *"What a tragedy"*. Graham, who had led the educational facility at Alston for seven years up to 2004, commented:

I really hope the Hall can be restored to its former glory. It was a beautiful building and inspirational place and 60 years of very happy learning took place there, the walls would echo to the sounds of music and choirs. Since it became a college many thousands of people will have some lovely memories about being there. The building may have been damaged, but hopefully those memories will live on. It's a very sad day for me personally and also for everyone connected with the Hall. The building started life as a private house. When it stopped being a college we were all very, very sad. But we were pleased when we heard someone had taken it on and was going to restore it to its former glory as a family home and it wouldn't slip into dilapidation and would be preserved.

At its height as a college it offered a very large programme of courses, both day courses and residential. We built the programme up and the place was open seven days a week, 51 weeks a year. There were 20,000 people a year coming down that lane. It was absolutely thriving. A lot of love went into that building and I hope the owners will manage to bring it back from this.

Fig. 16.1 Dining room (December 2017).

Jess Mortimer, Chair of the Friends of Aston Hall, would also express her sentiments:

> *We have heard the news of the fire with immense sorrow. Our thoughts are with the family who are hoping to make this beautiful, well loved building their home.*

Just before Christmas 2017 following the kind invitation of Mr Salim Habib Patel, the son of the new owner, to visit the Hall, Malcolm Tranter and I arrived during the morning of 14 December to see the building almost enveloped in scaffolding as at the time of the fire the cleansing of the Hall's external stonework had been well advanced.

Much of the roof had been destroyed and inside the Hall one was met with a scene of devastation, a reminder of that terrible night of 15 March

Fig. 16.2 Drawing room (December 2017).

nine months previous when fire had attempted to entirely destroy such a beautiful building. It seemed that no room including those on the ground floor had escaped the effects of either the inferno or subsequent water damage. Walls had been stripped of their décor, ceilings and floors damaged or destroyed, such a sad scene as one recalled how these rooms had once echoed the sounds of those who had experienced the sheer joy of learning and social interaction in the most friendly and beautiful of environments. Standing in the blackened and desolate interior of the mansion on that cold and grey December morning one had a feeling of deep sadness as one visualised happier times, especially open days and garden fêtes when staff, tutors and visitors enjoyed being about its rooms and grounds.

By the beginning of 2017 prior to the fire a considerable amount of work had been done to bring the Hall back into line as a domestic dwelling. Within its immediate surroundings, trees had been felled after careful selection to present a more open look to the grounds, whilst shrub and tree had been removed within the dell area to bring into full view the waterfalls and ornamental ponds that had been created in the 1870s. Near the dell area the old greenhouse that had been against the kitchen garden wall had been completely rebuilt.

The December visit was to be the first of many during which one would be allowed the opportunity to discover many of the mansion's structural and interior design features that had lay hidden for decades following the two major twentieth century periods of modernisation. Fortunately

Fig. 16.3 Rose bedroom (December 2017).

Fig. 16.4 West corner of the rose bedroom (December 2017). This area had been part of the rose suite's dressing room until the conversion work of the 1950s when its fireplace was removed. Its corner chimney breast can be seen as well as what was presumably the entrance to the suite's bathroom.

Fig. 16.5 Charred remains of the wooden beam from the dining room ceiling (December 2017).

Fig. 16.6 Originally the morning room and eventually the college lounge (April 2018).

Fig. 16.7 Main staircase area during restoration work (January 2019).

Fig. 16.8 Original stencilled wall decoration in the chapel (January 2019). Seen is the trompe l'oeil 'to deceive the eye' technique giving the impression of a wall of ashlar stone blocks.

Fig. 16.9 1950s girder work in what had originally been the bathroom area of the rose suite. Such work was undertaken to support a bathroom to be fitted in the tank room above in the Hall's obsolete water tower (January 2019).

the mahogany doors in the private rooms and also the entrance hall's impressive skylight had escaped damage and had been removed into safe storage. The main tasks were now to make secure what remained of the roof structure and gables followed by the urgent need to make the mansion's rooms weatherproof. Construction of a new roof would be an urgent and

Fig. 16.10 South-facing corner of the chapel and Hall (December 2017) Behind, chimneystacks and gables stand above a roofless interior.

Fig. 16.11 South-facing corner of the chapel and Hall (May 2019). The conservatory has gone whilst its doorway from the dining room can be seen.

Fig. 16.12 The 'new look' southeast-facing façade (May 2019).

Fig. 16.13 Looking in the direction of the stable yard from the top of the entrance tower (May 2019).

Fig. 16.14 Looking south across an area of recent tree felling (May 2019).

Fig. 16.15 Rear of the Hall (January 2019) following recent demolition of the servants' hall and the ground floor service rooms of c.1913–14 as seen in fig. 3.19.

major undertaking and once completed the long period of 'drying out' throughout the mansion began aided by the removal of water-sodden wall plaster and ceilings. The exposed inner brick walls somehow gave one the impression of how the rooms would have looked almost a century and a half ago when the mansion was under construction.

Fig. 16.16 The new walled garden (March 2019).

Fig. 16.17 Arches within the wall of the main staircase (November 2020).

Fig. 16.18 Carved plaster boss on the left-hand arch as seen in fig. 16.17. Water damage has revealed its intricate and fine carving upon which there are remains of paint.

A visit during the early summer of 2019 saw roofing work had been completed and inside restoration work was well advanced, especially on the first and second floors where new room layouts were taking shape. Outside where now peacocks freely roamed much work had been done in restoring the garden areas, in particular the walled kitchen garden that had been transformed into an Islamic style garden designed by Adam Frost of BBC's television *Gardeners' World* programme. Also the cleaning of the exterior stonework of the Hall had been completed as seen in figs 16.11 and 16.12.

During the 1950s the cleaning of stonework on our public buildings in particular would arouse much debate as there were many dissentient voices being heard as to whether cleaning should be encouraged as such might remove the surface and patina of the stone that had been formed by the natural process of weathering, such a removal possibly leading to

Fig. 16.19 The restored skylight area in the entrance hall awaiting the fitting of its stained-glass and leaded-light window (November 2020).

Fig. 16.20 The recently constructed lake within the lower one of two lawns (November 2020). The pathway to the left leads to the mound at the end of the 'pleasure ground terrace' where foundations were in place for a summerhouse.

disastrous consequences. Yet by the fifties especially in our northern towns and cities many nineteenth-century buildings in particular were in dire need of cleaning, having accumulated grim and chemical deposits over decades from what had seemed to be countless industrial furnaces and domestic fires. The cleaning campaign that would gather momentum by the sixties was not simply a matter of aesthetics but also one of arresting stone decay.

Different types of stonework require different techniques of cleaning, and with the hard sandstone of the exterior walls at Alston Hall much care would have been taken. On the more friable sandstones that can easily crumble only clean cold water should be used, but for hard sandstone if the cleaning operation is to be effective, grit blasting has been a successful technique. The grit, usually silica sand can be dry or mixed with water and applied by a spay gun operating on compressed air, but the lowest pressure should be used that will do the work effectively.

Today after careful cleaning the façades of Alston Hall represent the true hues of Longridge stone. By November 2020, plastering of the brick interior walls at the Hall had been completed and a more modernised look to suit the twenty-first century was being envisaged about its rooms. In the morning room the fireplace had been removed and its wall re-plastered whilst a connecting doorway had been made into what had originally been the study or smoking room. Fireplaces in other private rooms were not to become part of the new décor because of the damage done to them by the fire. In the entrance hall the original ceiling with its painted panels had been boarded up and a fireplace was to be installed within the wall shown in fig. 4.8 where at one period had been a doorway into the butler's pantry. Outside from the pleasure ground terrace and within the lower one of two lawns, was now a small lake, whilst a short distance away upon the mound, foundations for a summerhouse had been laid. Life was now returning to a building that on that terrible night in March 2017 by the help of professional and dedicated firefighters had simply refused to die.

Postscript

During the restoration work at the Hall it was decided to delay the publication of the book until the work was finished when the results of such work could be presented as a fitting end to its final chapter.

In early May 2023, a visit to the fully restored Hall and its grounds was a memorable one. Clearly the work had been undertaken adopting the highest standards of workmanship using the best of materials. Ground floor rooms had a pleasing modern décor and had been arranged to present community style living for members of the Patel family. The entrance hall had received a fireplace and the skylight window was back in its original position, whilst in the dining room its alcove now had a large and elegant mirror.

Outside, the old coach house had recently been demolished, and what had been the stable yard was now an area of gardens, including a kitchen garden. The plan to build a summerhouse on the mound had been cancelled, the mound now a feature of the lake was an open-air area with seating enclosed by an attractive stone balustrade.

The following photographs by Malcolm Tranter illustrate that the Hall was now ready to begin yet another lifestyle.

Fig. 16.21 The Hall after restoration (May 2023).

Fig. 16.22 Dining room (May 2023).

Fig. 16.23 Entrance hall (May 2023).

Fig. 16.24 New water feature (May 2023).

Fig. 16.25 Once the stable yard now an area of gardens (May 2023).

Fig. 16.26 Walled garden (May 2023).

Fig. 16.27 Walled garden (May 2023).

Fig. 16.28 Lake and mound (May 2023).

Acknowledgements

The writing of a book of this nature has to depend to a considerable extent on the help and good will of others and for such I have been most fortunate.

Many thanks must be expressed to Anne Russell (staff member at Alston Hall College in 2015) for allowing photographs to be taken externally and internally of the Hall some months before its closure as a college, and to present on loan the Hall's archives for the purpose of this publication. Such archive material has made a most valuable contribution to the book and will eventually be deposited in the Lancashire Archives' collection in Preston.

Another most valuable contribution has been the work of Malcolm Tranter, a long-standing friend and ex-tutor at Alston Hall College. His photographs of the Hall (2015) and those taken on the many visits to the Hall following the fire of 2017 have certainly enhanced this publication. To Malcolm I am most grateful and equally so to his wife Ouida who during the extensive period of research 'trawled' the internet to bring about new and relevant material, enhancing the content of the book to a considerable degree.

Many thanks must go to the following (not in any special order) for their valuable contribution to some of the illustrations;

a) The Wigan Archives for figs 1.2 and 1.3.

b) The Longridge Archives for figs 3.19 and 8.3. Also to Dorothy Little (ex-courses manager of Alston Hall College) who most kindly obtained these photographs for the book and her husband Fred who prepared them for publication by skilfully removing copyright wording.

c) Diane Robinson, staff member at Alston Hall College for allowing me to take photographs of 'Ribble View House' and the Birtwistle crest above its doorway.

d) Alan G. Crosby, ex-tutor at Alston Hall College, historian and author, for fig. 8.1.

e) The Lancashire Archives, Preston, for figs 3.1, 6.2, 14.3, 14.6, and the two plans figs 4.25 and 4.30 (to which additional information has been added for the purpose of this publication).

f) Sister Marguerite Boutezoup of The Society of the Holy Child Jesus Archives, Oxford, for fig. 10.2.

g) Chris Taylor of Cassidy and Ashton, architects for the restoration work at Alston Hall, for supplying the floor plans of Alston Hall drawn by Lancashire County Council in 2003.

h) Salim Habib Patel and his father for allowing me access to the Hall during post fire restoration work. The photography allowed during these visits has certainly presented a unique and valuable pictorial record not only of the damage done by the inferno of 2017 but also how the Hall's interior underwent changes in décor and layout during *c.*1912–14 and the time it was a college. Without these photographs this publication would have been much poorer in content. Salim also presented the aerial photographs (taken by drone), the one on the front cover and fig. 3.24.

I am also most grateful to the 'Friends of Alston Hall' under the Chair of Jess Mortimer for the considerable amount of money given by them as part of the cost of this publication and for supplying figs 3.10, 3.13, 3.20, 4.2, 4.18 and 15.25.

Thanks also to Anna Goddard, Lucy Frontani and the team at Palatine Books for their work in helping to produce and publish this book.

Index

Numerals in *italic* indicate pages with an illustration